The Great Nightfall

The Great Nightfall

*How We Win
the New Cold War*

J. William Middendorf II

With a Foreword by Bill Gertz

Heritage Harbor Foundation
East Providence, Rhode Island
2020

For information, write:
Heritage Harbor Foundation
1445 Wampanoag Trail, Suite #201
East Providence, RI 02915
tel: (401) 272–1776
fax: (401) 273–1791
heritageharborfoundation.org

Printed in the United States of America
ISBN 978-0-917012-11-2

Typeset in Minion Pro and Cooper Hewitt
Printed & bound by LSC Communications

Dedication

This book is dedicated to the men and women of the Armed Forces of the United States, past, present, and future, whose patriotism and valor have won liberty for freedom-loving people everywhere. While our adversaries have changed and will continue to change, as will weapons systems, weapons platforms, technologies, strategies, and tactics, it is the resourcefulness of our Armed Forces that will continue to achieve battleground superiority and success. The uncertainties and frustrations of asymmetric warfare in recent decades have severely tested our military personnel, but they have not faltered and never will. We must assure them of the support, both moral and financial, to preserve our freedom and way of life.

Contents

Acknowledgments

THIS BOOK WOULD NOT HAVE BEEN POSSIBLE without the contributions of a number of people, starting with author and playwright Ken Dooley. Ken did the research, conducted the interviews, and provided the latest information on very complex issues.

Bill Gertz and Gordon Chang gave us much of the information reflected in the chapters on China, North Korea, and Taiwan. The Heritage Foundation of Washington, D.C., allowed us to interview some of the leading military and civilian experts in the world. Special thanks to James Carafano, Bruce Klinger, Tom Callender, Ed Feulner, Oliva Enos, Thomas Spoehr, Federico Bartels, Peter Brookes, Daniel Kochis, Dakota Wood, John Venable, Patty Jane Geller, Edwin Meese III, and Charles Stimson of the Heritage Foundation for providing expert information.

John Odegaard, former special assistant to the secretary of the Navy, became involved with the project early, read every page, and came up with a number of excellent suggestions. Special thanks to Roger Pardo-Maurer, former U.S. deputy of defense for Western Hemisphere Affairs, for his advice and counsel and for Eric Russi for providing special insights. My son, John Middendorf, tracked down numerous articles, read them, and highlighted important information. Wayne Muller conducted many of the key interviews.

The contributions of U.S. Senator Jack Reed (RI) are invaluable. As a senior member of the Armed Services Committee, Senator Reed works hard to ensure that America's fighting men and women have the weapons and support they need to preserve our way of life. U.S. Representative Jim Langevin (RI) provided expert advice on cyberterrorism.

I am thankful for the sage advice of Admiral James Stavridis, former Supreme Allied Commander of NATO. Eric Russi provided incredible advice.

I am indebted to Bryan Clark of the Hudson Institute; Admiral Chris Parry (ret.) of the Royal Navy; Samuel LeGrone, U.S. Naval Institute;

Mark Lyles, Captain, USN; John Buche, U.S. State Department; Dr. Lyle J. Goldstein, Naval War College; Richard Kuchon, U.S. State Department; and Roger W. Robinson.

One of the great honors of my life was serving shoulder to shoulder with Admiral James L. Holloway III, Chief of Naval Operations while I was secretary of the Navy. Jimmy's steady, calm and brilliant leadership could always be counted on during the most difficult times.

The father-son team of Philip and Andrew Bilden provided valuable insights and motivation.

Margaret C. Satell rendered expert advice as a copyeditor and vigilant proofreader.

A special thanks to Edward Achorn, vice president of the *Providence Journal*, for his editorials warning of the threats from China, Russia, and North Korea.

Without the love and care of my late wife Isabelle and my daughters, Frances and Amy, this book could not have been completed. A special thanks to my administrative assistants, Frances Nadeau and Madeline Brumley.

Foreword

THE COLLAPSE OF THE SOVIET UNION in December 1991 was a seminal event in world history that inspired hope for some relief from the long and dangerous conventional military and nuclear standoff with Moscow and its satellites during decades of Cold War.

Yet that relief and a new era of peace did not materialize. The world today remains more dangerous than ever with threats to American national security seemingly emerging on every front — militarily, diplomatically, economically, and in the foreign intelligence sphere. New dangers are presenting themselves with a vengeance. The nation and our leaders are confronted with never before seen challenges from cyberattacks and electromagnetic pulse attacks, a coming war in space, aggressive gray zone information warfare, and economic and financial warfare.

J. William Middendorf warns in these pages that these threats are real and growing and must be dealt with. Bill is a veteran defense expert. He was among the premier "steel benders" — as defense leaders who got things done are called — in helping build some of the most important arms while Navy secretary from 1974 to 1977. During this period, he oversaw an increase in budgets for naval systems by more than 60 percent at a time when other military service budgets remained static.

More importantly, under his tenure some of the most important weapons systems in U.S. history were built and deployed. They include the Ohio-class ballistic missile submarine fleet and their Trident missiles that currently remain, nearly half century later, the backbone of the U.S. strategic nuclear deterrent. Under his tenure, the Navy also developed its advanced fleet of Aegis battle management system-equipped warships. Today, Aegis ships constitute most of the warships in the Navy fleet as well as its robust sea-based missile defenses. For aircraft carriers, Middendorf shepherded the F/A-18 warplane that remains a staple of American power projection capabilities worldwide. These weapon systems contributed to the ending of the Cold War.

At that time, we had only one major adversary — the Soviet Union. Today, we face threats from China, Russia, North Korea, and Iran. China and Russia are rapidly building up their military forces and are bent on achieving superiority to ours. Their goal is to create a three-dimensional strike capability that combines undersea, surface and aerospace capabilities. Both countries are developing directed-energy weapons that could make satellites useless by blinding sensitive optical sensors used for missile defense.

It takes a 10- to 12-year lead time to achieve a new weapon system. Middendorf warns we must accelerate our present research and develop weapon systems capabilities to match or exceed those of our potential adversaries. We must build against projected capabilities not the perceived intentions of a potential adversary. *The Great Nightfall* is a call to arms. Its publication comes at a time of great danger posed by adversary states such as the People's Republic of China under Supreme Leader Xi Jinping, the Russian Federation under Vladimir Putin, North Korea under Kim Jong Un, and Iran under theocratic, terrorist-supporting mullahs.

And despite nearly 20 years of war against Islamic extremists, the danger posed by terrorist groups remains very real. The United States under President Donald Trump is steadily emerging from a strategic slumber that has seen the threats from foreign adversaries dramatically increase. The president already has taken steps to stem the massive loss of American technology to China that for years involved an estimated trade deficit of $500 billion annually and another several hundred billion dollars of intellectual property rights stolen annually.

Prime among these current dangers outlined in *The Great Nightfall*, however, is the threat from China, a nuclear-armed Communist dictatorship bent on replacing the United States as the world's superpower. For the sake of world peace and freedom, a Communist Party–ruled China must never be allowed to become the global world domination its leaders desire. China's brand of communism remains subtler than that of the old Soviet Union. But make no mistake, it is more dangerous. Beijing's leaders are using the deception that China poses no threat to subvert the United States and other western nations. It is also using economic engagement to lull its avowed enemies into complacency. For the Chinese Communist Party leadership, the United States is the main enemy to be vanquished — even as Beijing seeks engagement worldwide.

The China threat is not new to Middendorf. In December 1945, his ship was stationed in Shanghai for occupational forces. He was there when General Marshall, Truman's envoy, came to China that had the unfortunate effect of undermining Chiang Kai-shek and moving our foreign policy toward the revolutionary Mao, who was described in the western press as the George Washington of the Pacific and an "Agrarian

Reformer." Too late, a year and half later the United States resumed aid to Chiang, but China was lost, 1949 perhaps the greatest geopolitical strategic error of all times. Later, Middendorf and Constantine Menges supporting the Monroe Doctrine by taking a proposed invasion of Grenada to the national security council. Two weeks later our successful military action brought the Cuban and Soviet expansion plans in Latin American to a halt. He participated with Danny Graham in an organization called "Peace Through Strength," which Ronald Regan fully endorsed in his military buildup.

The Great Nightfall provides two extremely valuable contributions to the current debate on how best to improve American national security. First is a clear-eyed assessment of the threats, from China, Russia, North Korea, Iran, and others. For without fully understanding the dangers solutions are nearly impossible. Middendorf outlines these threats in a comprehensive way. Second, *The Great Nightfall* warns the current weapons and strategies for using them are in urgent need of updating. Defense and national security in the 21st century require both new technologies and better ways of fielding weapons systems rapidly and efficiently.

The universal goal of freedom-loving people in America and throughout the world remains unchanged: Peace through strength. Achieving peace through strength demands not only new and exotic weapons such as hypersonic missiles, or artificial intelligence--powered drones. It will require new strategies and new ways of thinking about mitigating existing and future threats.

The Great Nightfall correctly emphasizes that China above all-other threats must be the most important priority of American defense leaders. Confronting China and preventing its global ambition to push aside the United States and ultimately defeat it must be done. Our national survival in this struggle depends on winning the new Cold War with Beijing.

Bill Gertz
June 2020

Introduction: A Full Blown National Emergency

THE COLD WAR ENDED because we were the strongest military force in the world, backed by a unified NATO and strong allies in the Pacific. Times have changed. China challenges us as the number one military, and Russia is not far behind. NATO is no longer the cornerstone of European security and stability, and our allies in the Pacific are not a unified block, with China influencing defections or promoting fence sitting.[1]

We are now emerging from a period of strategic atrophy, aware that our military advantage has been eroding. Meanwhile, China is intimidating its neighbors while militarizing islands in the South China Sea and talks openly about invading Taiwan. The Hong Kong protests that began in the summer of 2019 continue to escalate, and it may be only a matter of time before China eliminates the "one country, two systems approach."[2]

In this book, we will cover the details of China building one of the most advanced military powers in world history, including missiles, undersea weapons, anti-satellite weapons, and a whole range of non-traditional warfare weapons such as EMP, cyber, AI, and bio-terrorism.

Russia has violated the borders of nearby nations while it continues to build its nuclear arsenal, advance missiles, and build its submarine force. North Korea continues to build its nuclear program, despite the United Nations' censure and sanctions. Iran continues to sow violence and undermine stability in the Middle East. Terrorist groups, sponsored by Iran, continue to murder the innocent and threaten peace.

The greatest threat to U.S. military strength is the misconception that America can no longer afford military superiority. The force we need will not come cheaply, but the costs of weakness and complacency are far greater. The costs of failing to meet America's crisis of national defense and national security will be measured in American lives, American treasure, and American security and prosperity. It will be a tragedy if the United States allows its national interests and national security to be compromised through an unwillingness to make hard choices and necessary investments. That tragedy will be more regrettable because it is within our power to avoid it.

NATO has faced criticism from American president Donald Trump for failing to live up to pledges for military expenditures. He pointed out that each member of NATO has pledged to devote 2 percent of its GDP to defense. Most members have failed to live up to this commitment, with Germany investing 1.2 percent of its GDP. President Trump also criticized a trade agreement that calls for Germany to buy billions of dollars in natural gas from Russia. "It certainly doesn't seem to make sense that Germany paid billions of dollars to Russia and we have to defend them against Russia," Trump said.[3]

U.S. military superiority has bred complacency among a population that has never known military defeat. Our military has been stretched to its limits, making do with aging ships, planes, and tanks. The threats we face have grown increasingly sophisticated with cyber war, artificial intelligence and space weapons for which we have no defense.

Throughout our history, the United States has considered the Pacific and the Atlantic oceans wide and virtually impassable moats assuring our security. The time has arrived when we must be concerned that they are easy channels of access for enemies. To defend ourselves and carry out our urgent responsibilities around the world, we must fully commit to developing and maintaining the world's best navy. We are not going to make the mistakes of the Allied powers in the 1930s of appeasing dictatorships bent on crushing democracies. We must be ready and willing to commit the resources needed to defend our cherished way of life.

The United States' trade deficit with China has climbed to more than $500 billion in hard currency, money that China uses to develop an array of advanced high technology weapons designed to defeat the United States in a future conflict. They include maneuverable missile warheads, hypersonic weapons, laser and beam weapons, electromagnetic rail guns, space weapons, and artificial intelligence robots. Once characterized by slow development, China is moving rapidly in the area of special weapons in ways not for military parity with the United States but for military supremacy.

The Chinese have launched a massive campaign to become the world's leading economic superpower. We know about the "Belt and Road Initiative," a strategic undertaking to place huge segments of the world under China's influence or outright control with their debt traps.[4] We know about "Made in China 2025," a strategy designed to dominate key technology sectors from artificial intelligence and quantum computing to hypersonic missiles and 5G.[5] We know about China's practice of forced technology transfers, requiring American companies to share their trade secrets and R&D in order to do business in China. We know about China's predatory trade practices. We know many of these things only because President Trump has brought them to the forefront of national attention, for which he deserves credit. And the ongoing tariff war is a good thing in the sense that we've finally begun to take a stand.

But there is an issue more critical than trade that Americans, by and large, *do not* know about: China has more than 700 companies on our stock and bond markets or capital markets. It has about 86 companies listed on the New York Stock Exchange, about 62 in the NASDAQ, and more than 500 in the murky, poorly regulated over-the-counter market. Among these companies are some egregious bad actors. Hikvision, for example, is responsible for facial recognition technology that identifies and monitors the movement of ethnic Uyghurs, persecuted Muslims living in China's northwest. It also produces the surveillance cameras placed atop the walls of Chinese concentration camps holding as many as two million Uyghurs in Xinjiang. Both its parent company and Hikvision itself are on the U.S. Commerce Department Entity List (what many describe as the "Blacklist").

Many of these American listed companies have raised billions of hard currency dollars for China from American investors and pension funds. Do any of us have the financing of concentration camps in mind when we transfer money into our retirement and investment accounts? This sounds difficult to believe, but it is an empirical fact: the majority of American investors are unwittingly funding Chinese concentration camps, weapons systems for the People's Liberation Army (PLA), and more. This is because the United States has no security-minded screening mechanism for our capital markets, which have roughly $35 trillion under management.

Then there is the question of China's military. Is it better than the United States' now? How about Russia? The United States may not stand a chance against a united Russia or China should World War III break out, analysts from the RAND Corporation concluded after performing simulated war scenarios concerning battles on land, sea, and air and in space and cyberspace. In scenario after scenario, the United States suffered severe losses despite spending nearly $1 trillion annually on the military, exceeding the spending of any other country by more than double.

"We lose a lot of people. We lose a lot of equipment. We usually fail to achieve our objective of preventing aggression by the adversary," David Ochmanek, a researcher for RAND, said. Though hypothetical, the simulated games warn that the world order America has fought to protect for more than a century could be at risk. "The brain and nervous system that connects all of these pieces is suppressed, if not shattered," Ochmanek warns.[6]

Robert Work, a former Deputy Secretary of Defense and experienced war-gamer, warns that U.S. military bases across Europe and the Pacific are not equipped to handle the fire they would face in a high-end conflict. Work said China would focus on cyberspace with "system destruction warfare," which involves targeting U.S. communications satellites, command-and-control systems, and wireless networks.[7]

If you thought the deadly coronavirus that broke out in Wuhan, China, and afflicted millions of people around the world originated in China, you're wrong, according to the Chinese Communist Party. U.S. military athletes participating in sporting events in Wuhan in October 2019 brought the disease with them, China's propaganda machine claims. China has been involved in a strategy of blame shifting ever since the virus was first identified.

Dr. Li Wenliang will be remembered for the dangers of being a messenger of bad news in a dictatorship. A 34-year-old physician at Wuhan Central Hospital, he was examining a glaucoma patient on December 30, 2019, when he noticed symptoms of what was to become known as coronavirus infection. After several other patients exhibited these symptoms, which were like SARS — the virus that led to a global epidemic in 2003 — he sent out a warning over the We Chat messaging application advising fellow medical school grads to wear protective clothing to avoid infection.

While Dr. Wenliang was just one of eight whistleblowers who tried to sound an early alarm about the new virus, it was his warning that alarmed the authorities. Denounced for "rumormongering," he was summoned to the Public Security Bureau and required to sign a letter in which he professed to have made "false comments" that had "severely disturbed the social order."[8]

Initially, the Chinese Communist Party (CCP) silenced whistleblowers like Dr. Wenliang who tried to limit the spread of the disease domestically and abroad. The government subsequently repressed the freedom of speech of bloggers who tried to share accurate information about the spread of the disease, the mortality rate, and the challenges faced by medical professionals.

The CCP's ongoing, systematic repression of both freedom of association and freedom of religion has stunted civil society's capacity to respond to crises like infectious diseases — and the government has cracked down on private citizens' attempts to help each other, including the donation of medical supplies. The CCP's onerous requirements for international nongovernmental organizations and its current policies also prevented international humanitarian aid from reaching the Chinese people in their time of need.

The worldwide implications of the coronavirus virus should serve as a wake-up call for the United States and its allies. What if China were to develop another virus together with an antidote for its own people? It could release the virus and combine it with EMC attacks and space weapons that could compromise our global positioning stations.

The coronavirus pandemic also alerted the U.S. public to how dependent we have become on China for essential medical and health supplies. According to the Centers for Disease Control, most of the drugs in the United States are imported, some from Europe. However, Europe also places the production base of these drugs in China, so more than 90 percent of the United States' imported drugs are in some way connected to China. The implication is that should China announce all drugs are needed for domestic consumption and ban exports, the United States could be virtually helpless in combatting a viral epidemic.

"It does fit a kind of scenario we have worried about in the field for a while now," says Cornelius Clancy, associate professor of medicine and director of the XOR pathogen laboratory at the University of Pittsburgh. "It wouldn't take much to expose the vulnerabilities in the supply chain."[9]

This is yet another lesson on the dangers of overreliance on foreign sources and just-in-time inventories for supplies that may be required to meet urgent needs. We cannot rely on others to take care of us when the chips are down. We cannot place our essential needs in the hands of others, particularly others with whom we have years of enmity. Having our medical imports cut off at any time would be extremely threatening and having that occur during a disease outbreak that China allowed to start and to spread would be catastrophic.[10]

Of course, medical services are — or should be — primarily civilian operations. It is when the United States only sources vital military supplies and components from China that alarms must really go off. The chemical Butanetriol is a propellant used in the HELLFIRE missile, one of the most effective and widely used United States military weapons since its introduction in 1985. Since securing the contract nearly 20 years ago, the missile propellant manufacturer — Copperhead Chemical Company, located in Pennsylvania — has relied on Shanghai Fuda Chemicals in China for the key propellant ingredient, Butanetriol (BT). Now the U.S. Government Accountability Office has ordered the military to fund a factory to produce the chemical.

A Pentagon commission ordered by President Trump identified hundreds of instances where the U.S. military depends on foreign countries, especially China, for critical materials. The commission determined that the United States is too dependent on foreign suppliers for a range of items, including microelectronics, tiny components such as integrated circuits and transistors. These kinds of essential components are embedded in advanced electronics used in everything from satellites and cruise missiles to drones and cell phones. The focus on China reflects an effort under Trump to address the risks to the United States' national security from Beijing's growing military and economic clout. Pentagon officials want to be sure China is not able to hobble America's military by cutting off supplies of materials or by sabotaging technology it exports. The Trump Administration's "Buy American" initiative aims to help drum up billions of dollars more in arms sales for United States manufacturers and create more jobs. One recommendation is "to ensure a robust, resilient, secure and ready manufacturing and defense industrial base."[11] China, which has also become the main supplier of many of the rare earth minerals used by the United States, was given special emphasis in the report. An analysis from the United States Geological Survey states that this county had produced no rare earth minerals in 2017, while China accounted for 81 percent of global mine production. Rare earth minerals are used in magnets, radars and consumer electronics.

Aside from the risk that a foreign power could cut off vital supplies needed to keep the United States military up and running, other risks include the threat of sabotaged equipment or espionage. The Pentagon has long fretted that "kill switches"[12] could be embedded in transistors that could turn off our sensitive systems in a conflict. Our intelligence officials also warned about the possibility China could use Chinese-made mobile phones and network equipment to spy on Americans. U.S. shortcomings that contribute to purchases from foreign companies include roller-coaster defense budgets that make it difficult for companies to predict government demand. Another weakness is in our science and technology education. Ways must be found to address America's loss of manufacturing, whose toll on national security gets far less attention than the jobs lost.

Beijing's "Made in China 2025" plan is a model of astonishing economic ambition and potential global hegemony. Achieved, it would carry China to the top in 10 major areas: robotics, ships, railway transport, next-generation vehicles, air and space, medicine, new materials, electronics, energy equipment, and agriculture equipment. From the perspective of 2020, however, "Made in China 2025" appears to be more of a rally cry for political support than a potentially done deal.

Chief among the obstacles to the plan is the ongoing trade war with the United States, identified as the main cause of the fall in advanced industrial output as high tariffs cut into demand, causing business and consumer confidence to shrink and so perpetuating a downward spiral in economic activity. Of course, Beijing could still pursue dominance in these high-tech areas within a smaller and contracting global economy. But the country would be operating against the economic headwinds of a domestic population dissatisfied with government requirements and restrictions.

The plan triggered a backlash from the European Union as well as the United States, China's biggest trading partners, who complained that Beijing's state-subsidized industrial strategy was unfair to foreign firms and, worse, would lead to market distortions. The United States has already imposed tariffs on $250 billion in Chinese goods — and has threatened duties on double that value of products, responding to what Washington has claimed as unfair trade practices in China.

As of this writing, the traffic truce agreed to by presidents Trump and Xi Jinping in late 2019 had gone no further, and analysts believe even if the two nations agree on no additional tariffs, manufacturers may still contemplate making their products in other locations that are less sensitive politically. Clearly, that is not a path toward "Made in China 2025."

"People used to think you could outsource the manufacturing base without any repercussions on national security," noted one high-ranking official. "But now we know that's not the case." One alarmed and expert observer of the foreign supply problem is Army Brigadier General (ret.) John Adams who argues:

Outsourcing America's defense industry makes us vulnerable. The threat of military supply chain disruptions due to natural disasters, traversing disputes in the South China Sea, foreign unrest, regime change, or price manipulation could result in a lack of needed materials like the components that we import for night-vision goggles, communications equipment, missile guidance systems, and other mission critical assets. And if China (whom we rely upon heavily for defense components) decides to cut shipments, then America's military will be left non-mission capable.

Overseas production reduces standards in quality. Our soldiers, sailors, airmen, and marines depend on equipment that is reliable and of the highest quality. Foreign supply chains have allowed the infiltration of counterfeit parts into some of our most advanced machinery. An investigation by the Senate Armed Services Committee found upwards of one million counterfeit components destined for use in "critical" defense systems.

Eroding our defense industrial base costs innovation, knowledge base and jobs. America is losing the knowledge and innovation bases that are vital to staying on the cutting edge of new military technology that puts our warfighters a step ahead of our enemies. A

xxi

growing reliance on foreign suppliers for military needs is resulting in the closure of our factories, meaning fewer job opportunities for everyday Americans — including veterans, who are more likely to work in manufacturing than non-veterans.[13]

Ellen Lord, the Pentagon's top weapons buyer, has publicly spoken about the Defense Production Act (DPA) of 1950, which allows the president to incentivize domestic producers of critical materials through purchase commitments and other guarantees. Lord said the government should step in to offer such support if businesses would be unable to ensure a "reasonable profit."[14]

Politicians have long argued that the United States spends much more on defense than any other country. But those figures are misleading, according to Army Chief of Staff General Mark Milley. "I've seen comparative numbers of United States defense budget versus China and Russia," General Milley said. "What is not often commented on is the cost of labor. We're the best-paid military in the world. The cost of Russian or Chinese soldiers is a tiny fraction. Our military spends almost half its budget on pay and benefits for uniformed and civilian personnel. China and Russia spend the bulk of their budgets on weapons, R&D, operations and training. The purchasing power of China and Russia's defense budgets increases China's to $434.5 billion and Russia's to $157.6 billion."[15]

The "tooth to tail ratio" refers to the amount of money, personnel or other resources needed for a deployed ship, aircraft squadron, or ground force compared to the money, personnel or other resources needed to train, equip and sustain those deployed forces (training pipeline, major maintenance, etc.). China and Russia's "tooth to tail ratio" is far more efficient than that of the United States and its allies.

Understanding the connection between Chinese military spending and Chinese military power is complicated by a lack of transparency. Although Beijing provides figures for its defense spending each year, outside estimates of China's budget are often significantly higher than the official numbers. China provides limited information on the distribution of its military spending which further obscures spending patterns. Experts agree that China spends more on the military than Japan, South Korea, the Philippines, and Vietnam combined.

China's rising defense spending follows from more than two decades of modernization efforts. China began modernization in earnest after the 1995–1996 Taiwan Strait crisis, which exposed fundamental weaknesses in China's ability to deter foreign intervention in sovereignty disputes. The increase in China's defense spending during this period was a response to domestic policies that left China's budget relatively stagnant in the 2000s.

Russia is expected to begin gradually increasing its defense budget in 2020. After years of decline, Russia has been rebuilding its military power in recent years. Moscow claims that the share of new equipment in the Russian military is expected to reach 70 percent in 2020.

Flash Points That Could Trigger World War III

Chinese threat to Taiwan. China's long-standing threat to end the de facto independence of Taiwan and ultimately bring it under the authority of Beijing is a threat to the stability in the western Pacific.

Chinese threat to Hong Kong. The 2019 Hong Kong protests, also known as the Anti-Extradition Law Bill movement, triggered a wave of demonstrations in Hong Kong. If it had been signed into law, the bill would have required Hong Kong residents charged with crimes to be tried in China. Although the Hong Kong government withdrew the extradition bill, the protests continue and the violence increases. What began as peaceful mass marches has exploded into the city's biggest political crisis in modern times. Unrest is expected to continue, with protesters digging in for prolonged urban warfare against the government and police. The question is how long will Beijing wait before taking military action? On November 16, 2019, Chinese soldiers in black shorts and olive T-shirts jogged out of a barracks in Hong Kong and cleared streets of bricks, metal bars, and other debris left by demonstrators. The presence of the soldiers fueled speculation about the extent of their future role in Hong Kong.

Differences between the United States and China in the South China Sea have expanded significantly with Chinese militarization of the seven man-made Spratly Islands. China also routinely and vigorously protests routine United States Navy "freedom of navigation" operations in the area, which have increased in frequency and intensity during the Trump Administration.[16]

North Korea's conventional and nuclear missile forces threaten United States bases in South Korea, Japan, and Guam. Pyongyang has several different intercontinental ballistic missiles (ICBMs) with enough range to hit the continental United States. After President Donald Trump met with North Korean leader Kim Jong-un, both leaders declared there was no longer a nuclear threat in Korea. Since the meeting, our intelligence community assessed that Pyongyang had increased production of fissile material for nuclear weapons, and satellite imagery showed upgrades to missile, reentry vehicle, missile launcher, and nuclear weapon production facilities.

Iran. The world's foremost sponsor of terrorism, Iran has made extensive efforts to export its radical brand of Islamist revolution. It also possesses the largest number of deployed missiles in the Middle East. Iran has threatened to disrupt the flow of Persian Gulf oil by closing the Strait of Hormuz in the event of a conflict with the United States and its allies.

Russia vs. NATO. Russia has significant conventional and nuclear capabilities and remains the top threat to European security. Its aggressive stance in a number of theaters, including the Balkans, Georgia, Syria, and Ukraine, continues both to encourage destabilization and to threaten United States interests.

India vs. Pakistan. With continued violence in Kashmir and a heightened threat of terrorist activity by Pakistan-based militant groups, tensions and concerns over a serious military confrontation between nuclear-armed neighbors India and Pakistan remain high.

Japan vs. China. China has declared a formal Air Defense Identification Zone covering airspace over islands in the East China Sea called the Senkaku by Japan and Diaoyu by China.

Terrorist organizations. Radical Islamist terrorism in its many forms remains a threat to the safety and security of U.S. citizens at home and abroad. Most of the terrorist threats originate in the greater Middle East.

Venezuela. Since January 2019, the Trump Administration, joined by governments in Latin America and Europe, has called for President Nicolás Maduro to step down, partly because the country has suffered from an economic collapse and humanitarian crisis during his rule. With the country in flames, China and Russia are seeking claims in the rubble. For years, China and Russia have sought more influence in the Western Hemisphere but are increasingly motivated to bolster their economic and security positions in South America, Central America, and the Caribbean. China has pledged to invest $250 billion there and reach half a trillion in trade, while Russia has invested billions in Venezuela.

Although the Kremlin insists it has a right to send Russian troops to Venezuela, the United States disagrees. Elliott Abrams, our special representative for Venezuela, said the United States could impose sanctions in response to the presence of Russian troops in Venezuela. "We have options and it would be a mistake for the Russians to think they have a free hand."[17]

Another part of the problem in Venezuela is the presence of 20,000 to 25,000 Cuban security officials. Communist-run Cuba has been a key backer of the Venezuelan government since the Bolivarian Revolution that began under former leader Hugo Chávez in 1998.

John Bolton, former National Security Advisor, warned that the administration might use the Monroe Doctrine to force Russian troops to withdraw from Venezuela. Bolton was referring to an 1820 policy from President James Monroe, when the United States moved to prevent European colonization or intervention in the Western Hemisphere's newly independent nations. "This is a country in our hemisphere. It's been the objective of American presidents going back to Ronald Reagan to have a completely democratic hemisphere," Bolton said.[18]

Spending money on social programs at the expense of national defense has left the U.S. Navy in a vulnerable position to carry out its mission. In 1917, our navy had 245 active ships. The number peaked at a massive 6,758 ships during World War II. Then the number drifted down during most of the 20th century, with slight upticks during the Korean War and the Vietnam War. As of 2015, the number of active ships stood at 272, which is the lowest since 1917. After considering its future military needs, the navy has set a goal for a fleet of 308 ships by 2022 at the earliest.

There are two reasons why we need a strong military budget: (1) to make up for the savage cuts made by previous administrations and (2) to deal with the fact that the world has gotten so much more dangerous with Russia and China possessing precision-strike capabilities, integrated air defenses, cruise and ballistic missiles, advanced cyber warfare, and anti-satellite capabilities. If the United States had to fight Russia in a Baltic contingency or China in a war over Taiwan, we could face a decisive military defeat.

In a future war, we will not have the luxury of being a privileged sanctuary where we can be the model of democracy for others while they fight. Our entire country becomes a legitimate target, particularly with the space weapons being developed by China and Russia. Investing in the correct weapons systems is critical and must be done now.

The first American president, George Washington, enunciated a policy of peace through strength. The best example of the concept of peace through strength occurred when I was Secretary of the Navy in the Ford Administration. We addressed the threat from the Soviet Union by developing the Trident submarine, the Aegis missile system, and the F/A-18 fighter. We had sufficient lead-time to meet the apogee of the Soviet build-up, which we anticipated to be in the 1980s. Years later, a Russian admiral told me that his country could not match those weapons systems and thus the Cold War ended.

Over the past 80 years, I have had several direct and indirect brushes with communism. In the early 1940s, the communist John Reed Society and its dreams of nirvana were popular with a number of my classmates at Harvard. To entice me to join, I was visited by three beautiful young ladies wearing Hawaiian grass skirts, indicating possible promises of future benefits of membership. I did not join. Year later, I reflected on the importance of this decision when I appeared before the Senate Armed Services Committee as a candidate for Secretary of the Navy.

I was in China as an officer in the U.S. Navy in December 1945 when George Atcheson, Jr., Chargé d'Affaires in China and advisor to General MacArthur during World War II, tried to mediate the conflicts between the Chinese Communist Party and the Kuomintang led by General Chiang Kai-shek.

Atcheson did not try to hide his dislike for Chiang Kai-shek and labeled his government corrupt. He described Mao Zedong as "the George Washington of the Pacific."[19] Chiang Kai-shek also had a strained relationship with General Joseph W. Stillwell, who was assigned to China in January 1942 to represent our interests. Stillwell and Chiang Kai-shek clashed repeatedly about military strategy and the best use of military resources. Before Stillwell was replaced in 1944, he had shared much of his criticism of Chiang Kai-shek with his good friend, General George Marshall.

General Marshall arrived in China 1945, assigned by President Harry Truman to somehow unify the battling Nationalists and Communists into a strong non-Communist government that could serve as a bulwark against the Soviet Union. By great coincidence, my ship was stationed in China at that time, and I was temporarily assigned to the security forces during Marshall's visit.

After more than a year of negotiations, Marshall achieved no significant agreements. But the net effect was to weaken the Nationalists when, in a vain attempt to broker a ceasefire, he recommended that the sale of weapons and ammunition we had been making to the Nationalists be suspended between July 29, 1946, and May 1947. General Douglas MacArthur described Marshall's mission as "one of the greatest blunders in American diplomatic history for which the free world is now paying in blood and disaster."[20] A year later, Congress recognized the mistake and rushed aid to the Nationals, but it was too late, and China fell to the Communists in 1949. Millions of Chinese deaths were the result of the actions by Atcheson, Stillwell, and Marshall in suspending the delivery of weapons to the Nationals. A number of American deaths in the Korean War occurred directly after the Chinese came to the aid of North Korea.

Despite Marshall's impressive military career and good standing as a trustworthy man who worked hard for America's interests, public opinion became bitterly divided about him. In 1952, Dwight Eisenhower, while campaigning for president, denounced the Truman Administration's failures in Korea and refused to defend Marshall's policies.

My next brush with communism was on a personal level. With several partners, I owned a factory in Cuba manufacturing hardboard from sugar beet stalks (bagasse). Hardboard was in short supply in Cuba and the entire Caribbean. With 400 employees and a huge demand for our products, everything looked positive — until I made what turned out to be my final visit to Cuba in the late 1950s.

The plant manager, Bill Miller, was alarmed to see me and warned that I had to leave immediately. A man named Fidel Castro was in the countryside, burning and looting everything in his path. We could hear gunfire in the distance as one of our warehouses was set on fire. We left immediately in a small plane and heard bursts of gunfire as we took off. The pilot told me later that there were bullet holes in the tail of the aircraft. The factory was destroyed, the machinery was sold for scrap, and 400 people were put out of work.

By the end of 1959, Castro revolutionaries were making a final push to overthrow Fulgencio Batista's regime. Just days after Batista fled the country, Ed Sullivan, host of a popular American television show, interviewed Castro. When asked about the future of his country, Castro vowed that Cuba would "never again be governed by a dictator."[21] Free elections would be held and Cuba would become a democratic society, Castro promised. Later, Castro declared himself a Marxist-Lenist, and an iron curtain descended over Cuba.

In 1991, as communism was collapsing in the Soviet Union, President Boris Yeltsin invited a team from the Heritage Foundation to help draft a constitution for the new Russia. The team was headed by Dr. Edwin J. Feulner, the president of the Heritage Foundation, and included key members of the Heritage Foundation. As a member of the Board of Trustees of the Heritage Foundation, I was invited to participate.

Relations between Yeltsin and the Duma (Russian parliament) had been deteriorating for some time. The chief cause of Russia's low standard of living was the inefficiency of its government-owned and managed enterprises, which misused the country's skilled workforce, scarce capital and raw materials. Yeltsin realized that privatization, the process of transferring state-owned facilities to private sector owners, was the only way the new Russia could survive.

After a number of visits and working with the head of the Russian delegation appointed by Yeltsin, we wrote the "Russian Privatization Handbook."[22] Sergei Krasnachenko, head of the Russian delegation, sent me a note indicating that our privatization recommendations were now in place. He included an original copy of the *Privatization Handbook*, complete with annotations, a document I treasure.

Unfortunately, communist members of the Dumas prevented many of our key recommendations from going into effect. William Eggers, a member of the Russian Republic Heritage Privatization Team, and I wrote a letter to President Yeltsin and other leaders of the Soviet republic expressing our concern about the lack of progress in privatization efforts. Here are three paragraphs excerpted from our letter:

1. President Yeltsin, you are strongly committed to private property and a rapid move to a market economy. For the past year, a team from the Heritage Foundation has been working closely with the Russian Republic Privatization Team you created and which is totally orientated to converting the Russian Republic to free market principles. Numerous important laws have been passed this last year by your Parliament that go much further than the Soviet laws in laying the groundwork for the transition to a free market economy. However, to date, relatively little serious economic reform has taken place in Russia, because entrenched interests have sabotaged your efforts. Now it is time to use your tremendously increased powers and prestige to act quickly and decisively in introducing revolutionary economic changes to jump-start your economy.

2. Military spending must be radically cut back. No nation can devote 25 percent or more of GNP to the military over a prorated period. As the new Soviet Defense Minister Yevgeny Shaposhnikov is well aware, the military would be better served in the long run by a smaller piece of a growing pie, rather than the lion share of a shrinking pond.

3. The rapid breakup of the Soviet Empire means that freedom and democracy will finally come to billions of citizens — Lithuanians, Ukrainians, Armenians, Moldavians, Russians and the others who have lived under oppression all of their lives. The opportunities for increasing the economic well being of your people are immense. However, this will only happen if you adopt full-fledged free market reforms and seek ways to increase, not decrease, the free flow of goods and services between your borders.

Free trade and free markets are the only ways to lift your economy out of stagnation and give hope and promise to this and future generations of your people.

Some of the recommendations made by the Heritage team remain in the Russian constitution today. One of them spells out an election policy that contributed to the loss of multiple seats in Putin's ruling party in a September 2019 election. Russian opposition leader Alexei Navalny claimed a technical victory in the elections, saying that United Russia had suffered a major setback. Under Stalin's regime, voters who opposed him would have simply been shot. We must not make the mistakes of the Allied powers in the 1930s of appeasing dictatorships bent on crushing democracies. We should be ready and willing to commit the resources needed to defend our cherished way of life.

This book is not a call for war. The best way to prepare for war is to be prepared to win it. We need to stop underfunding the military, especially in areas of research, non-conventional war, space, cyber war, and artificial intelligence. War is changing, and we need to change with it. We cannot expect success fighting tomorrow's conflicts with yesterday's weapons.

I have been asked frequently why, at age 95, I am so concerned about a future that I will never see. It reminds me of an old Greek proverb: "A society grows great when old men plant trees whose shade they shall never sit in."[23] After serving in the U.S. Navy in World War II and leaving Wall Street for public service, I have long been concerned about the well-being of our nation and its citizens.

I remember when we appeased a dictator in Europe that brought Adolf Hitler to power and 73 million people died in World War II. I was in China in 1945 when General Marshall began undermining Chiang Kai-shek and four years later the country became communist. I was in Cuba shortly before Castro took over the country. I spent four years at the Navy Department devoting every minute to overcoming the rising Soviet threat. I, together with Dr. Edwin J. Feulner, then president of the Heritage Foundation, met with Boris Yeltsin after the fall of the Soviet Union and helped write a new constitution for what we hoped would become a new democracy.

My friend the poet Robert Frost honored me with a handwritten copy of his poem "Stopping by Woods on a Snowy Evening." Like the subject of the poem, I have miles to go before I sleep.

J. William Middendorf II
Little Compton RI

NOTES

1. Max Bergmann, "An Alliance in Crisis: Europe Needs to Act Quickly to Defend Itself," Center for American Progress, June 1, 2017.
2. Brian Wong and John Mak, "One Country, Two Systems Is Still the Best Model for Hong Kong But It Really Needs Reform," *Time*, October 20, 2017.
3. Kristine Wong, "Trump's NATO Criticism Wins Positive Reviews," *The Hill*, June 16, 2016.
4. "How Can Chinese Companies Benefit from the Belt and Road Initiative," *The Motley Fool*, Yahoo Finance, May 7, 2019.
5. Kristen Hopewell, "What Is 'Made in China 2025' and Why Is It a Threat to China's Trade Goals," *Washington Post*, May 3, 2018.
6. David Ochmanek, "Improving Force Development Within the Department of Defense," Rand Corporation, 2018.
7. Robert O. Work, "Artificial Intelligence in the Hypersonic Era," Center for a New American Security, June 30, 2019.
8. Bruce Simson, "Who Was Li Wenliang, the Chinese Doctor Who Warned About Coronavirus?" *Fox News*, March 20, 2020.
9. Dr. Cornelius Clancy, "Experts Say U.S. Surpassing Italy, China in COVID-19 Cases Was Inevitable," *Helio Infectious Disease News*, March 30, 2020.
10. John McShane, "Coronavirus Crisis Exposes U.S. Dependence on Other Nations for Drug Ingredients," CNBC, April 29, 2020.
11. Maegan Vasquez, "Trump Signs Measure Aimed at His 'Buy American Initiative,'" CNN, January 31, 2019.
12. Jonohan Zittrain, "The Case for Kill Switches in Military Weaponry," *Scientific American*, September 3, 2014.
13. Brig. Gen. John Adams, "Outsourcing America's Defense Industry Makes Us Vulnerable," Center for Climate and Security's Advisory Board, February 7, 2019.
14. Ellen Lord, "Lord Urges Defense Workers to Stay on the Job," *Breaking Defense*, April 1, 2020.
15. Sydney J. Freedberg, "Gen. Mark A. Milley: 'U.S. Defense Budget Not That Much Bigger Than China, Russia,'" *Breaking Defense*, May 22, 2018.
16. "U.S. Navy Conducts 'Freedom of Navigation' Exercises in South China Sea," *Orissa Post*, April 23, 2020.
17. Tom O'Connor, "U.S Takes New Action Against Venezuela as Russia and China Warn Trump Administration to Stay Away," *Newsweek*, March 1, 2019.
18. David Richardson, "John Bolton Reaffirms America's Commitment to the Monroe Doctrine with New Sanctions," *Observer*, January 17, 2020.
19. "George Atcheson Jr. Papers, 1937–1948," UC Berkeley, Bancroft Library.
20. H.W. Brands, *The General vs. the President: MacArthur and Truman at the Brink of Nuclear War* (New York: Random House, 2016).
21. "Cuban Revolution, Facts and Worksheets," kidsconnect.COM, 2018.
22. *Russian Privatization Handbook*, 1991, Middendorf Private Collection.
23. *Bartlett's Familiar Quotations*.

The Great Nightfall

1 | The Threat from China

On May 29, 2019, President Donald Trump held a news conference in the White House Rose Garden to announce to the world his administration's new policies on relations with Hong Kong, the Chinese city of seven million which, since being turned over to Chinese rule by the British in 1997, has operated under a "one-nation, two systems" protocol. The system in Hong Kong is far more democratic than in the People's Republic of China (PRC), and new security legislation proposed and then enacted by the PRC to severely limit democratic freedoms there has resulted in general unrest and protests in the streets.

The press corps received a surprise when Trump announced his administration would end almost all aspects of the American government's special relationship with Hong Kong, including those on trade and law enforcement. He then went on to blast China for its responsibilities in the still-spreading COVID-19 pandemic and announced that the United States was withdrawing from the World Health Organization, for which it has been by far the largest source of funds.

"My announcement today will affect the full range of agreements we have with Hong Kong," he said, including "action to revoke Hong Kong's preferential treatment as a separate customs and travel territory from the rest of China."[1]

President Xi made no immediate comment. There were, of course, complaints in the nationalistic press. *The Global Times,* a tabloid controlled by the Communist Party, all but dared the United States to carry out these threats, noting that the 85,000 Americans living in Hong Kong, and the many American companies there would suffer from it.[2]

Two days before President Trump's news conference, Foreign Secretary Michael Pompeo announced that the State Department no longer considers Hong Kong to have the significant autonomy under PRC rule that is required to qualify for special trade and economic relations with the United States. The news corps assembled in the Rose Garden were therefore genuinely uncertain about what they might hear. Confirming

Pompeo's announcement would be significantly out of keeping with the president's campaign to reform and improve trade relations with the PRC, which has largely defined his presidency.[3]

In 2019, after threatening a veto, he had reluctantly signed a U.S. bill toughening the Hong Kong Policy Act of 1992, explaining that it would interfere with his effort the achieve the China trade deal.[4] At the wrap-up news conference of the National People's Congress on the same week, Premier Li Keqiang twice called for "peaceful" relations with Taiwan, signaling that the Pompeo and Trump announcement had caused no strain in the U.S.–China relations.[5]

Only a week before he had omitted the traditional adjective "friendly" in describing what the PRC believes will be the eventual and inevitable reunification of the island nation with mainland China. He also went out of his way to praise the American company Honeywell's announced investment plans in Wuhan, the Chinese city now destined to be forever famous as the origin of the COVID-19 pandemic.[6]

In terms of military capabilities, economic ambitions and aggressive attitude, our most serious threat is from China. "Anyone who attempts to split any region from China will perish, with their bodies smashed and bones ground to powder," warned President Xi on October 13, 2019.[7]

But such violent language, intended for Chinese public consumption, can be misleading. To understand China and its strategies, it is crucial not to lose sight of the fact that, while our government looks to the short term, including the next election, the Chinese work toward 2050. These are two totally different views, which define the way in which the competition is being played.

Between 2020 and 2050 there could be as many as seven different U.S. presidential administrations working with as many as 14 different and often furiously partisan Congresses. In China President Xi is likely to be succeeded by no more than three or four presidents, each of them working with rubber stamp legislatures. Consistent policies and plans, so essential in the economy and especially in the military, are all but assured.

With a growing population and a slowing economy, public support can be an issue. But while there are protests — often about corrupt lower level officials — there is a fundamental national fervor PRC government can count on.

This ideal of Chinese nationalism is embodied in Lang Feng, hero of *Wolf Warrior 2*, the highest grossing film in Chinese history. Lang is a retired commando racing from one incredible triumph to another. After defeating a tank-equipped force of African mercenaries with his home-made cross bow, he dispatches their racist American boss, who proclaims with his dying breath, "People like you will always be inferior to people like me."[8]

Lang's China is both feared for its strength and admired for its generosity and for its respect for international law. A naval commander will not launch missiles to save the day until his radio operator tells him that the Chinese ambassador has relayed authorization for the launch from the United Nations. Some audiences of *Wolf Warrior 2* are so impressed that they sing the national anthem from their seats.[9]

With this degree of public support, the PRC government takes the exceptionally long view of international affairs. Over the next 30 years they can look to finally gobbling up Taiwan and some of the disputed outer islands to the east, likely undisputed control of the South and East China Seas to the south and satisfactory resolution of border disputes with India and total control of Muslim areas to the west. From that point of view the dustup over Hong Kong is of minor consequence and will soon be out of the way.

In the short term, the Chinese have started to fix their tremendous errors in handling COVID. They have developed a strategy based on the following principles:

1. efficiency in contagion control,

2. speed in the recovery of the economy,

3. speed in developing a virus vaccine, and

4. good internal coordination and active international cooperation in combating the pandemic and in supporting the poorest.

As far as it has been reported in open sources, currently China is ahead of the United States in these areas. China's main objective, outside COVID-19, is internal social stability. Its economy must grow at a rate that allows it to absorb entrants into the workforce, at a rate of 10 or 11 million a year. A decade ago, growth of 10 percent was required to achieve this goal. Today 5.5 percent is enough, a result of economic reforms.[10]

China still faces tough challenges: the high amount of debt and the housing bubble; a spectacular concentration of income; the demographic problem (it needs more better trained people in certain areas, more participation and more productivity); and the serious environmental problem, with high levels of contamination, an issue that has also become a source of protest from its citizens and internationally.[11]

Companies involved in artificial intelligence, big data, cloud storage, and so on depend critically on 5G networks. Experts maintain that China is ahead in this field, and in 2030 it hopes to launch 6G networks. The United States, of course, is also working feverishly on 6G technology and networks.[12]

President Xi, an engineer, is one of the world's most informed and concerned leaders regarding these issues. He understands how global value chains and new technologies work internally and internationally. We all understand that today the strength of leading countries is in the data economy, which requires education and qualified work, and it is part of that Chinese dream that comes from Sun Yat-sen, from Zhou Enlai, from Deng, and now continues with Xi. There is a continuity. What are we doing about this competition? Probably not enough.[13]

With its tightly organized, hard-working, and ever-better educated population of 1.4 billion, its extraordinary technological development, and the world's second largest and fastest growing military, China looks past the pain and humiliations of civil war in the 1940s, the Japanese occupation of the 1930s, and colonial occupations by England and the other European powers in the 19th and early 20th centuries to vast and rapidly growing global trade and eventual Asian and pan-Pacific and Indian Ocean economic and military dominance. Near term, that certainly explains its indifference to complaints by the United States and neighboring countries about its militarization of islands in the South China Sea, its ferocious ambitions over the "breakaway" province of Taiwan, and its recent threats against Hong Kong.

"As a major power, the United States cannot afford to take its eye off the ball as national threats loom beyond COVID-19," notes Thomas Spoehr, Director of the Center for National Defense, the Heritage Foundation, Washington, D.C. "Threats that existed before the emergence of the coronavirus have not magically disappeared. They must be reckoned with still. For the sake of our nation, we can and must both prepare for future pandemics and build a strong military. When in the grip of an epidemic, it may be tempting to suggest that the U.S. swiftly shift its priorities away from building a strong military and toward pandemic preparation. Beijing's duplicity in the early months of the COVID pandemic illustrates the Chinese Communist Party's real priorities that do not involve maintaining a stable international order."[14]

James J. Carafano, a leading expert in national security and foreign policy for the Heritage Foundation, warns about the variety of challenges the national faces. The *"free world"* is a term that is going to make a big comeback, Carafano predicts, pointing out that there is a defining difference between the United States and the Chinese Communist government. "Economic freedom, human rights and popular sovereignty, the cores of American beliefs are foreign to the Chinese Communist Party. Countries intent on preserving popular freedom will have to pick a side. By triggering a global disease outbreak, the Chinese Communist Party's reprehensible behavior crossed the last line, leaving other nations no recourse but to push back hard. No longer can responsible nations tolerate the regime's destabilizing interference around the world. China doesn't have a hammerlock on any part of the world other than North Korea and a handful of Southeast Asian countries."[15]

Carafano predicts that China may have difficulty keeping those countries under control in the future. Disputes like the one now going on over the Mekong River in Southeast Asia may lead to countries becoming independent from China. The Meekong is southeast Asia's longest river over 3,000 miles long. It flows southward through the Chinese province of Yunnan before passing through Myanmar, Thailand, Laos, Cambodia, and Vietnam. For the 70 million people who live in the Mekong basin, the river is a vital source of food and water.

"Even as COVID-19 is wreaking havoc and uncertainty around the globe, Vietnam's Meking Delta declared an emergency over the devastating drought in early March of 2020. Studies suggest that the frequency and severity of droughts in the Mekong region have increased in the past decades, and many blame upstream dams, particularly those in China, for exacerbating the droughts," Carafano says.[16]

"Beijing's partnerships with Russia, Iran, Venezuela and Cuba are only marginal, and all of these countries are embroiled in competition of their own, leaving them politically and economically isolated from various parts of the world. They are at best partnerships of convenience, not real strategic alliances," according to Carafano. He predicts that "the vast majority of the world is, and for the foreseeable future, will be divided into: (1) the free working world, which is resilient against Chinese meddling; (2) the "balancers," which are nations recognizing that engaging with both the United States and China, protecting their independence and minimizing the likelihood that they will become theaters of competition between great powers are the keys to their prosperity and security, and (3) "contested space", the battle grounds where the U.S., China and others compete for influence in some or all of the economic, political, security and information spheres." He breaks the world into five camps.

1. United States–Canada–Mexico
"The hemispheric triad is the base of American power. The prosperity, economics, infrastructure, security and public health of these three countries are intertwined. The newly implemented U.S.–Canada–Mexico Free Trade Agreement further cemented the three economies together. The U.Su. and Mexico have implemented unprecedented cooperation on immigration and border security. In addition, as more U.S. companies look to move manufacturing partnerships out of China, more of that business is likely to go to Mexico."

2. Transatlantic Community

"No strategic partnership is more important to the free world than the transatlantic community. The U.S. isn't going to give up on this partnership. Neither should Europe. If Europeans want to keep their freedoms, they can't be neutral observers in the competition between the U.S. and China. Expect renewed investments in the transatlantic community post-COVID, not just to restart our joint economic engine, but also to marginalize the malicious influences of China."

3. The Middle East

"China will never supplant U.S. influence and importance in this region. If anything, Washington has an opportunity to expand its influence and establish a sustainable footprint for contributing to peace, stability and propensity in the Greater Middle East post-COVID-19. The key to that is putting a security, political and economic structure in place."

4. The Indo-Pacific

"One of the positive developments of the COVID-19 outbreak is that it has promoted cooperation among the 'quad-plus' group in fashioning a response. The United States along with India, Japan, South Korea, Australia, New Zealand, Vietnam and Taiwan offer a formidable diplomatic framework for bringing peace and prosperity to this part of the world in the face of China's bullying influence."

5. The Arctic and Antarctic

"The Arctic and Antarctic are both areas where China would like to have a lot more sway. From economic and environmental perspectives, these regions must remain areas of open cooperation, not competition. The peoples of the region and the planet will only benefit if these areas remain places of mutual cooperation. The U.S. will have to be party of a joint effort to curt China's unreasonable Arctic ambitions."

"The rise of China is the most persistent and consequential challenge that will confront the United States for the next several decades, according to Dean Cheng, Senior Research Fellow, Asian Studies Center, Davis Institute for National Security, the Heritage Foundation. "Even before the outbreak of COVID-19, China served as an irresponsible global actor that threatened American interests and values worldwide. The threats that China poses are growing. Evidence of this is seen on a day-to-day basis on a range of American interests from freedom of the seas to the security of its allies and even security at home, particularly in cyberspace. Chinese authorities' sanction or direct attacks on U.S. government cyber networks, steal the intellectual property of American companies, and threaten the free travel of ships and planes over international waters. The Chinese regime encroaches on the security of America's allies and partners in the region and interferes in their democratic processes. State-directed Chinese investment in sub-Saharan Africa and other developing regions of the world give the Communist dictatorship enormous influence over those regions and over the directions of their governments. Most recently, Beijing is backing the Hong Kong government's violent crackdown on civil disobedience and unrest, which started as a result of China's interference in Hong Kong's guaranteed autonomy."[17]

The People's Republic of China (PRC) is in the process of building and deploying a sophisticated and modern missile arsenal, according to the 2019 Assessing Threats to U.S. Vital Interests. Appropriately, in the 2017 National Security Strategy the Trump Administration made clear that it was shifting the focus of American security planning away from counter-terrorism and back to great-power competition, necessary for defending against adversaries' escalating missile and other weapons capabilities.

In particular, it noted that "China is challenging American power, influence, and interests, attempting to erode American security and prosperity. "China is determined to make economies less free and less fair, to grow its military, and to control information and data to repress its society and expand its influence. The PRC has a far larger economy, as well as the world's second-largest gross domestic product (GDP), and is intertwined in the global supply chain for crucial technologies, especially those relating to information and communications technology (ICT)."

The Strategy continued that, "Supported by these enormous resources, the PRC's ongoing comprehensive military modernization program, spanning the conventional, space, and cyber realms, including a multi-pronged nuclear modernization effort, has been going on for two decades and is rapidly accelerating. Matching this armaments buildup has been a far more aggressive stance toward neighboring countries. Territorial claims in the South China Sea, on the border with India and, of course, "province" of Taiwan all have the potential for military conflict."

The Threats Assessment also noted that the Chinese People's Liberation Army (PLA) is one of the world's largest militaries and is now mainly armed with modern weapons and equipment. "Nearly two decades of officially acknowledged double-digit growth in the Chinese defense budget have resulted in a comprehensive modernization program that has benefited every part of the PLA," the Threat Assessment states. "This has been complemented by improvements in Chinese military training and, at the end of 2015, the largest reorganization in the PLA's history.

The overall size of the PLA has shrunk, including a 300,000-person cut in the past two years, but its overall capabilities have increased as older platforms have been replaced with newer systems that are much more sophisticated."

Of great concern are the advanced capabilities, such as maneuverable anti-ship ballistic missiles, multiple independently targetable reentry vehicles (MIRVs), and hypersonic glide vehicles under development, according to the 2020 Index of Military Strength. "The combination of these trends degrades the survivability of foundational elements of American power projection like the aircraft carrier and forward air bases. China also has a developing contingent of nuclear intercontinental ballistic missiles (ICBMs) capable of striking every major city in the United States as well as a growing fleet of nuclear ballistic missile submarines."

The Index further notes that the PLA is continuing to extend its reach and military activities beyond its immediate region and conduct larger and more comprehensive exercises. These exercises include live firing of weapons in the East China Sea near Taiwan. Probes of the South Korean and Japanese air defense identification zones have drawn rebukes from both Seoul and Tokyo.

China's pursuit of a range of "advanced weapons with disruptive military potential," is noted with particular concern in the 2019 Annual Report of the U.S.-China Economic and Security Review Commission. The report outlines six types of advanced arms programs that Beijing has made priority developments in seeking "dominance" in the high-tech weapons area. They include maneuverable missile warheads, hypersonic weapons, laser and beam weapons, electromagnetic rail guns, space weapons, and artificial intelligence-directed robots.

"China revealed two anti-ship ballistic missiles with maneuverable reentry vehicles in 2010 and 2015 and has also set up the sensors and satellites needed for striking moving targets at sea — weapons designed for use against U.S. aircraft carriers and other warships," the report noted. "Beijing's hypersonic missiles are in the developmental stage but are progressing rapidly, with seven hypersonic glide vehicle tests since 2014 and one reported scramjet engine flight test in 2015."(James Carafano)

General John Hyten, head of U.S. Strategic Command, warns in the report, "We don't have any defense against hypersonic missiles, estimated to have a speed of Mach 20 (about 15,000 mph). Directed energy weapons include work on high-power microwave anti-missile systems and high-energy chemical lasers that can blind or damage satellites."[18]

The DF-31 missile series, a solid-fueled, road-mobile system with a range of 6,835 miles and the DF-41 series with a range of 8,388 miles are the core of China's ICBM force today. Medium-range nuclear forces have also shifted to mobile, solid-fuel rocket systems making them easier to maintain and more survivable. Under development are electromagnetic rail guns firing projectiles that destroy targets with enormous impact instead of explosives.

"Space weapons include direct-ascent anti-satellite missiles, ground-based directed energy weapons, and rendezvous and proximity operations for destroying or grabbing satellites, the report continues. And smart weapons include robotic, self-thinking cruise missiles, autonomous vehicles, and swarms of drones. Weapons system improvement is supported by such technological advances as semiconductors, supercomputing, industrial robotics, and quantum information science. So the U.S. is threatened by potential attacks against ships at sea, hypersonic missiles penetrating missile defenses, rail guns, and space arms that could block U.S. military operations in a future conflict. Large numbers of unmanned smart weapons could also be used to saturate U.S. air defenses," according to the report.

Missiles of China. Credit: Center for Strategic and International Studies

"Given Beijing's commitment to its current trajectory, and the lack of fundamental barriers to advanced weapons development beyond time and funding, the U.S. cannot assume it will have an enduring advantage in developing next frontier military technology," the Report states. "In addition, current technological trends render the preservation of any advantage even more difficult."

China may still have the number two military but like that auto rental company, it is trying hard to move into first place. "Once characterized by decades-long development, China is moving rapidly in the area of specialized weapons in ways designed not for military parity with the United States but military supremacy," the Report continues. "Advanced weapons work today appears aimed at moving from a phase of 'catching-up' to pursuing 'leap-ahead' technologies."

Of particular concern are potential intelligence surprises, such as advanced arms, threatening the U.S. homeland and its forward-deployed forces and regional allies. "China's achievement of a surprise breakthrough in one of these technologies is possible, due to the secrecy surrounding these programs and the uncertain nature of advanced weapons development in general," the Report states, noting that "such a breakthrough could have significant strategic implications for the U.S., particularly in its potential to further existing access challenges and hold forward deployed U.S. forces at risk."

Several commissioners stress in the report the threat that China's advanced weapons pose to the Asia Pacific region. "There are a number of areas where the PLA could make breakthroughs that would be decisive in a conflict with the U.S. and its regional Allies. In short, China is not just a threat to the U.S., or even a near-peer competitor. It has become, in its region, the dominant military power."

That fact, perhaps more than any other, explains why over the last five years China's aggressions have been successful. "The successes include encroachment in the South China Sea, imposition of an air defense zone in the East China Sea, aggression against the Philippines, coercion of Vietnam, increasing pressure on Taiwan and Hong Kong, harassment of Japan and other provocations," the report concluded.

Chinese Naval Frigate. Credit: United States Navy

Chinese Destroyer Xian. Credit: Michael Fahey

In the race to develop technologies, systems, and forces to sway future global military balance, China's navy (PLAN), which will be twice the size of the U.S. Navy by 2030, is a particular sore spot. "The future size of the People's Liberation Navy will be about 550 warships and submarines by 2030," retired U.S. Navy Captain James Fanell told a House Intelligence Committee hearing. Fanell, former Director of Intelligence for the U.S. Navy's Pacific fleet, warned that the projected size of the Chinese fleet will put the U.S. Navy at great risk.

"The Chinese Navy currently consists of 330 surface ships and 66 submarines," he explained. "The U.S. Navy has 211 surface ships and 72 submarines. The United States plans to increase its size to 355 ships by 2030, but congressional sources question whether this is possible."[19]

The PLAN is augmented by a shadow navy of more than 2,000 fishing boats fishing illegally in other countries' coastal domains. Some of these boats are not fishing at all. Disguised as fishing boats and called "sea phantoms," they are fire support vessels equipped with 16-tube rocket launchers and anti-aircraft guns. Sea phantoms also resupply PLA offshore garrisons and perform such functions as intelligence gathering and counter surveillance.

"The growth of the Chinese Navy is seen as part of a plan to push the United States out of Asia to become the world's superpower by 2050," according to the National Institute for Defense Studies. "The Chinese Navy is the first in East Asia to deploy its own aircraft carrier since World War II. Both the *Liaoning* and its Chinese-made sister ship are expected to carry a mixed air group of J-15 fighters and helicopters. Three nuclear-powered 'super carriers' are now under construction and are expected to form the centers of carrier battle groups in the 2020s."[20]

The PLAN's ballistic submarine fleet is being improved and expanded with the older Type 092 Xia-class nuclear powered submersible ship ballistic missile (SSBN) replaced with several Type 094 Jin-class SSBNs. Four of these newer subs are already operational, and, according to the 2020 Index of U.S Military Strength, they are expected to be equipped with the new, longer-range JL-2 submarine-launched ballistic missile (SLBM) (range 5,281 miles).

"Such a system would give the PLA a second-strike capability, substantially enhancing its nuclear deterrent," the Index notes. "The Chinese nuclear arsenal also contains land-attack cruise missiles. The CJ-10 can carry a conventional or nuclear warhead with a range of 930 miles. The CJ-20, a long-range, air-launched cruise missile, is carried on China's H-6 bomber. Nuclear tipped, the CJ-20 could reach every city in the United States."

Most of China's 1960s era aircraft have been replaced and the People's Liberation Army Air Force (PLAAF) is now dominated by fourth-generation fighter aircraft. "These include the domestically designed and produced J-10 and the Su-27J-llSu-30/J-11 system, which is comparable to the F-15 or F-18 and dominates both the fighter and strike missions,"

USS *America* operating in the eastern China Sea. Credit: United States Navy

the 2020 Index reports. "China is also believed to be preparing to field two stealth fifth-generation fighter designs. The J-20 is the larger aircraft, resembling the American F-22 fighter. The J-31 appears to resemble the F-35 but with two engines rather than one. A variety of modern support aircraft has also entered the PLAAF inventory, including early warning command and control and electronic warfare (EW) aircraft."

China's air defenses are rapidly modernizing with the recently acquired advanced S-300 surface-to-air missile (SAM) system analogous to the American Patriot SAM system. "Key industrial and military centers such as Beijing are now defended by SAM systems," according to the Index. "It is also developing its own advanced SAM, the HQ-9, which is deployed both on land and at sea."

It is in the vicinity of the Spratly Islands that the United States and its Pacific allies face the most immediate military challenge. An archipelago of tidal reefs and tiny islands roughly midway between Vietnam and the Philippines in the South China Sea, these islands are the sites of China's most provocative military preparations. Six different Asian nations claim part or all of the islands, disputing oil, mineral, and fishing rights. It is the location of the islands, however, that threatens "conflict on a global scale," according to the 2020 Index.

"Nearly half of the entire world's maritime traffic steams by on the way to or from the Malacca Strait — a principal chokepoint of global commerce. Despite protests by the other claiming Asian nations, the United Nations and the United States, China has proceeded with extensive and threatening development. Dredging has expanded tidal reefs and islands to accommodate airfields and other military and logistical support facilities," the Index warns.

"China has reclaimed territory on seven of these man-made islands and has built airstrips on them, thereby expanding the potential reach of its navy. In 2017 and 2018, the Chinese deployed surface-to-air missiles and anti-ship cruise missiles on the 'islands' despite a promise by President Xi to President Barack Obama not to 'militarize them.'"[21]

In his February 14, 2018, statement to the House Committee on Armed Services, Admiral Harry Harris, Commander, U.S. Pacific Command, listed the structures on each of the three largest of these islands:

- 10,000-foot runways capable of launching and recovering all military aircraft;

- fighter aircraft hangers;

- large aircraft hangars, capable of supporting larger aircraft, such as bombers, AWACS and transports;

- protected air defense launcher sheds;

- protected anti-ship missile launcher sheds;

- water and fuel storage tank farms; and

16

- barracks communication systems, deep-water pier facilities, and military radars.

China has shrugged off U.S. protests about the continued militarization of the Spratly Islands. It appears that Beijing wants to assert that the entire sea is its preserve, even though U.S. and allied naval forces are legally entitled to waters within 200 miles of the Philippines.

China has transformed "what was a great wall of sand just three years ago into a great wall of SAMs," Admiral Phillip Davidson, Chief of Indo-Pacific Command, stated. "If war breaks out, the island bases become a strategic southward extension of China's land-based defense against U.S. ships and planes."[22]

Military officials claim the missiles threaten U.S. warships and aircraft conducting freedom of navigation operations near the islands in a bid to counter Chinese claims to control more than 90 percent of the South China Sea. Ships as distant as 340 miles could be targeted by the YJ-128 anti-ship cruise missiles and HQ-9B long-range surface-to-air missiles

Chinese Destroyer Haikou. Credit: Michael Fahey

with ranges up to 184 miles. Nuclear-capable H-6 bombers are deployed on Woody Island in the Paracels. Of particular concern is the DF-21D mobile missile, capable of destroying a U.S. super carrier at a distance of up to 1,000 miles.

More worrisome still is that the DF-21D appears to be only the tip of China's missile development iceberg. In one war game China's KT-2 anti-satellite missile knocked out 20 U.S. satellites, shutting down global positioning systems and most critical navigation, intelligence, and communications systems. Stunned by this, the U.S. Naval Academy has revived a course in celestial navigation. The WU-14, a hypersonic glide vehicle, is another awesome threat. From 60 miles above Earth, these could release precision-guided missiles achieving supersonic speeds.

Capabilities for coping with these threats and for handling other potential crises are hampered by the U.S. Navy's reduced size, with a fleet of 260 ships attempting to perform a 306-ship mission. U.S. allies are benefitting from burgeoning trade in the area, and they are depending more and more on satisfactory relations with China. They look the United States to maintain a balance of forces in the region, but so far, U.S. actions are not convincing — to them or to the Chinese.[23]

The problem has been complicated by the Ukraine conflict, which has taught the Chinese and the United States some unsettling lessons. Putting up with Putin's military support for the separatists in Ukraine's eastern provinces and caving in on Crimea has exposed weaknesses of the U.S./EU coalition. And Chinese achievements, particularly in naval operations, have boosted confidence. The Chinese submarine that embarrassed the U.S. Navy on October 24, 2006, by maneuvering undetected into the middle of a carrier battle group and surfacing just a few miles aft of the USS *Kitty Hawk* was one of 13 of the Song class now in active service.

"First launched in 1994 and completing sea trials a year later, this class was a breakaway from what had been almost exclusively Russian influences on PLAN submarine design," according to the Heritage Foundation's report "Assessing Threats to U.S. Vital Interests."

"A German propulsion system, seven blade skewed propellers and noise-reduction rubber tiles all contributed to the surprising of the *Kitty Hawk*. Armed with torpedoes and a submarine-launched variant of the YJ-8 anti-ship missile, Songs initially operated by the PLAN were the Russian Whiskey class, but all of these were removed from service by the mid–1990s. The Romeo class, also Russian, followed. There were growing problems apparent with the Kilo class, the first indigenously Chinese designed submarines built in 1993, and four had to be scrapped. But there were also significant advances. They were equipped with modern sonar and operating noise was significantly reduced by air independent propulsion (AIP). Seventeen remain as an important part of the fleet, reportedly making incursions into Japanese waters, and on at least one occasion surfacing in those waters," according to the Threats Assessment.

Nine years after the Kitty Hawk surprise, a Kilo-class sub was discovered shadowing the carrier USS *Ronald Reagan* near southern Japan. One defense official told *The Washington Free Beacon* that the submarine's appearance 'set off alarm bells on the *Reagan*,' though there was no sign of threatening behavior."[24]

"The U.S. still owns the undersea realm in the western Pacific right now and is determined to maintain it," a U.S. Navy spokesman told the press after the *Reagan* incident. "But China has grown — in terms of maritime power, maritime projection — more quickly than any country in the region," he added.

"By 2020, the Chinese submarine force will increase to about 70 submarines, with substantially more-capable submarines replacing older units. Current expansion at submarine production yards could allow higher future production numbers. The issue for the PLAN, however, is that such expansion would require the training of additional crews as well as keeping all of the remaining Ming-class hulls in service despite their age, high noise levels and relative lack of capability," according to the Threats Assessment.

China continues to modernize its submarine force, and most of its new submarines are built to modern Chinese designs. "The PLAN is likely to continue to use its submarine-production capacity to replace these older vessels in the near term," the Threat Assessment states. "This focus on improving quality rather than expanding quantity will limit the PLAN's requirement for heavy investment in extra personnel and infrastructure, although the 72nd Flotilla's Mings may need to be retained at Xiachuan Dao until its berths can be upgraded to accept newer submarine designs. Capable of launching the Russian Novator 3M-54E Klub S cruise missile and engaging land and sea targets at over 150 miles, the Kilo class may represent a huge leap forward in the PLAN submarine fleet. These are one of the world's quietest class of submarines, and 12 are now active in the PLAN fleet. The Yuan class, fitted with an AIP system and armed with advanced Russian and Chinese torpedoes and cruise missiles, is the more recent of the PLAN indigenous submarine."

With capabilities surpassing the Kilo and Song classes, 13 Yuans have gone into operation since production began in 2017, and seven more are under construction. All PLAN submarines from the Whiskey to the Yuan have been conventionally powered (diesel/electric), but both nuclear powered ICBM and attack versions have been under development.

Specifically, these are the Type 092 (one in service), the Type 094 (four in active service and one to be commissioned), and the Type 096 (in development). The Type 092 was built in the early 1980s, China's first-ever nuclear-powered ballistic missile submarine. Armed with the JL-1 SLBM, she has 12 launch tubes along with six 533 mm tubes for self-defense.

"After several failures, the JL-1 was first successfully launched in 1988, but its short range restricts it to regional targets. Major modernizations have increased this range somewhat, but its capabilities are nothing like the U.S. and Russian ICBMs. Russian assistance resulted in the development of the Type 094 or Jin-class ICBM. Its 12 tubes launch the 8,000 km range JL-2 missile that carries three to four MIRVs. So the Jins could launch missiles against targets in the continental United States from Chinese waters," the Threats Assessment warns.

The Type 093 or Shang class has been in development since the 1980s as a replacement for the Han class. Considered comparable to the Russian Victor III class, the Shang is a major step forward in the PLAN's nuclear attack submarines and has been the focus of much U.S. military analysis. "The mission of the Shangs, two of which are in service and four under construction, is expected to be escorting ICBM submarines and possibly attacking U.S. Navy carrier battle groups," according to the Threats Assessment.

China's submarines are now making distant cruises. When, in May 2016, a PLAN nuclear-powered attack submarine docked in Karachi, Pakistan, it was the first such port call in south Asia. Then, in January 2017, an attack submarine returning from anti-piracy patrols in the western Indian Ocean stopped in a Malaysian port on the South China Sea. A Shang-class nuclear-powered attack sub was detected in the contiguous zone around the Senkaku/Diaoyu Islands in the East China Sea in January 2018. That resulted in protest from Japan.[25]

The PLAN is expected to begin operating large unmanned submarines to perform a wide range of missions from reconnaissance to mine placement and even suicide attacks on enemy vessels as part of China's ambitious plan to boost its naval power with artificial intelligence technology, according to the 2019 Threats Assessment. "While not replacing manned submarines, these large submersible drones are expected to be deployed mainly to oppose U.S. naval forces in the South China Sea and the western Pacific. China is also developing an AI-assisted support system for submarine commanders. It is intended to help them make faster, more accurate judgments in the heat of combat situations. The new class of unmanned submarines will join the other autonomous or manned military systems on water or land and in orbit to carry out missions in coordinated efforts. The submersible drones will have no human operators on board. They will go out, handle their assignments and return to base on their own. They may establish contact with the ground command periodically for updates but are by design capable of completing missions without human intervention."[26]

Authors at the Chinese Qingdao Submarine Academy (QSA) contend that the new era requires a global submarine strategy. "As national maritime interests are expanding continuously, the ocean's significance for the survival of the Chinese nation is more and more important," the QSA authors explained in a report. As well as outlining the vulnerability of China's lengthy maritime strategic energy corridor, the report asserts that China faces a definite external threat and must therefore expand its maritime strategic space. "At bases in both Northeast Asia and in Southeast Asia, as well as the base on Guam, the U.S. has deployed advanced air and sea forces in order to control our country's maritime passages out into the Pacific. By constructing strategic arcs to contain our country, our space for maritime activities has been strictly confined."

The QSA asserts that the United States and Japan have developed an elaborate anti-submarine system that aims to achieve a permanent blockade of Chinese submarines. "China's submarine force must not only go to the Asia-Pacific but also to the Indian Ocean, and then to the Atlantic and to the Arctic oceans. In this way, the current problems of submarine operations can be alleviated and will provide a vast maritime strategic space for our country's rise," the QSA report states.[27]

As another hint that the PLAN may consider foreign submarine force basing, the QSR report points out that Chinese submarine base ports are all located along its ocean borderline. The speed of submarines is relatively slow, so operating time is too short, diminishing the actual impact of the submarine force going to the distant seas. The report seems to open the door to the permanent basing of Chinese submarines in distant countries.

Lyle J. Goldstein, associate professor in the China Maritime Studies Institute at the U.S. Naval War College in Newport, Rhode Island, believes that the report defines the PLA plans to use submarines as offensive forces to defend the Belt and Road, to mix it up with adversary forces and to gain intelligence about enemy doctrine and capabilities. "For U.S. strategists, there certainly are many troubling implications, such as the likelihood that a military conflict ignited in the western Pacific could spread rapidly into the Atlantic," he says. "There are dangers inherent in the increased intensity of cat-and-mouse games, which are set to become ever more common across the world's oceans. Such dangerous interactions could cause tragic accidents and also fuel crises and rivalry in unpredictable and costly directions."[28]

Deepening Chinese activities in the Arctic region could pave the way for a strengthened military presence, including the deployment of submarines to act as deterrents against nuclear attack," according to the Pentagon's China Security Report 2019: "Chinese Strategy for Reshaping the Asian Order and Its Ramifications." The report noted that China's military has made modernizing its submarine fleet a high priority. "The assessment follows Beijing's publication of its first official Arctic policy to develop shipping lanes opened up by global warming to form a 'Polar Silk Road'—building on President Xi Jinping's signature Belt and Road Initiative. China, despite being a non–Arctic state, is increasingly active in the polar region and became a server member of the Arctic Council in 2013. That has prompted concerns from Arctic states over Beijing's long-term strategic objectives, including possible military deployments."[29]

SUMMARY

"China's stated goal of becoming the world's predominant economic and military power by 2050 appears to be well within its reach," according to the Heritage Foundation's report, "Assessing Threats to U.S. Vital Interests." "Certainly, the PLA remains one of the world's largest militaries, its days of largely obsolescent equipment in the past. Double-digit growth in the Chinese defense budget for the past two decades has resulted in a comprehensive modernization program, enhancing every part of the PLA, which is in the process of building and deploying a sophisticated and modern missile arsenal, though one shrouded in secrecy due to an unwillingness to enter arms control or other transparency agreements."[30]

Missiles are featured most prominently in Beijing's developing anti-access/area denial doctrines. These use a combination of ballistic and cruise missiles launched from air, land, and sea, targeting U.S. and allied military assets in the Asia Pacific Theatre. President Xi's Belt and Road economic plan is creeping steadily across Asia, Africa, and Eastern Europe, and advanced unrivaled electronics capabilities and weaponry is surging ahead. There may be no area of rivalry, with the possible exception of democratic political reform, where China is not gaining on us. Approval by Congress to spend $22 billion building nine new Virginia-class attack submarines is the key to the U.S. fleet's capabilities over the next decade. But the PLAN's attack submarine force will grow far faster. To match China 30 years from now, we must create a stealthier, longer range fleet armed with harder-hitting weapons. Rapid transitions in modern naval operations require integrated, multi-domain capabilities of our fleets. We must respond to this transition with urgency. Our fleets must be ready to fight and win at sea — keeping that fight forward, far from the homeland. We must also succeed in sustained, day to-day competition, winning future fights before they become kinetic. We must remain steadfast in our alliances and partnerships, which remain indispensable in any future fight. We must apply time, effort and resources to grow naval power and think differently to find every competitive advantage."[31]

As we consider what actions to take regarding Communist China, we must keep in mind what kind of government we are dealing with. It is a totalitarian regime that knows only one rule, articulated by its still-revered leader, Mao Zedong, "Political power grows out of the barrel of a gun."[32] We must never forget the ultimate sacrifice that the students of Tiananmen Square made for freedom and justice. The Chinese Communists dismiss as "Western lies" any and all stories about an alleged massacre. They will not permit any public discussion of Tiananmen Square and block any mention of it on Chinese social media.

"We must commit to crafting the military budgets to support the U.S. in fighting two wars at roughly the same time. That requires more ships, planes and troops — a lot more. This is going to be a difficult conversation to have as the U.S. grapples with the debt it has incurred in dealing with COVID-19. But right sizing the military to protect American interests is not first and foremost a budget exercise. Would-be budget-cutters are going to have to identify which region of the world and what American interests they are willing to write-off. It certainly cannot be the Indo-Pacific if the U.S. is going to compete with China's rising military might."[33]

To successfully deal with China, the United States must rely on its own unique strengths while remaining committed to the principles of economic and political freedom. We must engage all our levers of power, including strong global presence and partnerships, economic engagement, and clear power projection on the world stage.

NOTES

1. Tucker Higgins, "Trump Holds News Conference About Relations with Hong Kong," *CNBC*, May 29, 2020.

2. Tian Feilong, "US interference in Hong Kong doomed to Fail," *Global Times*, Aug. 20, 2019.

3. Abigail Williams, "Pompeo Says Hong Kong No Longer Has Autonomy Under China," *CNBC*, May 27, 2020.

4. Trump Signs Bill Supporting Hong Kong Protesters Despite Strong Opposition from China," *Fox News*, Nov. 27, 2019.

5. Premier calls for peaceful development of cross-Strait relations," *Xinhua,* March 20, 2018.

6. Derek Grossman, "No Smiles Across the Taiwan Strait," *FP News*, Jan. 7, 2019.

7. "China's Xi Warns Attempts to Divide China Will End in 'Shattered Bones,'" *Reuters,* October 13, 2019.

8. Frank Scheck, "*Wolf Warrior 2* Review," *Hollywood Reporter*, July 27, 2017.

9. Katsuji Nakazawa, "China's 'Wolf Warrior' Diplomats Roar at Hong Kong and the World," Katsuji Nakazawa, *NIKKEI Asian Review*, May 26, 2020.

10. Mark Preen, "Economic Reform in China: Current Progress and Future Prospects," *China Briefing*, April 3, 2019.

11. Eleanor Albert and Beina XU, "China's Environmental Crisis," Council on Foreign Relations, Jan. 18, 2016.

12. Jon Brodkin, "Trump Demands Quick Rollout of "6G" Wireless Tech, Which Doesn't Exist," *Ars Technica,* Feb. 21, 2019.

13. "Profile: China's President Xi Jinping," *BBC News*, Feb. 25, 2018.

14. Thomas Spohr, "U.S. Can't Afford to Take Its Eye off the Ball as National Threats Loom Beyond COVID19," The Heritage Foundation, April 12, 2020.

15. James Carafano, "The Great U.S.-China Divorce Has Arrived," The Heritage Foundation, April 22, 2020.

16. Zhang Hongzhou, "China's 'Development Approach to the Mekong Water Disputes," *The Diplomat*, March 20, 2020.

17. Dean Cheng, "China Wants to Take Down the U.S. to Accomplish Its Goals," The Heritage Foundation, May 4, 2020.

18. John L. Dolan, "America's Hypersonic Danger – Missiles that Go 10 Times the Speed of Sound," *The National Interest*, April 23, 2019.

19. Captain James Fannel, USN (ret.), "China's Global Strategy and Expanding Force Strategy: Pathway to Hegemony," House Intelligence Hearing, May 21, 2018.

20. *NIDS Journal of Defense and Security*, No. 18, December 2017.

21. "Xi Denies China Turning Artificial Islands into Military Bases," *Reuters,* September 26, 2019.

22. Adm. Davidson, Indo-Pacific Commander," *Reagan Defense Forum*, December 11, 2019.

23. Caleb Larson, "Type 092: China's First Nuclear Powered Ballistic Missile Made Submarine History," *The National Interest*, May 3, 2020.

24. Kyle Mizokami, "A Chinese Submarine Stalked an American Aircraft Carrier," *Popular Mechanics*, Nov. 6, 2015

25. Christina Zhao, "China Sent Nuclear Missile Attack Submarine to Disputed Islands, Japan Says," *Newsweek*, Jan. 15, 2018.

26. Joe Pinkstone, "China Plans to Launch AI-Powered Unmanned Submarines in 2020 That Will Stay at Sea for Months Without Refueling and Can Embark on Suicide Missions to Enemy Targets," *MailOnline*, July 29, 2019.

27. China's Submarine Academy: PLAN Strengthens Training for Future Underwater Force," *CGTN*, April 22, 2019.

28. Interview, Lyle J. Goldstein, associate professor in the China Maritime Studies Institute at the U.S. Naval War College, May 5, 2019.

29. U.S.-China Economic and Security Review Commission, *2019 Annual Report.*

30. Assessing Threats to U.S. Vital Interests, 2020, *The Heritage Foundation.*

31. USNI News, "Report to Congress on Navy Force Structure," May 22, 2020.

32. Phrase contained in speech by Mao Zedong, Aug. 27, 1927, at the beginning of the Communist era.

33. James J. Carafano, "10 Steps America Should Take to Respond to the China Challenge, James J. Carafano," The Heritage Foundation, April 30, 2020.

2 | The Threat from Russia

"Russia is a gas station with Nukes," according to U.S. Congressman Denny Heck of Washington state. Heck was referring to Russia's declining economy, with the coronavirus crippling oil and gas prices dramatically. Russia continues to prioritize the rebuilding of its military despite economic problems, according to Heck. As a member of the House Permanent Select Committee on Intelligence, Heck warns that Russia continues to be a major threat to both the United States and to U.S. interests in Europe.[1]

From the Arctic to the Baltics, Ukraine, the South Caucasus, and increasingly, the Mediterranean, Russia continues to foment instability in Europe. China has vaulted past Russia as the world's second largest and most powerful military, but the forces President Vladimir Putin has built up and shaped in his 20+ years in power threaten massive destabilization, particularly in Europe and the Middle East. The nation was indeed a shamble economically, socially, and militarily on his ascent to power just as the 20th century ended. The Second Chechen War had erupted in 1999, a 10-year conflict pitting Russian Army forces against Islamic separatists that would drag on for 10 years with estimated 50,000 fatalities.

The army's deficiencies of outdated equipment and command capabilities as well as poor training and morale were holdovers from the waning days of the Soviet Union in the 1980s. They would become conspicuous again in the August 2008 conflict with the Republic of Georgia. The Russians had the good fortune of fighting poorly led and similarly under-equipped Georgian forces and they triumphed in five days. But the experience prompted Putin to launch major initiatives to bring the military up to 21st-century standards.

The Russian military also gained important experience not only in modernizing equipment but also in operating as a cohesive whole, testing their capabilities in Ukraine and Syria, where they demonstrated major improvements over their performance in their 2008 war in Georgia.

The August War of 2008 would thus be the last conflict of the Soviet

Union legacy force. The modernization of the Russian military, which would enable them to operate so effectively in Ukraine and Syria, had begun. Putin and his senior military team had come to realize the urgent importance of the initial period of a conflict — what they termed as standoff warfare. They saw aerospace operations and precision guided munitions as key factors in shaping battlefields and as enormous force multipliers. The significance of battle lines had disappeared as new weapons and weapons platforms could destroy targets throughout vast territories.

The costs of these military advances would be challenging for a country without manufacturing export and dependent entirely on selling oil and gas. Russians would have to tighten their belts, but Putin understood that his countrymen would put up with deprivation if they had something to be proud of, and he built that pride with an aggressive military. Today, these forces are at or approaching state of the art, particularly at sea, and they present a growing threat to the United States and our allies in the Atlantic, the Arctic, and beyond. Combined with Russia's potent nuclear arsenal, they are the stuff of strategic nightmares.

"The signs of how peace has been restored can be seen with the naked eye," commented Russian president Vladimir Putin as he drove through Damascus streets with Syrian president Bashar al-Assad on January 6, 2020.[2] Those signs of peace were probably not evident in Idlib Province, where Russian fighter jets were supporting Syrian government forces in mopping-up operations against rebel forces and tens of thousands of civilians were fleeing for their lives.

Any authoritarian regime in need of help, with economic and military advantages to offer, probably has Putin's personal phone number. In Syria, with assistance from Iran, Russian air power has devastated civilian areas in the process of securing an ally and a naval port on the Mediterranean. Russia has also patched up differences with China, and now the two burgeoning naval powers are holding joint fleet exercises in the Baltic.

"Despite economic problems, Russia continues to prioritize the rebuilding of its military and funding for military operations abroad. Russia's military and political antagonism toward the United States continues unabated, and its efforts to undermine U.S. institutions and the NATO alliance are serious and troubling. Russia uses its energy position in Europe along with espionage, cyber-attacks, and information warfare to exploit vulnerabilities and seeks to drive wedges into the transatlantic alliance and undermine people's faith in government and societal institutions."[3]

Overall, Russia has significant conventional and nuclear capabilities and remains the top threat to European security. Its aggressive stance in a number of theaters, including the Balkans, Georgia, Syria, and Ukraine, continues both to encourage destabilization and threaten U.S. interests.

"Russia has two strategies for nuclear deterrence. The first is based on a threat of massive launch-on-warning and retaliatory strikes to deter a nuclear attack. The second is a threat of limited demonstration and de-escalation of nuclear strikes to deter or terminate a large-scale conventional war."[4]

Moscow has repeatedly threatened U.S. allies in Europe with nuclear deployments and even preemptive nuclear strikes. Russia also continues to violate the Intermediate-Range Nuclear Forces Treaty banning the testing, production, and possession of intermediate-range missiles. Russia first broke the treaty in 2008 and then systematically escalated its violations, moving from testing to producing to deploying the prohibited missile into the field. United States withdrew from this treaty on August 2, 2019.[5]

"Key weapons in Russia's inventory are 334 intercontinental ballistic missiles; 2,750 main battle tanks; more than 5,140 armored infantry fighting vehicles; more than 6,100 armored personnel carriers; and more than 4,342 pieces of artillery. The navy has one aircraft carrier, 58 submarines including 13 ballistic missile submarines, five cruisers, 15 destroyers, 13 frigates, and 100 military patrol and coastal combatants. The air force has 1,223 combat-capable aircraft. The IISS counts 280,000 members of the army. Russia also has a total reserve force of 2,000,000 for all armed forces."[6]

Hamstrung by low oil prices, economic sanctions, and deep structural

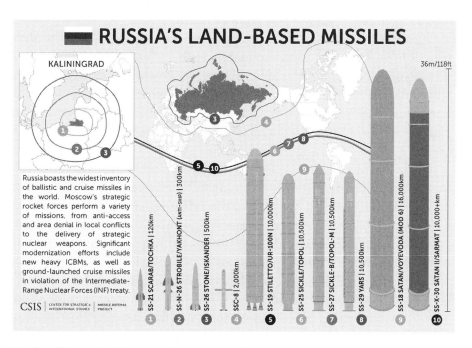

Missiles of Russia. Credit: Center for Strategic and International Studies

issues, Russia's economy produced only a tepid growth of 1.5 percent to 2.0 percent in 2018. Though Russia cut defense spending by 20 percent from $70 billion in 2016 to $66.3 billion in 2017, it has invested heavily in modernization of its armed forces.

"In early 2018, Russia introduced the new State Armament Program 2018–2027, a $306 billion investment in new equipment and modernization. The new armaments program is likely to be distributed more evenly between military branches and the emphasis of the 2018–2027 program is on procurement of high-precision weapons for air, sea and land battles, including hypersonic missiles, unmanned air strike complexes, individual equipment for servicemen and advanced reconnaissance, communication and electronic warfare systems."[7]

Because of this modernization, former U.S. Deputy Assistant Secretary of Defense for Strategy and Force Development Elbridge Colby said in 2018 that the U.S. military advantage over Russia was eroding.[8] In January 2018, Chairman of the Joint Chiefs of Staff and U.S. Marine Corps General Joseph Dunford noted that "there is not a single aspect of the Russian armed forces that has not received some degree of modernization over the past decade."[9]

The new armaments program will also focus on development of unmanned vehicles and robotics. Russia's counter-space and counter-satellite capabilities are formidable and both Russia and China continue to pursue anti-satellite (ASAT) weapons as a means to reduce U.S. and allied military effectiveness. The program will form the basis of Russia's defense procurement and military priorities until 2027.[10]

"Russia's nuclear arsenal has been progressively modernized. The Strategic Rocket Force continues to rearm, with a number of regiments receiving new Yars missiles and launchers. Meanwhile, tests of the heavy Sarmat liquid fuel intercontinental ballistic missile have been resumed. The new RS-28 ballistic missile came into service in 2019, and Russia also plans to deploy the RS-28 (Satan 2) ICBM by 2021 as a replacement for the RS-36, which is being phased out in 2020."[11]

Russia is expected to continue to focus on developing high end-systems, such as the S-500 surface-to-air missile systems. In May 2018, it was reported that Russian testing of the S-500 system struck a target 299 miles away. This is the longest surface-to-air missile test ever conducted, and the S-500's range could have significant implications for Europe when the missile becomes operational.[12]

Reinvigorating submarine construction has been one of the visible accomplishments of the Russian Navy's modernization program for 2011–2020. The first Project 09852 submarine, described as a nuclear-powered Belgorod, was launched from Sevmash shipyard in northern Russia on April 23, 2019. The submarine will be finished while afloat, and sea trials are set for 2020 and deployment by the end of that year. U.S. defense officials claim it carries drones, called Kanyons, that are capable of blowing up entire ports and cities, such as Groton, Connecticut, Kings Bay, Georgia, and Puget Sound in Washington, where U.S. nuclear missile submarines are based. The U.S. Navy has no unmanned underwater vehicles similar to the Kanyon.[13]

Yasen Class Submarine. Credit: General Dynamics Electric Boat

"The nuclear drone is one of several new Russian strategic weapons designed to threaten the United States and highlight the need to modernize U.S. nuclear arms and those of our NATO allies. But while the Kremlin is investing heavily in its submarine fleet, NATO countries have let their underwater firepower lag. The dangers are wide-ranging and alarming. Russia may be attempting to tap into or sever some of the 550,000 miles of underwater fiber-optic cables that span the Atlantic and Arctic sealanes. More than 95 percent of the global Internet traffic is transmitted across the network of submerged cables along the ocean floor. The scale and scope of global communications — military and civilian — moving through the network of cables present an inviting target that is vulnerable to attack by Russian submarines."[14]

The transatlantic cable links are particularly vital for an alliance that links the United States and Europe. A transatlantic alliance must be able to transport troops and equipment safely across the Atlantic. On any given day, the cables carry some $10 trillion of financial transfers as well as millions of nonfinancial communications. The *Yantor*, a mother ship to two Russian mini submarines, is often seen near undersea cables capable of being tapped or cut. It has also been observed collecting intelligence near U.S. naval facilities, including submarine bases at Kings Bay, Georgia, and Groton, Connecticut.[15]

Among the reactions to the potentially destructive firepower of the Yasen class submarines has been the reestablishment of the U.S. Second Fleet. Headquartered in Norfolk, Virginia, where NATO's new Joint Force Command for the Atlantic is also located, the Second Fleet will exercise operational and administrative authority over assigned ships, aircraft, and landing forces on the East Coast and northern Atlantic Ocean. It will also contribute to the planning, training, and provision of maritime forces for global contingencies. The fleet's primary focus will be the Russian Navy, in particular its submarine forces, augmented by long-range missile-armed bombers and strike aircraft. The fleet will also be contending with mine warfare and special forces operations, plus non-kinetic activities such as cyber-attacks. The re-established Second Fleet, together with NATO's formation of Joint Force Command for the Atlantic, will enable naval forces to focus on ensuring the security of the Atlantic. They also demonstrate how important it is to challenge increased competition in the Indo-Pacific from a rising Chinese People's Liberation Army Navy and regional security threats from the Korean peninsula to the Middle East.[16]

Submarine building will focus on completing the series of Borey-A ballistic-missile boats armed with Bulava missiles. Russia is looking to the future with the Khaski-class fifth generation stealth nuclear-powered

Severodvinsk class. Credit: General Dynamics Electric Boat

Russian Yasen-M submarine. Source: Twitter account Chris Cavas

submarines slated to begin construction in 2023 and to be armed with Zircon hypersonic missiles which have a reported speed of 3,708 mph.[17]

Russia is bolstering its underwater battle capabilities in a direct challenge to U.S. forces in the Atlantic and Mediterranean, and their increasingly active submarine fleets in the Atlantic and Arctic are threatening to overwhelm an aging U.S. submarine fleet. Russian naval modernization continues to prioritize submarines, including upgrades to its diesel electric Kilo class. According to one analyst, the submarines' improvement in noise reduction has led them to be nicknamed "Black Holes."[18]

"Russia is expected to produce a fifth-generation stealth nuclear-powered submarine by 2030 and arm it with Zircon hypersonic missiles, which have a reported speed of from Mach 5 (about 3,806 mph) to Mach 6 (about 4,567 mph) with a range of 620 miles. The first ship in the Yasen class, Severodvinsk, is approximately 393 feet long and displaces 11,800 tons submerged. An OK-650KPM pressurized water nuclear reactor provides 200 megawatts of power, driving her to speeds of up to 31 knots submerged. An Irtysh-Amfora sonar system provides all-around sonar coverage. The Severodvinsk's combat systems are formidable with 10 533-millimeter torpedo tubes armed with UGST-M heavyweight guided torpedoes."[19]

While modernization of the Russian submarine force is ramping up, it retains a potent core of ex-Soviet warships. The Northern, Baltic. and Black Sea fleets operate 38 submarines comprising 15 diesel-electric submarines (eight Kilos, six Caliber-armed Impro Kilos and a Lada); 4 nuclear-powered guided missile-armed submarines (three Oscar II and a Graney class); 12 nuclear-powered attack submarines (four Victor III, four Akula, two Akula II, a Sierra and a Sierra II); and 7 nuclear-powered ballistic missile-armed submarines.[20]

"The Northern Fleet, the most powerful of the Russian Navy's four fleets, operates all submarines. The submarine fleet had always had priority in defense budgeting, but the highest priority has gone to ballistic missile submarines. Commissioned near the end of the Cold War, the keel of the first Yasen-class submarine boat, the Severodvinsk, was laid down in 1993. Post-Soviet budget cuts halted the program in the mid–1990s. The program was revived in the mid–2000s with the boom in oil and gas prices, and the K-329 Severodvinsk, a fourth-generation multipurpose submarine, was launched at the Sevmash shipyard. The Yasen design went through a significant overhaul when construction resumed more than a decade ago."

"The cost of a Yasen has been reported in the Russian press at about $1.5 billion per hull. The design's capabilities are unknown, but Russian news reports paint a picture of a capable boat. The Yasen class measures 390 feet long, with a displacement just under of 14,000 tons. A relatively small crew of 64 indicates that the ship's systems are highly automated. Maximum operating depth is reported to be almost 2,000 feet, and it can travel up to 20 knots beneath the surface without breaking silence. The weapons array, featuring guided cruise missile launching capabilities, shows that a primary role will be keeping U.S. carrier battle groups away from the coast. Combined with land-based bombers armed with standoff cruise missiles, these submarines are designed to overwhelm missile defenses."[21]

Most Russian submarines will be cruise missile carriers, intended to be used in conventional strikes. But Russia has the ability to deploy nuclear long-range, sea-launched cruise missiles as well. The Oscar submarines would be modernized for Caliber launches.

"Russia's 27 nuclear-powered multipurpose and fast-attack submarines now in service compare with 60 similar subs in the U.S. Navy. The Russians plan to add six more Yasen-class boats. Should a conflict erupt with NATO, the role of the Russian Navy will be to secure a favorable operational regime in such critical waters as the Barents and the Norwegian, Baltic and Black Seas; to ensure access through chokepoints such as the Greenland-Iceland gap; to conduct strikes against opposing cruise missile-armed ships and submarines and carrier strike groups; to target the deployment of U.S. reinforcements transiting the Atlantic; and to ensure the security of the vital ballistic missile-armed submarines. U.S. intelligence agencies estimate the unmanned underwater vehicle known as the Kanyon will be outfitted with a warhead on the order of tens of megatons of nuclear yield. The U.S. Navy has no weapon similar to the Kanyon"[22]

Russian military exercises, especially snap exercises, are a source of serious concern because they have masked real military operations in the past. Their purpose is twofold: to project strength and to improve command and control, according to Army General Curtis M. Scaparrotti, former Commander, U.S. European Command, "Their exercise program demonstrates increasingly sophisticated command and control and integration across multiple warfare areas. Snap exercises have been used for military campaigns as well. The annexation of Crimea took place in connection with a snap exercise by Russia."[23]

Exercises in the Baltic Sea in April 2018, a day after the leaders of the three Baltic nations met with President Donald Trump in Washington, were meant as a message.[24] Russia stated twice in April that it planned to conduct three days of live-fire exercises in the Exclusive Economic Zone of Latvia, which forced a rerouting of commercial aviation as Latvia closed some of its airspace. It turned out that Russia did not actually fire any live missiles, and the Latvian Ministry of Defense described the event as "a show of force, nothing else."[25]

Russia's snap exercises are conducted with little or no warning and often involve thousands of troops and pieces of equipment. In February 2017, Russia ordered snap exercises involving 45,000 troops, 150 aircraft, and 200 anti-aircraft pieces.[26]

"The reintroduction of snap exercises has "significantly improved the Russian Armed Forces' warfighting and power-projection capabilities," These, in turn, support and enable Russia's strategic destabilization campaign against the West, with military force always casting a shadow of intimidation over Russia's sub-kinetic aggression."[27]

Russia conducted its VOSTOK ("East") strategic exercises, held primarily in the Eastern Military District, mainly in August and September of 2018 and purportedly with 300,000 troops, 1,000 aircraft, and 900 tanks taking part. Russia's Defense Minister claimed that the exercises were the largest to take place in Russia since 1981. Chinese and Mongolian forces also took part, with China sending 3,200 soldiers from the People's Liberation Army along with 900 tanks and 30 fixed-wing aircraft.[28]

Russia has increasingly deployed paid private volunteer troops trained at Special Forces bases and often under the command of Russian Special Forces, to avoid political blowback from military deaths abroad. Russia has used such volunteers in Libya, Syria and Ukraine and they take casualties the Russian authorities do not report.[29] In January 2020, reports surfaced that 400 Russian mercenaries were in Venezuela to bolster the regime of Nicolas Maduro. Russian propaganda has supported the regime and claims that Washington's recognition of Juan Guaido is part of a centuries old process of meddling by the United States in the region.[30] As the crisis metastasized and protests against the Maduro regime grew, Russia began to deploy Russian troops and supplies to bolster Maduro's security forces. In December 2018, Russia temporarily deployed two TU-160 nuclear-capable bombers to Caracas. Russia exports billions of dollars in arms to Venezuela and has loaned the regime money to purchase Russian arms along with $70 million to $80 million yearly in nonmilitary goods.[31]

SUMMARY

The resurgence of an aggressive, belligerent Russia has thrown conventional post–Cold War thinking into the waste bin. Russian President Vladimir Putin's decision to invade Ukraine and annex Crimea has changed post–Cold War norms. From the Arctic to the Baltics, Ukraine, and the South Caucasus, Russia has proven to be the source of much instability in Europe. Despite economic problems, Russia continues to prioritize the rebuilding of its military and funding for its military operations abroad. Russia's military and political antagonism toward the United States continues unabated, and its efforts to undermine U.S. institutions and the NATO alliance are serious and troubling. Russia's aggressive stance in a number of theaters, including the Balkans, Georgia, Syria, and Ukraine, continues to contribute to destabilization and run counter to U.S. interests.

Russia's nuclear capabilities have been prioritized for modernization, and 82 percent of its nuclear forces have been modernized. Russia plans to deploy the RS-28 (Satan 2) ICBM by 2021 as a replacement for the RS-36, which is being phased out in the 2020s. The missile, which can carry up to 15 warheads, underwent flight development tests from April–June 2019. The armed forces also continue to undergo process modernization, which was begun by Defense Minister Anatoly Serdyukov in 2008.

Russia's naval modernization continues to prioritize submarines. According to the IISS, "Submarine building will focus on completing the series of Borey-A ballistic-missile boats armed with Bulava missiles and Project 08851 Yasen-M multi-role submarines, though from the early 2020s construction is expected to begin on the first Khaski-class successor. The Khaski-class submarines are planned fifth-generation stealth nuclear-powered submarines. They are slated to begin construction in 2023 and to be armed with Zircon hypersonic missiles, which have a reported speed of from Mach 5 to Mach 6. According to a Russian vice admiral, these submarines will be two times quieter than current subs.

NOTES

1. "Denny Heck tells Olympia Rotary Russia Has Become A 'Gas Station with Nukes,'" *The Olympian*, Aug. 19, 2019.

2. Richard Hall, "Russian President Vladimir Putin Lands in Damascus on Unannounced Visit," Independent, Jan. 7, 2020.

3. *Assessing Threats to U.S. Vital Interests*, Washington, D.C.: Heritage Foundation.

4. *Assessing Threats to U.S. Vital Interests*, Washington, D.C.: Heritage Foundation.

5. "President Donald Trump to Withdraw the United States from the Intermediate-Range Nuclear Forces (INF) Treaty," The White House, Feb. 1, 2019.

6. International Institute for Strategic Studies, The Military Balance, 2017.

7. *Assessing Threats to U.S. Vital Interests*, Washington, D.C.: Heritage Foundation.

8. Tom Bowman, "U.S. Military Advantage over Russia and China 'Eroding,' Pentagon says" *NPR*, Jan. 19, 2018

9. Damien Sharkov, "Russia's Military Expansion Makes It Greatest Threat to Europe and NATO Must Defend It," *Newsweek*, Jan. 16, 2018.

10. Richard Connolly and Mathieu Boulegue, "Russia's New State Armament Programme: Implications for the Russian Armed Forces and Military Capabilities to 2027," Chatham House, May 2018.

11. Franz-Stefan Gady, "Russia's Most Powerful Intercontinental Ballistic Missile to Enter Service in 2021," *The Diplomat*, March 30, 2018.

12. Amanda Macias, "Russia Quietly Conducted the World's Longest Surface-to-Air Missile Test," *CNBC*, May 24, 2018.

13. Franz-Stefan Grady, "Russia Launches Project 09852 Special Purpose Submarine," *The Diplomat*, April 24, 2019.

14. Michael Birnbaum, "Russian Submarines Are Prowling Around Vital Undersea Cables. It's Making NATO Nervous." *The Washington Post*, Dec. 22, 2017.

15. Stuart Peach, "Russia a 'Risk' to Underwater Cable, Defense Chief Warns," *BBC*, Dec. 15, 2017.

16. U.S. Second Fleet Conducts NAVEUR Convoy Exercises in the Atlantic, U.S. Second Fleet, Feb. 28, 2020.

17. Charles Gao, "Russia's Husky Class submarines Armed with Nuclear Torpedoes and Hypersonic Missiles," *The National Interest*, May 10, 2018.

18. International Institute for Strategic Studies, *The Military Balance*, 2017.

19. *Assessing Threats to U.S. Vital Interests,* Washington, D.C.: Heritage Foundation.

20. *Assessing Threats to U.S. Vital Interests*, Washington, D.C.: Heritage Foundation.

21. "Next Generation Russian Submarines Better and Cheaper than Newest U.S. Submarines," *Military Intelligence*, March 3, 2017.

22. International Institute for Strategic Studies, *The Military Balance*, 2019.

23. General Curtis M. Scaparrotti, United States European Command statement on EUCOM posture before the Committee on Armed Services, U.S. Senate, March 5, 2019.

24. Michael Birnbaum, "Russia Tests Missiles in the Baltic Sea a Day After Baltic Leaders Met with Trump," The Washington Post, April 4, 2018.

25. "The Dangerous Tool of Russian Military Exercises," Association, June 7, 2017. Foreign Policy

26. Damien Sharkov, "Putin Calls 45,000 Troops to Snap Air Drill," *Newsweek,* Feb. 8, 2017.

27. Dave Johnson, "Ten Years of Russian Strategic Exercises and Warfare Preparation," *NATO Review*, Dec. 20, 2018.

28. Andrew Higgins and Sam LaGrone, "300,000 Troops and 900 Tanks: Russia's Biggest Military Drills Since the Cold War," U.S. Naval Institute, June 17, 2018.

29. "Private Military Companies Forming Vanguard of Russian Foreign Operations," Pavel Felgenhauer, *Eurasia Daily Monitor*, March 16, 2017.

30. "The Latin American Front: Russian Propaganda in Venezuela and Western Response," Brian Whitmore, *Center for European Policy Analysis,* February 2019.

31. "Russians in Venezuela: As Moscow Accuses U.S. of 'Information War,' What is Putin's Role in the Standoff?" Daria Litvinova, *CBS News*, May 1, 2019.

3 | The Threat from North Korea

THE PREMISE OF ANY NEGOTIATION is that both sides have something to gain or lose, something each may be willing to give up in order to secure some concession or agreement. By that definition, North Korea's talks with the United States, over the decades and increasingly since 2017, have never qualified as negotiations. Instead they have been rhetorical exercises not very cleverly designed to frustrate arriving at any meaningful concession or agreement. Always ambitiously publicized in advance, reports of the non-results are cynically distorted.

This is only what should be expected from the ruling dynasty, begun in 1948 by World War II hero Kim Il-sung, passed on to his son, Kim Jong-il in 1994 and, upon his death in 2011, to his grandson, Kim Jong-un. A family dynasty with total authority — so long as they do not lose the backing of the military — the Kims are buttressed by *Juche*, the state religion which roughly translates as self-reliance, and is a blend of Marxism, Confucianism, Japanese imperialism and traditional Korean nationalism. The fundamental idea is that North Korea can only survive and prosper by remaining totally separate and distinct from the world. The country's strength and very existence, according to Juche, depend entirely on its godlike leaders, the Kim family.[1]

To what extent the North Korean people believe any of this is not known; the vast majority of the population living in terrified and impoverished misery. What is known is that Kim Jong-un is free to negotiate as he likes, so long as he does not provoke the military by committing to giving up weapons.

The history of negotiations between the United States and North Korea is not encouraging.

"Expect lies. Do your homework, because they will have. Choose your words very carefully. And have Job-like patience." This warning comes from U.S. ambassador-at-Large Robert Gallucci, who served as the chief

U.S. negotiator of the Agreed Framework between President Bill Clinton's administration and Kim Jong-un's father, Kim Jong II.[2]

In 2017, North Korea successfully tested an ICBM, the Hwasong-14, capable of flying between 6,213 and 6,835 miles. At that range, Los Angeles, Denver, and Chicago, and possibly New York, Boston, and Washington, D.C., are within range.[3] South Korean Minister of Unification Cho Myoung-gyon commented in October 2018 that North Korea could have as many as 60 nuclear weapons.[4] North Korea successfully tested a hydrogen bomb in 2017, clearly signaling that it had no intention of following a U.N. resolution requiring a cessation of Pyongyang's nuclear and missile programs. With its active and growing ballistic missile capability, North Korea also threatens U.S. bases in South Korea, Japan, and Guam.[5]

North Korea has 1 million soldiers with reserves numbering several million more, making it the world's fourth-largest military. About 70 percent of its ground forces and 50 percent of its air and naval forces are deployed within 60 miles of the Demilitarized Zone between South and North Korea.[6]

Tensions escalated when President Trump referred to Kim Jung-un as "rocket man" in a tweet with South Korean president Moon Jae-in on September 17, 2017.[7] Trump also agreed to impose stronger sanctions on North Korea following recent nuclear and missile tests. In response to Pyongyang's missile program, the U.N. Security Council passed a resolution imposing stricter sanctions on North Korea. In response, Kim Jong-un vowed to expand his country's nuclear program until it established a military equilibrium with the United States.

After conducting its longest-range missile test on November 29, 2017, Korea declared itself a globe-spanning nuclear weapons power and insisted the United States deal with it on those terms.[8] What Jeffrey Lewis, director of the East Asia Nonproliferation Program at the Middlebury Institute of International Studies, finds most significant about the test is that it was fired from an 18-wheel truck manufactured in North Korea. "It enables North Koreans to build more long-range missiles since they're no longer restricted to missiles small enough to fit on imported Chinese vehicles," Lewis said.

With tensions between the United States and North Korea mounting, Trump met with Kim Jong-un in Singapore on June 21, 2018. Immediately following the meeting, Trump declared "there is no longer a nuclear threat from South Korea and that total denuclearization was already taking place." Secretary of State Michael Pompeo claimed that Kim Jong-un had accepted a U.N. mandate for complete, verifiable, and irreversible dismantling of his nuclear, missile and biological and chemical weapons program. Later it became clear that Kim Jong-un had no intention of dismantling his country's nuclear arsenal.[9]

Missiles of North Korea. Credit: Center for Strategic and International Studies

There were high expectations when Trump and Kim Jong-un met in Vietnam in 2019. Not only were they not able to deliver an agreement on denuclearization, they cancelled the ceremonial lunch and failed to issue a joint statement. Trump said Kim had been willing to denuclearize some of the country, but only if sanctions were lifted in their entirety, something Trump was unwilling to do. In summarizing the meeting, Trump said, "Sometimes you have to walk, and this was just one of those times."[10]

Following the meeting, Kim Jong-un announced that he no longer felt bound by his promise to President Trump to not conduct nuclear or ICBM tests. Instead, North Korea indicated it would "shift to a shocking actual action to make the U.S. pay for the sanctions pains sustained by our people."[11]

On July 1, 2019, President Trump crossed into North Korea for a meeting with Kim Jong-un, the first sitting U.S. president to set foot on North Korean soil. After the 45-minute-long meeting, Trump announced that he and Kim Jong-un had agreed to restart negotiations for full denuclearization of the peninsula.[12]

Despite two U.S.–North Korean summit meetings, there has been no decrease in North Korea's weapons of mass destruction or production capabilities. The U.S. Intelligence Community assesses that Pyongyang has increased its production of fissile materials for nuclear weapons and satellite imagery shows upgrades to missile, reentry vehicles, missile launchers and nuclear weapon production facilities.[13]

Pyongyang has repeatedly warned Washington that until it abandons its "hostile policy" and current negotiating position, there will be no diplomatic talks at either the working or summit level, according to Bruce Klinger, Senior Research Fellow, Northeast Asia, Heritage Foundation. Pyongyang has made clear it isn't interested in discussing its nuclear and missile programs, Klinger said.

To underscore that message, in 2019 North Korea launched 26 missiles, the largest annual total since such tests were forbidden by U.N. resolutions. Another seven were launched in March 2020, all in violation of U.N. resolutions. Several large-scale military exercises were conducted, even though the United States and South Korea had curtailed their scheduled combined exercises.

"Even if negotiations resumed, the two sides are far apart on even the basis for an agreement," says Klinger. "Crafting a good agreement would require extensive diplomatic meetings that would go beyond the U.S. presidential election. If North Korea altered its negotiating position, including in return for economic relief, President Trump might be willing to accept a small deal that, while flawed, could be seen as a first step to final denuclearization."[14]

It is more likely, however, that Trump would prefer the quiet status quo of 2019 where, despite a record high number of North Korean violations of U.N. resolutions, the lack of major provocations is seen as an improvement over the high tensions of 2017," Klinger continues. "But, knowing that, North Korea might threaten or carry out escalatory provocations. Pyongyang may assess that Washington, facing both health and economic crises, would be more malleable to avoid a concurrent foreign policy crisis. The Trump administration must chart a course between the twin flaws of overreacting and underreacting to a North Korean ICBM test. America should not return to 'fire and fury' rhetoric, nor initiate an attack on North Korea for crossing a technological threshold, since that would risk precipitating a full-scale war with a nuclear nation, leading to massive casualties."[15]

Despite the failure of the Trump-Kim Jong-un meetings, a more positive tone was set by an inter-Korean summit on April 27, 2018. It is only the third time leaders from the two countries have met and the first since Kim Jong-un took power in 2011 after the death of his father.[16]

The inter-Korean summit in April 2018 led to bilateral pledges of non-aggression and mutual force reduction, similar to those contained in the 1972, 1992, 2000, and 2007 joint statements. All of them Pyongyang subsequently violated or abrogated, and none prevented North Korea from conducting provocations, attempted assassinations of South Korea's president, terrorist acts, military attacks and cyberattacks, and acts of war. The two Koreas signed a Comprehensive Military Agreement in September 2018 to ease military tension and build confidence."[17]

According to the Heritage Foundation's Fellow, Bruce Klinger, North Korea is ramping up its vitriol toward South Korea. The push to sever inter-Korean ties is being led by Kim Jung-un's sister, Kim Yo Jong, rumored heir apparent to her brother. She is now responsible for overseeing North Korea's relations with the South. "Pyongyang is putting pressure on South Korea through increasingly acerbic means, including aggressive missives, breaking off communications, and threatening to take future steps against its enemy to the south. These hostile threats came after the Moon administration sought to improve relations with North Korea by making security concessions to reduce tensions. The Moon administration willingly agreed to constrain some military training as part of the inter-Korean Comprehensive Military Agreement. The Moon administration also repeatedly offered economic incentives to Pyongyang, despite the fact that the regime continues to reject U.S. resolutions requiring it to cease missile and nuclear tests and to abandon its weapons of mass destruction programs. The regime may attempt to capitalize on growing tensions between Washington and Seoul over stalled negotiations to determine the amount South Korea will contribute for the cost of stationing U.S. forces on the peninsula," Klinger warned.

Meanwhile, the Kim regime remains an information black hole. The secrecy led to unfounded rumors in May 2020 that Kim Jong-un was seriously ill and speculation about his successor. He had failed to attend a celebration on the birth of his grandfather, North Korea's founder, and the most important day in the country's political calendar. Kim's sudden death would have left Pyongyang facing an unplanned succession for the first time in its history.[18]

The 'bamboo curtain' extends to the COVID-19 crisis, with North Korea claiming to have no victims despite all neighboring countries having outbreaks. Some South Korean news agencies with access to sources in North Korea report that major cities in North Korea have been hit by the coronavirus epidemic and many regions suffer from a shortage of daily necessities.

According to several sources, people are starving in both border regions and inland areas, and more than 100 North Korean soldiers have died of coronavirus.[19]

Klinger notes that President Trump's offer of COVID-19 assistance to North Korea was quickly rebuffed by the regime, but that the disclosure of Trump's secret message has generated debate over policy options. "Some see a bigger assistance package and reducing sanctions as a way to get negotiations back on track," he says. "Others urge even stronger measures against North Korean cybercrime and missile launches. Even before the outbreak of COVID-19, Kim Jong-un in late December 2019 warned North Koreans to expect dire economic conditions brought on by international sanctions. The regime resurrected earlier campaigns calling on the public to "tighten their belts" after several years of promising an improving economy. "North Korea's subsequent draconian response to the COVID-19 outbreak in China may ameliorate a health crisis, but at the cost of further degrading the economy," Klinger says.

He reports that the quarantine measures North Korea rapidly implemented were far more extensive than those imposed during the 2003 SARS, 2014 Ebola, and 2015 MERS outbreaks. Borders were closed and travel suspended into and out of the country, officials stationed in China were recalled, and a quarantine imposed on all inbound cargo. "All items transiting North Korean ports or crossing border bridges are kept in isolated areas for 10 days. Pyongyang also imposed severe restrictions on internal travel within the country, cracking down on people crossing provincial borders without special permits."

Pyongyang also cracked down on smuggling, he says, and this included even reducing their own state-run smuggling. Many North Korean commercial vessels that had previously carried sanctioned material to and from China, including via illicit ship-to-ship fuel transfers at sea, appeared on satellite imagery idled in their home ports.

"North Korea's economy has been decimated by the combined impact of sanctions restricting trade, the regime isolating the country from both legal and covert foreign supply chains, Pyongyang's strong domestic COVID-19 isolation measures, and its repressive socialist economy. Furthermore, North Korea's foreign currency reserves were already dwindling, and the country is now approaching the lean food months before the fall harvest. Pyongyang's isolation measures have indirectly enhanced enforcement of U.N. economic sanctions. Chinese entities had engaged in prohibited economic activity with North Korea, but both countries have now curtailed smuggling in order to reduce the risk of contagion. Shipments to and from China accounting for 90 percent of North Korea's foreign trade were cut off by the regime. Combined exports to China in the first two months of 2020 declined by 71.9 percent to $10.7 million, while North Korean imports from China over the same period declined by 23 percent," Klinger said.

"North Korea faces potential disaster," Klinger reports. "Food prices are soaring, with the cost of rice increasing by 25 percent. The populace, impoverished and malnourished, is at high risk for a devastating outbreak of the disease. The country's decrepit medical system, even in normal circumstances, is undersupplied. Kim has acknowledged that his country lacks modern medical facilities and called for urgent improvements."[20]

Kim has appealed to South Korea President Moon Jae-in for help in combating coronavirus and has received a rush order for medical supplies from China. He is also believed to have secretly requested urgent international help to increase COVID-19 testing.

"Pyongyang announced on March 22 that Kim had received a personal letter from President Trump offering U.S. assistance in combating COVID-19 and providing a plan to develop bilateral ties," Klinger reports. "President Trump later confirmed the North Korean statement but did not provide details. North Korea responded with dismissals and missiles. Pyongyang commended Trump for sending the letter but affirmed previous messaging that the strong personal relationship between Trump and Kim had no bearing on the poor relations between the two countries nor the ongoing nuclear impasse."

Pyongyang has made clear that, while communications remain possible, it has no interest in discussing its nuclear and missile programs. In response to a request from the World Food Program, the U.N. approved an exemption so diagnostic and medical equipment can be transported into North Korea.

Six-month waivers have been approved by the U.N. for the World Health Organization, the International Federation of Red Cross and Red Crescent Societies, and Doctors Without Borders to send thermometers, portable ventilators, resuscitators, gloves, face shields, surgical masks, gowns, and goggles. While the first shipments of this international medical aid have arrived at North Korea's borders, the regime's strict quarantine restrictions have hampered delivery. On June 13, 2020, Kim Yo Jong warned that the North–South liaison office in North Korea would be destroyed in retaliation for South Korean activists who are launching propaganda leaflets across their border.[21] Two days later, the building was destroyed in a move that raised tensions on the Korean Peninsula. North Korea's official Korean Central News Agency said it has also cut off all government and communication channels with the South and threatened to abandon bilateral peace agreements reached in 2018. Inter-Korean relations have worsened since the breakdown of the second summit between President Trump and Kim Jong-un. The negotiations fell apart when North Korea demanded the lifting of all sanctions prior to a dismantling of its nuclear weapons.[22]

Some experts say North Korea is more concerned about a lack of progress in nuclear talks with Washington than any propaganda problems with South Korea. "North Korea has suspended communications lines with South Korea and threatened to nullify 2018 agreements that led the Koreas to halt firing exercises, remove some land mines and tear down guard posts in front-line area. The end of the 2018 deals could allow North Korea to send ships across the disputed sea boundary, float mines on a border river or take other provocative steps at the border area. The South Korean Defense Ministry said the 2018 deals must be maintained to prevent accidental armed clashes and establish peace on the Korean Peninsula."[23]

44

SUMMARY

"There was never a good war or a bad peace," Benjamin Franklin once wrote.[24] The maxim certainly hails from a different time, but despite some notable exceptions, it is hard to argue with Franklin's assessment. "Yet peace should not be rushed. And patience should temper the prospects of a possible U.S.–North Korea 'peace declaration,' a political agreement that would rhetorically declare an end to hostilities between Washington and Pyongyang. Such a peace declaration would be little more than a symbolic gesture of potential better political relations between Washington and Pyongyang. It might also significantly reduce the political, economic and military pressure on the Kim regime, possibly undermining its willingness to address issues essential to peace and security. It might also lead to significant political tensions with our South Korean and Japanese allies if it does not protect and advance their national interests sufficiently."[25]

The international community has long tried, and failed, to moderate North Korean behavior and bring about political and economic reform by offering concessions to Pyongyang. Threats and sanctions have also been unsuccessful. With its active and growing ballistic missile capability, North Korea poses definite threats to the United States in addition to contributing to the general threat of regional war in Asia and threatening U.S. bases in South Korea, Japan, and Guam. North Korean belligerence toward the United States has included military and diplomatic threats. Pyongyang's provocative behavior also includes nuclear and missile tests and tactical-level attacks on South Korea, a critical American ally that remains under active threat of attack and invasion from the North. In addition, Japan faces both intimidation attacks intended to deny the United States its base access to Japan and nuclear attacks on U.S. bases in the case of conflict on the Korean peninsula.

"Calls for relaxing sanctions in return for only a partial, flawed agreement should be rejected by the Trump Administration. What should be required is a comprehensive strategy of diplomacy, military deterrence, containment, pressure, law enforcement, and confrontation of North Korean human rights violations, including targeting North Korean entities engaged in cybercrimes. North Korea gained an estimated $2 billion using "widespread and increasingly sophisticated" cyberattacks to steal from banks and cryptocurrency exchanges according to U.N. assessments, and the regime so far has shown no sign of abandoning its nuclear and missile arsenal nor its continued defiance of the international community. While it is possible that North Korea's mounting economic problems could lead it back to nuclear talks, the amount of pressure North Korea feels in the months ahead will depend, not so much on international sanctions, as on the extent of COVID-19 in the country and Pyongyang's response measures.[26]

NOTES

1. Zack Beauchamp, *Fox News*, June 18, 2018.

2. Amanda Macias, "The last US diplomat to secure a nuclear deal with North Korea warns: They will cheat," Amanda Macias, *CNBC*, March 10, 2018.

3. "North Korean ICBM Appears Able to Reach Major US Cities, David Wright, *Union of Concerned Scientists*, July 29, 2017.

4. "North Korea is Believed to Have Up to 60 Nuclear Weapons, South Korea Says," *NBC News*, Oct. 2, 2018.

5. Josh Smith, "How North Korea's Latest ICBM Test Stacks Up," *Reuters*, Nov. 28, 2017.

6. Report to Congress: Military and Security Developments Involving the Democratic People's Republic of Korea, May 22, 2018.

7. Niamh McIntyire, "Donald Trump Calls North Korean Leader Kim Jung-un 'Rocket Man,'" *Independent*, Sept. 17, 2017.

8. Uri Friedman, "North Korea Says It Has Completed Its Nuclear Program," *The Atlantic*, Nov. 29, 2017.

9. David Brunnstrom and James Oliphant, "Trump: North Korea Total Denuclearization Started; Officials see No New Moves," *Reuters*, June 21, 2018.

10. Patrick Goodenough and Susan Jones, "Trump Ends Summit: 'Sometimes You Have to Walk, and This Was Just One of Those Times,'" *CNS News*, Feb. 28, 2019.

11. Bruce Klinger, "North Korea Starts the New Year with a Threatened Bang," The Heritage Foundation.

12. Caroline Linton, "Trump Crosses into North Korea, Meets with Kim Jong Un, *CBS News*, July 1, 2019.

13. Jonathan Cheng, "North Korea Expands Key Missile-Manufacturing Plant," *Wall Street Journal*, June 25, 2019.

14. Assessing Threats to U.S. Vital Interests: North Korea, Washington, D.C.: Heritage Foundation, Oct. 30, 2019.

15. Bruce Klinger, "Once Again, North Korea Is Reaching Out to the South. We Should Be Receptive, but Wary." Heritage Foundation, Washington, D.C., June 4, 2018.

16. Benjamin Haas, "Everything You Need to Know about the Inter-Korean Summit," *The Guardian*, April 26, 2018.

17. *Assessing threats to U.S. Vital Interests: North Korea*, Washington, D.C.: The Heritage Foundation, Oct. 30, 2019.

18. Claire Lee, "North Korea's Kim Reappears After Weeks of Speculation," *AFP*, May 2, 2020.

19. Deidre Shesgreen, "A Near Impossibility: Experts Doubt North Korea's Claim of Zero Coronavirus Cases," *USA Today*, April 30, 2020.

20. Bruce Klinger, "North Korea Remains Self-Isolated and Defiant Amidst the Coronavirus," *The Heritage Foundation*, April 3, 2020.

21. Kim Tong-Hyung, "Kim Jong Un's sister threatens South Korea with military action. Kim Tong-Hyung," *Associated Press*, June 13, 2020.

22. Kim Tong-Hyung and Hyung-Jin Kim, "North Korea Blows Up Inter-Korea Liaison Office, Raising Tensions," *Associated Press*, June 16, 2020.

23. "There Was Never A Good War or a Bad Peace," *Good News Network, Oct. 19, 2019.*

24. Peter Brookes, "This Is No Time for an Artificial Peace in Korea," The Heritage Foundation, Feb. 6, 2019.

25. *Assessing Threats to U.S. Vital Interests: North Korea*, The Heritage Foundation, Washington, D.C., Oct. 30, 2019

26. Bruce Klinger, "The U.S. Should Implement Maximum Pressure After Failed Hanoi Summit," *The Heritage Foundation*, May 22, 2019.

4 | The Threat from Iran

WITHOUT ANY BASES ON THE PERSIAN GULF, how were China, Russia, and North Korea to effect military and economic influence on this epicenter of global oil production? The simple answer has been to arm and equip Iran, the virulently anti-West country occupying the entire eastern shore of the Persian Gulf. It has been a strategy with many high and low points since Iran's Islamic Revolution began in 1979, but it has consistently managed to foster political, economic, social and, of course, military upheaval throughout the Middle East over four decades.

On January 7, 2020 sixteen short and medium-range Fatah 110 and Shahabad missiles rained down on the U.S. bases at al-Asad and Erbil in Iraq, a strike threatening all-out war between the United States and Iran.[1] That confrontation started four days earlier when a U.S. drone strike at Baghdad airport killed Qassim Soleimani, an Iranian major general in the Islamic Revolutionary Guard Corps, and Abu Mahdi al-Muhandis, commander of the Kata'ib Hezbollah Militia.[2]

Once called the most powerful operative in the Middle East, Soleimani was one of the key architects of the Iranian regime's efforts to reshape the country's influence in the region. He directly armed and trained Iraq's Shiite militias and other proxy groups in Lebanon, the Palestinian territories, Syria, and Yemen. Retired U.S. general David Petraeus, commander of American forces during the war in Iraq, called "Soleimani "our most significant and evil adversary in the greater Middle East."[3]

President Trump defended his order to kill a top Iranian general by accusing Soleimani of plotting imminent and sinister attacks on American civilian and military personnel. "We took action last night to stop a war. We did not take action to start a war," Trump said a day after the attack.[4]

Soleimani's death ignited furious demands in Iran for retaliation from a population in deep and angry mourning. "The great nation of Iran will take revenge for this heinous crime," Iranian President Hassan Rouhani said immediately after the attack.[5]

Iran fired more than a dozen ballistic missiles at Iraqi bases housing U.S. troops at al-Asad and Irbil, on January 7, 2020. "The brave soldiers of IRGC's aerospace unit have launched a successful attack with tens of ballistic missiles on Al Assad military base in the name of martyr General Qassem Soleimani," a spokesman for the IRGC said in a statement released after the attack.[6] Initially, the DOD reported no American casualties and minimum damage as a result of the missile attack. Within a month, more than 100 troops were being treated for brain injuries. The number underscores the effects of traumatic brain injuries, which may not show up for days or weeks after such an attack.[7]

Would Iran consider the missile attack as sufficient retaliation for the death of Soleimani? And how would Trump respond to any further military action from Iran? Both questions were answered when Iran's president Hassan Rouhari said the necessary retaliation for Soleimani's death had been accomplished. In a sense, the general's assassination had resulted in an eerie calm instead of the predicted turmoil.[8]

Iran's major military buildup began in July 2015 when a nuclear agreement lifted sanctions on Iran, giving it about $100 billion in restricted assets and allowed it to expand its oil and gas exports. The following year, Tehran increased its military budget to $19 billion, 90 percent more than the previous year.[9]

Relief from the burden of sanctions helped Iran's economy and enabled it to improve its military capabilities and support for terrorist groups. It also allowed Tehran to emerge from diplomatic isolation and strengthen strategic ties with Russia. This growing relationship has strengthened Iran's military capabilities. Tehran announced in April 2016 that Russia had begun deliveries of S-300 Favorit long-range surface to air missile systems.

Iran and Russia also escalated their strategic operations in supporting Syria's embattled Assad regime. "Iran's growing military intervention in Syria was partly eclipsed by Russia's military intervention and launching of an air campaign against Assad's enemies in September 2015. By October 2015, Iran had deployed an estimated 7,000 IRGC troops in Syria, along with an estimated 20,000 foreign fighters from Iran-backed Shiite militias from Lebanon, Iraq, Afghanistan, and Pakistan."[10]

President Trump did the right thing when he withdrew from the agreement with Iran and restored sanctions on May 8, 2018. Iran, Britain, France, Germany, the European Union, China, and Russia have tried to salvage the nuclear deal but without success to date.

"We will be instituting the highest level of economic sanction," Trump said. "Any nation that helps Iran in its quest for nuclear weapons could also be strongly sanctioned by the United States," he warned.[11]

Iran had accumulated enough low-yield uranium to build eight nuclear bombs before the 2015 nuclear deal was reached. Iranian President Rou-hani announced on May 8, 2019, that Iran would no longer comply with 2015 nuclear agreement restrictions on the size of Iran's stockpile of en-riched uranium and heavy water.[12]

It has recently attempted to buy technology to build weapons of mass destruction, according to reports from the German states of Mecklen-berg, Vorpommen, and Bavaria. Iran attempted to bypass the German law that prohibits the export to Iran of welding machines that can be used to manufacture military vehicles to launch missiles. According to the report, Iran claimed the end user was in Malaysia.[13]

Iran continues to pose a major threat to Saudi Arabia and other mem-bers of the Gulf Cooperation Council, including Bahrain, Oman, Qatar, and the United Arab Emirates. Tehran has supported groups that launch terrorist attacks against the Gulf States. Saudi Arabia has criticized Iran for supporting radical Saudi Shiites, intervening in Syria, and supporting Shiite Islamists in Lebanon, Iraq, and Yemen.[14]

Iran threatens to cut off the free flow of oil exports from the Gulf if it is attacked or if a cutoff of its own oil exports is threatened. Iran's leaders have threatened to close the Strait of Hormuz, the jugular vein through which most Gulf oil exports flow to Asia and Europe. Major General Mo-hammad Baqeri warned on April 28, 2019, that if "our oil does not pass, the oil of others shall not pass the Strait of Hormuz either."[15]

During the Iran-Iraq War, each side targeted the others oil facilities, ports, and oil exports. Iran attacked neutral Kuwait oil tankers and ter-minals and laid mines in Persian Gulf shipping lanes. The United States defeated Iran's tactics by reflagging Kuwaiti oil tankers, clearing mines and escorting ships through the Persian Gulf.[16]

"Since the Iran-Iraq war, Tehran has invested heavily in developing its naval forces, particularly the IRGC Navy, along unconventional lines. Today. Iran boasts an arsenal of Iranian-built missiles based on Russian and Chinese designs that pose significant threats to oil tankers as well as warships. Iran has deployed mobile anti-ship missile batteries along its 1,500-mile gulf coast and on many of the 17 Iranian-controlled islands in the gulf. Six of these islands are particularly important because they are located close to the shipping channels that all ships must use near the Strait of Hormuz."[17]

Iran has a large supply of anti-ship mines, including significant stocks of "smart mines including versions of the Russian MDM-6 and Chinese EM-11, EM-31 and EM-55 mines.[18]

Iran can deploy mines or torpedoes from its three Kilo-class subma-rines, purchased from Russia and based at Bandar Abbas, the country's largest seaport and naval base. These submarines could be difficult to detect while running silent and remaining stationary on a shallow bottom outside the Strait of Hormuz. In these shallow waters, heavyweight nuclear submarines lose their advantage to small diesel submarines, which Iran has in numbers."[19]

IRGC naval forces frequently challenged U.S. naval forces in a series of incidents. IRGC missile boats launched rockets within 1,500 yards of the carrier Harry S. Truman near the Strait of Hormuz. Iran detained and humiliated 10 American sailors in a provocative January 12, 2016, incident. Rep. Randy Forbes, (R-VA) claims the Iranians forced 10 American sailors to apologize at gunpoint.[20]

Iran has escalated its intimidation tactics against international shipping near the gulf. On May 12, 2019, four oil tankers were damaged by mysterious explosions off the coast of the UAE in the Gulf of Oman. Then U.S. National Security Adviser John Bolton stated that "naval mines almost certainly came from Iran." Two more tankers were attacked in the Gulf of Oman on June 13, 2019. On June 19, 2019, an IRGC surface-to-air missile shot down a U.S. surveillance drone in international airspace.[21]

"Iran looms large over its weak and divided Arab rivals. Iraq and Syria have been destabilized by insurgencies and civil war and may never fully recover. Egypt is distracted by its own internal problems, economic imbalances and the Islamist extremist insurgency in the Sinai Peninsula, and Jordan has been inundated by a flood of Syrian refugees and is threatened by the Islamist extremist groups from Syria."[22]

At the heart of many of the region's conflicts is the friction within Islam between Sunni Muslims, who form the majority of the world's Muslim population, and Shias. Iran has exacerbated Shia–Sunni tensions to increase its influence on embattled regimes and has undermined adversaries in Sunni-led states.[23]

"Tehran attempts to run an unconventional empire by exerting great influence on sub-state entities like Hamas (Palestinian territories); Hezbollah (Lebanon); the Mahdi movement (Iraq); and the Houthi insurgents (Yemen). In Afghanistan, Tehran's influence on some Shia groups is such that thousands have volunteered to fight for Bashar al-Assad in Syria."[24]

"The Middle East is deeply sectarian and these long-standing divisions, exacerbated by the constant vying for power by religious extremists, are central to many of the challenges that the region faces today. In some cases, these sectarian divides go back centuries. Contemporary conflicts, however, have less to do with these histories than they do with moderate extremist ideologies and the fact that today's borders often do not reflect the region's cultural, ethnic, or religious realities."[25]

The economic situation in the Middle East is part of what drives the political environment. The lack of economic freedom was an important factor leading to the Arab Spring uprisings, which began in early 2011 and

Missiles of Iran. Credit: Center for Strategic and International Studies

disrupted economic activity, depressed foreign and domestic investment and slowed economic growth.[26]

The popular uprisings in Tunisia, Libya, Egypt, Bahrain, Syria, and Yemen did not usher in a new era of democracy and liberal rule as many in the West were hoping. At best, they made slow progress toward democratic reform. At worst, they added to political instability, exacerbated economic problems, and contributed to the rise of Islamic extremists. Years later, the economic and political outlooks remain bleak.[27]

Meanwhile, Tehran continues to build up its missile arsenal. Iran has more ballistic missiles than any other middle eastern country as well as the greatest number of all types of missiles, and can strike targets up to 2,000 kilometers (1,242 miles) from Iran's borders. Russia's delivery of the SA-20c SAM system in 2016 has provided Iran with its most advanced long-range air defense system. Iran's ballistic missiles pose a major threat to U.S. bases and allies from Turkey, Israel, and Egypt in the west to Saudi Arabia and the other Gulf states to the south and Afghanistan and Pakistan to the east. Israel is most at risk from an Iranian missile attack. In case the Israeli government had any doubt about Iran's implacable hostility, they displayed a message written in Hebrew on the side of one of the Iranian missiles that Israel must be "wiped off the earth."[28]

The development of nuclear warheads for Iran's ballistic missiles would significantly reduce Israel's ability to deter attacks, an ability that the existing (but not officially acknowledged) Israeli monopoly on nuclear weapons in the Middle East currently provides. Israel is within range of Iran's Shahab-3 missiles. Moreover, all of Israel can be hit with the thousands of shorter-range rockets that Iran has provided to Hezbollah in Lebanon and to Hamas and Palestinian Islamic Jihad in Gaza.

"Iran is not a member of the Missile Technology Control Regime, and it has sought aggressively to acquire, develop, and deploy a wide spectrum of ballistic missiles, cruise missiles, and space launch capabilities. During the 1980–1988 Iran-Iraq war, Iran acquired Soviet-made Scud-B missiles from Libya and later used North Korean–designed Scud-C and No-dong missiles, which it renamed the Shahab-2 (with an estimated range of 500 kilometers or 310 miles) and Shahab-3 (with an estimated range of 900 kilometers or 560 miles). It now can produce its own variants of these missiles as well as longer-range Ghadr-1 and Qiam missiles.[29]

"Iran's Shahab-3 and Ghadr-1, which is a modified version of the Shahab-3 with a smaller warhead but greater range (about 1,600 kilometers or 1,000 miles), are considered more reliable and advanced than the North Korean No-dong missile from which they are derived. In addition to its growing missile and rocket inventories, Iran is seeking to enhance lethality and effectiveness of existing systems with improvements in accuracy and warhead designs. Iran is developing the Khalij Fars, an anti-ship ballistic missile which could threaten maritime activity throughout the Persian Gulf and Strait of Hormuz," Michael Flynn, former White House national security adviser warned.[30]

Iran is a declared chemical weapons power that claims to have destroyed all its chemical weapons stockpiles. U.S. intelligence agencies have assessed that Iran maintains the capability of producing chemical weapons. It continues to develop and improve a range of new military capabilities to target U.S. and allied military assets in the region, including armed unmanned aerial vehicles, ballistic missiles, advanced naval mines, unmanned explosive boats, submarines, torpedoes, and anti-ship and land-attack cruise missiles.

Key weapons in Iran's inventory are up to 50 medium-range ballistic missile launchers, as many as 100 short-range ballistic missile launchers, 336 combat-capable aircraft, 1,513 or more main battle tanks, 640 or more armored personnel carriers, 21 tactical submarines, six corvettes, and 15 amphibious landing ships. There are 523,000 personnel in the armed forces, including 350,000 in the Army, upwards of 125,000 in the Islamic Revolutionary Guard Corps, 30,000 in the Air Force, and 18,000 in the Navy.[31]

Meanwhile Iran, with over 3,000 deaths attributed to COVID-19 as of April 2, 2020, is one of the most severely affected countries in the world. A lack of trust in state institutions has led to weakened public adherence to restrictions aimed at reducing the spread of COVID-19. Syria and

Yemen also stand to be gravely affected by the pandemic because of lack of medical facilities after years of conflict.[32]

SUMMARY

Iran represents by far the most significant security challenge to the United States, its allies, and its interest in the greater Middle East. Its open hostility to the United States and Israel and sponsorship of terrorist groups such as Hezbollah pose the greatest threat to U.S. citizens, at home and abroad. Hezbollah has murdered more Americans than any other terrorist group. Tehran's revolutionary ideology has fueled hostility to other Middle Eastern states, many of which it seeks to overthrow and replace with radical allies. The leader of Iran's 1979 revolution, Ayatollah Khomeini, called the United States the "Great Satan."[33]

"For the foreseeable future, the Middle East region will remain a key focus for U.S. military planners. Overall, regional security has deteriorated in recent years. Even though the Islamic State appears to have been defeated, the nature of its successor is unclear. Iraq has restored its territorial integrity after the defeat of ISIS, but the political situation and future relations between Baghdad and the U.S. will remain difficult as long as a government that is sympathetic to Iran is in power."[34]

NOTES

1. Julian Borger and Patrick Winters, "Missiles Launched by Iran against US Airbase in Iraq," *The Guardian*, Jan. 7, 2020.

2. Quassin Aboul-Zahra and Zeina Karam, "U.S. kills Iran's Most Powerful General in Baghdad Airstrike," , *Associated Press*, Jan. 2, 2020.

3. "Who was Qussem Soleimani, the Iranian General Killed in a U.S. strike," *CBS*, Jan. 3, 2020.

4. Katherine Faulders, "Trump Defends Killing of Iranian General, Accuses Him of Plotting Sinister Attacks on Americans," *ABC*, Jan. 3, 2020.

5. Alexander Smith, "Iran Vows Revenge and Retaliation After U.S. Kills Its Top General," *NBC News*, Jan. 2, 2020.

6. "Iran Warns U.S.: Aggression Against Tehran Will Not Be Tolerated," *Fox News*, Jan. 7, 2020.

7. Bill Chappel, "109 Troops Suffered Brain Injuries in Iran Strike, Pentagon Says," *NPR*, Feb. 11, 2020.

8. Martin Chulov, "Impact of Soleimani's Death Is Playing Out in Unexpected Ways," *The Guardian*, Jan. 12 ,2020.

9. Saeed Ghasseminejad, "Iran Doubles Down on Its Military Budget," *FDD*, June 3, 2016.

10. *Assessing Threats to U.S. Vital Interests*, Washington, D.C.: Heritage Foundation, Oct. 30, 2019.

11. Tom Di Christopher, "Trump Announces He Will Withdraw US from Iran Nuclear Deal and Restore Sanctions," *CNBC*, May 8, 2020.

12. *Assessing Threats to U.S. Vital Interests*, Washington, D.C.: Heritage Foundation, Oct. 30, 2019.

13. Gursimran Haas, "Iran Is Buying Technology to Build Nuclear Weapons, Claims Shock German Intelligence," *Express*, June 4, 2019.

14. Carlo J.V. Caro, "Fighting Radical Islamic Terrorism Begins with Saudi Arabia," *The National Interest*, April 1, 2019.

15. *Assessing Threats to U.S. Vital Interests – Iran*. Washington, D.C., The Heritage Foundation, Oct. 30, 2019.

16. Jon Gasmbrell, "Oil Tanker Attacks Echo Persian Gulf's 1980s 'Tanker War,'" *Associated Press*, June 14, 2019.

17. *Assessing Threats to U.S. Vital Interests, Iran*, Washington, D.C.: The Heritage Foundation, Oct. 30, 2019.

18. Sune Engel Rasmussen, "Iran's Fast Boats and Mines Bring Guerilla Tactics to Persian Gulf," *The Wall Street Journal*, May 30, 2019.

19. Caleb Larson, "Danger: Iran's Submarines Could Easily Control the Arabian Gulf and the Strait of Hormuz," *The National Interest*, April 15, 2020.

20. Adam Kredo, "Congressman: Classified Details of Iran's Treatment of U.S. Sailors Will Shock the Nation," *Washington Free Beacon*, May 16, 2016.

21. Natasha Turak, "Iran Shoots Down American Drone in International Airspace in 'Unprovoked Attack,' U.S Says," *CNBC*, June 20, 2019.

22. *Assessing the Global Operating Environment: Middle East*, Washington, D.C.: The Heritage Foundation, Oct. 30, 2019.

23. "What Is the Difference Between Sunni and Shia Muslims?" *The Economist*, May 8, 2019.

24. Sune Engel Rasmussen, "Iran Covertly Recruits Afghan Shias to Fight in Syria," *The Guardian*, June 30, 2016.

25. *Assessing the Global Operating Environment, Middle East*, Washington, D.C.: The Heritage Foundation, Oct. 30, 2019.

26. "The Arab Spring," Heritage Foundation, April 13, 2011.

27. "The Arab Winter," *The Economist*, Jan. 9, 2016.

28. "Israel Must be Wiped off the Earth: Iran Launches Missiles Marked Threat," *The Tower*, March 9, 2016.

29. *Assessing Threats to U.S. Vital Interests*, Washington, D.C.: The Heritage Foundation, Oct. 30, 2019.

30. Kevin Liptak, "White House National Security Adviser: Iran Is 'On Notice,'" Kevin Liptak, *CNN*, Feb. 2, 2017.

31. "Iran, Its Partners and the Balance of Effective Force," International Institute for Strategic Studies, IISS, March 19, 2020.

32. Emile Hokayem and Mahas Rouhi, "COVID-19 in the Middle East: Iran in Crisis and the Urgent Risks for Countries in Conflict, IISS, April 2, 2020.

33. "Who is the 'Great Satan,'" Hamid Abash, *Al Jazeera*, Sep. 20, 2015.

34. *2020 Index of Military Strength*, The Heritage Foundation, Oct. 29, 2019.

5 | The Threat from Terrorism

Since 9/11, four terrorist attacks have occurred on American soil. On November 5, 2009, 13 people were killed, and more than 30 others wounded when Major Nidal Malik Hasan, an Army psychiatrist, went on a shooting rampage at Fort Hood, Texas. The Virginia-born Hasan shouted in Arabic, "Allah Akbar" ("God is Great) as he opened fire with a semi-automatic pistol on unarmed soldiers. Later he told a judge that America's war on terrorism was really a war against Islam.[1]

Two bombs went off near the finish line of the Boston Marathon on April 15, 2013, killing three spectators and wounding more than 260 people. Two brothers, Tamerlan and Dzhokhar Tsarnaev, who spent most of their childhoods in the former Soviet republic of Kyrgyzstan, planned and carried out the attack. That night, a 27-year old police officer at the Massachusetts Institute of Technology, Sean Collier, was shot dead in his patrol car by Tamerlan Tsarnaev. Three days later, Tamerlan was killed in a shootout with Boston police, but the other brother escaped. Dzhokhar was captured on April 19, 2013, and is now under a death sentence in a federal prison. He had left a note claiming the attack was in retaliation for U.S. wars on Muslim countries.[2]

On December 6, 2019, a Saudi Arabian pilot, al-Shamrani, opened fire at the Naval Air Station in Pensacola, Florida, killing three U.S. service members and wounding eight others. He was shot dead by security personnel immediately after the shooting. The FBI used two cell phones to connect al-Shamrani with AQAP. The evidence shows that the Pensacola attack was the culmination of years of planning by a longtime AQAP associate. He made a cell phone call to an AQAP operative the night before he started shooting. FBI director Christopher Wray said that al-Shamrani associated with Abdullab al-Maliki, one of the overseas AQAP operatives, while in the Florida.[3]

On May 2, 2020, Adam Salim Alsahli was shot and killed after wounding one sailor during an attack on Naval Air Station Corpus Christi,

Texas. The FBI said the shooter, a U.S. resident who was born in Syria, had been "neutralized" and labeled the attack as terrorism related. According to social media accounts traced to Alsahi, he was a supporter of ISIS and Al Qaeda.[4]

While the FBI is vigilant in its tracking of terrorists on American soil, the major battles are being fought in the Middle East. On October 26, 2019, helicopters carrying between 50 and 70 members of the U.S. Army Delta Force landed on the compound of Islamic State leader Abu Bakr al-Baghdadi by the town of Barisha in northwest Syria. With military jets circling overhead, the commandos blew a hole in the complex wall, starting a firefight in which five residents were killed and two taken prisoner. Baghdadi was left inside trying to escape through a tunnel. With a Delta dog in pursuit, the world's most wanted man detonated his suicide vest, killing two children along with him. Abu Hassan al-Muhajir, spokesman for ISIS, was also killed in the attack. After vital ISIS documents and electronics were collected, the compound was destroyed in an airstrike to prevent it from becoming an extremist shrine. The man who built a caliphate and inspired millions of followers worldwide reportedly spent his last minutes fleeing from a dog in a tunnel, blowing himself up along with his children. Baghdadi's death is of major moral significance and exemplifies a meaningful milestone in ISIS's demise.[5]

Since 9/11, America has targeted several al-Qaeda leaders. The highest-profile target, Osama bin Laden, was killed in a May 2011 raid.[6] The United States also killed Abu Musab al-Zarqawi, leader of al-Qaeda in Iraq in 2006.[7] In November 2002, a U.S. drone killed Qaed Salim al-Harethi, al-Queda leader in Yemen who was implicated in the bombing of the U.S. Cole on October 12, 2000.[8] Muhammad Atef, al-Qaida's military chief, was killed in a drone attack in Afghanistan in October 2001."[9]

"The Defense Intelligence Agency (DIA) and U.S. Central Command (CENTCOM) assess that the death of Baghdadi did not disrupt the group's command structure of operations. Abu Ibrahim al-Hashimi al-Qurayshi has been named Baghdadi's successor and the fight against the Islamic State is far from over. Little is known about al-Hashimi, although his last name (al Qurayshi) claims a lineage to the Prophet Muhammad, a position that offered legitimacy in some quarters."[10]

"Baghdadi's death in northern Syria is a long way from where it began for the Islamic State and its forerunners in the deserts in Iraq, was the latest in a series of blows for the group. It has been stripped of all the land it once held and has lost nearly all its founding leaders after more than five years of war. The direction of the organization is now largely up to a new generation of leaders, who must determine whether to pursue the goals set out by Baghdadi or set a new course. Central to the debate is whether to continue with the insurgency that made it such a lethal presence in the region, or to boost affiliates elsewhere in the world. Isis's capacity to launch spectacular terror attacks in Europe and beyond is thought to have been diminished by the grueling war that drastically eroded its ranks and leadership."[11]

ISIS has lost its Caliphate, but it remains a highly dangerous adversary capable of planning and executing attacks regionally and — at the very least — inspiring them in the West. It appears to be transitioning from a quasi-state to an insurgency, relying on its affiliates to project strength far beyond its former Syrian and Iraqi strongholds.

Meanwhile, despite sustained losses to its leadership, al-Qaeda remains resilient. It has curried favor with other Sunnis in particular areas of strategic importance to it, has focused its resources on local conflicts, has occasionally controlled territory, and has de-emphasized (but not eschewed) focus on the global jihad.[12]

Regardless of any short-term tactical considerations, both groups ultimately aspire to attack the U.S. at home and U.S. interests abroad. While the U.S. has hardened its domestic defenses, making this a tricky prospect for both groups, they can rely on radicalized individuals living within the U.S. to take up the slack. Furthermore, as has been demonstrated time and again, there are ample opportunities to target Americans based in countries that are more vulnerable to terrorist attack.

In general, terrorists operate in a very local context, usually within a specific country or sub-region. Sometimes a terrorist group's objectives extend beyond the internationally recognized borders of a state because their identity as a group transcends such legal or geographic boundaries. Al-Qaeda was founded in 1988 by foreign veterans from among those who flocked to Afghanistan to join the war against the Soviet occupation in the 1980s. With Osama bin Laden appointed emir, al-Qaeda was envisaged as a fighting force that could defend Sunnis across the world and expand the Islamist struggle into a global revolutionary campaign.[13]

After 9/11, al-Qaeda's leadership fled Afghanistan. Much of the original cadre has now been killed or captured, including Osama bin Laden, and other key al-Qaeda leaders have been killed by targeted strikes in Afghanistan, Pakistan, Syria, Yemen, and Somalia. However, segments of al-Qaeda's leadership, including its emir, Ayman al-Zawahiri, survived. Some al-Qaeda lieutenants are believed to remain in the Afghanistan–Pakistan region; others have taken refuge in Iran.[14]

Al-Qaeda also dispersed its fighters further afield, allowing for the development of regional affiliates that shared the long-term goals of al-Qaeda's general command and largely remained loyal to it. These affiliates have engaged with some success in local conflict environments. In particular, the Arab Spring uprisings that began in 2011 enabled al-Qaeda to advance its revolutionary agenda, taking advantage of failed or failing states in Iraq, Libya, Mali, Syria, and Yemen. It is through these affiliates that al-Qaeda is able to project regional strength most effectively.[15]

Yemen has long been a bastion of support for militant Islamism. Yemenis made up a disproportionate number of the estimated 25,000 foreign Muslims in the Afghan jihad against the Soviet Union in the 1980s. After that conflict ended, Yemen also attracted Westerners into the country to carry out terrorist operations there. In 1998, several British citizens were jailed for planning to bomb Western targets, including hotels and a church.[16]

Al-Qaeda's first terrorist attack against Americans occurred in Yemen in December 1992 when a bomb was detonated in a hotel used by U.S. military personnel. Al-Qaeda launched a much deadlier attack in Yemen in October 2000 when it attacked the USS *Cole* in the port of Aden with a boat filled with explosives, killing 17 American sailors.

The first U.S. drone strike outside Afghanistan after 9/11 also took place in Yemen, targeting those connected to the attack on the *Cole*.[17]

After 9/11, and following crackdowns in other countries, Yemen became increasingly important as a base of operations for al-Qaeda. In September 2008, it launched an attack on the U.S. embassy in Yemen that killed 19 people, including an American woman. Yemen's importance to al-Qaeda increased further in January 2009 when al-Qaeda members who had been pushed out of Saudi Arabia merged with the Yemeni branch to form Al-Qaeda in the Arabian Peninsula. This affiliate quickly emerged as one of the leading terrorist threats to the U.S.

Much of this threat initially centered on AQAP's Anwar al-Awlaki, a charismatic American-born Yemeni cleric who directed several terrorist attacks on U.S. targets before being killed in a drone air strike in September 2011. He had an operational role in the plot executed by Umar Farouk Abdulmutallab, the failed suicide bomber who sought to destroy an airliner bound for Detroit on Christmas Day 2009.[18] Awlaki was also tied to plots to poison food and water supplies, as well as to launch ricin and cyanide attacks, and is suspected of playing a role in the November 2010 plot to dispatch parcel bombs to the U.S. in cargo planes. Additionally, Awlaki was in contact with Major Nidal Hassan, who perpetrated the 2009 Fort Hood shootings that killed 13 soldiers. Since Awlaki's death, the number of AQAP-sanctioned external operations in the West has diminished. However, his videos on the Internet have continued to radicalize and recruit young Muslims, including the perpetrators of the April 2013 bombing of the Boston Marathon.

AQAP's threat to Western security, while seemingly slightly reduced by Awlaki's death, is still pronounced. Another attempt to carry out a bombing of Western aviation using explosives concealed in an operative's underwear was thwarted by a U.S.–Saudi intelligence operation in May

2012.[18] In August 2013, U.S. interception of al-Qaeda communications led to the closure of 19 U.S. embassies and consulates across the Middle East and Africa because of fears that AQAP was planning a massive attack.[19]

In January 2015, two AQAP-trained terrorists murdered staff members and nearby police at *Charlie Hebdo* magazine in Paris.[20] Then, in 2017, aviation was targeted once again by a plan to conceal bombs in laptop batteries.[21]

Much of AQAP's recent activity has focused on exploiting the chaos of the Arab Spring in Yemen. AQAP acquired a significant amount of territory in 2011 and established governance in the country's South, finally relinquishing this territory only after a Yemeni military offensive in the summer of 2012.[22] AQAP further intensified its domestic activities after the overthrow of Yemen's government by Iran-backed Houthi rebels in 2015, seizing the city of al-Mukalla and expanding its control of rural areas in southern Yemen. AQAP withdrew from al-Mukalla and other parts of the South in the spring of 2016, reportedly after the U.S.-backed Saudi–United Arab Emirates coalition had cut deals with AQAP, paying it to leave certain territory and even integrating some of its fighters into its own forces targeting the Houthis.[23]

More substantive progress has been achieved in the targeting of AQAP's leadership. Said al-Shehri, a top AQAP operative, was killed in a drone strike in 2013. The group's leader at the time, Nasir al-Wuhayshi, was killed in a drone strike in June 2015.[24] Perhaps most significantly, Ibrahim al-Asiri, AQAP's most notorious bomb maker, was killed in a U.S. strike in 2017.[25] Since then, the tempo of U.S. drone strikes against AQAP has slowed.

Despite U.S. drone activity, it is estimated that AQAP still has between 6,000 and 7,000 fighters. It therefore remains a potent force that could capitalize on the anarchy of Yemen's multi-sided civil war to seize new territory and plan more attacks on the West.

Al-Qaeda's Syrian affiliate, the al-Nusra Front, was established as an offshoot of the Islamic State of Iraq, al-Qaeda's Iraq affiliate, in late 2011 by Abu Muhammad al-Julani, a lieutenant of ISIS leader Abu Bakr al-Baghdadi.[26]

ANF had an estimated 5,000 to 10,000 members and emerged as one of the top rebel groups fighting the Assad dictatorship in Syria. ANF had some success in attracting Americans to its cause. An American Muslim recruited by ANF, Moner Mohammad Abusalha, conducted a suicide truck bombing in northern Syria on May 25, 2014, in the first reported suicide attack by an American in that country.[27]

At least five men have been arrested inside the U.S. for providing material assistance to ANF, including Abdirahman Sheik Mohamud, a naturalized U.S. citizen who was arrested in April 2015 after returning from training in Syria and was planning to launch a terrorist attack on U.S. soldiers based in Texas.[28]

In recent years, the al-Qaeda movement in Syria has undergone several name changes, allying itself with various Islamist rebel groups. This has made the degree of direct threat posed outside of Syria's borders harder to assess. In a May 2015 interview, al-Julani stated that al-Nusra's intentions were purely local and that, "so as not to muddy the current war" in Syria, ANF was not planning to target the West.[29]

Then, in July 2016, al-Nusra rebranded itself as Jabhat Fath Al Sham (JFS), and al-Julani stated that it would have "no affiliation to any external entity," a move that some regarded as a break from al-Qaeda and others regarded as a move to obscure its ties to al-Qaeda and reduce U.S. military pressure on the group.[30] In January 2017, JFS merged as part of an alliance with other Islamist extremist movements into a new anti-Assad coalition: Hayat Tahrir al-Sham (HTS) (Organization for the Liberation of the Levant). It was estimated that HTS had 12,000 to 14,000 fighters in March 2017.[31]

Further complicating matters surrounding al-Qaeda's presence, another group in Syria connected to al-Qaeda, Hurras al-Din (Guardians of the Religion), was formed in March 2018. Among its ranks are those who defected from HTS, and its suspected emir is an Ayman al-Zawahiri acolyte.

HTS has adopted a more pragmatic course than its extremist parent organization and has cooperated with moderate Syrian rebel groups against the Assad regime, as well as against ISIS. However, the leadership of Abu Muhammad al-Julani and his tactical approach to the conflict, as well as the clear divisions within the Syrian jihad, have led to rebukes from Ayman al-Zawahiri and those loyal to him. Zawahiri has stressed the need for unity while lambasting the jihadist movement in Syria and its emphasis on holding territory in northwest Syria at the expense of intensifying the struggle against Assad.[32]

One entity that did pose a direct threat to the West was the Khorasan group, which was thought to comprise dozens of veterans of al-Qaeda's operations in Afghanistan and Pakistan. "Al-Zawahiri had dispatched this cadre of operatives to Syria, where they were embedded with ANF and — despite al-Julani's statement that ANF was not targeting the West — charged with organizing terrorist attacks against Western targets. However, a series of U.S. air strikes in 2014– 2015 degraded Khorasan's capacity to organize terrorist attacks." [33]

Al-Qaeda's presence and activities in Syria, as well as the intent of those once aligned with it, are sometimes opaque, most likely on purpose. Even if offshoots of al-Qaeda are not currently emphasizing their hostility to the U.S., however, that will likely change if they succeed in further consolidating power in Syria.

Al-Qaeda in the Islamic Maghreb (AQIM) "has an estimated 1,000 fighters operating in the Sahel, including Algeria, northern Mali, southwest Libya, and Nigeria," and "is based in southern and eastern Algeria (including isolated parts of the Kabylie region), Burkina Faso, Cote D'Ivoire, Libya, northern Mali, Niger, and Tunisia."[34]

"AQIM's roots lie in the Algerian civil war of the 1990s, when the Algerian government cancelled the second round of elections following the victory of the Islamic Salvation Front (FIS) in the first round. The armed wing of the FIS, the Armed Islamic Group (GIA), responded by launching a series of attacks, executing those even suspected of working with the state. The group also attempted to implement sharia law in Algeria.

The GIA rapidly alienated regular Algerians, and by the late 1990s, an offshoot, the Salafist Group for Preaching and Combat (GSPC), emerged. Its violence, somewhat less indiscriminate than the GIA's, was focused on security and military targets. Having failed to overthrow the Algerian state, the GSPC began to align itself with al-Qaeda, and Ayman al-Zawahiri announced its integration into the al-Qaeda network in a September 2006 video. The GSPC subsequently took the AQIM name."[35]

AQIM has carried out a series of regional attacks and has focused on kidnapping Westerners. Some of these hostages have been killed, but more have been used to extort ransoms from Western governments.[36]

Like other al-Qaeda affiliates, AQIM also took advantage of the power vacuums that emerged from the Arab Spring, particularly in Libya where Islamist militias flourished. The weak central government was unable to tame fractious militias, curb tribal and political clashes, or dampen rising tensions between Arabs and Berbers in the West and Arabs and the Toubou tribe in the South. The September 11, 2012, attack on the U.S. diplomatic mission in Benghazi underscored the extent to which Islamist extremism had flourished in the region. The radical Islamist group that launched the attack, Ansar al-Sharia, had links to AQIM and shared its violent ideology. AQIM and likeminded Islamist allies also grabbed significant amounts of territory in northern Mali in late 2012, implementing a brutal version of sharia law, until a French military intervention helped to push them back."[37]

AQIM continues to support and works alongside various jihadist groups in the region. In March 2017, the Sahara branch of AQIM merged with three other al-Qaeda or al-Qaeda–linked organizations based in the Sahel to form the Group for Support of Islam and Muslims (JNIM), an organization that has pledged allegiance to al-Qaeda emir Ayman al-Zawahiri. AQIM is not known to have explicitly targeted the U.S. homeland in recent years, but it does threaten regional stability and U.S. allies in North Africa and Europe, where it has gained supporters and operates extensive networks for the smuggling of arms, drugs, and people.[38]

"The Islamic State of Iraq and al-Sham (ISIS) is an al-Qaeda splinter

Missiles of Hezbollah. Credit: Center for Strategic and International Studies

group that has outstripped its parent organization in terms of its immediate threats to U.S. national interests. The Islamic State of Iraq (ISI), the precursor to ISIS and an al-Qaeda offshoot, was perceived by some Western policymakers as having been strategically defeated following the U.S. "surge" of 2006–2007 in Iraq. However, the group benefited from America's effectively having withdrawn — both politically and militarily — from Iraq in the 2010–2011 period, as well as from the chaos in Syria where Bashar al-Assad responded to the Arab Spring protests with bloody persecution. In both Iraq and Syria, ISIS had space in which to operate and a large disaffected pool of individuals from which to recruit."[39]

In April 2013, ISI emir Abu Bakr al-Baghdadi declared that the al-Nusra Front, the al-Qaeda affiliate operating in Syria, was merely a front for his operation and that a new organization was being formed: the Islamic State of Iraq andal-Sham (ISIS). ISIS sought to establish an Islamic state governed by its interpretation of sharia law, posing an existential threat to Christians, Shiite Muslims, Yazidis, and other religious minorities. Its long-term goals continue to be a jihad to drive Western influence out of the Middle East; diminish and discredit Shia Islam, which it considers apostasy; and become the nucleus of a global Sunni Islamic empire.[40]

With both al-Qaeda leader Ayman al-Zawahiri and ANF emir Abu Mohammed al-Julani unsuccessful in reining in al-Baghdadi, ISIS was expelled from the al-Qaeda network in February 2014. Despite this, ISIS swept through parts of northern and western Iraq and in June 2014 declared the return of the Caliphate, with its capital in the northern Syrian city of Raqqa. It subsequently kidnapped and then murdered Westerners working in Syria, including American citizens." [40]

A U.S.-led international coalition was assembled to chip away at ISIS's control of territory. The Iraqi Army and Iranian-backed militias broke its control of Mosul in July 2017, and the U.S.-backed Syrian Democratic Forces militia liberated Raqqa in October 2017, with ISIS's last town (Baghouz) falling in March 2019. ISIS fighters have retreated, have adopted insurgent tactics, and will continue to pose a regional terrorist threat with direct implications for the U.S. In January 2019, for example, U.S. troops were killed in a suicide bombing at a market in Manbij in northern Syria. [41]

Although ISIS's territorial control has now been broken in Iraq and Syria, its presence has spread far beyond that territory. Terrorist groups around the world have pledged allegiance to Abu Bakr al-Baghdadi, and ISIS now has affiliates in the Middle East, in South and Southeast Asia, and throughout Africa. ISIS poses a threat to stability in all these regions, seeking to overthrow their governments and impose Islamic law. In pursuit of this cause, ISIS has shown itself willing to kill Christians and other non-Muslims while committing attacks on the police and soldiers. In addition, ISIS has made threats against government embassies, including those of the United States, in its areas of influence. ISIS poses an ongoing threat to life in the West. [42]

In the United States, on May 3, 2015, two extremists in contact with an ISIS operative in Syria were fatally shot by police before they could commit mass murder in Garland, Texas. [43]

More commonly, however, the ISIS ideology has inspired individuals and small groups to plan attacks in the U.S. Tashfeen Malik, one of the perpetrators of the December 2, 2015, shootings that killed 14 people in San Bernardino, California, pledged allegiance to al-Baghdadi. [44] ISIS then claimed responsibility for the June 12, 2016, shootings at a nightclub in Orlando, Florida, that killed 49 people. Omar Mateen, the perpetrator, had pledged allegiance to al-Baghdadi, although there is no evidence to show that the attacks were directed by ISIS. [45] The group also claimed responsibility for the October 31, 2017, vehicular attack by Sayfullo Saipov in New York that killed eight. Saipov, too, had pledged allegiance to ISIS's emir but did not appear to be operationally guided by ISIS. [46] Such terrorist attacks, incited but not directed by ISIS, are likely to continue for the foreseeable future.

ISIS has also attempted complex attacks on aviation. It claimed responsibility for the October 31, 2015, downing of a Russian passenger jet over Egypt's Sinai Peninsula that killed 224 people and also tried to bring down a flight heading from Sydney to Abu Dhabi by concealing an explosive device inside a meat grinder. ISIS had well-publicized success in attracting the support of foreign fighters. Approximately 250 from the United States traveled or attempted to travel to Syria.[47] There is the potential for an ongoing threat from these individuals, who are likely to have received military training, upon return to the United States either in terms of attack planning or in recruiting future generations of jihadists. ISIS had greater success attracting those from Europe, with approximately 6,000 departing from European countries.[48]

The foreign fighter threat in Europe has led to several attacks. Mehdi Nemmouche, a French citizen of Algerian origin who shot and killed four civilians at the Jewish Museum in Brussels in May 2014, for example, was an ISIS-aligned terrorist who had fought in Syria.[49] In August 2015, Ayoub el-Khazzani, a Moroccan, attempted to gun down passengers in a train travelling between Amsterdam and Paris. Passengers, including two members of the U.S. Army, restrained him.[50] Similarly, a group of ISIS foreign fighters teamed with local Islamist terrorists to launch a series of suicide and gun attacks on a music venue, restaurants, cafes, and a football stadium, killing 130 and injuring 368 people in Paris, France, in November 2015.[51]

ISIS ideology has also inspired a wave of attacks in Europe, including one carried out by a Tunisian who used a truck to kill 86 people and injure 434 more at a Bastille Day celebration in Nice, France, in July 2016.[52] In another such attack, in June 2017, three men killed eight people and injured 47 on or near London Bridge by running over them or stabbing them.[53]

ISIS has demonstrated an interest in carrying out chemical attacks. Sief Allah H., a Tunisian asylum seeker who was in contact with ISIS, and his German wife Yasmin H. were arrested in Cologne in June 2018 after they successfully produced ricin as part of a suspected attack. This was the first time that ricin was successfully produced in the West as part of an alleged Islamist plot.

Overall, as of May 2019, ISIS had had some involvement — ranging from merely inspirational to hands-on and operational — in over 150 plots and attacks in Europe since January 2014 that led to 371 deaths and over 1,700 injuries.[54] This includes the loss of American lives abroad. An American college student was killed in Paris in November 2015, four Americans were killed in the Brussels attack of March 2016, and another three were killed in the Nice attack of July 2016.[55]

ISIS's threat is by no means confined to Europe: Americans were also killed in ISIS-claimed attacks in Tajikistan in July 2018[56] and Sri Lanka in April 2019.[57]

SUMMARY

ISIS has lost its Caliphate, but it remains a highly dangerous adversary capable of planning and executing attacks regionally and — at the very least — inspiring them in the West. It appears to be transitioning from a quasi-state to an insurgency, relying on its affiliates to project strength far beyond its former Syrian and Iraqi strongholds.

Meanwhile, despite sustained losses to its leadership, al-Qaeda remains resilient. It has curried favor with other Sunnis in particular areas of strategic importance to it, has focused its resources on local conflicts, has occasionally controlled territory, and has de-emphasized (but not eschewed) focus on the global jihad. This approach has been particularly noticeable since the Arab Spring.

Regardless of any short-term tactical considerations, both groups ultimately aspire to attack the United States at home and U.S. interests abroad. While the United States has hardened its domestic defenses, making this a tricky prospect for both groups, they can rely on radicalized individuals living within the United States to take up the slack. Furthermore, as has been demonstrated time and again, there are ample opportunities to target Americans based in countries that are more vulnerable to terrorist attack.

Iran has adopted a political warfare strategy that emphasizes irregular warfare, asymmetric tactics, and the extensive use of proxy forces. Iran is the world's foremost state sponsor of terrorism and has made extensive efforts to export its radical Shia brand of Islamist revolution. It has established a network of powerful Shia revolutionary groups in Lebanon and Iraq; has cultivated links with Afghan Shia and Taliban militants; and has stirred Shia unrest in Bahrain, Iraq, Lebanon, Saudi Arabia, and Yemen. The Islamic Revolutionary Guard Corps has trained, armed, supported, and collaborated with a wide variety of radical Shia and Sunni militant groups, as well as Arab, Palestinian, Kurdish, and Afghan groups that do not share its radical Islamist ideology. The IRGC's elite Quds (Jerusalem) Force has cultivated, trained, armed, and supported numerous proxies, particularly the Lebanon-based Hezbollah; Iraqi Shia militant groups; Palestinian groups such as Hamas and Palestinian Islamic Jihad; and groups that have fought against the governments of Afghanistan, Bahrain, Egypt, Israel, Iraq, Jordan, Kuwait, Morocco, Saudi Arabia, Turkey, the United Arab Emirates (UAE), and Yemen.

Pakistan is home to a host of terrorist groups that keep the region unstable and contribute to the spread of global terrorism. Its continued support for terrorist groups that have links to al-Qaeda, the Taliban, and the Haqqani Network undermines U.S. counterterrorism goals in the region.

Pakistan's military and intelligence leaders maintain a short-term tactical approach of fighting some terrorist groups that are deemed to be a threat to the state while supporting others that are aligned with Pakistan's goal of extending its influence and curbing India's.

If the United States wishes to contain and ultimately end Islamist violence, it must continue to bring effective pressure to bear on these groups and those that support them.

NOTES

1. "Army Major Kills 13 People in Fort Hood Shooting Spree," *History Newsletter*, Nov. 5, 2009.

2. "Boston Marathon Bombing," *History.com*, March 28, 2014.

3. "FBI Director Wray's Remarks at Press Conference Regarding Naval Air Station Pensacola Shooting Investigation," FBI National Press Office, May 18, 2020.

4. Howard Altman and Geoff Ziezulewicz, "FBI Identifies Suspect Identified In NAS Corpus Christi Shooting It Believes To Be 'Terrorism Related,'" *Navy Times*, May 7, 2020.

5. "Isis Leader Abu Bakr al-Baghdadi Killed in U.S. Raid," *The Guardian*, Oct. 26, 2019

6. "Death of Osama bin Laden Fast Facts," *CNN*, May 2, 2011.

7. "Abu Musab al-Zarqawi Killed in Bombing Raid," *Fox News*, June 8, 2006.

8. John Esterbrook, "US Kills top Al Qaeda Suspect," *CBS News*, Nov. 7, 2002.

9. Khaled Dawoud, "Mohammed Atef, Egyptian militant who rose to the top of the al-Qaida, killed," *The Guardian*, Nov. 18, 2001.

10. Martin Chulov, "Islamic State Names New Leader after Death of Abu Kakr al-Baghdadi," *The Guardian*, Oct. 31, 2019.

11. Eyal Tsir Cohen and Eliora Katz, "What We Can Learn about US Intelligence from the Baghdad Raid," Brookings Institute, Nov. 6, 2019.

12. Luis Martinez, "Pentagon Report Says Al-Baghdadi's Death Has Little Impact on ISIS Leadership and Operations," *ABC News*, Feb. 4, 2020.

13. Peter I Bergen, *The Osama Bin Laden I Know: An Oral History of al Qaeda's Leader*, New York, Free Press, 2006.

14. Daniel Klaidman, *Kill or Capture: The War on Terror and the Soul of the Obama Presidency*, Houghton Mifflin Harcourt, 2012.

15. *Assessing Threats to U.S. Vital Interests: Non-State Actors*, Washington, D.C.: The Heritage Foundation, Oct. 30, 2019.

16. *The 2020 Index of U.S. Military Strength*, Washington, D.C.: The Heritage Foundation.

17. "U.S. Kills Cole Suspect," *CNN*, Nov. 5, 2002.

18. Jeremy Pelofsky, "Prosecutors Say al Qaeda Leader Awlaki Directed Underwear Bomber," *Reuters*, Feb. 10, 2012.

19. "Yemen Terror Threat Prompts State Department to Evacuate Some Embassy Staff, Warn Americans to Leave Country 'Immediately,'" *CBS*, August 6, 2013,

20. Thomas Joscelyn, "Al Qaeda in the Arabian Peninsula Claims Responsibility for Charlie Hebdo Attack," Foundation for Defense of Democracies, Long War Journal, January 14, 2015.

21. Barbara Starr and Rene Marsh, "AQAP Trying to Hide Explosives in Laptop Batteries, Official Says," *CNN*, March 22, 2017.

22. Maggie Michael, Trish Wilson, and Lee Keath, "AP Investigation: US Allies, al-Qaida Battle Rebels in Yemen," *Associated Press*, Aug. 7, 2018.

23. Robin Simcos, "Ansar al-Sharia and Governance in Southern Yemen," *Current Trends in Islamist Ideology*, Jan. 2013.

24. Kareen Shaheen, "US Drone Strike Kills Yemen al-Qaida Leader Nasir al-Wuhayshi, Kareen Shaheen," *The Guardian*, June 16, 2015.

25. "White House Confirms top al-Qaeda Bomb-Maker Killed in 2017," White House statement, Oct. 10, 2019.

26. United Nations Security Council, *Twenty-Second Report of the Analytical Support and Sanctions Monitoring Team,* Aug. 2018.

27. Adam Goldman, Greg Miller, and Nicole Rodriguez, "American Who Killed Himself in Syria Suicide Attack Was from South Florida," *The Washington Post*, May 31, 2014.

28. Adam Goldman, "Ohio Man Who Trained with Jabhat al-Nusra Is Indicted on Terrorism Charges," *The Washington Post*, April 16, 2015.

29. Agence France-Presse, "Chief of Al-Qaeda's Syria Affiliate Pledges No Attacks on the West," May 27, 2015.

30. Thomas Joscelyn, "Analysis: Al Nusrah Front Rebrands Itself as Jabhat Fath Al Sham," Foundation for Defense of Democracies *Long War Journal*, July 28, 2016,

31. "Foreign Terrorist Organizations," in U.S. Department of State, Bureau of Counterterrorism, Country Reports on Terrorism 2017.

32. Thomas Joscelyn, "Zawahiri Criticizes Jihadists in Syria for Clinging to Territory Under Turkey's Protection," Foundation for Defense of Democracies, *Long War Journal*, Feb. 3, 2019.

33. James Phillips, "The Rise of Al-Qaeda's Khorasan Group: What It Means for U.S. National Security," *Heritage Foundation Issue Brief* No. 4281, Oct.6, 2014.

34. *2020 Index of Military Threats*, Washington, D.C.: The Heritage Foundation.

35. *Assessing Threats to U.S. Vital Interests: Non-State Actors*, Washington, D.C.: The Heritage Foundation, Oct. 30, 2019

36. Raissa Kasolowsky and Kate Kelland, "Al Qaeda Kills British Hostage in Mali," *Reuters*, June 3, 2009.

37. Michael Bay, *13 Hours: What Actually Happened at the US Consulate in Benghazi*, documentary film, Feb. 5, 2016.

38. U.S. Department of State, Bureau of Counterterrorism, Country Reports on Terrorism 2017.

39. *Assessing Threats to U.S. Vital Interests: Non-State Actors*, Washington, D.C.: The Heritage Foundation, Oct. 30, 2019.

40. Zachary Cohen, "4 Americans Among Those Killed in Syria Attack," *CNN*, Jan. 17, 2019.

41. Tom O'Connor, "Manbij Attack: U.S. Soldiers Reported Killed in Syria Suicide Bomb Claimed by ISIS," *Newsweek*, Jan. 16, 2019.

42. U.S. Department of State, Bureau of Counterterrorism, Country Reports on Terrorism 2017.

43. Adam Chandler, "A Terror Attack in Garland, Texas," *The Atlantic*, May 4, 2015.

44. Laura Wagner and Bill Chappell, "FBI: San Bernardino Shooting Is Being Investigated as a Terrorist Act," *NPR*, December 4, 2015,

45. Thomas Joscelyn, "Orlando Terrorist Swore Allegiance to Islamic State's Abu Bakr al Baghdadi," Foundation for Defense of Democracies, *Long War Journal*, June 20, 2016.

46. Jeremy B. White, "New York Truck Attack Suspect 'Left Note Pledging Allegiance to Isis,'" *The Independent*, Nov. 1, 2017.

47. Lisa Curtis, "Combatting the ISIS Foreign Fighter Pipeline: A Global Approach," *Heritage Foundation Special Report* No. 180, Jan. 6, 2016.

48. "More than 6,000 Have Left Europe for Isis Jihad: EU," *Agence France-Presse*, The Local, April 13, 2015.

49. "Brussels Jewish Museum Murders: Mehdi Nemmouche Jailed for Life," *BBC News*, March 12, 2019.

50. Paul Cruickshank, "Train Attack Suspect Confesses After Revelations in Academic Journal," *CNN*, Dec. 19, 2016.

51. "Paris Attacks: What Happened on the Night," *BBC News*, Dec. 9, 2015.

52. "Nice Attack: What We Know About the Bastille Day Killings," *BBC News*, Aug. 19, 2016.

53. "London Bridge Attack: What Happened," *BBC News*, May 3, 2019.

54. U.S. Department of State, Bureau of Counterterrorism, Country Reports on Terrorism 2017.

55. "European Islamist Plots and Attacks Since 2014 — and How the U.S. Can Help Prevent Them," *Heritage Foundation Backgrounder No. 3236*, August 1, 2017.

56. "Tajikistan 'Attack' Leaves Four Foreign Cyclists Dead," BBC *News*, July 30, 2018.

57. "ISIS Claims Responsibility for Sri Lanka Easter Bombings that Killed over 350," *ABC News*, April 23, 2019.

Chapter 6 | The Chinese Threat to Taiwan

THE OVERWHELMING VICTORY scored by the democratic opposition in Hong Kong's district elections in November 2019 and the rioting in the streets that followed for months gave Taiwan's president Tsai Ing-wen a boost just when she appeared vulnerable to a humiliating defeat in the island's regional elections. Her campaign was also invigorated by China's undisguised belligerence to her as a vigorous and articulate champion of Taiwanese independence.

"We know the responsibility we bear," she told supporters at a rally in New Taipei City, where she pledged to preserve Taiwan as "a beacon of democracy" in the face of efforts by China to undercut it. "Taiwan is on the front line," she said.[1] A victory for Ms. Tsai would be regarded as a rebuke of Beijing, which is widely seen as favoring her Nationalist Party opponent. The Nationalist Party, also known as the Kuomintang, has generally pursued policies that would ensure steady economic relations with the mainland.

The "beacon," located only 112 miles off the coast of mainland China, is in a strategic position to block most of China's vast trading empire. China sees Taiwan as a breakaway province that will eventually be part of the mainland, but many Taiwanese want their country to remain as a separate nation. China's long-standing policy to end the de facto independence of Taiwan and ultimately to bring it under the authority of Beijing is a threat to a major American security partner in the Western Pacific.

After easing for eight years, tensions across the Taiwan Strait resumed as a result of Beijing's reaction to the outcome of Taiwan's 2016 presidential election. Regardless of the state of the relationship at any given time, however, Chinese leaders from Deng Xiaoping and Mao Zedong to Xi Jinping have consistently emphasized the importance of ultimately reclaiming Taiwan. The island, along with Tibet, is the clearest example of a geographical core interest in Chinese policy. China has never renounced the use of force, and it continues to employ political warfare against Taiwan's political and military leadership.[2]

On May 28, 2020, while speaking on Hong Kong opposition to China's new security law, Premier Li Keqiang reiterated Beijing's position of firm opposition to the independence of Taiwan, warning that the Taiwan question is China's internal affair. "We are opposed to any foreign interference," Li said. "The Chinese nation has the wisdom and the ability to handle appropriately its own affairs."[3]

The U.S. involvement with Taiwan began in 1949, when Chiang Kai-shek's Kuomintang (KMT) government and 1.3 million supporters abandoned the Chinese mainland and relocated to the island of Taiwan (also known as Formosa). On June 25, 1950, President Harry Truman sent the U.S. Navy's Seventh Fleet into the Taiwan Strait to prevent any conflict between the Republic of China (Taiwan) and the People's Republic of China (PRC), effectively putting Taiwan under American protection.[4]

Questions are emerging as to whether the Seventh Fleet is up to the challenges it now faces in the Pacific, from both a nuclear-armed North Korea and a strengthening China. The U.S. military acknowledges it lacks the money, manpower, and weapons to ensure success. At a Congressional hearing into the series of fatal collisions at sea in recent years, naval officials acknowledged they were trying to do too much with too little and have a supply-and-demand problem placing a heavy strain on the force.[5]

For the Chinese leadership, the failure to effect unification, whether peacefully or using force, would reflect fundamental political weakness in the PRC. For this reason, there is no realistic means by which any Chinese leadership can back away from the goal of unifying the island with the mainland.

In 1998, as the Taiwanese were preparing to hold their country's first direct presidential election, China fired missiles within 35 miles of the ports of Keelung and Kaohsiung, causing panic in Taiwan. President Clinton responded by deploying a carrier battle group in international waters near the Taiwan Strait. There were fears of a possible invasion of Taiwan, fueled by PLA exercises simulating an amphibious assault and live-fire exercises near the outlying island of Penghu. A crisis was averted, likely due to the U.S. intervention. Beijing's efforts to coerce the Taiwanese backfired when pro-independence Lee Teng-hui was elected in 1998. The threat also convinced Washington of the necessity of providing Taiwan with more weapons to defend itself. Humbled by the U.S. naval deployment, Beijing did not resort to similar intimidation as the Taiwanese continued to exercise their democratic rights. Beijing's rhetoric remains harshly opposed to Taiwan independence, but it has learned that coercion by military means can be counterproductive. It shifted its strategy and for the past decade and a half has attempted to win the hearts and minds of the Taiwanese through business and trade.[6]

The injury to Chinese pride also convinced Beijing to modernize its military. The result was an intensive program of double-digit investment, foreign acquisitions, and indigenous resourcing to turn China into a nation capable of imposing its will within its immediate neighborhood and beyond. Two decades of double-digit increases in China's defense budget have produced a significantly more modern PLA, much of which remains focused on a Taiwan contingency. This modernized force includes more than 1,000 ballistic missiles, a modernized air force, and growing numbers of modern surface combatants and diesel-electric submarines capable of mounting a blockade. As the 1995–1996 Taiwan Strait crisis demonstrated, Beijing is prepared to use open displays of force.[7]

Over the last year, the Chinese have sought to intimidate Taiwan with a growing number of military exercises, including live-fire drills and bomber flights around the island. In the absence of a strong American presence, China might be willing to go further. By holding at risk key American platforms and systems such as aircraft carriers, the Chinese seek to delay or even deter American intervention in support of key friends and allies.

The growth of China's military capabilities is specifically oriented toward countering America's ability to assist in the defense of Taiwan. Chinese efforts to reclaim Taiwan are not limited to overt military means. Chinese political warfare methods include legal warfare, public opinion, and psychological warfare. The PLA employs such approaches to undermine both Taiwan's will to resist and America's willingness to support Taiwan. The Chinese goal is to win without fighting, to take Taiwan without firing a shot or with only minimal resistance, before the United States can organize an effective response.[8]

Democratically-ruled Taiwan poses an existential threat to China's Communist leaders because the island serves as a beacon of freedom for ethnic Chinese people everywhere. China regards Taiwan as a renegade province and considers reuniting the island with the mainland part of China's goal of achieving global dominance. If a new Taiwan crisis erupts, what will China's President Xi do? He has many rivals and outright enemies within China's power structure. Any sign of weakness on his part may cause him serious problems and could even bring him down. He would lose face if he backed down if challenged by the Seventh Fleet.[9]

The danger of a Taiwan conflict has grown in recent years, even as current tensions between Washington and Beijing are mainly the result of U.S. opposition to Chinese militarization in the South China Sea, its support of North Korean's nuclear and missile programs and a trade war.

According to Ian Easton, a China affairs analyst, China will invade

Taiwan by 2020 with massive missile attacks along with a naval and air blockade, followed by amphibious beach assaults using up to 400,000 troops. "Of all the powder kegs out there, the potential for a war over Taiwan is the largest and most explosive," Easton claims.[10]

Parts of the PLA invasion plan were first revealed publicly by the Taiwan defense ministry in 2013 when Chinese leaders committed to using force against Taiwan by 2020, if non-military means were not successful. China currently is using non-lethal means — psychological, diplomatic, propaganda, and informational warfare — against Taiwan. Once these are exhausted, the plan for large-scale amphibious assaults may be carried out. The war plan calls for rapidly capturing the capital Taipei and destroying the government, seizing other major cities, and clearing out surviving defenders. Military operations will emphasize speed and surprise to overwhelm coastal defenses and create so much destruction in the early phase that Taiwan would surrender before the U.S. military could deploy forces to the area.[11]

Just how vulnerable Taiwan may be to Chinese conquest remains, however, the subject of intense debate. There is little question that the Xi regime is making intensive preparations. Since June 2011, Chinese tourists have been free to travel anywhere on the island. Within three years, the number of Chinese visitors annually totaled more than three million. How many of them came as agents of the PLA can only be speculated, but it may have been in the hundreds of thousands.[12]

None of this is a secret to Taiwan president Tsai Ing-wen or other Republic of China (ROC) officials. A deft politician and fluent in five languages, she has been working for years to maintain a viable relationship between an independent Taiwan and its massive neighbor. She has also established contacts in high government circles in major Western countries. Tsai got worldwide attention when she phoned congratulations to President Donald Trump soon after his election, a call that infuriated Chinese officials. For some time, she and her fellow senior officials have been well aware of the aggressive plans beyond the infiltration strategy that the Chinese leadership and the PLA have been formulating and implementing for Taiwan. And she, of course, has discussed them with the United States.

As background for the Taiwanese officials' thinking, the restricted PLA manual, *Course Book on the Taiwan Strait's Military Geography*, warns that Taiwan could cut off China's trade lines. The manual also emphasizes that many of China's seaborne oil imports pass through the Taiwan Strait and are highly vulnerable to military interdiction. Protecting the security of this strategic maritime passageway is not just a military activity alone but also an act of national strategy, the manual claims.[13] Other internal PLA writings have surfaced indicating that China is ready to use force when it believes non-military means would not be successful in forcing capitulation to Beijing's demands — with the very important condition that the United States should be kept out of the battle. It is crucial that the United States be given no reason to relax and reduce its naval and air capabilities in the region. Fortuitously, Beijing's odd and ambitious build-up of military facilities in the Spratly Islands convinced Washington that the Seventh Fleet is entitled to most of the available ships in its smaller navy.

Taiwan has a fleet of Tuo Jiang–class missile corvettes, offering a potent defense against the People's Liberation Army Navy (PLAN) surface fleet. As the Tuo Jiang corvettes were being built, launched, and commissioned, Taiwanese senior naval officers warned that they would be vulnerable to air attack or anti-ship missiles since their air-defense capabilities are minimal. Naval experts are dubious that their other air defense systems — Oliver Hazard Perry class frigates and Kidd class destroyers — could prevail against China's more modern ships.

As to air cover, Taiwan's aging fighter fleets had already fallen well behind their Chinese counterparts in quality and quantity, and their airfields have been primary targets of the PLA infiltrators. Land-based surface-to-air missiles, such as Patriot and Tien-Kung (Sky Bow) systems, could cover coastal areas but would not provide the corvettes with any protection if they were operating some distance from the coast.[14]

SUMMARY

The biggest question, of course, is what would the U.S. reaction be if China tried to take Taiwan by force? Under the 1979 Taiwan Relations Act, the United States is required to provide defensive weaponry to Taiwan to prevent the use of force against the island. The invasion of Taiwan could lead to a nuclear war between the United States and China. While polls in the United States show only a minority of Americans would favor U.S. military personnel fighting to defend Taiwan, members of Congress are more supportive. They realize America's leadership position in the region would be compromised if the United States stood aside while a large communist state gobbled up a small democracy.

NOTES

1. "President Tsai Lauded Taiwan as a Beacon of Democracy, *The China Post*, Oct. 10, 2018.
2. Gordon Chang, Interview, Dec. 10, 2019.

3. "China Premier Comments on New Security War and Taiwan," *Associated Press TV News*, May 28, 2020.

4. Bill Gertz, Interview, Nov. 11, 2019.

5. Gina Harkins, "New Report Points to Acute Fatigue as Factor in Deadly Ship Collisions," *Military.Com.*, August 2019.

6. Gordon Chang, Interview, Dec. 10, 2019.

7. Bill Gertz, Interview, Nov. 11, 2019.

8. Thomas Callender, Senior Fellow for Defense Programs, Heritage Foundation, Interview, Oct.4, 2019.

9. Michael J. Cole, "A Chinese Invasion of Taiwan: What happens? Who wins?" *The National Interest*, Jan. 27. 2019.

10. Ian Eason, "The Chinese Invasion Threat," *The National Interest*, March 27, 2019.

11. Kyle Mizokmi, "China Has Secret Plans to Invade Taiwan by 2020," *Popular Mechanics,* Oct. 4, 2017.

12. Chris Horton, "Rather Than Talk to Taiwan, China Sends in the Spies," *Quartz*, March 15, 2017.

13. *Course Book on the Taiwan's Strait's Military Geography*, PLA, Oct. 5, 2017.

14. Gordon Chang Interview, Dec. 10, 2019.

7 | The Threat of India-Pakistan Conflict

INDIA AND PAKISTAN were created out of the bloody partition of British India in 1947. The tensions before and after the drawing of new borders uprooted 14 million people and erupted in mob violence that killed as many as one million Hindus, Muslims, and Sikhs. The two countries have gone on to fight three major wars since independence. Pakistan's founders believed India saw the subcontinent's partition as temporary and hoped to absorb the territory that had become Pakistan at the first opportunity. India has been frustrated by what it sees as Pakistan's support for terrorists that continue to strike inside its territory, particularly in Kashmir.

India and Pakistan are now engaged in an ongoing military confrontation across the de facto border to Kashmir, a disputed region claimed by both countries. The heightened tensions stemmed from a suicide car bombing carried out on February 14, 2019, in which 40 Indian security personnel were killed. Twelve days later, the two countries conducted airstrikes against targets in each other's territory.[1]

Many nuclear experts are concerned about a war between India and Pakistan that could start a nuclear exchange that could kill one billion people worldwide. Both countries are engaged in a nuclear competition that threatens stability throughout the world. Pakistan has been said to have the world's fastest-growing nuclear stockpile. Islamabad currently has an estimated 140 nuclear weapons and has developed tactical nuclear weapons capabilities to counter perceived Indian conventional military threats. This affects India's nuclear use threshold, which could affect China and possibly others.

"The possibility that terrorists could gain effective access to Pakistani nuclear weapons is contingent on a complex chain of circumstances. In terms of consequence, however, it is the most dangerous regional threat scenario. Concern about the safety and security of Pakistan's nuclear weapons increases when India-Pakistan tensions increase. When armed conflict broke out in the Kargil district of Kashmir, for example, U.S. intelligence indicated that Pakistan had made 'nuclear preparations' and this spurred greater U.S. diplomatic involvement in defusing the crisis."[2]

"If Pakistan were to move around its nuclear assets or, worse, take steps to mate weapons with delivery systems, the likelihood of terrorist theft or infiltration would increase. Increased reliance on tactical nuclear weapons (TNWs) is of particular concern because launch authorities for TNWs are typically delegated to lower-tier field commanders far from the central authority in Islamabad. Another concern is the possibility that miscalculations could lead to regional nuclear war if top Indian leaders were to lose confidence that nuclear weapons in Pakistan are under government control or, conversely, were to assume that they were under Pakistani government control after they ceased to be."[3]

There is concern that Islamist extremist groups with links to the Pakistan security establishment could exploit those links to gain access to nuclear weapons technology, facilities, and/or materials. The realization that Osama bin Laden stayed for six years within a half-mile of Pakistan's premier defense academy has fueled concern that al-Qaeda can operate relatively freely in parts of Pakistan and might eventually gain access to Pakistan's weapons-grade materials. There is the additional scenario of extremists gaining access through a collapse of the state. While Pakistan remains unstable because of its weak economy, regular terrorist attacks, sectarian violence, civil-military tensions, and the growing influence of religious extremist groups, it is unlikely that the Pakistani state will collapse altogether. The country's most powerful institution, the 550,000-strong army that has ruled Pakistan for almost half of its existence, would almost certainly intervene and take charge once again if the political situation began to unravel. The potential breakup of the Pakistani state would have to be preceded by the disintegration of the army, which currently is not plausible.

"Pakistan continues to expand its nuclear arsenal with more warheads, more delivery systems, and a growing fissile materials production industry. Analysis of a large number of commercial satellite images of Pakistani army garrisons and air force bases shows what appear to be mobile launchers and underground facilities that might be related to nuclear forces. It is estimated that Pakistan now has a nuclear weapons stockpile of 140 to 150 warheads. This stockpile exceeds the projection made by the U.S. Defense Intelligence Agency in 1999 that Pakistan would have 60 to 80 warheads by 2020."[4]

With several delivery systems in development, four plutonium production reactors, and its uranium enrichment facilities expanding, however, Pakistan has a stockpile that will likely increase further over the next 10 years. The size of the increase will depend on many factors. Two key factors will be how many nuclear-capable launchers Pakistan plans to deploy and how much the Indian nuclear arsenal grows. The country's stockpile could more realistically grow to 220 to 250 warheads by 2025 if the current trend continues. If that happens, it would make Pakistan the world's fifth-largest nuclear weapon state. But unless India significantly expands its arsenal or further builds up its conventional forces, it seems reasonable to expect that Pakistan's nuclear arsenal will not continue to grow indefinitely but might begin to level off as its current weapons programs are completed.

"Pakistan is modifying its nuclear posture with new short-range nuclear-capable weapons systems to counter military threats below the strategic level. The efforts seek to create a full-spectrum deterrent that is designed not only to respond to nuclear attacks but also to counter an Indian conventional incursion into Pakistani territory. This development has created considerable concern in other countries, including the United States, which fears that it lowers the threshold for nuclear use in a military conflict with India. Pakistan also continues to develop new types of nuclear weapons, including short-range tactical weapons, sea-based cruise missiles, air-launched cruise missiles, and longer-range ballistic missiles."[5]

Another major review expressed full confidence in both Pakistan's command and control systems and existing security measures meant to ensure comprehensive stewardship and security of strategic assets and materials. But this review noted that Pakistan's evolving arsenal — particularly its growing inventory of short-range nuclear weapons systems — could lead to problems with warhead management and command and control during a crisis. Satellite images showed that security perimeters around many bases and military facilities have been upgraded over the past seven years in response to terrorist attacks.[6]

Over the past decade, the U.S. assessment of nuclear weapons security in Pakistan appears to have changed considerably from confidence to concern, particularly as a result of the introduction of tactical nuclear weapons. The Trump Administration assessment in 2018 expressed concern that, by the development of tactical nuclear weapons that are designed for use on the battlefield, these systems can be more susceptible to terrorist theft and increase the likelihood of nuclear exchange in the region.[7]

Pakistani officials reject such concerns, noting that nuclear warheads are assembled only at the eleventh hour should they need to be launched and are stored in three to four different parts at three to four different locations. They contend they have opted to develop a variety of short-range, low-yield nuclear weapons as defensive, deterrence response to an offensive doctrine by India.

"Officials argue that Pakistan's understanding of India's strategy is that

Delhi envisioned launching quick strikes into Pakistan within two to four days with eight to nine brigades. Such an attack force might involve roughly 32,000–36,000 troops. They contest that by introducing the variety of tactical nuclear weapons in Pakistan's inventory, and in the strategic stability debate, they have blocked the avenues for serious military operations by the other side."[8]

Pakistan has a well-established and diverse fissile material production complex that is expanding. It includes the Kahuta uranium enrichment plant east of Islamabad, which appears to be growing with the addition of what could be another enrichment plant, as well as the enrichment plant at Gadwal to the north of Islamabad. Meanwhile, a second reprocessing plant located at Chashma in the northwestern part of Punjab province is being completed. Nuclear-capable missiles and their mobile launchers are developed and produced at the National Defense Complex in the Kala Chitta Dahr mountain range west of Islamabad. The complex is divided into two sections. The western section south of Attock appears to be involved in development, production, and test launching of missiles and rocket engines. The eastern section north of Fateh Jang is involved in production and assembly of road-mobile transporter erector launchers (TELs), which are designed to transport and fire missiles.

"Satellite images show the presence of launchers for Shaheen I and Shaheen II ballistic missiles and Babur cruise missiles. The Fateh Jang section has been expanded significantly over the past 10 years, with several large launcher assembly buildings. Other launcher and missile-related production and maintenance facilities may be located near Tarnawa and Taxila. Little is publicly known about warhead production, but experts have suspected for many years that the Pakistan Ordnance Factories near Wah, northwest of Islamabad, serve a role. One of the Wah factories is located near a unique facility with six earth-covered bunkers inside a multi-layered safety perimeter with armed guards. The security perimeter was expanded significantly between 2005 and 2010, possibly in response to terrorist attacks against other military facilities. At the end of 2016, it is estimated that Pakistan had an inventory of approximately 3,400 kilograms (kg) of weapons-grade (90 percent enriched) highly enriched uranium, and about 280 kg of weapons-grade plutonium. This material is theoretically enough to produce between 236 and 283 warheads, assuming that each first-generation implosion-type warhead's solid core uses either 15 to 18 kg of weapon-grade HEU or 5 to 6 kg of plutonium. However, calculating stockpile size based solely on fissile material inventory is an incomplete methodology that tends to produce inflated numbers. Instead, warhead estimates must take several factors into account, including the amount of weapons-grade fissile material produced, warhead design choice and proficiency, warhead production rates, numbers of operational nuclear-capable launchers, how many of those launchers are dual-capable, nuclear strategy, and statements by government officials."[9]

Estimates must assume that not all of a country's fissile material ends up in warheads. Like other nuclear weapon states, Pakistan probably maintains a reserve. Moreover, Pakistan simply lacks enough nuclear-capable launchers to accommodate 200 to 300 warheads, and all of Pakistan's launchers are thought to be dual-capable, which means that some of them, especially the shorter-range systems, presumably are assigned to non-nuclear missions as well. Despite these uncertainties, Pakistan is clearly engaged in a significant build-up of its nuclear forces and is believed by some to be producing nuclear weapons at a faster rate than any other country in the world.[10]

"Pakistan has six currently operational nuclear-capable land-based ballistic missiles: the short-range Abdali (Hatf-2), Ghaznavi (Hatf-3), Shaheen-1 (Hatf-4) and NASR (Hatf-9), and the medium-range Ghauri (Hatf-5) and Shaheen-2 (Hatf-6). Three other nuclear-capable ballistic missiles are under development: the medium-range Shaheen-1A, Shaheen-3, and the MIRVed Ababeel. The Pakistani road-mobile ballistic missile force has undergone significant development and expansion over the past decade and a half. This includes possibly eight or nine missile garrisons, including four or five along the Indian border for short-range systems (Babur, Ghaznavi, Shaheen-1, NASR) and three or four other garrisons further inland for medium-range systems (Shaheen-2 and Ghauri). The short-range, solid-fuel, single-stage Abdali (Hatf-2) has been in development for a long time."[11]

The Pentagon reported in 1997 that the Abdali appeared to have been discontinued, but flight-testing resumed in 2002 and it was last reported test launched in 2013. The 200-km (124-mile) missile has been displayed at parades several times on a four-axle road-mobile transporter TEL. The three-year gap in flight-testing indicates the Abdali program may have encountered technical difficulties. After the 2013 test it was reported that Abdali carries nuclear as well as conventional warheads and provides an operational-level capability to Pakistan's strategic forces. The test launch may have consolidated Pakistan's deterrence capability both at the operational and strategic levels. The short-range, solid-fuel, single-stage Ghaznavi (Hatf-3) was last reported test launched in 2014. Its short range of approximately 300 km (186 miles) means that the Ghaznavi cannot strike Delhi from Pakistani territory, and army units equipped with the missile are probably based relatively near the Indian border.

The Shaheen-1 (Hatf-4) is a single-stage, solid-fuel, dual-capable, short-range ballistic missile with a maximum range of 750 km (466 miles) that has been in service since 2003. The Shaheen-1 is carried on a four-axle, road-mobile TEL similar to the one used for the Ghaznavi. Since 2012, Shaheen-1 test launches have involved an extended-range version widely referred to as Shaheen-1A. The Pakistani government, which has declared the range to be 900 km (560 miles), has used both designations.

One of the most controversial new nuclear-capable missiles in the Pakistani arsenal is the NASR (Hatf-9), a short-range, solid-fuel missile originally with a range of only 60 km (37 miles) that has recently been extended to 70 km (43 miles). With a range too short to attack strategic targets inside India, NASR appears intended solely for battlefield use against invading Indian troops.

Pakistan is also developing a sea-launched version of the Babur known as Babur-3. The weapon is still in development and has been test launched twice. It has a range of 450 km (279 miles). The Babur-3 will most likely be deployed on the diesel-electric Agosta-class submarines. Once it becomes operational, the Babur-3 will provide Pakistan with a triad of nuclear strike platforms from the ground, air, and sea. The Pakistani government said the Babur-3 was motivated by a need to match India's nuclear triad and the "nuclearization of [the] Indian Ocean Region."[12]

It also said the Babur-3's stealth technologies would be useful in the emerging regional ballistic missile defense environment. The future submarine-based nuclear capability is managed by Naval Strategic Forces Command, which the government said would be the custodian of the nation's second-strike capability to strengthen Pakistan's policy of credible minimum deterrence and ensure regional stability.

"India has 130 to 140 nuclear warheads and is estimated to have enough military plutonium for 150 to 200. Additional plutonium will be required to produce warheads for missiles now under development, and India is reportedly building several new plutonium production facilities. In addition, India continues to modernize its nuclear arsenal, with at least five new weapons systems now under development to complement or replace existing nuclear-capable aircraft, land-based delivery systems, and sea-based systems."

"Unlike the missile-centric U.S. and Russian nuclear forces, India still heavily relies on bombers, maintaining three or four nuclear strike squadrons of Cold War–vintage, French-made Mirage 2000H and Jaguar IS/IB aircraft targeted at Pakistan and China. While these planes have been upgraded, they are getting old and India is probably searching for a modern fighter-bomber that could potentially take over the air-based nuclear strike role in the future. These will include 36 Rafale fighters bought from France that carry nuclear weapons in French service and presumably could do so for India."[13]

India's nuclear missile force is only 15 years old, but it already has four types of land-based ballistic missiles: the short-range Prithvi-II and Agni-I, the medium-range Agni-II and the intermediate-range Agni-III. Two other longer-range Agni missiles are under development and it remains to be seen how many of these missile types India plans to fully develop and keep in its arsenal. Some may serve as technology development programs toward longer-range missiles.

"Although the Indian government has made no statements about the future size or composition of its land-based missile force, short-range and redundant missile types could potentially be discontinued, with only medium- and long-range missiles deployed in the future to provide a mix of strike options against near and distant targets. India is also developing the Nirbhay ground-launched cruise missile, similar to the U.S. Tomahawk. In addition, there is the Dhanush sea-based, short-range ballistic missile, which is fired from two specially configured patrol vessels. Three or four nuclear-powered ballistic missile submarines under construction will be equipped with a short-range missile or a bigger missile with a range of 2,000 miles."[14]

The broader military and strategic dynamic between India and Pakistan remains volatile and has arguably grown more so since the May 2014 election of Bharatiya Janata Party leader Narendra Modi as India's prime minister. While Modi initially sought to extend an olive branch by inviting Pakistani Prime Minister Nawaz Sharif to his swearing-in ceremony, he subsequently called off foreign secretary–level talks that were scheduled for August 2014 to express anger over a Pakistani official's meeting with Kashmiri separatist leaders.[15]

During the same month, the two sides engaged in intense firing and shelling along their international border (called the working boundary) and across the Line of Control that divides Kashmir. The director of India's Border Security Force noted that the firing across the international border was the worst it had been since the war between India and Pakistan in 1971. A similar escalation in border tensions occurred again on December 5, 2014, when a series of firing incidents over a one-week period resulted in the deaths of eight Indian soldiers.16

On December 25, 2015, a meeting did occur when Prime Minister Modi made an impromptu visit to Lahore to meet with Pakistani Prime Minister Sharif, the first visit to Pakistan by an Indian leader in 12 years. The visit created enormous goodwill between the two countries and raised hope that official dialogue would soon resume.17 Again, however, violence marred the new opening. Six days after the meeting, JeM militants attacked the Indian airbase at Pathankot, killing seven Indian security personnel. India has provided information on the attackers to Pakistan and has demanded action against Jaish-e-Mohammed (JeM), but to no avail. On March 22, 2019, Indian forces killed seven militants in Kashmir.[18]

As a result, official India-Pakistan dialogue remains deadlocked even though the two sides are reportedly communicating quietly through their foreign secretaries and national security advisers. Since 2015, there has also been an uptick in cross-border firing between the Indian and Pakistani militaries, raising questions about whether a cease-fire that has been in place since 2003 is being rendered ineffective.

"Pakistan continues to harbor terrorist groups like Lashkar-e-Taiba and Jaish-e-Mohammed. The latter was responsible for a January 2, 2016, attack on an Indian airbase at Pathankot as well as a February 2018 attack on an Indian army camp in Jammu. Media reports indicate that some JeM leaders were detained in Pakistan following the Pathankot attack, but no charges were filed. Hafiz Muhammad Saeed, LeT's founder and the leader of its front organization Jamaat-ud-Dawa (JuD), has periodically been placed under arrest only to be later released. Previously, he had operated freely in Pakistan, often holding press conferences and inciting violence against India during large public rallies. In December 2014, Saeed held a two-day conclave in Lahore that received support from the Pakistani government, including security from 4,000 police officers and government assistance in transporting attendees to the gathering of more than 400,000."[19]

India condemned the Pakistani government's support for the gathering as "blatant disregard" of global norms against terrorism.[20] There is some concern about the impact on Indian-Pakistani relations of an international troop drawdown in Afghanistan. Such a drawdown could enable the Taliban and other extremist groups to strengthen their grip in the region, further undermining stability in Kashmir and raising the chances of another major terrorist attack against India. Afghan security forces thwarted an attack on the Indian consulate in Herat, Afghanistan, in May 2014. However, a successful future attack on Indian interests in Afghanistan along the lines of the bombing of the Indian embassy in Kabul in 2008 would sharpen tensions between New Delhi and Islamabad.

Indian military retaliation against a Pakistan-backed terrorist strike against India could include targeted air strikes on terrorist training camps inside Pakistan. This would likely lead to broader military conflict with some prospect of escalating to a nuclear exchange. Neither side desires another general war. Both countries have limited objectives and have demonstrated their intent to avoid escalation, but this is a delicate calculation.

"Pakistan's continued support for terrorist groups that have links to al-Qaeda undermines U.S. counterterrorism goals in the region. Pakistan's military and intelligence leaders maintain a short-term tactical approach of fighting some terrorist groups that are deemed to be a threat to the state while supporting others that are aligned with Pakistan's goal of extending its influence and curbing India's. A December 16, 2014, terrorist attack on a school in Peshawar that killed more than 150 people, mostly children, shocked the Pakistani public and prompted the government led by Prime Minister Nawaz Sharif to introduce a National Action Plan (NAP) to reinvigorate the country's fight against terrorism. The action plan includes steps like lifting the moratorium on the death penalty for terrorists, establishing special military courts to try terrorists, curbing the spread of extremist literature and propaganda on social media, freezing the assets of terrorist organizations, and forming special committees of army and political leaders in the provinces to implement the NAP."[21]

The NAP has been criticized for being poorly implemented, but in the summer of 2018, the leaders of the PPP and PTI opposition parties, Bilawal Bhutto and Imran Khan, called for the NAP to be strengthened and extended across the country. There are few signs that Pakistan's crackdown on terrorism extends to groups that target India, such as the Lashkar-e-Taiba (LeT), which was responsible for the 2008 Mumbai attacks, and the Jaish-e-Mohammed, which carried out an attack on the Indian airbase at Pathankot on January 2, 2016. In early April 2015, Pakistan released the mastermind of the Mumbai attacks, Zakiur Rehman Lakhvi, who had been in Pakistani custody since 2009.[22]

U.S.–Pakistan relations have grown more acrimonious since 2011, when U.S. special forces conducted a raid on Osama bin Laden's hideout in Abbottabad not far from facilities run by the Pakistani military. President Trump suspended U.S. military assistance to Pakistan and increased pressure on Islamabad for its continued support of the Taliban.[23] As frustration with Pakistan increased, the Trump Administration has signaled a series of measures designed to hold Pakistan to account for its "double game."[24] In 2018, the U.S. military suspended all $800 million in Coalition Support funds "due to a lack of Pakistani decisive actions in support of the US. South Asia Strategy. The Administration has also added Pakistan to a "grey list for failing to fulfill its obligations to prevent the financing of terrorism and its designation on a special watch list for violations of religious freedom."[25]

Military ties between the United States and India have improved significantly over the past decade as the two sides have moved toward establishment of a strategic partnership based on their mutual concern about rising Chinese military and economic influence and converging interests in countering regional terrorism. Defense ties between the two countries are expected to expand further as India moves forward with an ambitious military modernization plan. The signing of the Logistics Exchange Memorandum of Agreement in June 2016 marked a major milestone in the Indo-U.S. defense partnership.[26] The Trump Administration granted India Strategic Trade Authorization (STA) which eases export control regulations on arms sales. India is only the third Asian country after Japan and South Korea to be granted STA status. Three years later, the Trump Administration stripped India of its STA status.[27]

India sent a blunt message to Pakistan on March 27, 2019, when it successfully tested the country's first space weapon, an anti-satellite missile. Prime Minister Modi said that India is the fourth country to acquire the ability to shoot down satellites, after the United States, Russia, and China.

SUMMARY

With terrorist groups operating relatively freely in Pakistan and maintaining links to the country's military and intelligence services, there is a risk that India and Pakistan might eventually engage in all-out conflict. Pakistan's recent focus on incorporating tactical nuclear weapons into its warfighting doctrine has also raised concern that conflict now involves a higher risk of nuclear exchange. the likelihood of miscalculation and escalation has grown considerably since 2016 when India ended its policy of not responding to Pakistani-backed terrorist attacks. In addition, despite the broad U.S. relationships with Pakistan's governing elites and military, it is likely that the political–military interplay in Pakistan and instability in Afghanistan will continue to result in an active threat to world security.

"Some observers remain concerned about the impact of an international troop drawdown in Afghanistan. Such a drawdown could enable the Taliban and other extremist groups to strengthen their grip in the region, further undermining stability in Kashmir and raising the chances of another major terrorist attack against India. A successful future attack on Indian interests in Afghanistan along the lines of the bombing of the Indian embassy in Kabul in 2008 would sharpen tensions between New Delhi and Islamabad."[28]

NOTES

1. George Steer, "From Suicide Bombing to Captured Pilot: A Timeline of the Latest Crisis in Kashmir," *Time*, Feb. 28, 2019.
2. "Kargil Conflict Timeline," *BBC News*, July 13, 1999.
3. *Assessing the Global Operating Environment, Asia*, Washington, D.C.: Heritage Foundation, Oct. 30, 2019.
4. James Carafano, "Preparing National Security Strategy for 2020 and Beyond," Heritage Foundation Special Report N. 224, May 23, 2019.
5. *Assessing Threats to U.S. Vital Interests*, Washington, D.C.: Heritage Foundation, Oct. 30, 2019.
6. Rajhatta Chidanarad, "Pakistan's Nuclear Proliferation in News Again,", *TNN*, Oct. 22, 2019.
7. Hans Kristensen, Robert Norris, and Julia Diamond, "Pakistani Nuclear Forces," *Federation of American Scientists*, 2018.

8. Sonia Naz, "Pakistan's Nuclear Safety and Security," *Modern Diplomacy*, Aug. 14, 2018.

9. International Panel on Fissile Materials, Dec. 18, 2016.

10. Hans Kristensen and Robert Morris, "Pakistani Nuclear Forces," *Bulletin of Atomic Scientists*, Nov. 4, 2016.

11. Tom Hundley, "The Nuclearization of the Indian Ocean," Pulitzer Center, April 2, 2018.

12. Daniel R. Coats, "Worldwide Threat Assessment of the U.S. Intelligence Community," statement before the Select Committee on Intelligence, U.S. Senate, May 11, 2018.

13. *Assessing Threats to U.S. Vital Interests*, Washington, D.C.: Heritage Foundation, Oct. 30, 2019.

14. "PM Modi's Nod to Hit Terrorists Hard in Kashmir, No Soft Approach Towards Pakistan-Sponsored Terrorism," *New Delhi News*, Sep. 21, 2016.

15. Mukhtar Ahmad, "8 Indian soldiers killed in gunfight with militants in Kashmir," *CNN*, Dec. 5, 2014.

16. "PM Modi Back in Delhi After Meeting Nawaz Sharif in Lahore," *NDTV*, Dec. 25, 2015.

17. Fayaz Bukhari, "Indian Forces Kill Seven Militants in Kashmir as Crackdown Deepens," *Reuters*, March 22, 2019.

18. *Assessing Threats to U.S. Vital Interests*, Washington, D.C.: Heritage Foundation, Oct. 30, 2019.

19. "India slams Pakistan for Backing Saeed," *Express News Service*, New Delhi, Dec. 4, 2014.

20. "Pakistani Nuclear Forces, 2018," *Bulletin of Scientists*.

21. *Assessing Threats to U.S. Vital Interests*, Washington, D.C.: Heritage Foundation, Oct. 30, 2019.

22. "Mumbai Attack Suspect Lakhvi Released on Bail in Pakistan."

23. Sarmad Ali Khan, "Nuclearization of Indian Ocean: Ramifications on Regional Security," *Strategic Foresight for Asia*, June 2, 2019.

24. *2020 Index of U.S. Military Strength*, Washington, D.C.: Heritage Foundation.

25. Deepshikha Ghosh, "India Calls Off Talks with Pakistani Over their Envoy Meeting Kashmiri Separatists, *NOTV*, Aug. 17, 2014.

26. "Pakistan's Support for JuD Meet Blatant Disregard of Global Norms," *India TV*, Dec. 4, 2014.

27. Rachel Frazin, "Trump Moves to Strip India of Special Trade Status, *The Hill*, June 1, 2019.

28. *Assessing Threats to U.S. Vital Interests*, Washington, D.C.: Heritage Foundation, Oct. 30, 2019.

8 | The Threat of China–India Conflict

AT LEAST 20 INDIAN SOLDIERS WERE KILLED in a clash with Chinese forces on June 15, 2020, in an area of the Himalayas known as Doklam in India and Donglang in China. The deaths are reportedly the first in a 45-year border confrontation between the two nations. India and its close ally, Bhutan, view this land as Bhutanese territory, while China claims it as its own. The land is highly strategic, leading to the Siliguri Corridor, a narrow area of land that connects northeastern India to the rest of the country.[1]

India's external affairs ministry accused China of violating an agreement to respect the Line of Actual Control (LAC) in the Galwan Valley. Zhao Lijian, Chinese foreign ministry spokesman, accused India of crossing the border onto the Chinese side, the day before the incident. China did not confirm any casualties, and both sides claim that no bullets had been fired and the battle was fought with rocks and clubs.

The two nuclear-armed neighbors have a long history of skirmishes and overlapping territorial claims along the more than 2,100 mile poorly drawn border separating the two sides. Tensions increased after India built a new road along the disputed border, and China responded by deploying troops and building infrastructure of its own.

"We routinely see both armies crossing the LAC — it's fairly common and such incidents are resolved at the local military level. But this time, the build-up is the largest we have ever seen," says former Indian diplomat P. Stobdan, an expert in Ladakh and India-China affairs. "The stand-off is happening at some strategic areas that are important for India. If Pangong Lake is taken, Ladakh can't be defended. If the Chinese military is allowed to settle in the strategic valley of Shyok, the Nubra Valley and even Siachen can be reached."[2]

The two sides have sought to reduce tensions in the past, and an informal summit between President Xi and Prime Minister Modi was held in April 2018. The latest incident is likely to trigger a fresh wave of anti-

China sentiments in India, which struggles with COVID-19 infections and an economy that looks headed for a recession. "We never provoke anyone," Modi said on national television the day after the hand-to-hand fighting. "There should be no doubt that India wants peace, but if provoked, India will provide an appropriate response."[3]

90

The roots of the distrust between the two nations go back to India's decision to shelter the Dalai Lama in 1959, when the spiritual leader fled Tibet after China invaded his country in 1962.[4] There was a marked deterioration in relations after India signed a nuclear cooperation agreement with the United States in 2005 and ties deepened between the two large democracies.

Narendra Modi came into office in 2014 as the most pro-China Indian prime minister since 1962, wanting not only to emulate China's economic progress but also to attract Chinese investment, analysts say. But he found Chinese president Xi Jinping an unreliable partner when he blocked India's application to join the Nuclear Suppliers Group and blocked efforts at the United Nations to declare Pakistani militant Masood Azhar a terrorist.[5]

Tensions rose sharply when China's sweeping Belt and Road development initiative added an economic corridor through parts of Pakistani-administered Kashmir, a region that India claims. Modi snubbed a major summit in Beijing that launched the Belt and Road plan. Meanwhile, India alarmed China in 2018 for allowing the Dalai Lama to visit an important Buddhist monastery in India's northeastern state of Arunacha, a region Beijing claims is part of Tibet.[6]

"India has tolerated and supported Tibetan separatists, allowing the Tibetan independence groups to set up an exile government in India," said Long Xingchun, Director of the Center for Indian Studies at China West Normal University in Nanchong.[7]

Xu Guangyu, a retired PLA major general, said China had been preparing to evict Indian troops if New Delhi did not back down but hoped that China's objective could be realized without bloodshed. "We won't be the first to fire. We are very clear about this line, and this shows China's sincerity," he said. "But it's not up to China to decide. Whether there is to be war depends on the Indians. However, if they fire the first shot, they would lose control and the initiative."[8]

Meanwhile, Chinese media has kept up its overheated rhetoric, culminating in the release by a state-run news agency of a video mocking India as a bad neighbor — with an actor wearing a turban, fake beard speaking in a put-on Indian accent. Indian citizens immediately denounced the video as racist.[9]

Watching Chinese escalation, India has undertaken a variety of preparedness measures including advancing the operational alert status of several units to begin acclimatizing to higher altitudes. Clearly, they are being as discreet as possible to shield themselves from Chinese offenses.[10]

"The possibility of armed conflict between India and China could raise nuclear tensions in the region. It would also risk straining the maturing India-U.S. partnership if the level of U.S. support and commitment in a conflict scenario did not meet India's expectations. Meanwhile, a border conflict between India and China could prompt Pakistan to try to take advantage of the situation, further contributing to regional instability. The Chinese continue to enjoy an advantage over India in terms of military infrastructure and along the Line of Actual Control (LAC) that separates Indian-controlled territory from Chinese-controlled territory and continue to expand a network of road, rail, and air links in the border areas. To meet these challenges, the government of India's Prime Minister Modi has committed to expanding infrastructure development along India's disputed border with China, especially in the Indian states of Arunachal Pradesh and Sikkim, but progress has been slow. Although China currently holds a decisive military edge over India, New Delhi is engaged in an ambitious military modernization program."[11]

A visit to India by Chinese president Xi Jinping in September 2014 was overshadowed by another flare-up in border tensions when hundreds of Chinese forces reportedly set up camps in the mountainous regions of Ladakh, prompting Indian forces to deploy to forward positions in the region. The border standoff lasted three weeks and was defused when both sides agreed to pull their troops back to previous positions.[12]

The Border Defense and Cooperation Agreement (BDCA) signed during then-prime minister Manmohan Singh's visit to China in October 2013 affirms that neither side will use its military capabilities against the other, proposes a hotline between the two countries' military headquarters, institutes meetings between border personnel in all sectors, and ensures that neither side tails the other's patrols along the LAC. The agreement also includes language stipulating that in the event the two sides come face to face, they "shall exercise maximum self-restraint, refrain from any provocative actions, not use force or threaten to use force against the other side, treat each other with courtesy and prevent exchange of armed conflict."[13]

"However, the agreement failed to reduce specific border issues or restore momentum to border negotiations that have been largely stalled since the mid-2000s. Some analysts have even contended that the Chinese intend to buy time on their border disputes with India through the BDCA while focusing on other territorial claims in the Asia-Pacific."[14]

SUMMARY

India and China each have more than one billion people, nuclear weapons, an historical animosity toward one another, and a strong sense of nationalist pride. So far both sides seem to be digging in their heels. China believes Indian troops invaded its territory and will not pursue reconciliation until they leave. India charges that China invaded its land for the explicit purpose of threatening their national security. The two countries have fought only one war so far, in 1962, when India suffered a humiliating defeat. Stakes are considerably higher now, with both sides armed with nuclear missiles.

The first major opponent of China's Belt and Road Initiative, India continues to oppose China's grand infrastructure initiative because one of its subcomponents, the China-Pakistan Economic Corridor, traverses Indian-claimed Kashmir. Meanwhile, China has significantly expanded its economic, political, and military footprint in the Indian Ocean and South Asia, contributing to a sense of encirclement in Delhi. Beijing has achieved major diplomatic breakthroughs and landmark investments in Nepal, Sri Lanka, and the Maldives, and the PLA navy has begun regular conventional and nuclear submarine patrols in the Indian Ocean, complementing the anti-piracy naval task force it regularly rotates through the Indian Ocean. China opened its first "overseas logistics supply facility," which closely resembles a full military base, in Djibouti, in 2017 and reportedly has expressed interest in building a naval base in Pakistan near the Chinese-operated Gwadar port.[15]

"Both India and China apparently want to avoid allowing minor incidents to escalate into a more general war. The Chinese seem to use border tensions for limited diplomatic and political gain vis-à-vis India, and India responds in ways that are intended to contain minor incursions and maximize reputational damage to China. The unsettled situation and gamesmanship along the border could result in miscalculation, accidents, or overreaction. Relations between India and China are expected to remain tense and possibly to deteriorate further, elevating the risk of unintentional escalation."[16]

NOTES

1. "India-China Clash: 20 Indian Troops Killed in Ladakh Fighting," *BBC News*, June 16, 2020.

2. "India-China Clash: Modi Says Soldiers' Deaths Will Not Be in Vain, *BBC News*, June 17, 2020

3. Sanjeev Miglani and Yew Lun Tian, "India, China Want Peace but Blame Each Other After Deadly Border Clash," *Reuters*, June 17, 2020.

4. Greg MacGregor, "Dalai Lama Asks Asylum of India," *New York Times*, April 3, 1959.

5. "China Blocks India's Bid to Enter Nuclear Suppliers Group," *The New Indian Express*, June 21, 2019.

7. Sutirtho Patranobis, "China Angry at Dalai Lama's Nalanda Visit, *World News*, Nov. 17, 2016.

8. "China Is Preparing to Evict Indian Troops If New Delhi Does Not Back Down," *Washington Post*, Aug. 17, 2017.

9. "China, India Dangerously Close to Nuclear Conflict In The Himalayas," *Washington Post*, Aug. 18, 2017.

10. Deepshikha Ghosh, "Chinese State Media Video Mocks India in Bizarre Propaganda on Doklam," *NDTV*, Aug. 17, 2017.

10. "With an Eye on China, Modi's India to Develop Disputed Border Region," *Reuters*, Sep. 14, 2014.

10. *Assessing Threats to U.S. Vital Interests*, Asia, Washington, D.C.: Heritage Foundation, Oct. 30, 2019.

11. Fayaz Bukhari, "China, India Troops Set Up Rival Camps in Himalayan Desert," *Reuters*, April 20, 2013.

12. Ajith Vijay Kumar, "India, China Sign Key Pact to Address Border Tensions," *Planet Deep*, Oct. 23, 2013.

13. *Assessing Threats to U.S. Vital Interests, Asia*, Washington, D.C.: Heritage Foundation, Oct. 30, 2019.

14. Sara Zheng, "China's Djibouti Military Base: Logistics Facility or Platform for Geopolitical Ambitions Overseas?" *South Coast Morning Post*, Oct. 1, 2017.

15. *Assessing Threats to U.S. Vital Interests, Asia*, Washington, D.C.: Heritage Foundation, Oct. 30, 2019.

9 | Pledging Peace While Rapidly Pursuing Space Weapons Development

THE U.S. GLOBAL POSITIONING SYSTEM (GPS) — produced by some 24 satellites orbiting Earth at an altitude of 12,500 miles and sending a synchronized signal from each individual satellite — has become indispensable to many vital military and civilian functions. "There are also nine 'spares' up there ready to be added to the GPS system as needed, and we have more on the ground ready to be launched eventually," according to Dave Tremper, a program manager at the Strategic Technology Office for DARPA, the military's advanced research branch. Even so, the GPS system has become "a single point of failure," according to Tremper. "Up until the early 2000's, there was a variety of other alternatives. But after GPS came along, "they all went away."[1]

GPS could also "go away" almost instantly and without anything happening to those 24 satellites. jammed temporarily by widely available equipment on the civilian market or permanently by the equipment developed and under development by China, Russia, North Korea, Iran and a host of other countries, both friendly and hostile and probably by terrorist groups as well. The point is that space and the thousands of satellites that are now in orbit have become essential to civilian and military operations on land and sea and in the air but are vulnerable to any number of deliberate and even accidental interferences from the ground, from the air or from other satellites.[2]

"Space is essential to our nation's security, prosperity and our very way of life," Vice President Mike Pence said in a speech at the Pentagon. "China has launched a missile that tracked and destroyed one of its own satellites, a highly provocative demonstration of its growing capability to militarize space. Russia has been designing an airborne laser to disrupt our space-based system," he warns. "Both China and Russia have been conducting highly sophisticated on-orbit activities that could enable them to maneuver their satellites into close proximity of ours, posing unprecedented new dangers to our space systems."[3]

Chinese space capabilities gained public prominence in 2007 when the PLA conducted an anti-satellite (ASAT) test in low-Earth orbit against a defunct Chinese weather satellite. The test became one of the worst debris-generating incidents of the Space Age, with several thousand pieces of debris generated, many of which will remain in orbit for over a century. However, the PRC has been conducting space operations since 1970 when it first orbited a satellite. Equally important, Chinese counter-space efforts have been expanding steadily. The PLA has not only tested ASATs against low-Earth orbit systems, but is also believed to have tested a system designed to attack targets at geosynchronous orbit (GEO), approximately 22,000 miles above the Earth. As many vital satellites are at GEO, including communications and missile early-warning systems, China's ability to target such systems constitutes a major threat."[4]

The major 2015 reorganization of the PLA included the creation of the PLA Strategic Support Force (PLASSF), which brings the Chinese military's electronic warfare, network warfare (including cyber), and space warfare forces under a single service umbrella. Previously, these capabilities had been embedded in different departments across the PLA's General Staff Department and General Armaments Department. By consolidating them into a single service, the PLA has created a Chinese information warfare force that is responsible for offensive and defensive operations in the electromagnetic and space domains. The creation of the PLASSF, incorporating counter-space forces, reflects the movement of counter-space systems, including direct-ascent ASATs, out of the testing phase to fielding them with units. A recent report from the U.S. National Air and Space Intelligence Center (NASIC) notes that Chinese units are now training with anti-satellite missiles.[5]

The Pentagon is establishing its own space force that will be under the air force. The United States appears to be lagging behind China in developing space weapons. An anti-satellite missile program was killed in the 1980s. However, a navy anti-missile interceptor was used to shoot down a falling U.S. satellite in 2008, demonstrating some anti-satellite weapons capabilities.[6]

Anti-satellite weapons (ASATs) are space weapons designed to incapacitate or destroy satellites for strategic military purposes. Several nations possess operational ASAT systems. Although no ASAT system has yet been utilized in warfare, a few nations have shot down their own satellites to demonstrate their ASAT capabilities.

China's strategy for developing advanced space weapons was disclosed in August 2019 in Beijing's first defense white paper issued in years. The defense strategy report produced by the PLA bluntly identifies the United States as Beijing's main adversary undermining world peace. The report, part policy statement and part propaganda, also claims the United States seeks absolute military superiority.

"The U.S. has adjusted its national security and defense strategies, and adopted unilateral policies," the white paper said. "It has provoked and intensified competition among major countries, significantly increased its defense expenditure, pushed for additional capacity in nuclear, outer space, cyber and missile defense, and undermined global strategic stability."[7]

Chinese propaganda outlets sought to portray the white paper as furthering Beijing's questionable assertion that its large-scale build-up of conventional, nuclear, space, and cyber weapons poses no threat. On space warfare, the PLA report states that threats to space "loom large" and as a result space security is now among the most vital Chinese strategic interests. "Outer space is a critical domain in international strategic competition," the white paper said.

"Space capabilities and potential conflicts are not confined to the United States, Russia and China. The National Air and Space Intelligence Center (NASIC) reports that, in addition to the "big three," six countries and one international organization can independently launch spacecraft: India, Iran, Israel, Japan, North Korea, South Korea and the European Space Agency."[8]

There are currently 5,009 identified payloads in orbit. These include space systems that are tractable as well as those reported by their operators. The number includes payloads that are no longer active. The Union of Concerned Scientists reports that as of November 30, 2018, there were 1,957 operating satellites. Of these 849 are American, 167 of which are designated for military use. Of all active total satellites 430 are currently designated as having some military use.

This total was reduced from 5,010 on March 27, 2019, when India announced it had successfully conducted an ASAT missile test called Mission Shakti. This test made India the fourth country after the United States, China, and Russia to demonstrate this capability. While the destroyed satellite was one of India's own, the test has caused concerns about the space debris generated, which potentially threatens the operation of functional satellites. Worse yet, the test is a loss for global security, as nations and regulatory bodies struggle to maintain a view of space as a neutral and conflict-free arena in the face of escalating technological capabilities.

According to the official press release, India destroyed its own satellite by using technology known as "kinetic kill" or hit to kill. No explosive warhead is needed because of the extraordinary speed of the missile interceptor. Hitting at several thousand miles an hour it "atomizes" the satellite. The same technology was used by China in its test 11 years earlier.[9]

Many countries have developed space launch capabilities to compete in the international market or to advance national security strategies that require domestic access to space. Iran and North Korea maintain independent space launch capabilities that could also test ballistic missile technologies. China and Russia are updating their space launch capabilities to increase responsiveness, reduce launch timelines, improve manufacturing efficiencies, and support future human space flight and deep space exploration missions. While the North Korean and Iranian capabilities are disquieting, China and Russia's activities concern us most.[10]

China's journey toward a space capability began in 1958, less than 9 months after the launch of Sputnik-1. China's aspirations to match the Soviet Union and the United States soon faced self-imposed delays due to internal political dynamics that lasted until the late 1960s. China did not launch its first satellite until April 1970. In the early 1980s, China's space program began moving with purpose.

According to "Challenges to Security in Space" published by the U.S. Defense Security Agency, Beijing's present goal is building China into a space power in all respects. Its rapidly growing space program — China is second only to the United States in the number of operational satellites — is a source of national pride and part of President Xi Jinping's "China Dream" to establish a powerful and prosperous China. The space program supports both civil and military interests, including strengthening its science and technology sector, international relationships, and military modernization efforts. China seeks to achieve these goals rapidly through advances in the research and development of space systems and space-related technology.[11]

"Challenges notes that while China officially advocates for peaceful use of space and pursues agreements at the United Nations on the non-weaponization of space, it nonetheless continues to improve its counter-space weapons capabilities and has enacted military reforms to better integrate cyberspace, space, and EW into joint military operations."[12]

The PLA views space superiority, the ability to control the information sphere, and denying adversaries the same, key components of conducting modern wars. Since observing the U.S. military's performance during the 1991 Gulf War, the PLA embarked on an effort to modernize weapons systems and update doctrine to place the focus on using and countering adversary information-enabled warfare.

"We assess that if a future conflict were to occur involving China or Russia, either country would justify attacks against U.S. and allied satellites as necessary to offset any perceived U.S. military advantage derived from military, civil or commercial space systems. That justification, might well occur within the next few years."[13]

A key point in the history of this conflict occurred on January 11, 2007, with China's destruction of one of its own weather satellites. This ASAT test involved a fairly primitive system, limited to high-inclination low Earth orbit (LEO) satellites. (Note: There are three orbital regimes: Low Earth Orbit, 999.42 miles to 1,242.74 miles; Medium Earth orbit, 1,242.74

miles to 22,236.39 miles; High Earth or Geostationary Orbit, above 22,236.39 miles.)[14]

Many countries use space satellites for military and intelligence purposes. In addition to the United States and Russia, several European countries, Israel, India, and Japan also maintain reconnaissance satellites in LEOs vulnerable to China's KT-1 and KT-2 direct-ascent ASAT missiles.

China's 2007 ASAT test was widely viewed as a direct challenge to U.S. space superiority, since the United States maintains by far the largest fleet of military and intelligence satellite systems in the world. The mission of the U.S. Space Command is to maintain control of space. The transformation of the U.S. military for network-centric warfare and information operations is increasing its reliance on space-based assets. American satellites are inviting targets in the Chinese strategy of asymmetric warfare.[15]

As one Chinese defense analyst noted at the time of the test, "For countries that can never win a war with the U.S. with tanks and planes, attacking the U.S. space system may be an irresistible and most tempting choice." Even a limited ASAT capability was seen as extremely useful to the PLA in contingencies involving the Taiwan Strait.[16]

China's test strengthened the arguments in the United States for an improved ASAT program and prompted further development of countermeasures. Funding for a proposed constellation of space sensors, capable of tracking the entire life of a missile and allowing precise targeting, remains tied up in the Congressional approval process. But adversaries' achievements like this one will hopefully move it along.[17]

China's test prompted India to develop ASAT capabilities. Both the Defense Research and Development Organization (DRDO) and the Indian air force proposed various ASAT systems. Israel raised concerns about transfers of ASAT technology from China to countries in the Middle East, especially Iran.

Long a prominent advocate of the prevention of an arms race in outer space (PAROS), China, in one move, albeit a fairly primitive one, provided a major stimulus to such a race. The PLA can only have calculated that the inevitable reactions were worth risking for a demonstrable capability to threaten a relatively few valuable LEO imaging and ELINT satellites in some critical contingency.

"Challenges" points out that Russia, as a pioneer in space, dating back to its launch of the first satellite, Sputnik-1, and placing the first person into orbit around Earth, Yuri Gagarin, views its space program as a long-standing example of its leadership on the international stage. Reliance on Russian launch vehicles to send astronauts to and from the International Space Station reinforces Moscow's perspective that it remains a global leader in space. In the years following the end of the Cold War, however, a combination of budgetary constraints and technological setbacks caused a setback in Russian space capabilities, including space-based remote sensing and satellite navigation.[18]

"Russia's space program is robust but more narrowly focused and its budget more limited than China's because of competing priorities with broader military modernization efforts. Nonetheless, over the last two decades, Moscow has been developing a suite of counter-space weapons capabilities, including EW to deny, degrade, and disrupt communications and navigation and DEW to deny the use of space-based imagery. Russia is probably also building a ground-based missile capable of destroying satellites in orbit. Similar to China, Russia supports space arms control agreements to prevent weaponization of space even as it views space as a war-fighting domain."[19]

As Russia continues to modernize its military, it will increasingly incorporate space-provided services across its forces. Moscow views space as a key enabler of U.S. precision strike and military force projection capabilities. Russia believes that U.S. space-enabled, conventional precision strike capabilities undermine strategic stability. At the same time, Russia views America's perceived dependence on space as the "Achilles' heel" of U.S. military power, which can be exploited to achieve Russian conflict objectives. Russia is therefore pursuing counter-space systems to neutralize or deny U.S. space-based services, both military and commercial, as a means of offsetting a perceived U.S. military advantage and is developing an array of weapons designed to interfere with or destroy an adversary's satellites.[20]

It should be noted that attacking this Achilles' heel would not eliminate the retaliatory threat of U.S. intercontinental missiles. The United States has backup targeting capabilities should the space-enabled, precision-strike capabilities be knocked out.

Russia's counter-space doctrine involves employing ground-, air-, and space-based systems to target an adversary's satellites, with attacks ranging from temporary jamming or sensor blinding to destruction of enemy spacecraft and supporting infrastructure. Moscow believes developing and fielding counter-space capabilities will deter aggression by adversaries reliant upon space. If deterrence fails, Russia trusts that its counter-space forces will provide the ability to control escalation of a conflict through selective targeting of adversary space systems.[21]

China and Russia continue to pursue anti-satellite weapons knowing that, if successfully employed, they could undermine U.S. military capabilities. Both countries aim to have nondestructive and destructive counter-space weapons available for use during a potential future conflict. U.S. intelligence predicts that "destructive" Russian and Chinese anti-satellite weapons probably will reach initial operational capability in the next few years. China's military is setting up specialized units and has begun initial operational training with counter-space capabilities, such as ground-launched anti-satellite missiles.[22]

"As part of the military reforms announced in 2015, China established the Strategic Support Force (SSF) to integrate cyberspace, space, and EW capabilities into joint military operations. The SSF forms the core of China's information warfare force, supports the entire PLA, and reports directly to the Central Military Commission. The SSF likely is responsible for research and development of certain space and counter-space capabilities. The SSF's space function is focused primarily on satellite launch and operations to support PLA navigation, and communication requirements. Currently, the state council's State Administration for Science, Technology, and Industry for National Defense (SASTIND) is the primary civil organization that coordinates and manages China's space activities, including allocating space research and development funds. It also maintains a working relationship with the PLA organization that oversees China's military acquisitions. SASTIND guides and establishes policies for state-owned entities conducting China's space activities, whereas the state-owned Assets Supervision and Administration Commission provides day-to-day management."[23]

The China National Space Administration (CNSA) serves as the public face of China's civil space efforts. China is increasingly using these efforts to bolster relationships with countries around the world, seeking opportunities to lead the space community. By April 2018, China had signed 21 civil space cooperation agreements with 37 countries and international organizations.

In the commercial space sector, mixed-ownership enterprises such as Zhuhai Orbital, Expace, and OK-Space offer remote sensing, launch, and communication services. Many of these space technologies can serve a civilian and military purpose and China emphasizes civil-military integration to the leveraging of dual-use technologies, policies, and organizations for military benefit. Both countries also are advancing directed-energy weapons that could make satellites useless by blinding sensitive optical sensors, such as those used for remote sensing or missile defense.[24]

China and Russia are soon expected to launch experimental satellites for on-orbit activities, not necessarily hostile but enabling them to advance their counter-space capabilities. Some technologies with peaceful applications, such as satellite inspection, refueling and repair, can also be used against adversary spacecraft. Especially infuriating is that both countries are continuing their pursuit of space warfare capabilities while publicly maintaining that space must be a peaceful domain.[25]

Russia has been accused of deploying a suspicious satellite intended to be part of Moscow's plan to attack orbiting satellites in a future conflict, according to Yleem Poblete, U.S. Assistant Secretary of State for Arms Control, Verification, and Compliance. In a speech at the Geneva Disarmament Forum, she declared that Moscow is promoting a draft treaty aimed at banning arms in space while advancing an array of space weaponry. Poblete claimed that in October 2017, Russia conducted tests of a space apparatus inspector that was detected by U.S. intelligence maneuvering and taking other unusual actions in space. "Its behavior in-orbit was inconsistent with anything seen before from in-orbit inspection or space situational awareness capabilities, including other Russian inspection satellite activities," she stated. U.S. intelligence agencies are uncertain about Moscow's intentions regarding the use of the suspicious satellite. But Poblete said the satellite is "obviously a very troubling development."[26]

Recent comments by senior Russian aerospace officers tend to confirm these suspicions that assimilating new prototypes of weapons into space force military units is a main task facing the Aerospace Forces space troops. These concerns and suspicions have now been addressed by Pentagon plans to create a new Space Force as a separate branch of the U.S. military. At this point few details have been disclosed about plans for U.S. space weapons and the war-fighting doctrine of the new forces. But they will certainly be formulated to counter China as well as Russia.[27]

It is known that China has a well-developed space warfare capability that includes three types of ground-launched anti-satellite missiles, anti-satellite lasers, and maneuvering satellites. U.S. intelligence agencies have observed small Chinese maneuvering satellites with robotic arms capable of grabbing and crushing satellites. Russia launched a "small space apparatus" from the Plesetsk Commodore in June 2017 to be used for "examining the condition of a Russian satellite," according to the Russian Ministry of Defense. According to the Ministry, the satellite was coupled to a larger satellite, Kosmos-2519, which then conducted autonomous flight, a change in orbit, and a satellite inspection before returning to the base station. The test is "yet another example that the threats to US and allied space programs are for real, serious, and growing," according to US Space Command General John Raymond.[28]

The test itself remains a mystery. No satellites, target or otherwise, were destroyed. The missile system in question, known as Nudol, has been in development for decades and has been tested at least five times over the past few years. The weapon is believed to be a possible successor to the A-135 system, the core of the ballistic missile defense deployed in the Moscow region.

The secretive Kosmos-2519 satellite was delivered to orbit on June 23,

2017, by a Soyuz 2–1V rocket flying with a Volga upper stage that dropped the spacecraft off in orbit and deorbited itself later on the day of launch. No official identification on the satellite was provided, though rumors prior to launch indicated Soyuz may have been carrying the first napry-azhenie geodetic satellite.

Orbital data, however, showed the Kosmos-2519 satellite in a highly unusual orbit for a geodetic satellite and more in tune with a remote sensing mission. The Russian defense ministry confirmed the successful launch and described a twofold mission of remote sensing of Earth and photographing objects in space. But these two objectives seemed to have been reconciled in a single mission.

"Experts noted that a peculiarity about the Kosmos-2519 mission was its planar proximity to the Kosmos-2486 satellite, the second Persona image reconnaissance satellite that has been in orbit since June 2013. Kosmos-2486 flies about 30 miles above Kosmos-2519's initial orbit. Given the military nature of the mission, it remains to be seen what the inspector satellite will do with respect to Kosmos-2486. The best source of information on the mission will come from public tracking data released by the U.S. Joint Space Operations Center. Few doubt this will fail to confirm the military implications."[29]

Russian space weaponry includes a new anti-satellite missile fired from aircraft and a mobile attack anti-satellite system. Russia's development of a future MiG-41, billed as hypersonic, is touted as capable of destroying targets in space. Additionally, Russia recently announced that its space troops have been equipped with a mobile laser system that was cited in a speech by Russian president Vladimir Putin.[30]

"In November 2017, Russian officials announced development of a mobile anti-satellite strike system called Rudolf, along with a mobile anti-communications satellite electronic warfare system known as Tirada-2S, which will be used to conduct radio-electronic attacks on satellites. Then in July 2018, Russia revealed plans for an advanced aircraft called Porubshik-2 reportedly capable of blinding orbiting satellites with electronic strikes. The electronic warfare system will be deployed in a modified IL-76 transport. Russia's anti-satellite missile known as the Nudol or PL-19 has been tested at least six times since 2015. The Nudol will utilize a high-speed interceptor missile that destroys satellite targets using kinetic energy."[31]

Brian Weeden, Director of Program Planning at the Secure World Foundation, has been researching China's space weapons for years. He believes that China's arsenal includes ground-based direct ascent missiles that can physically destroy a satellite, jammers that can interfere, and lasers that can be used to dazzle or perhaps even blind imaging satellites. Weeden insists that China has conducted a series of tests of on-orbit proximity and rendezvous operations, although the publicly available evidence does not indicate they are explicitly aimed at offensive capabilities.

Russia had several operational anti-satellite systems right up until the end of the Cold War, Weeden noted, and there is "strong evidence to suggest they too are active again." There are indications that Russia has also resurrected an airborne laser dazzler system known as the A-60, Weeden said. There are multiple reports of Russia using GPS jammers in Eastern Ukraine, and Russia has also done a series of its own on-orbit proximity and rendezvous operations demonstrations, both in Low-Earth and geosynchronous orbits.

"What's driving this is the desire to blunt the ability of the U.S. to use space in a future conflict," said Weeden. "If a war broke out in the Baltic region or in East Asia, the U.S. would be heavily reliant on its space capabilities. China and Russia think that by developing these systems they can deter the U.S., and if that doesn't work then they hope to take out enough U.S. space capabilities to win the war."

"What is very worrisome," Weeden sums up, "is that all parties have strong incentives to go after the other side's space capabilities early in a conflict. That could lead to some very unstable crisis dynamics and an outcome — armed conflict — that everyone says they want to avoid."[32]

While most attention is understandably focused on China and Russia, experts express some concern about Iranian space efforts. Three years after joining the Asia-Pacific Space Cooperation Organization in 2005, Iran launched a two-stage Safir SLV. It has also some launched the larger two-stage Simorgh SLV, which could serve as a test for developing ICBM technologies. Because of the inherent overlap in technology between ICBMs and SLVs, Iran's development of larger, more capable SLV boosters remains a concern for a future ICBM capability. These advancements could also be applied to developing a basic ground based ASAT missile, should Iran choose to do so in the future.[33]

North Korea's National Aerospace Development Administration operates a space launch complex at the Sohae Satellite Launching Station and associated space tracking facilities in Pyongyang, which supported satellite launch cycles in 2012 and 2016. The space strategy is defensive, attempting to deny adversaries the use of space during a conflict, as well as demonstrating non-kinetic counter space capabilities, including GPS and satellite communication jamming. North Korea also has ballistic missiles and space launch vehicles that can reach orbit and could, be used to target satellites in a conflict.

Having placed two satellites in orbit and articulated further space ambitions, its program has enabled North Korea to test technology used in ballistic missiles under the guise of peaceful use of space. These systems have provided them with valuable data applicable to the development of long-range, multi-stage ballistic missiles.[34]

For China and Russia, potential for conflict will soon extend well beyond close earth orbits, both countries having conducted lunar missions as key demonstrations of technological sophistication and economic prosperity. In 2013, China became the first country to land a mission on the moon's surface since the Soviet Union did so in 1976. While insisting China favors the peaceful use of space, it warns it will develop technologies and capabilities for safeguarding satellites while maintaining the ability to safely enter, exit, and openly use space.[35]

When asked if the United States is falling behind China in military space systems, Army Lt. Gen. Robert Ashley, Director of the Defense Intelligence Agency said, "I can't tell you who's in front and who's behind. China, like Russia, now has direct ascent ASAT missiles that 'literally can go up and target a satellite,'" Ashley said on January 15, 2020.

On the threat from co-orbital satellites, Ashley said small satellites are being outfitted with robotic arms. "If that satellite nestles up against yours, then you have the ability to damage a sensor," he said. "You can cut lines. You in fact could disable that with a co-orbital satellite. There's a multitude of things that are potentially at risk," the DIA chief said, declining to discuss U.S. efforts to harden satellites against attack, to stockpile rapidly deployable replacements, "and that is being addressed," he said.[36]

China's other space weapons include ground-based lasers that blind or damage orbiting satellites, and orbiting robot satellites capable of grabbing and crushing satellites. China continues development of multiple counter-space capabilities designed to degrade and deny adversary use of space-based assets during a crisis or conflict. Chinese military writers have stated the goal of PLA space warfare is "destroying, damaging, and interfering with the enemy's reconnaissance and communications satellites" along with navigation and early warning satellites. The objective is to blind and deafen the enemy. The PLA Air Force is in charge of integrating air and space forces and coordinating offensive and defensive operations. The service is accelerating the transition of its tasks from territorial air defense to both offensive and defensive operations.[37]

"China also has created a Space Corps within a new service-level Strategic Support Force. The corps is believed to be the key space war-fighting unit. A 2018 intelligence report by the National Air and Space Intelligence Center (NASIC) stated that China is among the most advanced nations in building space weapons. Through military reforms, China and Russia have organized new military forces devoted to the employment of space and counter-space capabilities and regularly integrate them into military exercises. Meanwhile, these countries continue to develop, test, and proliferate sophisticated anti-satellite weapons to hold U.S. and allied space assets at risk. The weapons include kinetic kill interceptors that destroy satellites by slamming into them at high speeds. Other space weapons include satellites armed with radiofrequency jammers, lasers, chemical sprayers, high-power microwaves, and robotic arms. Orbiting satellite maintenance and debris removal systems now in the testing and research phase could also be used to damage satellites."[38]

Steve Lambakis, a former official at the Pentagon's Missile Defense Agency, said a key PLA objective is to use space weapons to cripple operations of the Hawaii-based Indo-Pacific Command during a future conflict by attacking American satellites. "These operations would likely start with disruption and destruction of command, control, communications, and intelligence capabilities with cyber and kinetic attacks on satellites and ground assets in support of other Chinese kinetic capabilities," Lambakis said.[39]

"China plans to become an international leader in lunar research and exploration with goals to assemble a lunar research station beginning in 2025, perform a crewed moon-landing mission in 2036, and establish a Lunar Research and Development Base around 2050. Russia plans to launch a robotic moon mission in 2021. China and Russia have active Mars and deep space exploration programs. During the mid–2020s, China intends to launch its first Mars rover mission and an asteroid sample return mission. Russia's Mars program can be traced back to Soviet ambitions in the 1960s. Since then, it has launched several Mars exploration missions, with the only two successful missions occurring in 1971. China is proceeding with ambitious space plans backed by multi-step procedures and impressive funding for reusable space plans, nuclear-powered spaceships, and robotic moon bases. China Aerospace Science and Technology Corporation's (CASC) three planned stages are

- a reusable carrier rocket plane

- a reusable rocket plane and a second-stage rocket, and

- a hypersonic carrier aircraft with a turbine-rocket-combined cycle engine.

The reusable space plane is expected to fly for the first time in 2020, and to carry astronauts and freight into space by 2025. The two-stage space plane would be rocket-powered at first and able to fly off a runway at hypersonic speeds to near space. It would then detach a reusable second-stage rocket that would carry passengers and cargo and reach an altitude of 180 to 310 miles in orbit. In line with previous space plane plans, CASC will fly a scramjet-powered version of the first-stage carrier by 2030."[40]

Competing with the CASC program, the rival China Aerospace Science and Industry Corporation's (CASIC) has a space plane program with engines and other core technologies in advanced testing. CASIC's concept spaceship uses a nuclear power source to provide thrust through its plasma engines. CASIC's plans for deep-space exploration include a nuclear-powered spacecraft, slated to enter service in 2040, most likely to support a manned Chinese Martian mission. CAISC also has plans for China to engage in deep-space economic activity, like building orbit solar power plants, and mining asteroids and the moon.[41]

"Potential adversaries' deep space ventures, however, will not deter defense against threats from space here on earth. "Dual-use capabilities will challenge U.S. ability to provide advanced warning of nefarious intentions or discern between peaceful and potential hostile activity, for example, future satellite servicing and recycling capabilities incorporate a variety of technologies, such as robotic arms, to inspect, repair, or dispose of damaged satellites. However, the same technologies have inherent counter-space capabilities that could be used to inspect non-consenting satellites or to cause physical damage, steal parts, or grapple with a satellite."[42]

Several concepts for future technologies promise to provide new enhancements to space capabilities. For instance, advanced artificial intelligence and improved sensors will provide satellites with the situational awareness for autonomous self-protection. Additionally, 3D printing in space could alloy elimination of the cost of space launch by servicing, repairing, or manufacturing new systems entirely on orbit.

Reconnaissance and remote sensing satellites collect images, electronic emissions, and other data across the globe to meet a variety of needs. There are several civil and commercial applications for remote sensing data, such as environmental monitoring, urban planning, and disaster response. High demand for this data and falling costs for capable technology have spurred the rapid growth and proliferation of these satellites.[43]

"China and Russia have the largest remote sensing satellite fleets outside the U.S. In 2010 foreign remote sensing satellites numbered about 100. By mid-2018 that number reached over 300.

In addition to civil and commercial uses, these satellites provide military and intelligence collection capabilities. They have reduced the ability of all countries to perform sensitive military activities undetected. Additionally, the Chinese PLA and the Russian Ministry of Defense are reportedly capable of employing their respective civil and commercial remote sensing satellites to supplement military-dedicated capabilities. As of May 2018, the Chinese reconnaissance and remote sensing fleet consisted of more than 120 satellites designed to collect data for civil, commercial, or military owners and operators. Reportedly, the PLA owns and operates about half of these systems, most of which could support monitoring, tracking, and targeting of U.S. forces. These satellites also allow the PLA to maintain situational awareness of China's regional rivals (e.g., India and Japan) and potential regional flashpoints (e.g., Korea, Taiwan, and the East and South China Seas."[44]

Many countries developed space launch capabilities to compete in the international market or to advance national security strategies that require domestic access to space. Iran and North Korea maintain independent space launch capabilities that could also test ballistic missile technologies. China and Russia are also updating their space launch capabilities to increase responsiveness, reduce launch timelines, improve manufacturing efficiencies, and support future human spaceflight and deep space exploration missions.

China and Russia are updating their medium- and heavy-lift launch fleets to include new, modular launch vehicles with common designs that increase manufacturing efficiency, launch vehicle reliability, and overall cost savings for space launches. China has developed and fielded light, quick response space launch vehicles capable of expedited launches. Compared to medium- and heavy-lift launch vehicles, quick response systems require little launch infrastructure, can relocate by road or rail and can be stored launch-ready for longer periods. However, they are capable only of launching small satellite payloads into low orbits.[45]

China designed quick response space launch vehicles to increase its attractiveness as a commercial small satellite launch provider and to rapidly reconstitute space capabilities in Low Earth orbit during disasters or conflicts. China and Russia are currently in the early stages of developing super heavy-lift space launch vehicles similar to the U.S. Space Launch System. These super heavy-lift vehicles could support future Chinese and Russian crewed lunar and Mars exploration.

U.S space programs have been mainly civilian controlled. That does not appear to be the case with China's space programs. "China's space endeavors are subordinate to the PLA," insists Richard Fisher, Senior Fellow, Asian Military Affairs International Assessment and Strategy Center. Although China's combat intentions in its manned space program were revealed in the first Shenzhou-5 mission in 2005, Fisher believes that China's new leadership has escaped attention regarding its plans for exploiting space technology for military advantage, but that it too sees space as the domain for warfare.[46]

"President Xi-Jinping has personally ordered services of the PLA to prepare for space combat. The motivation behind the space program is to sustain the Chinese Communist Party AND eventually displace the U.S. from its position of global leadership. Chinese doctrine assumes fighting and winning modern wars lies in the ability to establish information dominance, which is acquired through gathering and communicating battlefield information while preventing an opponent from doing the same. The Chinese have seen that the essential data, ranging from meteorological information to weapons guidance and communications, is increasingly gathered via satellites. A Chinese study of the NATO intervention in Kosovo noted that 98 percent of precision-guided weapons were guided with space-based information. The Chinese military concluded that information dominance is dependent on space dominance."[47]

China in the late 1990s developed its own military modernization built around information assets, such as higher resolution optical and radar satellite surveillance, space-based data relay and new infrared-multi-spectral early warning satellites. "At the same time, China invested in counter-space capabilities intended to exploit U.S. military dependence on space, which the Chinese see as a critical U.S. vulnerability," said Dr. Phillip Saunders, Director of the Center for the Study of Chinese Military Affairs. The PLA's apparent goal is to exercise denial and then dominance in LEO and then extend control into the Earth-moon system."[48]

The National Air and Space Intelligence Center (NASIC) warns that China and Russia are developing and proliferating a variety of weapons that could disrupt or deny civil and military space services. Although many of these weapons are intended to degrade space services only temporarily, others could damage or destroy satellites permanently. These include:

- Funding and developing the long-proposed constellation of space sensors capable of tracking the entire life of a missile and enabling precise targeting.

- Jamming global navigation and communications satellites used for command and control of naval, ground, and air forces, to include manned and unmanned vehicles.

- Developing weapons designed to target intelligence, surveillance, and reconnaissance capabilities that may deny the ability to locate, monitor, track, and target the enemy.

- Using anti-satellite missiles to shoot down satellites in Low Earth orbit.

- Testing on-orbit, space-based anti-satellite technologies and concepts. China and Russia continue to conduct sophisticated on-orbit activities that may advance counter-space capabilities.

- Physically attacking ground sites and infrastructure that support space operations and thereby threatening satellite services.

- Using cyber capabilities to target space systems and their supporting infrastructure.

110

The U.S. missile defense system comprises three critical physical parts: sensors, interceptors, and command and control infrastructure that provide data from sensors to interceptors. Of these, interceptors receive much of the public's attention because of their very visible and kinetic nature. Different physical components of a ballistic missile defense system are designed to recognize the phase of flight in which an intercept occurs although some of them — for example, the command and control infrastructure or radar — can support intercepts in various phases of a ballistic missile flight. Interceptors can shoot down an adversarial missile in the boost, ascent, midcourse, or terminal phase of its flight.[49]

"Another way to consider ballistic missile defense systems is by the range of an incoming ballistic missile (short-range, medium-range, intermediate-range, or long-range) that an interceptor is designed to shoot down. The length of the interceptor's flight time determines how much time is available to conduct an intercept and where the various components of a defense system must be placed to improve the probability of such an intercept. With long-range ballistic missiles, the U.S. has no more than 33 minutes to detect the missile, track it, provide the information to the missile defense system, come up with the most optimal firing solution, launch an interceptor, and shoot down an incoming missile, ideally with enough time to fire another interceptor if the first attempt fails. The timeframe is shorter when it comes to medium-range and short-range ballistic missiles."[50]

Missile defense can be framed by the origin of interceptor launch. At present, U.S. interceptors are launched from the ground or from the sea. In the past, the U.S. explored concepts to launch interceptors from the air or from space, but limited efforts have been made on that front since the U.S. withdrawal from the Anti-Ballistic Missile Treaty in 2002. There is renewed interest in boost-phase missile defense concepts within the present Administration.[51]

The platform carrying air-launched ballistic missile interceptors has to be close to the launch area, aloft, oriented in a proper way, and within the range of enemies' anti-access/area-denial systems because of payload limits on airborne platforms themselves. These requirements make airborne intercepts particularly challenging.

"The current U.S. missile defense system is a result of investments made by successive U.S. Administrations. President Ronald Reagan's vision for the program was to have a layered ballistic missile defense system that would render nuclear weapons impotent and obsolete," including ballistic missile defense interceptors in space. These layers would include boost, ascent, midcourse, and terminal interceptors, including directed-energy interceptors, so the U, S. would have more than one opportunity to shoot down an incoming missile."[52]

SUMMARY

We have stopped far short of our space goals, even though the Strategic Defense Initiative Program resulted in tremendous technological advances and benefits. Instead of a comprehensive layered system, we have no boost phase ballistic missile defense systems and are unable to handle more qualitatively and quantitatively advanced ballistic missile threats like those from China or Russia. As technological trends progress and modern technologies become cheaper and more widely available, North Korean or Iranian ballistic missiles may rival those of Russia or China in sophistication if not numbers. Consequently, we must remain aware of how such threats are evolving and alter our missile defense posture accordingly.

NOTES

1. U.S. Department of Defense, Missile Defense Agency, "Ballistic Missile Defense Challenge," *MDA Forum*, May 27, 2018.

2. Garett Evans, "A Simple Point of Failure: The Problem with GPS," *Global Defense Technology*, March 2016.

3. Jeff Foust, "Pence Reaffirms Administration's Support for Space," *SPACE NEWS*, May 6, 2019.

4. "National Air and Space Intelligence Center's 'Competing in Space' Assessment,"*Covault*, Jan. 12, 2018.

5. *Assessing Threats to U.S. Vital Interests — Space*, Washington, D.C.: Heritage Foundation, Oct. 30, 2019.

6. Bill Gertz, "China Outlines Space War Plans," *Washington Free Beacon*, July 26, 2019.

7. Full text of white paper on China's space activities, The State Council, The People's Republic of China, Dec. 26, 2016.

8. *Assessing Threats to U.S. Vital Interests – Space*, Washington, D.C.: Heritage Foundation, Oct. 30, 2019.

9. "India Destroys Its Own Satellite with a Missile, Still Says Space Is For Peace," *The Conversation,* April 1, 2019.

10. "2018 U.S. Worldwide Threat Assessment," *USNI News*, Feb. 16, 2018.

11. "Challenges to Security in Space," *U.S. Defense Security Agency*, Feb. 26. 1019.

12. *Assessing Threats to U.S. Vital Interests – Space*, Washington, D.C.: Heritage Foundation, Oct. 30, 2019.

13. *Space Threat Assessment, 2020*, Washington, D.C.: Heritage Foundation.

14. Lt. General Michael Maples, "Chinese Anti-Satellite Missile Test," Senate Armed Services Committee Hearing, Feb. 27, 2007.

15. Space Threat Assessment 2018, Aerospace Security Project. "Challenges to Security in Space," *U.S. Defense Security Agency*, Feb. 26. 2019.

16. "Sensors and Systems for Space Applications," *SPIE*, April 27, 2020.

17. Space Threat Assessment 2018, Aerospace Security Project. U.S. Department of Defense, Missile Defense Agency, "Ballistic Missile Defense Challenge," *MDA Forum*, May 27, 2018.

18. James Carafano, "Preparing National Security Strategy for 2020 and Beyond, *Heritage Foundation Special Report 214*, May 23, 2019.

19. Bill Gertz, "China Outlines Space War Plan," *Washington Free Beacon*, July 26, 2019.

20. Ajey Lele, "China's 2016 Space White Paper: An Appraisal," *IDSA Issue Brief*, Jan. 6, 2017.

21. "Challenges to Security in Space," *U.S. Defense Security Agency*, Feb. 26. 2019.

22. Namrata Gosuwami, The U.S. Space Force and the Implications," *The Diplomat,* Jan 22. 2018.

23. Vleem Poblete, "Russia, China Propose Space Treaty," speech to Disarmament Conference, Geneva, Switzerland *Prophecy in the News*, Aug. 16, 2018.

24. Bill Gertz, "US Says Small Russian Satellite A Space Weapon," *Fortuna's Corner,* Aug. 15, 2018.

25. Namrata Gosuwami, "The U.S. Space Force and the Implications," *The Diplomat,* Jan 22. 2018.

26. Ben Kesling, "Nominee to Head Space Command Warns of Threats to U.S. Power," *The Wall Street Journal*, June 4, 2019.

27. James Carafano, "Preparing National Security Strategy for 2020 and Beyond," *Heritage Foundation Special Report 214*, May 23, 2019.

28. "'Final Test of New Hypersonic Missile Successful,' Putin says," *CBS News*, Dec. 26, 2018.

29. Dave Majumdar, "Get ready, America: Russia and China Have Space Weapons," *The National Interest*, Jan. 26, 2016.

30. Brian Weeden, "Russia and China Are Developing Counter-Space Capability and Anti-Satellite Weapons That Could Interfere with U.S. Space Systems in Future Conflicts," *Think*, Sep. 3, 2019.

31. Michael R. Pompeo Secretary of State, U.S. Department of Defense, "Iran's Space Program Is Dangerous, Not Peaceful," April 25, 2020.

32. Elizabeth Shim, "North Korea Highlights Space Program in State Media," *UPI*, April 2, 2020.

33. Full text of white paper on China's space activities, the State Council, the People's Republic of China, Dec. 26, 2016.

34. Robert Ashley talks with Michael Morell on "Intelligence Matters," *CBS News*, Jan. 15, 2020.

35. Ajey Lele, "China's 2016 Space White paper: An Appraisal," *IDSA Issue Brief*, Jan. 6, 2017.

36. "NASIC Report on Space Competition, Threats," *Inside Defense*, Jan. 16, 2019.

37. Steve Lambakis, "Thinking About Space Deterrence and China," *National Institute for Public Policy*, Issue No. 443, July 2018.

38. Alexander Bowe, *China's Pursuit of Space Power Status and Implications for the United States*, U.S.-China Economic and Security Review Commission, April 11, 2019.

39. Bill Gertz, "China Outlines Space War Plans," *Washington Free Beacon*, July 26, 2019.

40. "Challenges to Security in Space," *U.S. Defense Security Agency*, Feb. 26, 2019.

41. "National Air and Space Intelligence Center's 'Competing in Space' Assessment, *Covault*, Jan. 12, 2018.

42. *Space Threat Assessment, 2020*, Washington, D.C.: Heritage Foundation.

43. NASIC report on space competition, threats, *Inside Defense*, Jan. 16, 2019.

44. Gary Feuerberg, "China's Space Program Dominated by Chinese Military," *The Epoch Times*, Feb. 22, 2015.

45. "Chinese Military Reforms in the Age of Xi: Drivers, Challenges and Implications," *Journal of Strategic Studies*, March 2017.

46. Philip C. Saunders, *Chairman Xi Remakes the PLA*, NDU Press, 2020.

47. "NASIC Report on Space Competition, Threats," *Inside Defense*, Jan. 16, 2019.

48. *Assessing Threats to U.S. Vital Interests – Space*, Washington, D.C.: The Heritage Foundation, Oct. 30, 2019.

49. Wade Boese, *U.S. Withdraws from ABM Treaty*, Arms Control Association, July 2002.

50. NASIC report on space competition, threats, *Inside Defense*, Jan. 16, 2019.

51. *Assessing Threats to U.S. Vital Interests: Space*, The Heritage Foundation, Oct. 30, 2020.

52. *U.S. Withdraws From ABM Treaty*, Wade Boese, Arms Control Association, July, 2002.

53. *Assessing Threats to U.S. Vital Interests: Space*, The Heritage Foundation, Oct. 30, 2020.

113

10 | Cyber Warfare Threat

IN THE FUTURE, wars will not just be fought by soldiers with guns or with planes that drop bombs. They will also be fought with the click of a mouse a half-a-world away that unleashes carefully weaponized computer programs that disrupt or destroy critical industries like utilities, transportation, communications and energy. Such attacks could also disable military networks that control the movement of troops, the path of jet fighters, or the command and movement of warships.

No issue has emerged so rapidly as the militarization of cyberspace, and yet no issue is more poorly understood as cyber-security. Ignorance is not bliss when it comes to cyber-security. Cyber issues affect literally everyone: the military protecting the nation; business executives defending firms from once unimaginable threats and politicians wrestling with everything from voter fraud, cybercrime and online freedom.

Unlike the Cold War, cyberwar is fuzzy. The Cold War featured two superpowers pursuing ideological goals. The Internet features millions of users and, given the mass of their sheer number, they provide cyber attackers with camouflage. Nations can cybersiege their enemies constantly without ever firing a shot or engaging in open hostilities.

Russia, China, Iran, and North Korea. Four adversaries and authoritarian states that are rapidly improving already formidable proficiencies in making attacks for which neither our military, our government agencies or our civilian organizations and corporations have developed adequate defenses: cyber warfare.

In recent years, the role of cyber warfare in the United States and other westernized democracies expanded from simply protecting military networks to defending our entire economic system from cyber attacks. While tightly integrated civil-security forces relations have emerged, more efforts are crucial for the survival of democratic societies in an increasingly cyber-enabled authoritarian world. What's been accomplished so far is not nearly enough.

Cyber defense is a momentous issue that has prompted a massive array of suggested strategies. "We must build a NATO/EU equivalent for the cyber conflict age — to defend across the whole of the democratic community." This warning comes from Dr. Chris C. Demchak, the Grace Hopper Chair of Cyber Security and Senior Cyber Scholar, Cyber and Innovation Policy Institute at the U.S. Naval War College.

"The difference between arms races in the cyber sphere and the physical world is that in cyberspace, any player can potentially become a superpower: The capital costs are alarmingly low, compared to funding a physical war machine. Even some of the world's most impoverished regions proved their ability to make a global impact through cyber campaigns in 2018, and this is one genie that is not going back in the bottle," according to Demchak.[1]

CrowdStrike has experienced daily the role defenders play in the cyber arms race and introduced more effective endpoint protection to the market, raising the stakes for determined adversaries. CrowdStrike has documented cases where bad actors discovered encountering an effective defense have simply gone away, presumably to ply their tradecraft on a more vulnerable victim. In other cases, patient attackers simply go back to the drawing board, adding new weapons to their cyber arsenals as they probe for a novel, less defended point of entry.[2]

The cyber capabilities of four adversaries are of major concern.

Russia

Russian cyber capabilities are sophisticated and active, regularly threatening economic, social, and political targets around the world. Moscow appears to be increasingly aggressive in its use of digital techniques, often employing only the slightest veneer of deniability in an effort to intimidate targets and openly defy international norms and organizations. Russia clearly believes that these online operations will be essential to its domestic and foreign policy for the foreseeable future.

Former Chief of the Russian General Staff General Yuri Baluyevsky observed that "cyber attacks are much more important than victory in a classical military conflict, because it is bloodless, yet the impact is overwhelming and can paralyze all of the enemy state's power structure."[3]

Russia launched coordinated cyber-attacks against the Ukrainian government and military targets before and during the seizure of Ukrainian ships and sailors on November 25, 2018, according to Stealthcare, a cyber threat intelligence group. The attacks were aimed at stealing information relevant to planning the attack. It began when a Russian entity known as Carbanak sent deceptive emails to convince its targets to click links and download malware around October 25, 2018, a month before the attack. Attached to the emails were PDFs with links and other pieces of code that, when executed, allowed the attacker to steal data and gain control over important computer functions.[4]

The 2020 Worldwide Threat Assessment of the U.S. Intelligence Community (WWTA) identifies the cyber threat as one of our nation's major concerns and cites Russia specifically. Russia is expected to conduct bolder and more disruptive cyber operations in the future, most likely using new capabilities. It is likely to build on the wide range of operations it is already conducting, including disruption of energy distribution networks, hack-and-leak operations and distributed denial-of-service attacks. Russian intelligence and security services are expected to continue to probe U.S. and Allied infrastructures.[5]

In June 2018, the U.S. Treasury Department sanctioned five Russian entities and three Russian individuals for maligning and destabilizing cyber activities, including "the destructive NotPetya cyber-attack against the U.S. energy grid." These sanctions were based on a joint assessment by the Department of Homeland Security and the FBI noting Russian hackers were behind a series of attacks against U.S. energy and critical infrastructure sectors.[6]

The U.S. is not Russia's only target. In April 2018, Germany's Director of Domestic Intelligence accused Moscow of attacking his government's computer networks, and the U.K.'s National Cyber Security Center warned that Russian hackers were targeting Britain's critical infrastructure supply chains. Russia continues to employ cyber as a key tool in manipulating and undermining democratic elections in Europe and elsewhere.

In addition to official intelligence and military cyber assets, Russia employs criminal organizations (so-called patriotic hackers) to help it engage in cyber aggression. Using these hackers gives Russia greater resources and can help shield their true capabilities. Patriotic hackers also give the Russian government deniability when it is desired. In June 2017, for example, Putin stated, "If hackers are patriotically-minded, they start to make their own contribution to what they believe is the good fight against those who speak badly about Russia."[7]

Russia's cyber capabilities are advanced and are a key tool in realizing the state's strategic aims. Russia has used cyber-attacks to further the reach and effectiveness of its propaganda and disinformation campaigns, and its ongoing cyber-attacks against election processes in the United States and European countries are designed to undermine its citizens's belief in the veracity of electoral outcomes and erode support for democratic institutions.

"Most attacks against U.S. space assets are likely to be non-kinetic, focusing on electronic attacks and cyber warfare. They will focus on jamming capabilities against dedicated military satellite communications (SATCOM), Synthetic Aperture Radar (SAR), imaging satellites and enhanced capabilities against Global Navigation Satellite Systems (GNSS), such as the U.S. Global Positioning System (GPS). Blending of EW (electronic warfare) and cyber-attack capabilities will likely expand in pursuit of sophisticated means to deny and degrade information networks, according to some experts. Russian researchers have discussed methods to enhance robust jamming capabilities with new systems to disrupt commonly used frequencies. Russia is also modernizing its EW forces and plans to field a new generation of EW capabilities by 2020. If electronic warfare and cyber-weapons fail to achieve their desired objectives, Russia may be prepared to use kinetic force to physically destroy American space assets."[8]

China

In 2015, a Chinese cyber-attack against the United States resulted in the loss of 21.5 million records, including sensitive information concerning weapons development. Chinese government hackers stole massive amounts of highly sensitive data related to undersea warfare, including secret plans to develop a supersonic anti-ship missile for use on U.S. submarines by 2020. The hacks took place in January and February 2018 and targeted an unidentified contractor who works for the Naval Under Seas Warfare Center in Newport, Rhode Island.[9]

Taken were 614 gigabytes of material relating to a closely held project known as "Sea Dragon," as well as signals and sensor data, submarine radio information relating to cryptographic systems and the Navy submarine development unit's electronic warfare library. U.S. Senator Jack Reed, a member of the Senate Armed Services Committee, described the incident as very serious. He warned that this is another example of how the Chinese are focused on getting advanced weapons technology through all kinds of means, including stealing secrets from defense contractors and that China has made closing the gap in undersea warfare one of its top military priorities.[10]

The Verizon Risk Center found that China was responsible for the largest percentage (30 percent) of external breaches in which the threat actor's country of origin was discoverable and that 96 percent of espionage cases were attributed to China and the remaining 4 percent were unknown. Given the difficulties of attribution, country of origin should not necessarily be conflated with the perpetrator, but forensic efforts have identified at least one Chinese military unit with cyber intrusions. The

Verizon report concluded that China was the source of a huge percentage of state-sponsored cyber-espionage attacks.

Since the 2015 Xi–Obama summit at which the two sides reached an understanding to reduce cyber economic espionage, Chinese cyber trends have been difficult to discern. While Chinese economic cyber-espionage is reported to have declined, the overall level of cyber activity appears to have remained relatively constant. FireEye, a cyber-security consulting firm, has observed an increase in attacks against U.S. companies attempting to obtain sensitive business information, and it warns that this may be due to Chinese activity.[11]

"China's cyber-espionage efforts are often aimed at economic targets, reflecting the Chinese view of both security and information. Rather than creating an artificial dividing line between military security and civilian security, the PLA plays a role in attacking both, and it seeks to obtain economic intellectual property as well as military electronic information. The PLA continues to emphasize the military importance of cyber warfare. Chinese military writings emphasize a fundamental transformation in global military affairs. Future wars will be conducted through joint operations involving multiple services rather than through combined operations focused on multiple branches within a single service. These future wars will span not only the traditional land, sea, and air domains, but also outer space and cyberspace. The latter two arenas will be of special importance because warfare has shifted from an effort to establish material dominance to establishing information dominance. This is due to the rise of the information age and the resulting introduction of information technology into all areas of military operations."[12]

According to PLA analysis, the ability to gather, transmit, analyze, manage, and exploit information will be central to winning future wars. The side that is able to do these things most accurately and most quickly will be the side that wins. Chinese military writings suggest that a great deal of attention has been focused on developing an integrated computer network and electronic warfare (INEW) capability. This would allow the PLA to reconnoiter a potential adversary's computer systems in peacetime, influence opponent decision-makers by threatening those same systems in times of crisis and disrupt or destroy information networks and systems by cyber and electronic warfare means in the event of conflict. INEW capabilities would complement psychological warfare and physical attack efforts to secure information dominance, which Chinese military writings emphasize as essential for fighting and winning future wars. Attacks on computer networks in particular have the potential to be extremely disruptive. The indictment of five serving PLA officers on the grounds of cyber espionage highlights how active the Chinese military is in this realm.[13]

"A major Chinese military reform includes the establishment of the PLA Strategic Support Force (PLASSF), which brings together China's space, electronic warfare, and cyber warfare areas.

This reflects the importance that the PLA is placing on computer network operations. The PLA views computer network operations as part of the larger body of information operations. They are conducted in both peacetime and wartime, with the peacetime focus on collecting information, improving its flow and application, influencing opposing decision-making, and effecting information deterrence.

Information operations involve four mission areas:

1. **Command and Control Missions.** An essential part of information operations is the ability of commanders to control joint operations by disparate forces. Command, control, communications, computers, intelligence, surveillance and reconnaissance structures constitute a key part of information operations, providing the means for collecting, transmitting and managing information.

2. **Offensive Information Missions.** These are intended to disrupt the enemy's battlefield command and control systems and communications networks, as well as to strike the enemy's psychological defenses.

3. **Defensive Information Missions.** These missions are aimed at ensuring the survival and continued operation of information systems. They include deterring an opponent from attacking China's own information systems, concealing information, and combating attacks when they occur.

4. **Information Support and Information Safeguarding Missions.** The ability to provide the myriad types of information necessary to support extensive joint operations and to do so on a continuous basis.

Computer network operations are integral to all four of these overall mission areas. They can include both strategic and battlefield network operations and can incorporate both offensive and defensive measures. They also include protection not only of data, but also of information hardware and operating software. Computer network operations will not stand alone, however, but will be integrated with electronic warfare operations aimed at weakening or destroying enemy electronic facilities and systems while defending one's own."[14]

The combination of electronic and computer network attacks will produce synergies that affect everything from finding and assessing the adversary to locating one's own forces to weapons guidance to logistical support and command and control. The creation of the PLASSF is intended to integrate these forces and make them more complementary and effective in future wars.

North Korea

On May 27, 2016, North Korea conducted the first government-sponsored digital bank robbery when its hackers gained access to the Society for Worldwide Interbank Financial Telecommunication (SWIFT), the system used by central banks to authorize monetary transfers, to steal $81 million. The regime had attempted to send money transfer requests of $951 million from the Central Bank of Bangladesh to banks in the Philippines, Sri Lanka, and other parts of Asia.[15]

On April 26, 2018, North Korea was suspected in a cyber-attack on a Turkish bank as part of a hacking campaign identified as Operation GhostSecret that spanned 17 countries and numerous industries. Years earlier, North Korean hackers have also targeted the World Bank, the European Central Bank, 20 Polish banks, and large American banks such as Bank of America, as well as financial institutions in Costa Rica, Ecuador, Ethiopia, Gabon, India, Indonesia, Iraq, Kenya, Malaysia, Nigeria, Poland, Taiwan, Thailand, and Uruguay.[16]

In 2014, North Korea conducted the largest cyber-attack on U.S. soil, targeting Sony Pictures in retaliation for the studio's release of a satirical film depicting the assassination of Kim Jong-un. The cyber-attack was accompanied by physical threats against U.S. theaters and citizens.[17] So, contrary to the perception of North Korea as a technologically backward nation, the regime has an active cyber warfare capability. As far back as 2009, the country declared that it was fully ready for any form of high-tech war.

The Reconnaissance General Bureau, North Korea's intelligence agency, oversees Unit 121 with approximately 6,000 "cyber-warriors" dedicated to attacking Pyongyang's enemies. Defectors from the unit have told South Korean intelligence officials that hackers are sent to other countries for training as well as to conduct undercover operations. The unit's hackers never operate primarily within North Korea, and this makes both attribution and retaliation more difficult. North Korea has been expanding both the scope and sophistication of its cyber-weaponry, laying the groundwork for more devastating attacks, according to a February 2018 report by cyber-security firm FireEye.[18]

Seoul has concluded that North Korea was behind cyber-attacks using viruses or distributed denial-of-service tactics against South Korean government agencies, businesses, banks, and media organizations in 2009, 2011, 2012, and 2013. The most devastating attack, launched in 2013 against South Korean banks and media outlets, deleted the essential Master Boot Record from 48,000 computers. North Korea also jammed GPS signals in 2012, putting hundreds of airplanes transiting Seoul's Incheon Airport at risk.[19]

Iran

"Iranian's cyber capabilities present a significant threat to the U.S. Iran has developed offensive cyber capabilities as a tool of espionage and sabotage and claims to possess the fourth largest cyber force in the world — a broad network of quasi-official elements as well as regime-aligned "hacktivists," who engage in cyber activities broadly consistent with the Islamic Republic's interests and views."[20]

The creation of the Iranian Cyber Army in 2009 marked the beginning of a cyber offensive against those whom the Iranian government regards as enemies. A hacking group dubbed the Ajax Security Team, believed to be operating out of Iran, has used malware-based attacks to target U.S. defense organizations and has successfully breached the Navy-Marine Corps Intranet.[21]

"The group also has targeted dissidents within Iran, seeding versions of anti-censorship tools with malware and gathering information about users of those programs. Iran has invested heavily in cyber activity, reportedly spending over $1 billion on its cyber capabilities in 2012 alone. Hostile Iranian cyber activity has increased significantly since the beginning of 2014 and could threaten U.S. critical infrastructure. The Islamic Revolutionary Guard Corps and Sharif University of Technology are two Iranian institutions that investigators have linked to efforts to infiltrate U.S. computer networks."[22]

Iran allegedly has used cyber weapons to engage in economic warfare, most notably the sophisticated and debilitating "denial-of-service" (DOS) attacks against a number of U.S. financial institutions, including Bank of America, J.P. Morgan Chase, and Citigroup. In February 2014, Iran launched a crippling cyber-attack against the Sands Casino in Las Vegas, owned by Sheldon Adelson, a leading supporter of Israel who is known to be critical of the Iranian regime. In 2012, Tehran was suspected of launching both the "Shamoon" virus attack on Saudi Aramco, the world's largest oil-producing company, an attack that destroyed approximately 30,000 computers, and an attack on a Qatari natural gas company.[23]

In the fall of 2015 that included a series of cyber-attacks against State Department officials. U.S. officials warned of a surge of sophisticated computer espionage by Iran. In March 2016, the Justice Department indicted seven Iranian hackers for penetrating the computer system that controlled a dam in the state of New York.[24] The sophistication of these and other Iranian cyber-attacks, together with Iran's willingness to use these weapons, has led various experts to characterize Iran as one of America's most cyber-capable adversaries. Iranian cyber forces have gone so far as to create fake online personas in order to extract information from U.S. officials through accounts such as LinkedIn, YouTube, Facebook, and Twitter.[25]

Significantly, the FBI alerted American businesses that foreign cyber actors operating in the Islamic Republic of Iran could use a range of computer network operations, from scanning networks for potential vulnerabilities to data deletion attacks, against U.S.-based networks in response to the U.S. government's withdrawal from the Joint Comprehensive Plan of Action.[26]

The FBI assesses that cyber actors operating in the Islamic Republic of Iran could potentially use a range of computer network operations — from scanning networks for potential vulnerabilities to data deletion attacks against U.S. based networks in response to the U.S. government's withdrawal from the Joint Comprehensive Plan of Action (JCPOA). Iran will continue working to penetrate U.S. and Allied networks for espionage to position itself for potential future cyber-attacks, although its intelligence services primarily focus on Middle Eastern adversaries — especially Saudi Arabia and Israel. Iran views cyber-attacks as a versatile tool to respond to perceived provocations. Iranian cyber capabilities present significant espionage and sabotage threats to the U.S. and its allies, and Tehran has shown both a willingness and skill in using them.[27]

A National Cyber Strategy

"New threats and a new era of strategic competition demand a new cyber strategy that responds to new realities, reduces vulnerabilities, deters adversaries and safeguards opportunities for us to thrive. President Trump signed into law a National Cyber Strategy in September 2018. The strategy explains how we will:

- **Defend the homeland** by protecting networks, systems, functions and data.

- **Make Cybersecurity part of our DNA.**

- **Promote American prosperity** by nurturing a secure, thriving digital economy and fostering strong domestic innovation.

- Expand American influence abroad to extend the key tenets of an open, interoperable, reliable and secure Internet.

- Strengthen federal contractor cyber-security. The United States cannot afford to have sensitive government information on systems inadequately secured by contractors. Among the acute concerns in this area are contractors researching and developing key systems for the DOD. The responsibility to secure the nation's critical infrastructure and manage its cyber security risk is shared by the private sector and the Federal government. We will use a risk-management approach to mitigating vulnerabilities to raise the level of cyber-security across critical infrastructure.

- Detect, prevent, disrupt and investigate cybercrime. We will apprehend and prosecute offenders, disable criminal infrastructure, and prevent cyber criminals from benefiting from these activities by seizing their assets.

- Improve incident reporting and response. We will encourage reporting of intrusions and theft of data by all victims, especially critical infrastructure partners. The prompt reporting of cyber incidents to the federal government is essential to an effective response.

- Strengthen our allies's law enforcement capacity to combat criminal cyber activity. The borderless nature of cybercrime, including state-sponsored and terrorist activity requires strong international law enforcement partnerships. We will help build cyber-crime-fighting capacity that facilitates stronger international law enforcement cooperation."[28]

NOTES

1. Cyber & Innovation Policy Institute, Dr. Chris C. Demchak, U.S. 1. Naval War College, April 3, 2019.
2. *Threats to U.S. Vital Interests, Russia, 2020,* Washington, D.C.: Heritage Foundation.
3. "Russian Military Admits Significant Cyber-War Efforts," *BBC News,* Feb. 23, 2017.
4. Patrick Tucker, "Russia Launched Cyber Attacks Against Ukraine Before Ship Seizures," *Defense One,* Dec. 7. 2018.
5. "Russian Malicious Cyber Activity," U.S. Department of Homeland Security Cybersecurity and Infrastructure Security Agency, June 20, 2019.
6. "Treasury Sanctions Russian Federal Security Service Enablers," U.S. Department of the Treasury, June 11, 2018.

7. "Patriotic Russians May Have Staged Cyber Attacks on Own Initiative Plan," V. Putin, *Reuters*, June 1, 2017.

8. *2020 Index of Military Strength*, Washington, D.C.: Heritage Foundation.

9. Ellen Nakashima, "China Hacked Navy Contractor, Secured Trove of Sensitive Data," *The Chicago Tribune*, June 9, 2018.

10. "Senator Says Chinese Hack Of Navy Contractor 'Very Serious,'" *Washington Times*, June 11, 2018.

11. Tom Davenport, "Cyber Threat Attribution at FireEye," *Forbes*, May 28, 2020.

12. Dean Cheng, "U.S.-China Competition in Space," testimony before the Subcommittee on Space, Science and Technology, U.S. House of Representatives, Sep. 27, 2016.

13. "U.S. Charges Five Chinese Military Hackers for Cyber Espionage Against U.S. Corporations and a Labor Organization for Commercial Advantage," U.S. Department of Justice, May 19, 2014.

14. *2020 Index of Military Strength*, Washington, D.C.: Heritage Foundation.

15. Chris Arnold, "North Korea Linked to $81 Million Bangladesh Bank Heist," *NPR*, May 27, 2016.

16. Kelly Higgins, "North Korea Ramps Up 'Operation GhostSecret' Cyber Espionage Campaign," *DarkReading*, April 26, 2018.

17. Update on Sony Investigation, FBI National Press Office, Dec. 19, 2014.

18. Tom Davenport, "Cyber Threat Attribution at FireEye," Forbes, May 28, 2020.

19. Choe Sang-Hun, "Computer Networks in South Korea Are Paralyzed in Cyberattacks," *The New York Times*, March 20, 2013.

20. *Threats to U.S. Vital Interests, Iran, 2020*, Washington, D.C.: Heritage Foundation.

21. Ilan Berman, "The Iranian Cyber Threat, Revisited," statement before the Subcommittee on Cybersecurity, U.S. House of Representatives, March 20, 2013.

22. *Threats to U.S. Vital Interests, Iran, 2020*, Washington, D.C.:Heritage Foundation.

23. Christopher Bronk and Eneken Tikk-Ringas, "The Cyber Attack on Saudi Aramco," *Survival:Global Politics and Strategy*, April/May 2013.

24. Ellen Nakashima and Matt Zapotosky, "U.S. Charges Iran-Linked hackers with Targeting Banks," *The Washington Post*, March 24, 2016.

25. "Iranian Hackers Attack State Dept. via Social Media," *The New York Times*, Nov. 24, 2015.

26. Carl Stinebower, "Implications of the U.S. Withdrawal from the Joint Comprehensive Plan of Action and the Re-imposition of U.S. Sanctions on Iran," *International Trade Law*, May 14, 2018.

27. "FBI" Iran to Launch New Cyber Attacks. The National Strategy to Secure Cyberspace, Department of Homeland Security, Feb. 2003.

28. The National Strategy to Secure Cyberspace, Department of Homeland Security, Feb. 2003.

11 | Artificial Intelligence and the Future of Warfare

THIRTEEN DAYS PASSED in October 1962 while President Kennedy and his advisors perched at the edge of the nuclear abyss, pondering their response to the discovery of Russian missiles in Cuba. Today, a president may not have 13 minutes. Indeed, a president may not be involved at all.

"Artificial intelligence is the future, not only for Russia, but for all humankind. It comes with colossal opportunities but also threats that are difficult to predict. Whoever becomes the leader in this sphere will become the ruler of the world."[1]

This statement from Vladimir Putin, Russian president, comes at a time when artificial intelligence is already coming to the battlefield and some would say it is already here. Weapons systems driven by artificial intelligence algorithms will soon be making potentially deadly decisions on the battlefield. This transition is not theoretical. The immense capability of large numbers of autonomous systems represents a revolution in warfare that no country can ignore.

The Russian Military Industrial Committee has approved a plan that would have 30 percent of Russian combat power consist of remote controlled and autonomous robotic platforms by 2030. For example, Russia's new T-14 Armata tank has a completely automated turret, with the entire three-man crew in the heavily armored hull. It replaces a human ammunition loader with a mechanical one, allowing for a smaller turret. Smaller vehicles have advantages for mobility as well as for survivability. They are easier to transport to the battlefield by ship, plane, or rail.[2]

China has vowed to achieve AI dominance by 2030. It is already the second-largest R&D spender, accounting for 21 percent of the world's total of nearly $2 trillion in 2015. Only the United States at 26 percent ranks higher. If present growth rates continue, China will soon become the biggest spender. From 2000 to 2015, Chinese R&D outlays grew an average of 18 percent annually, more than four times faster than the U.S. rate of 4 percent. If China makes a breakthrough in crucial AI technology —

satellites, missiles, cyber-warfare or electromagnetic weapons — it could result in a major shift in the strategic balance. China has dramatically expanded its technical workforce. From 2000 to 2014, its annual number of science and engineering degrees grew from about 359,000 to 1.65 million. Over the same period the comparable number of U.S. graduate degree rose from about 483,000 to 742,000.[3]

Despite expressing concern on AI arms races, most of China's leadership sees increased military usage of AI as inevitable and is aggressively pursuing it. China already exports armed autonomous platforms and surveillance AI. At the Beijing Xiangshan Forum on October 24, 2018, Major General Ding Xiangrong, Deputy Director of the General Office of China's Central Military Commission, defined China's military goal as narrowing the gap between the Chinese military and global advanced powers by taking advantage of the ongoing military revolution centered on information technology and intelligent technology.[4]

Chinese military leaders increasingly refer to AI as their confident expectation for the future basis of warfare. Zeng Yi, a senior executive at China's third largest defense company, gave a speech in which he described China's expectations for the future implementation of AI weapons: He predicted that in future battlegrounds there will be no people fighting, and, by 2025, lethal autonomous weapons would be commonplace, and the ever-increasing military use of AI is inevitable. "In future wars, AI systems will be just like the brain."[5]

His comments are consistent with ongoing autonomous military vehicle development programs and China's current approach to exports of military unmanned systems. "China is already exporting many of its most advanced military aerial drones to Middle Eastern countries such as Saudi Arabia and the UAE. China's government has stated that it will export its next generation of stealth drones when they are available. Though many current drones are remotely operated, Chinese officials expect drones and military robotics to feature ever more extensive AI and autonomous capabilities in the future."[6]

Chinese weapons manufacturers are already selling armed drones with significant amounts of combat autonomy. Ziyan, a Chinese military drone manufacturer, has sold its Blowfish A2 model to the UAE and is reportedly in negotiations with Saudi Arabia and Pakistan for Blowfish Ziyan's website. The 38 kg Blowfish A2 performs complex combat missions, including fixed-point timing detection, fixed-range reconnaissance, and targeted precision strikes. Depending on customer preferences, Ziyan offers to equip Blowfish A2 with either missiles or machine guns.[7]

China's aerospace industry is developing tactical missiles with in-built intelligence that would seek targets in combat. This would allow its military commanders to launch missiles tailor-made for specific combat conditions. There is no question that AI's concept of future warfare has gained traction with all U.S. armed services. "Everything from submarines to satellites, tanks to jets, destroyers to drones, is being impacted by AI. The Army is developing autonomous vehicles that scout ahead of manned machines or provide supporting fire alongside them. These machines would be smart enough that a single human could supervise a whole pack of them. By replacing humans with electronics, combat vehicles will be more fuel-efficient, harder to hit, and cheaper to build and operate. With AI at the helm, a central command could launch a multi-pronged attack from land, air and water simultaneously without any humans at the warfront. All combat decisions, such as targets and how much to fire to minimize collateral damage, would be made by robots. It could come to humans just monitoring the battlefield situation while sitting away safely in a central command center taking corrective action as needed. AI vastly increases the speed at which tactical and even strategic decisions will be made."[8]

The rise in the use of unmanned aerial vehicles (UAVs) — commonly known as drones — in both military and commercial settings has been accompanied by a heated debate as to whether there should be an outright ban on what some label "killer robots." Such robots, which could be in the air, on the ground, or in and under water, theoretically incorporate AI that would make them capable of executing missions on their own. The debate concerns whether AI machines should be allowed to execute military missions, especially if there is a possibility that human life is at stake.[9]

To understand AI, it is important first to understand the difference between an automated and an autonomous system. An automated system is one in which a computer reasons by a rule-based system and the output will always be the same. An autonomous system (AI) is one that reasons probabilistically given a set of inputs, meaning it will produce a range of behavior. AI means the human faculties of judgment; feelings and belief may no longer be taken into consideration.

AI technologies are now widely used in tactical warfare situations, such as target acquisition for missiles launched from drones. But the actual command to fire the missile is reserved for the human operator. What might happen if the decision time is reduced from minutes to seconds, removing the human operator from the process entirely? And might that scenario be adopted by one of our less responsible adversaries? Or might it just happen accidentally — an accident far more plausible than ever before?

There is confusion between the theoretical definition of AI and its popular interpretation. Technically AI is any onboard intelligence that allows machines in combat to execute regular tasks, allowing humans more time to focus on demanding and complex missions. Modern-day combat requires warfighters to operate with the active assistance from sensors and systems. AI provides the technology to augment human analysis and decision-making by capturing knowledge that can be reapplied in critical situations. It is a technology that purports to change the human role from "in-the-loop" controller to "on-the-loop" thinker, who can focus on a more reflective assessment of problems and strategies, guiding rather than being buried in details of execution.[10]

It is probably clearer to regard AI as a term used for a combat system capable of making targeting decisions. "The launch of a missile from an enemy platform is an act of war. The decision to execute a missile launch is the exclusive right of the command team, which must independently assess the threat and act in pursuit of war objectives. Despite several advancements allowing for a more precise targeting of platforms, the logic of maritime operations has not fundamentally changed. As a result, U.S missiles have not been invested with any serious intelligence to make command decisions to target enemy units. Although their ability to strike targets has been radically enhanced — using superior onboard gyros, computing systems, and track radars — the basic mode of operation of cruise missiles has remained the same."[11]

U.S. Chief Technology Officer Michael Kratsios cited the use of AI by China and other adversaries in a way that is in dramatic conflict with Western values. He explained this was part of the reason the United States decided to join the Global Partnership on Artificial Intelligence — a pact led by G-7 countries focused on ensuring that technology serves democratic interests, not authoritarian ones.

"AI is considered indispensable in the development of hypersonic missiles. After China's recent high-speed extreme maneuvers, future combat missions will require a human-machine interface on an unprecedented scale, this is why four other Asian countries–Japan, India, South Korea, and Taiwan — have been developing supersonic and hypersonic systems. Each country has expressed aspirations for a sophisticated maritime force, with long-range sensors, armor protection, precision weapons, and networking technologies. Yet none has been developing missile systems with AI."[12]

On February 16, 2019, the U.S. Defense Department released its first AI strategy calling for the increased use of AI systems throughout the military, from decision-making to predicting problems in planes or ships. It urged the military to provide AI training to change its culture skills and approaches. It supports investment and partnership with education and industry in AI research. "It is paramount for our country to remain a leader in AI, and it will not only increase the prosperity of our nation, but also enhance our national security," Dana Deasy, DOD's chief information officer, said. "Increasing speed and agility is the central focus on the AI strategy."[13]

Congress may pump $100 billion into the National Science Foundation for research into artificial intelligence under a bipartisan proposal led by Senate Minority Leader Chuck Schumer and Sen. Todd Young. *The Endless Frontier Act* would rename the *National Science Foundation* as *The National Science and Technology Foundation* and add a technology directorate to oversee research and make contract awards in select technology areas. "We must remain mindful that Beijing's authoritarian leaders aim to capitalize on this moment with an eye toward outpacing the United States by investing in technological innovations essential to Americans' future safety and prosperity," Sen. Schumer said.[14]

Recently, a group of 116 leading AI experts wrote an open letter to ban AI's use for developing autonomous weapons. These experts are calling use of AI as the third revolution in warfare after gunpowder and nuclear weapons. Technology has always been an integral part of the defense sector. Precision-guided missiles unmanned and remotely controlled drones and many more such advancements are all testament to the military's readiness to leverage technology. With the emergence of AI, however, military weapons could add capabilities that will bring a paradigm shift in modern warfare.

Well-intentioned scientists have also called for rules that will always keep humans in the loop of the military use of AI. Elon Musk, founder of Tesla, has warned that AI could be humanity's greatest existential threat for starting a third world war. Musk warns that AI could decide that a pre-emptive strike is the most probable path to victory and once developed, lethal autonomous weapons will permit armed conflict to be fought at a scale greater than ever, and at times faster than humans can comprehend. These can be weapons of terror that despots and terrorists use against innocent populations and weapons hacked to behave in undesirable ways. Musk is one of 100 signatories calling for a UN-led ban of lethal autonomous weapons.[15]

As well intentioned as they may be, they forget that countries like China, Russia, North Korea, and Iran will use every form of AI if they have it. Preventing expanded military use of AI is almost impossible. AI has the potential to be on a par with nuclear weapons, aircraft, computers, and biotech. Advances in AI will accelerate the shift from manned to unmanned combat missions. The robotic systems that are possible will be capable enough to transform military power.

Recently Diane Greene, CEO of Google, announced that her company will not renew its contract to provide recognition software for U.S. military drones. Google had agreed to partner with the DOD in a program aimed at improving America's ability to win wars with computer algorithms and AI. The program, known as Project Mavern, would upgrade the military's ability to analyze drone footage. Greene withdrew from the program after more than 4,000 Google employees signed a letter demanding that the company back out of the contract. "We believe that Google should not be in the business of war," the letter stated.[16]

Some of these protestors include employees from other countries who are uncomfortable creating tools for the American military. Google's decision comes at a time when both China and Russia are developing new tools for artificial intelligence. What might happen if, in the interest or perceived necessity of reducing the decision time from minutes to seconds, the human operator was removed from the process entirely? And might that scenario be adopted by one of our less responsible adversaries? Or might it just happen accidentally — an accident far more plausible than ever before.

American technology was crucial to U.S. military success in World War II. It also kept the Soviet Union at bay during the Cold War and enabled the United States to deter untold armed conflicts over the past half-century. We can no longer take this technology leadership for granted. Companies like China, Russia, North Korea, and Iran are investing heavily in AI. We believe that the decision to take a human life should not be made without human direction. To assert a moral high ground, we must first hold the technological high ground.

"Terrorists are now using remotely controlled aerial drones in their military operations. Self-driving cars could make suicide car bombs more frequent, since they no longer require a suicidal driver. AI will dramatically augment autonomous weapons and espionage capabilities and will provide a key aspect of future military power. An example is the Long-Range Anti-Ship Missile (LRASM) guided by the Global Positioning System (GPS). It is jam resistant and can continue even if it loses contact with the GPS. As part of its AI targeting system, the missile can be set to fly to a series of way points, swerving around land features and commercial shipping, detecting threats between those waypoints and navigating around them. Should it decide it is entering the engagement range of an enemy ship not on its target list, it passes around the ship. After locating the enemy fleet, the LRASM dives to sea-skimming altitude to avoid close-in defenses, sizes up the fleet, locates its target, and calculates the exact spot the missile should aim for. These calculations almost ensure it does not miss. Such is the future of naval warfare in the era of AI. The LRASM replaces the venerable, 50-year-old Harpoon cruise missile, which has become standard weaponry for navies across the world and is now countered by myriad anti-missile defenses. The U.S. is not alone in developing LRASM type weaponry."[17]

SUMMARY

Chinese President Xi and Russian President Putin are right: A global leader in Artificial Intelligence will emerge, achieving enormous international clout and the power to dictate the rules governing AI. The world will be safer and more peaceful with strong U.S. leadership in AI. To employ AI effectively, we must:

- **Convince technological companies** such as Google that refusal to work with the U.S. military could have the opposite effect of what they intend. If technology companies want to promote peace, they should stand with, not against, the U.S. defense community.

- **Increase federal spending on basic research** that will help us compete with China, Russia, North Korea, and Iran in AI research.

- **Be aware that a Chinese breakthrough in AI technology** could affect a major shift in the strategic balance and possibly lead to war.

- **Reinvigorate America's own technological base** by overhauling immigration to favor high-skilled newcomers.

- **Guard against subversion of AI systems.** These systems are vulnerable to being "fooled." Vulnerabilities of networks include model stealing and data poisoning. Until these attacks are understood and defended against, we should avoid applications that are exposed to input from adversaries.

- **Be constantly alert to the advantages of attackers** over defenders in the current balance of power in AI applications. Until that changes, AI applications will necessarily be running on insecure platforms, and this will remain a grave concern for command, control, and intelligence, as well as autonomous and partially autonomous weapons.

- **Remain ever alert to the serious risk of accidental conflict,** or accidental escalation of conflict, in the military applications of machine learning or algorithmic automation. Ignorant or unintended use of AI is understandably feared as a major potential cause of a dreaded accidental war.

NOTES

1. James Vincent, "Putin says the nation that leads in AI 'will be the ruler of the world,'" *The Verge*, Sep. 4, 2017.

2. Jeremy Bender, "These Are the Plans for Russia's New 3rd Generation Tank," *Business Insider*, March 30, 2015.

3. "Lists of Countries by Research and Development Spending," *World Bank*, 2015.

4. Gregory C. Allen, Understanding China's AI Strategy, *Center for a New American Security*, Feb. 6, 2019.

5. John Lockdett, "China Unveils Terrifying New Armoured Truck Which Launches Swarms of Killer Drones to Attack its Enemies," *The Sun*, May 17, 2019.

6. *Assessing Threats to U.S. Vital Interests – AI*, Washington, D.C.: Heritage Foundation, Oct. 30, 2019.

7. "Weirdly Shaped Chinese Attack Drone Revealed at LIMA-2019," *Defense World. net*, April 5, 2019.

8. *2020 Index of Military Strength*, Washington, D.C.: Heritage Foundation.

9. "Should Artificial Intelligence Be Regulated?," *Amitai, Issues in Science and Technology*, Summer, 2017.

10. Ville Hulkko, "Most Value from AI with Human-In-The-Loop Solutions," SILOAI, Dec. 17, 2018.

11. *Assessing Threats to US. Vital Interests – AI*, Washington, D.C.: Heritage Foundation, Oct. 30, 2019.

12. Brooke Singman, "US Technology Chief Warns China 'Twisting' Artificial Intelligence, *Fox News*, May 30, 2020.

13. *Threats to U.S. Vital Interests, China*, 2020, Washington, D.C.: Heritage Foundation.

14. Terri Moon, "DOD Unveils Its Artificial Intelligence Strategy," *Defense*, Feb. 16, 2019.

15. Joe Gould, "Congress May Unite on Fighting China With 100B Tech Industry Boost," *Defense News*, May 31, 2020.

16. Samuel Gibbs, "Elton Musk Leads 116 Experts Calling for Outright Ban Of Killer Robots," *The Guardian*, Aug. 20, 2017.

17. Brandon Specktor, "Google Will End Its 'Evil' Partnership with the US Military, But Not Until 2019," *Live Science*, June 4, 2018. LRASM: Long-range anti-surface cruise missile, Lockheed Martin, December 2018

12 | The Threat of an Electromagnetic Pulse Attack

AN ELECTROMAGNETIC PULSE ATTACK (EMP: a high-density electrical field attack) would fry the Pentagon's electronics, leaving the U.S. military unable to retaliate. Imagine a city, county, or state without power. No communications of any kind — not a landline, mobile, nor Internet. Hospitals would have no power — main or emergency. The safety of the water supply would rapidly deteriorate. There would be little to no access to money. ATMs wouldn't function, and banks would close out of security concerns. Food shortages would develop, followed by rioting and civil unrest.

Experts predict ninety percent of all Americans would die a year after an EMP event. Though an EMP is not directly harmful to people, it could lead to deaths by shutting down hospitals, transportation, communication, banking, finance, and food and water systems. In the worst possible scenario, a large-scale EMP could have effects like Hurricane Katrina, but on a national scale.[1]

The first EMP component of the detonation occurs within a few billionths of a second of detonation and produces a very brief but intense electromagnetic field that can induce very high voltages in electrical conductors. E1 has the power to disrupt or damage micro-electronic systems, electronics-based control systems, sensors, communication systems, protective systems, computers and similar devices. Individual items such as cars and trucks could also be damaged or disabled and damage could occur to electronic devices in homes and businesses. An attack could cut power to health care facilities and cripple municipal facilities and utilities.

Then comes E2, covering roughly the same geographic area as E1. This would not be an issue for critical infrastructure systems since they have existing protective measures for defense against lightning strikes. The most significant risk derives from the fact that it follows a fraction of a second after E1, which may have already impaired or destroyed protective and control features. The energy associated with E2 therefore may be allowed to pass into and damage systems.

Forty-two years after Starfish Prime, in 2004, the first time the United States tested an EMP weapon, Congress held hearings to try to figure out how to defend against the EMP threat.[3] The commission reported that several nations, including reported sponsors of terrorism, might currently have the capability to use EMP as a weapon to disrupt communications and other parts of the U.S. critical infrastructure. It was also reported that some equipment and weapons used by the U.S. military might be vulnerable to the effects of EMP. "The threat of an EMP attack against the United States is hard to assess," the report continued, "but some observers indicate that it is growing along with worldwide access to newer technologies and the proliferation of nuclear weapons."[4]

The Commission worried that, while in the past, the threat of mutually assured destruction had provided a lasting deterrent against the exchange of multiple high-yield nuclear warheads, now even a single, low-yield nuclear explosion high above the U.S., or over a battlefield, could produce a large-scale EMP effect that could result in a widespread loss of electronics, but no direct fatalities, and may not necessarily evoke a large nuclear retaliatory strike by the U.S. military.[5]

The Commission acknowledged that the widely understood vulnerability of U.S. critical infrastructure control systems to the effects of EMP might create a new incentive for other countries to rapidly develop or acquire a nuclear capability. Policy issues raised by this threat could include what the U.S. is doing to protect civilian critical infrastructure systems against the threat of EMP, whether the U.S. military would be affected if an EMP attack directed against U.S. civilian infrastructure, whether other nations would be encouraged by U.S. vulnerabilities to develop or acquire nuclear weapons, and how likely are terrorist organizations would be to launch a smaller-scale EMP attack against the U.S. This report would be updated as events warrant, the Commission promised. But 13 years later no update had been issued.[6]

The effects of EMP will immediately disable a portion of the 130 million cars and some 90 million trucks. Since millions of vehicles are on the road at any given time, there will be accidents and congestion that will impede movement, particularly in large metropolitan areas. Stoplights and train crossing signals will shut down or malfunction. The longer-term effects on the automobile and trucking infrastructure will hinge on the ability to obtain fuel and the recovery of commercial power. Police may be needed to replace automated traffic controls at the same time that they are critically needed for other emergency services.[7]

We can no longer assume that that America is safe from an EMP attack due to the doctrine of mutually assured destruction. For instance, Iran could undertake the attack for religious reasons. North Korea could give a nuclear bomb to terrorists. China could coerce North Korea into attacking and then deny all responsibility. If an EMP attack was launched from a ship off the coast of the United States, and the ship was registered in Liberia and crewed by Hezbollah terrorists from Lebanon, assigning blame would be no easy matter.[8]

There is no reason why America cannot take steps now to protect the American grid. It would only take two or three billion dollars to protect the core components, which are difficult to replace. The U.S. cannot continue to ignore the EMP threat. While some progress has been made in hardening potential U.S. targets against attack, including critical military and government systems, the vast majority of electrical systems are unshielded and unprotected, especially in the civilian sector. If properly shielded, electrical devices and systems can generally survive even the strongest EMP attacks.[9]

Recommendations

Here are recommendations from James Carafano and Richard Weitz of the Heritage Foundation:

- **Perform More Research on the Threat.** Further research is needed in order to ensure that we can respond to the EMP threat appropriately without flimsy or useless security measures. We must gain knowledge of the capabilities of EMP and understand the amount of money, time and effort that will be required for meaningful prevention.

- **Build a Comprehensive Missile Defense System.** The most likely method of EMP attack would be a ballistic missile armed with a nuclear warhead. Such a system would allow the U.S. to intercept and destroy a missile. The implementation of such a system would go a long way to prevent an attack.

- **Incorporate EMP Attacks into National Planning Scenarios.** The National Planning Scenarios are 15 all-hazards planning scenarios used by federal, state and local officials in disaster response exercises. EMP should be added to the mix.

- **Develop a National Recovery Plan.** The U.S. must identify the key power grid and telecommunications infrastructure that is critical to preserving our nation's core capabilities and create a National Recovery Plan. This risk-based approach recognizes that certain infrastructure is key to recovery after an EMP attack. By taking measures to protect the infrastructure, we can lessen the recovery time from an attack.

138

- **As individuals, we should also be preparing at the family level.** Ensure that our families know and can recognize the signs of an EMP event. Storing emergency supplies including food, water, a first-aid kit and manual and medications. The average U.S. city has only 3 days' worth of food and health care provisions. Most Americans don't have enough batteries to keep flashlights working for any period. Only a few have generator capabilities.

- **Educating ourselves and raising the awareness** of the EMP threat in our communities. We should be finding out how an EMP event would affect our local infrastructure by questioning local industries and utilities. Raise questions about the hazards of both natural and man-made EMP events.

- **Finding out whether our states have an EMP emergency response plans** and working to develop them if they don't.

Many states have established commissions that analyze the danger of EMPs and develop plans to protect citizens, respond to the aftermath, and recover after the event. A nuclear detonation in space is not the only danger. Our knowledge of the electromagnetic spectrum is becoming so sophisticated that we know that our adversaries can design tactical electromagnetic weapons that can target very tactical and specific things. Electronic attacks can be as simple as you zapping somebody's computer, or a base, or a local area. The advanced arms can also be a very discriminating weapon that has no attribution, meaning you wouldn't know who did it."[10]

President Trump has taken steps to protect electric grids and other life-sustaining critical infrastructures in his new National Security Strategy. Congress also passed the Critical Infrastructure Protection Act, which codifies criminal penalties for a person convicted of willfully trespassing or entering property containing a critical infrastructure facility without permission by the owner of the property and holds a person liable for any damages to personal or real property while trespassing.[11]

SUMMARY

On March 26, 2019, President Trump signed the first of its kind executive order calling for a government-wide war on EMP and the types of electromagnetic pulses that can wipe out every computer, electric grid, and jet.[12]

In joining the voices of those warning of EMP attacks, Trump called on his government to quickly generate a plan to detect EMP, protect critical infrastructure like water and electric sources, and also to recover if a hit lands.

"It is the policy of the United States to prepare for the effects of EMPs through targeted approaches that coordinate whole-of-government activities and encourage private-sector engagement," said the executive order released by the White House.[13]

"The federal government must

- **Provide warning** of an impending EMP;

- **Protect against, respond to, and recover** from the effects of an EMP through public and private engagement, planning, and investment; and

- **Prevent adversarial events** through deterrence, defense, and nuclear nonproliferation efforts.

- **To achieve these goals,** the federal government will engage in risk-informed planning, prioritize research and development (R&D) to address the needs of critical infrastructure stakeholders, and, for adversarial threats, consult Intelligence Community assessments."[14]

NOTES

1. David T. Pyne, "The Threat of EMP Attack Is Very Real," *The National Interest*, Dec. 15, 2019.

2. James Carafano and Richard Weitz, *EMP Attacks – What the U.S. Must Do Now*, The Heritage Foundation, Nov. 17, 2010.

3. Phil Platt, "The 50th Anniversary of Starfish Prime: The Nuke That Shook the World," *Discover*, July 9, 2012.

4. *Report of the Commission to Assess the Threat to the United States from an EMP Attack*, The Graham Commission, Vol. 1, 2004.

5. David T. Pyne, "The Threat of EMP Attack Is Very Real," *The National Interest*, Dec. 15, 2019.

6. *Report of the Commission to Assess the Threat to the United States from EMP Attack*, Nov. 8, 2010.

7. Jerry Emanuelson, "EMP Effects on Vehicles," *Futurescience*, Nov. 4, 2017.

8. "EMP Threat: How Likely Is an EMP Attack," *Tech Protect*, Oct. 29, 2019.

9. *Worldwide Threat Assessment of the U.S. Intelligence Community 2020*, Washington, D.C.: Heritage Foundation.

10. James Carafano and Richard Weitz, EMP Attacks – What the U.S. Must Do Now, The Heritage Foundation, Nov. 17, 2010.

11. Critical Infrastructure Protection Act, American Legislative Exchange Center (ALEC), Dec. 7, 2017.

12. *Worldwide Threat Assessment of the U.S. Intelligence Community 2020*, Washington, D.C.: Heritage Foundation.

13. "Trump Issued an Executive Order to Prepare for an EMP Attack," *Washington Post*, May 29, 2019.

14. Ariel Cohen,"Trump Moves to Protect America From Electromagnetic Pulse Attack," *Forbes*, March 27, 2019.

13 | China's Military Sends Undercover 'Students' to Western Universities to Steal Technology

NOT ALL CHINESE THEFT of military and scientific information comes through computer hacking or internal leaks. Universities in the United States, United Kingdom, Australia, and other countries may have been unknowingly collaborating with China's military. That's according to a study by Canberra-based think tank Australian Policy Institute (ASPI), which found that dozens of scientists and engineers linked to China's People's Liberation Army had obscured their military connections when applying to study overseas. About 2,500 PLA-sponsored military scientists have gone abroad since 2007, according to ASPI. Such collaborations are encouraged by cash-strapped foreign universities, some of which have increasingly turned to China for scientific funding.[1]

In January 2015 Hu Xianoziang was expelled from Norway. The Chinese scientist wore out his welcome in the Scandinavian country when officials at the University of Adner discovered that, besides his affiliation with the academic Xi'an Research Institute, there was a large body of evidence tying Hu to the Rocket Force Engineering University (RFEU) a Chinese military organization. They also realized that his work at Adner could be used to develop hypersonic cruise missiles.[2]

In a strategy described by the PLA as "picking flowers in foreign lands to make honey in China," the Chinese military deliberately obscures the connections of those it sends to study overseas, which are different from transparent military-to-military exchanges that also take place between China and other countries.[3] The five papers he wrote while at the university focused on air-breathing hypersonic vehicles, which travel at over five times the speed of sound and can carry more payload than ordinary flight vehicles. His work was supported by a Norwegian Government grant for offshore wind energy research.

Hu won an award for his Ph.D. thesis on hypersonic aircraft, supervised by PLA General Hu Changhua. The website also says that in 2014 he received 250,000 renminbi ($50,000) from the Chinese Government for a three-year research project on hypersonic aircraft. In 2016, he was described as a lecturer at the center, which received 14 awards for missile research between 2010 and 2014. Huang also listed the Harbin Institute of Technology, a civilian university in China engaged in military research.

A year after his expulsion Norway, Huang Xianjun was in the United Kingdom completing his Ph.D. at the University of Manchester, where he had been working with the discoverers of graphene, a material with extraordinary strength, electrical conductivity and flexibility. Huang then returned to China to work on key projects for the PLA.

Graphene has been described by the European Defense Agency as a material with enormous potential for revolutionizing military equipment. The substance is light and flexible but 200 times stronger than steel, and its electrical and thermal conductivity is extraordinary. It can be used to produce radar-absorbent coatings that make military vehicles, planes, submarines or ships almost undetectable.[4] Huang could have stayed in the United Kingdom or elsewhere in the West. He got generous job offers from industry, and the University of Manchester urged him to stay on as a researcher. But almost immediately after receiving his Ph.D., he returned to China where he is now a researcher at the PLA's National University of Defense Technology (NUDT), the agency that originally sent him to the United Kingdom.

There was nothing particularly unusual about Hu Xianoziang or Huang Xianjun. The United States, the United Kingdom, Canada, Australia, and Germany are, in that order, the top countries for research collaboration with the PLA. Globally, the number of peer-reviewed articles published as part of this collaboration has grown seven-fold in a decade. Over the decade before 2015, Beijing had used a covert agenda to strengthen its military by sending scientists to study at colleges and universities around the world, posing a risk to the West's strategic advantages, according to the Australian Strategic Policy Institute (ASPI), an independent think tank partially funded by Australia's Department of Defense.[5]

In October 2018, the ASPI issued a report detailing Beijing's scheme to send scientists with ties to the People's Liberation Army (PLA) abroad, mostly to the "Five Eyes" alliance countries– Australia, Canada, New Zealand, United Kingdom, and the United States — as well as Singapore, Germany, and Norway. The report estimated that since 2007, more than 2,500 Chinese military scientists and engineers have traveled abroad, often masking their military ties. Scientists would use the common name of a Chinese military institute when disclosing their academic affiliations instead of the formal name (i.e., the National University of Defense Technology, a military academy which would be referred to as Changsha Institute of Technology). They also used names of non-existent research institutions as their cover. They created LinkedIn profiles listed with their fake academic affiliations in order to establish a credible cover. They also claimed affiliation with real civilian institutions in the same regions as their military units.[6]

"Unlike in standard military exchanges, PLA scientists have very little or no interaction with military officials in their host countries. About half of the 2,500 PLA scientists are Ph.D. scholars, going abroad to complete their doctoral degrees, or spending up to two years overseas as visiting scholars. Typically, they study in fields with military applications, such as hypersonic missiles, navigation technology, quantum physics, signal processing, and cryptography at overseas campuses. Other Chinese schools sending scientists include the Army Engineering University in Nanjing City, Northwestern Institute of Nuclear Technology, the RFEU in Shaanxi Province, the Navy Submarine Academy in Qingdao, the Armored Forces Engineering Academy and Chemical Defense Institute of the Academy of Military Sciences in Beijing."[7]

Several of the best known Chinese military scientists from the RFEU spent time studying overseas, including Major General Hu Changhua, who heads the REFU's missile testing and simulation center.[8] He attended Germany's University of Duisburg–Essen for four months in 2008. RFEU scientists Zhou Zhijie and Wang Zhaoqiang claimed to be from the nonexistent Xi'an Research Institute when they were visiting scholars at universities in England. Similarly, Zhu Yijun, an associate professor at China's PLA Information Engineering University, claimed to be from the Zhengzhou Information Science and Technology Institute when he studied wireless communications technology with wide-ranging military applications at Canada's McMaster University.[9]

For universities that decided to collaborate with Chinese military scientists on scientific research, the report warned of many risks and costs, including Chinese military scientists who are unlikely to share any major breakthroughs of military value with their foreign colleagues. The report provided several suggestions such as improving the scrutiny of visa applications so that military scientists are identified and properly vetted. It also suggested that regulations should be put in place to limit the scientific training that foreign military personnel can receive while studying abroad.

Not surprisingly, the assessment of the costs and benefits of research collaboration with the PLA shows that it comes with significant security risks while offering unclear benefits. It was pointed out, for example, that helping build the capabilities of a rival military would not be in the national interest for any of the countries. The ASPI stressed that a number of benefits usually associated with research collaboration with militaries and foreign countries have not been observed in PLA collaboration. While overseas, PLA scientists remain under the close watch of the CCP, which works to ensure that they remain loyal and are not influenced by their experience living in free societies. PLA scientists often engage in deception in their interactions with foreign institutions and their staff, making it difficult for those collaborating with them to take appropriate security precautions.[10]

Not all leaks of sensitive military information are the result of cyber activities from China, Russia, North Korea or Iran. A former National Security Agency contractor, Harold Martin, convicted of stealing the largest collection of government secrets in U.S. history, received a nine-year sentence. Martin was found guilty of 20 counts of unauthorized and willful retention of national defense information in 2017. A former Navy officer, Martin worked in a supporting role for multiple intelligence agencies — including the National Space Agency and the Office of the Director of National Intelligence — during his employment at several different federal consulting firms.

Investigators found that Martin removed a staggering amount of sensitive material, including documents, removable media and computer files about internal NSA policy and cyber-operations, from various classified environments. More than 50 terabytes of material, some marked "Top Secret," were recovered as part of the investigation.[11]

Criminal referrals for leaks of sensitive government Information have surged. The uptick in leak cases doesn't necessarily mean more leaks are happening today than before, but it does shine a light on the reality of the Justice Department's battle to enforce criminal prosecutions against leaks. The figures obtained by the Federation of American Scientists only reveal leaks of classified information subject to criminal prosecution, not leaks that weren't referred for criminal prosecution, and which may have been handled administratively. The figures also don't break down the leaks by agency.[12]

In 2010, Jeffrey Sterling, another former CIA operations officer, shared information about "Operation Merlin," a covert operation under the Clinton Administration against Iran's nuclear program. He spent three years in prison.[13]

Chelsea Manning, who leaked 750,000 classified and sensitive documents, pled guilty to 10 charges and was convicted at trial of a total of 17 charges, and sentenced to 35 years in prison. She served just 7 years before President Obama commuted her sentence.[14]

Manning is a rare example of a leaks case that actually went to trial. Few cases do. Most are resolved through plea arrangements. Whether that's due to the government's desire to preserve secrecy or the need for expediency, plea deals, not extended court battles, are the norm. The number of criminal prosecutions for leakers only scratches the surface of those who disclose government secrets, however. Some hide under the umbrella of whistleblowing; in other cases, the government is just uninterested or perhaps unable to move the case to prosecution. When it comes to whistleblower cases, it's important to remember that, just as there are official protections for whistleblowers under the law, there are also procedures for properly reporting information. Revealing classified or sensitive information to anyone without a clearance or the authorization to receive it is not whistleblowing — it's leaking.

"Disclosing classified information without authorization is a crime even if the leaker had good intention and was motivated by a larger public interest. Evidence of the defendant's views of military and intelligence procedures would needlessly distract the jury from the question of whether he had illegally retaining and transmitted classified documents and instead convert the trial into an inquest of U.S. military and intelligence procedures."[15]

The case of Julian Assange, Wikileaks founder, put the contrast between leaks and whistleblowing in the spotlight. After Ecuador withdrew Assange's asylum in 2019, British authorities arrested him, and the U.S. government unsealed an indictment. The charges don't directly relate to the classified information published by Wikileaks, but rather Assange's alleged conspiracy to bypass protocols in the Secret Internet Protocol Router Network, better known as the SIPRNET.[16]

"On or about March 8, 2010, Assange agreed to assist Manning in cracking a password stored on Department of Defense computers connected to the [SIPRNet]," the indictment alleges. The decision not to prosecute Assange for espionage related to the leaking of classified information highlights how difficult enforcing those charges can be. Despite the ramifications of leaking classified information, securing criminal convictions remains rare, even as the number of cases being criminally prosecuted increases.[17]

SUMMARY

Helping a rival military develop its expertise and technology isn't in the national interest, yet it's not clear that Western universities and governments are fully aware of this phenomenon. Some universities have failed to respond to legitimate security concerns in their engagement with China. Current policies by governments and universities have not fully addressed issues like the transfer of knowledge and technology through collaboration with the PLA. Clear government policies toward universities working with the PLA is lacking. We need to explore a wider range of tools for limiting technology transfer, including better scrutiny of visa applications by Chinese military scientists and further legislation targeting military end users. We should also consider increasing funding to strategic science and technology fields while actively limiting problematic foreign investment in those fields. Universities must recognize the risks of such collaboration and try to learn the extent and nature of their collaboration with the PLA by actively working with government and security professionals.[18]

"The Foreign Intelligence Surveillance Act (FISA) is a critical national security authority that has kept us safe from terrorist attacks for the past two decades. Maintaining the core authorities, it provides is critical to the security of our national and its people. Congress should not adopt amendments that would fundamentally undermine those authorities. We believe that is it unconscionable and a very threat to the daily lives of all Americans that we are currently operating under authorities that date back to before the terrorist attacks of Sep. 11, 2001. Making changes that have little real benefit fort the American public is unwise."[19]

Here are six steps recommended by the Australian Strategic Policy Institute:

- **"Determine what kinds of collaboration** with the PLA should be further controlled or even prohibited and establish clear policy on engagement with PA research organizations and personnel.

- **Foster international discussions** on PLA collaboration to develop multilateral responses.

- **Picking flowers, making honey.** Check on the status of all Chinese students.

- **Develop interagency responses** to PLA collaboration to ensure better integration of efforts by defense and export control agencies, intelligence agencies and immigration agencies.

- **Share information about cases and trends** in PLA collaboration, particularly cases of deception by PLA scientists, with partners across the glove.

- **Create a list of Chinese and other non-allied military** and military-linked research institutions, including civilian universities heavily engaged in military research, for use by immigration officials."[19]

NOTES

1. John Morgan, "Western Universities Urged to Rethink Chinese Military Ties," *The World University Standings*, Nov. 8, 2018.

2. Echo Huang, "Foreign Universities Are Unwittingly Collaborating with Chinese Military Scientists, *The Diplomat*, Oct. 29, 2018.

3. Alex Joske, "Picking Flowers, Making Honey," *ASPI*, Oct. 30, 2018.

4. "The Ultimate Gide to Graphene's Potential Applications for 2019," *nanografi*, April 1, 2020.

5. Alex Joske, "The Chinese Military's Collaboration with Foreign Universities, *ASPI*, Oct. 30, 2018.

6. Christina Masa, "China's Military Sends Undercover 'Students' to Western Universities to Steal Technology, Research Reveals," *Newsweek*, Nov. 11, 2018.

7. *Assessing the Global Operating Environment*, Washington, D.C.: Heritage Foundation, Oct. 30, 2019.

8. Changhua Hu, *Biography*, IEEE Xplore, 2020.

9. Steven Aftergood, "Leakers May Be Worse Than Spies, Gov't Says," *Federation of American Scientists*, Oct. 3, 2019.

10. Echo Huang, "Foreign Universities Are Unwittingly Collaborating with Chinese Military Scientists," *The Diplomat*, Oct. 29, 2018.

11. Merrit Kennedy, "Ex-NSA Contractor Who Stole Top Secret Documents Is Sentenced to 9 Years in Prison," *NPR*, July 19, 2019,

12. "CIA officer Jeffrey Sterling Sentenced to Prison," *The Nation*, May 12, 2015.

13. Bill Chappell, "Chelsea Manning, Once Sentenced to 35 Years, walks Free After 7," *NPR*, May 17, 2017.

14. Steve Aftergood, "A Leaker's Motives Are Irrelevant, Government Says," *Federation of American Scientists*, Oct. 3, 2019.

15. Kevin Breuniger, "US charges WikiLeaks Co-Founder Julian Assange with Conspiracy to Commit Computer Hacking," *CNBC*, April 11, 2019.

16. "US Indictment against WikiLeaks Founder Julian Assange," *CNN*, April 11, 2019.

17. Alex Marquardt, "US Intelligence Warns China Is Using Student Spies to Steal Secrets," Zachary Cohen and Alex Marquardt, *CNN*, Feb. 1. 2019.

18. Zachary Cohen and Alex Marquardt, "US Intelligence Warns China Is Using Student Spies to Steal Secrets," *CNN*, Feb. 1. 2019.

19. "What's the Solution?" *Australian Strategic Policy Institute*, Oct. 30, 2019.

CHINA'S MULTIBILLION-DOLLAR ONE BELT, ONE ROAD INITIATIVE (BRI) has been called a state-backed campaign for global dominance. Since Chinese President Xi Jin Ping introduced BRI in October 2013, China has poured nearly $700 billion worth of Chinese money into more than 60 countries, much in the form of infrastructure projects and loans to governments with shaky credit. The idea was to draw those countries closer to Beijing, while boosting Chinese soft power abroad.[1]

Beijing insists the BRI is intended to increase global integration and boost growth, but some analysts question China's motivations, particularly those behind its investments in ports. During the first half of 2017 alone, Chinese companies announced plans to buy or invest in nine overseas ports, five of which are in the Indian Ocean. Those critical of the BRI typically argue that while some economic factors may be at play, these investments are driven primarily by strategic objectives. At the heart of this critique is a concern that China will use ports associated with the BRI to service military assets deployed to the region in support of China's growing security interests. These concerns have focused on several port projects, including those in Gwadar, Pakistan; Hambantota, Sri Lanka; Kyaukpyu, Myanmar; and Israel.[2]

The BRI Initiative consists of infrastructure projects connecting China to countries around the globe. It has two main strands. The first is the Silk Road Economic Belt, a series of overland corridors connecting China with Europe via Central Asia and the Middle East. The second is the Twenty-First Century Maritime Silk Road, a sea route linking China's southern coast to East Africa and the Mediterranean. The costs involved are dizzying. By some estimates, China plans to pump $159 billion into such projects each year. A report released in 2018, shows that a remarkable $900 billion in projects are already planned and underway. Yet, for all the fanfare, the Belt and Road Initiative has proved difficult to conclusively define.[3]

"President Xi Jinping's 'Chine Dream' is about making China great again, which is not so different from what President Trump is talking about in the United States, or Prime Minister Modi in India today. It's the idea that China used to be the great civilization-state in Asia, and that China should launch a 'Great Rejuvenation.'"[4]

Some experts have suggested that "Belt and Road" is more of a slogan than a policy, encompassing all Chinese investment overseas. Unlike Western lenders, China does not require its partners to meet stringent conditions related to corruption, human rights, or financial responsibility. This approach has fueled corruption and piled loans on countries that cannot afford to repay them. Countries that received these loans are now reacting in anger to the politicians who accepted Chinese loans. Disgruntled citizens have voted many of them out of office

"In Malaysia's election in May 2018, Mahathir Mohamad defeated incumbent Prime Minister Najib Razak by campaigning against Chinese influence. Raznak had approved expensive infrastructure projects that required considerable borrowing from China. Mohamad cancelled two of the largest Chinese projects in Malaysia — a $20 billion railroad and a $2.3 billion natural gas pipeline. Instead of expanding Chinese soft power, Belt and Road appears to be achieving the opposite. The deal's collapse adds urgency to a debate already growing in Beijing about the potentially $1 trillion program, the main engine of Xi's effort to convert China's economic might into global influence."[5]

In recent months, countries across Asia have suspended, scaled back, or terminated projects amid concerns over corruption, influence peddling and rising debt. Countries have become wiser to the financial terms associated with Chinese loans. Originally thought to be low-cost money, China often charges higher rates than traditional lenders. Critics also have concerns about China's role as an investment partner. China has demonstrated that it expects to be repaid on time or it will take punitive measures.[6]

Recently, China's official news agency Xinhua described the Belt and Road Initiative as "a Chinese solution to global economic blues." Meanwhile, commentators have expressed concern about "debt trap diplomacy," suggesting that China's generous loans are illustrative not of largesse but instead of imperialist ambitions.[7]

Some nations that find themselves unable to pay back loans agree. In December 2017, struggling to make repayments, the Sri Lankan government agreed to lease the port and 1,500 acres of surrounding land to China, for 99 years. The lease of the port to China prompted alarm both inside Sri Lanka and internationally. Within the country, it angered locals, who fear that Sri Lanka is caught in a debt trap and will be forced to lease more assets in the future. Internationally, it alarmed policy makers who suspect that China has gained a strategic hold in the Indian Ocean along an important commercial and military waterway.[8]

The port opened in 2010 with China funding 85 percent of the estimated $361 price tag (all dollars in U.S. currency). Predictably, the port was a failure. Although it is next to one of the world's busiest shipping lanes, Hambantota drew only 34 of the tens of thousands of ships that passed by in 2012. Hambantota was one of many Chinese investments in Sri Lanka. In the rush of development that followed the end of the civil war in 2009, Rajapaksa borrowed $8 billion from China to fuel a series of ambitious infrastructure projects, with varying levels of success. Large-scale Chinese funding is not unique to Sri Lanka. Beijing's interests in Bangladesh are estimated to be $35 billion.[9]

China has funded more than 20 projects in the Maldives, with the largest three projects alone worth nearly 40 percent of Maldivian GDP. The China-Pakistan Economic Corridor is a $62 billion network of motorways, railways, and power plants that will link China's Xinjiang region to Gwadar Port in southern Pakistan. Pakistani politicians claim it will create up to one million jobs. Other major infrastructure projects include a high-speed rail link in Indonesia and a massive industrial park in Cambodia.[10]

There is some anxiety — particularly in India — that the scale of Sri Lanka's debt crisis could lead to further concessions, such as letting China use Hambantota as a military base. It is a widespread theory that China is deliberately trapping countries in debt in order to gain concessions and military advantage. The first major opponent of China's Belt and Road Initiative, India, continues to oppose China's grand infrastructure initiative. China has significantly expanded its economic, political, and military footprint in the Indian Ocean and South Asia. It has made landmark investments in Nepal, Sri Lanka, and the Maldives.[11]

The PLA Navy makes regular conventional and nuclear submarine patrols in the Indian Ocean, complementing the anti-piracy naval task force it regularly rotates through the Indian Ocean. China opened a military base in Djibouti in 2017 and has expressed interest in building a naval base in Pakistan, near the Chinese-operated Gwadar port. When China acquires ports, it does so under the guise of maintaining a trade route from the Indian Ocean via the Suez Canal to Europe, such as the port of Piraeus in Greece.

A recent study by the Center for Strategic & International Studies (CSIS) Global Development found that the risk of debt distress is rising in 23 countries with Belt and Road funding. Eight of these countries — Pakistan, Djibouti, the Maldives, Laos, Mongolia, Montenegro, Tajikistan, and Kyrgyzstan — already have unsustainable levels of sovereign debt. This means poor returns on loans for China, as well as potentially disastrous economic outcomes for the countries involved. The affected nations are among the poorest in their respective regions and will soon owe more than half of all their foreign debt to China.[12]

China has an excess capacity in key industries such as steel, and Belt and Road projects allow it to export expertise, manpower, factories, and machinery. Most Belt and Road Initiative projects involve Chinese engineers being flown in to carry out the work. The investment creates new economic markets for Chinese industry. Chinese firms are engaging in construction work around the world on an unparalleled scale: to date, Chinese companies have secured more than $340 billion in construction contracts along the Belt and Road.

"Although the underlying aims of the Belt and Road Initiative are disputed, it is clear that China's seemingly endless loans do not come without strings attached. Around the world, including countries that were previously extremely enthusiastic, a pushback has begun. Malaysia, a big recipient of Belt and Road Initiative investments, cancelled about $3 billion-worth of pipeline projects this year. Kuala Lumpur had already suspended another $20 billion in Belt and Road schemes. Pakistan is in a payment crisis, in part brought on by the scale of its borrowing from China. In October 2018, Pakistan asked the International Monetary Fund for a bailout. A spokesperson for the US State Department said the request would be closely examined, as "part of the reason that Pakistan found itself in this situation is Chinese debt."[13]

Despite the widespread payment hardship felt by the Belt and Road countries, governments — even those already struggling with debt crises — continue to turn to China. Sri Lanka, which owes its debt crisis in no small part to its borrowing for Belt and Road infrastructure projects, is asking China for a further $1.25 billion in funds to finance its liabilities. Pakistan, too, is seeking loans worth somewhere between $1 billion and $2 billion from China to help alleviate its economic crisis. Notably, this ramping up of Chinese funding for Pakistan comes as the United States cuts aid to its occasional ally. The United States has led efforts to have some Pakistani interests placed on the global terror-financing watch list, which could have serious economic ramifications.[14]

Not all countries that have fallen prey to China's debt-trap initiative are impoverished. Israel ranks as the second lowest investment risk on the Economist Intelligence Unit risk index, making investment in the market highly attractive for China. Massive developments of energy resources in the Eastern Mediterranean, new ports coming online on its Mediterranean shores, new trade routes between Israel and its Arab neighbors, and growing alliances between Israel, Cyprus, and Greece make it a highly attractive market for China.[15]

Israel's population is expected to double its size over the next 30 years.

It will require an investment of over $200 billion to meet the needs of its population's real estate, transportation, energy, telecommunications, and other infrastructure needs. Its new ports and trade routes to the Arab world will make it significant as an overland gateway to Europe for the Middle East. Its current energy funds and future potential funds will require major infrastructure investments to allow for their full commercialization. An estimated $15 billion in Chinese investments have poured into Israel, from 2011 to 2018.

One Chinese company (China Harbor) is building a new port in Ashdod, while another — Shanghai International Port Group — won a 25-year concession to operate a new port in Haifa. The Chinese company won the bid to expand the Haifa Port four years ago. The project is slated to start in 2021 and calls for the Chinese company to run the Haifa Port for 25 years. Another Chinese firm won the bid to build a new port in Ashdod.[16]

It seems no one involved in the security or diplomatic arenas of Israel stopped to think through the strategic consequences of Chinese control of ports. The port of Haifa abuts the exit routes from the adjacent navy base, where the Israeli submarine fleet is stationed. It is also a strategic port of call for the U.S. Sixth Fleet. There is a question as to whether the U.S. Sixth Fleet can continue to use Haifa as a homeport under Chinese management. Chinese personnel would be in close proximity to U.S. naval ships and installations as well as the main base of the Israeli Navy. There is no question that China is acquiring vast influence over essential infrastructures in Israel's military capabilities.[17]

While the loudest criticism of the Belt and Road Initiative has come from overseas, there are also growing doubts over the project within China. Since the BRI was launched, critics have warned the scheme could leave China overextended, with billions of dollars wasted on projects that never pay off. While Beijing may acquire control of certain projects in return for forgiving debts, any strategic wins could be outweighed by a host of white elephant investments that offer little benefit to China.

"The BRI is facing pressure from Washington and other rival nations keen to restrain China from supplanting their influence over developing countries, as well as a potential funding shortfall for future projects. While boosters for the BRI remain plentiful, and the project is not on the verge of failing any time soon, there are signs that a shift is underway. The number of contracts signed in 2018 was down on previous years, and many countries have reportedly been told to partner with the World Bank and other international lenders on future projects."[18]

The Belt and Road Initiative was supposed to be Xi's signature project, one that would drive China back to its traditional position of power and dominance both in Asia and wider afield. But as the country enters

2019, the plan is looking shakier than in ever — and appears in need of a rethink. Failure to do so, according to Bloomberg analyst Nisid Hajari, risks that "this plan to project Chinese power, influence and trade across much of the world could undermine all three."[19]

The growing wariness toward Chinese largess adds another complication to Xi's effort to manage an economic slowdown at home and a more confrontational U.S. abroad. The Trump administration has seized on the doubts to bolster its own regional clout, with Vice President Mike Pence telling an Association of Southeast Asian Nations summit in November 2018 that U.S. wouldn't "offer a constricting belt or a one-way road." [20]

"The One Belt One Road covers a lot of countries and regions in the world. Here is the One Belt One Road 64 countries list.

- 8 countries in South Asia: Pakistan, Bangladesh, Sri Lanka, Afghan, Nepal, Maldives, Bhutan

- 11 countries in southeast Asia: Mongolia, Russia, Indonesia, Thailand, Malaysia, Vietnam, Singapore, Philippines, Myanmar, Cambodia, Laos, Brunei, east Timor

- 5 Central Asia countries: Kazakhstan, Uzbekistan, Turkmenistan, Kyrghyzstan, Tajikistan

- 16 countries of west Asia and north Africa: Saudi Arabia, UAE, Oman, Iran, Turkey, Israel, Egypt, Kuwait, Iraq, Qatar, Jordan, Lebanon, Bahrain, Yemen, Syria, Palestine

- 16 central and eastern European countries: Poland, Romania, Czech Republic, Slovakia, Bulgaria, Hungary, Latvia, Lithuania, Slovenia, Estonia, Croatia, Albania, Serbia, Macedonia, Bosnia and Herzegovina

- The other six states of the CIS: Ukraine, Azerbaijan, Armenia, Belarus, Georgia, Moldova

- One Belt One Road Impact on Kenya — Mombasa — Nairobi Railway

- Kenya is the only pivot of China's One Belt and One Road Initiative in Africa and the largest recipient of Chinese financial aid in the construction of a new silk road. In May 2014, China and Kenya signed a cooperation agreement on the Mombasa–Nairobi Railway. It is the first new railway to be built in Kenya in the past 100 years, which is the pharynx of the east African railway network.

- One Belt One Road Impact on Pakistan–Karachi–Lahore Highway.

- On December 22, 2015, Chinese construction co., LTD. formally signed the EPC general contract of the Karachi — Lahore Highway project with Pakistan's National Highway Administration. The Karachi–Lahore highway project is the largest transportation infrastructure projects for China–Pakistan economic corridor. It is about 1152 km in total and designed with two-way six lanes at a speed of 120 km/h.

- On January 10, 2016, Chinese engineers built the main project of the Karot hydropower station. The Chinese government has pledged to invest at least $35 billion in Pakistan by 2030 to finance the construction of power plants.

- One Belt One Road Impact on Indonesia — Ya-Wan High-speed Rail. The Ya-Wan high-speed rail will connect Djakarta, the capital of Indonesia, with its fourth largest city, Bandung. According to a report jointly prepared by the two countries, the total length of the line will be about 150 kilometers, with China's technology, Chinese standards and Chinese equipment to be adopted, with a design speed of 250–300km/h. After completion of this high-speed rail, the journey from Jakarta to Bandung will be reduced to about 40 minutes.

- One Belt One Road Impact on Iran — Tehran — Mashhad High-speed Rail. On February 6, 2016, Iranian President attended the opening ceremony of Tehran–Mashhad High-speed Rail project. The Iranian infrastructure-engineering group MAPNA and China's company will build the project.

- One Belt One Road Impact on Laos–China-Laos Railway. On December 25, 2016, China–Laos railway started construction. According to the plan, the railway will be completed by 2021, and it will take four hours from the Chinese border to Vientiane.

- One Belt One Road Impact on Bangladesh — Sheila GanJie Power Station. The second phase of the Sheila GanJie Power Station project has landed smoothly and is now in the construction phase. The completion of the project will alleviate the local electricity shortage in Bangladesh.

Each of the 44 countries in seven broad regions — Africa, Central Asia, Eastern Europe, the Middle East, Russia, South Asia and Southeast Asia — offer its own challenges to BRI. BRI projects confront national and regional risks arising from politics and local conditions. For example, charges of corruption abound in the building of Kenya's railway to connect inland Nairobi with coastal Mombasa. Sparse populations located across long distances pose physical and financial return obstacles to developing transportation links across central Asia."[21]

SUMMARY

To counter China's BRI, the United States and its democratic partners should work to create conditions that will enable fledgling democracies to succeed. Vice President Mike Pence's recent announcement of an Indo-Pacific Transparency Initiative, backed by $400 million in U.S. funding, is the right approach. A first step would be to provide development assistance to bolster the anti-corruption capabilities of countries that have recently experienced a peaceful transition of power. If these newly elected governments propose infrastructure projects that meet international standards, the United States and its partners should provide high-quality alternatives to Belt and Road.[22]

NOTES

1. Helen Chin and Winnie He, "The Belt and Road Initiative: 65 Countries and Beyond," *Global Sourcing Fung Business Intelligence Centre*, May 2018.

2. Sam Beatson, "The Power of Ports: China's Maritime March," *The Diplomat*, March 18, 2017.

3. Wade Shepherd, "How China's Belt and Road Became A 'Global Trail of Trouble,'" *Forbes*, Jan. 29, 2020.

4. Tom Miller, *China's Asian Dream: Empire Building along the New Silk Road*, Zed Books, 2017.

5. *Assessing Threats to U.S. Vital Interests — Asia*, Washington, D.C.: Heritage Foundation, Oct. 30, 2019.

6. Christopher Balding, "Why Democracies Are Turning Against Belt and Road," by *Foreign Affairs*, Nov. 20, 2018.

7. Christopher Balding, "The Backlash to BRI," *Foreign Affairs*, Dec. 18, 2019.

8. Christopher Balding, "How Did China's Big Soft Power Investment End Up Alienating the Very Countries It Was Supposed to Help," by *Foreign Affairs*, Oct. 23, 2018.

9. Christopher Balding, "Corruption, Debt and Backlash," *Foreign Affairs*, Nov. 3, 2018.

10. Elizabeth C. Economy, "China's New Revolution," *Foreign Affairs*, Dec. 6, 2018.

11. Sana Hashmi, "India's Response to China's BRI Linked to Territorial Concerns, *The Indian Express*, April 23, 2019.

12. Dylan Gerstel, "It's a DEBT Trap! Managing China-IMF Cooperation Across the Belt and Road," *CSIS*, Nov. 2019.

13. "One Belt, One Road, An Economic Roadmap," *The Economist Intelligence Unit*, Nov. 2018.

14. Christopher Balding, "Reports of Belt and Road's Death Are Greatly Exaggerated," *Foreign Affairs*, Oct. 24, 2018.

15. Mercy A Kuo, "China and Israel in the Belt and Road Initiative," *The Diplomat*, Sep. 19, 2018.

16. Mercy A. Kuo, "Israel-China Innovation Infrastructure, Investment," *The Diplomat*, July 17, 2018.

17. Amos Harel, "Israel is Giving China the Keys to Its Largest Port — and the U.S, Navy May Abandon Israel," *U.S. News*, Sept. 17, 2018.

18. 2020 Index of Military Strength, Asia, Washington, D.C.: Heritage Foundation.

19. Nisidi Hajari, "End of the Road?," *Bloomberg Opinion*, Nov. 1, 2018.

20. Jane Lanhee Lee, "U.S. Should Create Fund to Counter China's Belt and Road Push," *Reuters*, Feb. 23, 2018,

21. *Assessing Threats to U.S. Vital Interests — Asia*, Washington, D.C.: The Heritage Foundation, Oct. 30, 2019.

22. Abigail Grace and Max Hill, "How the U.S. Should Respond to China's Belt and Road," *The Diplomat*, Dec. 21, 2018.

15 | A Growing Threat: Chinese Aircraft Carriers

IN THE PAST DECADE, Chinese shipbuilders have produced more than 100 warships, a build-rate easily outstripping the U.S. Navy's. The Type 055 destroyer program alone demonstrates China's extraordinary warship development capabilities. Within just three years of the program's initiation in 2014, six Type 055s were under construction simultaneously. What's more, the Type 055 development, important in its own right, is the harbinger of something much more concerning. These ships, like the U.S. Ticonderoga missile cruisers they resemble in size, electronics, and armament, will undoubtedly be key components of powerful aircraft carrier strike groups in the near future.

China's carrier strike groups are suddenly materializing out of seemingly primitive origins. For decades, China has been buying largely discarded carriers from other countries, including Australia, but mainly Russia. Originally laid down in 1985 for the Soviet Navy is the Kuznetsov-class aircraft cruiser *Riga*, renamed *Varyga* in 1990, the rusting hulk of what was to become Chinese Navy's Type 001 carrier. It was purchased in 1998 and towed to the Dalian naval shipyard in northeast China. Rebuilt and renamed the *Liaoning*, she completed sea trials in August 2012 and loaded Shenyang J-15 aircraft and KJ-88, YJ-83K, and YJ-91 missiles in preparation for weapons systems trials.

Designated as a training ship, she was not assigned to any of China's operational fleets, but at the time of her commissioning, analysts noted that she and future Chinese carriers could be used to intimidate smaller countries that have territorial claims in the South China Sea, as well as extending air control further south.

The Liaoning, or type 001, was followed by the first carrier to be built in China, unnamed but designated Type 001A. Prior to the decision not to name this ship, there was popular sentiment to name her "Wei Wen." after a military general from the Three Kingdoms period (CE 184/220–280). He was the first man in history to arrive at Taiwan and whose name on this pivotal entry to the fleet would prove the historical fact of Taiwan being an integral part of China. There was also considerable sentiment for naming the carrier "Shi Lang," an admiral who recaptured Taiwan for the Qing Dynasty. This displays the high expectations among the Chinese people over solving the Taiwan question, because they want the country to use the first domestically built aircraft carrier as a symbol to announce its determination and ability to achieve this aim. It also sends a tough warning signal to secessionists in Taiwan.[1]

The speed with which the Type 001A was built was the fastest in the history of aircraft carrier construction, taking only two years from the laying of the hull in the shipyard to its launch. Initial work began in November 2013, and in March 2015 the first definite signs of the vessel's carrier role appeared when construction of a hangar deck began on the hull. She was launched on April 26, 2017, and fitting out was completed in November 2017. On April 17, 2018, she left dock for her first round of sea trials and was delivered to the Navy nearly a year ahead of schedule in late 2019.

The 001A's design is based largely on that of the *Liaoning*, with a same ski jump takeoff limiting her air wing to helicopters and Shenyang J-15 fighter jets. Powered by conventional oil-fired boilers driving eight steam turbines, she is 1,032 feet long and displaces 70,000 tons.

Modifications and upgrades over the *Liaoning* include increased storage for ammunition and fuel and capacity for 44 aircraft, 8 more than the *Liaoning*. Her shorter island structure allows more space for aircraft movements. The island also has redesigned radars and bridge, while the fleet command and flight control tower are on separate levels for increased efficiency. The Academy of Military Sciences announced that China needed at least three aircraft carriers. To defend its maritime interests effectively. Two aircraft carriers are being built at the Jiangnan Shipyard in Shanghai, with launched scheduled in 2020 and 2022, respectively.[2]

The first of these two carriers, known as Type 002, is to be a design entirely different from Type 001 and Type 001A. With a displacement of 85,000 tons, the ski-jump will be replaced by a steam-powered catapult permitting CATOBAR (Catapult-Assisted Take-Off but Arrested Recovery) takeoffs and landings, which will allow use of heavier and longer ranged planes. The Type 003 is planned to be larger than the Type 002, and may also feature nuclear propulsion, which could power weapons like lasers and railguns.

Russian Sukhoi Su-33 carrier-based aircraft were expected to be acquired for operation off these carriers, but instead China has developed the Shenyang J-15, featuring Chinese technology and avionics from the J-11B program, as a derivative of the Su-33. The Type 003 is the first Chinese carrier constructed using a modern, modular construction method. The modules, known as "super lifts," each weighing hundreds of tons, are assembled on land and then hoisted onto the ship in dry dock. Large American and British warships, including carriers such as the USS *Gerald R. Ford* and HMS *Queen Elizabeth* are assembled using the super-lift method. Although there are few hard details on Type 003, it is certain that CATOBAR will replace the ski ramp method allowing the carrier to launch heavier aircraft with greater fuel and weapons loads, making the carrier more effective as a power projection platform.

Thousands of launches have reportedly been made testing the 003's new electromagnetic aircraft launch system (EMALS) which enables the launch of heavier combat jets and also propeller-driven aircraft similar to the U.S. Navy's E-2D Hawkeye airborne early warning and control aircraft and the C-2 Greyhound cargo transport. The new carriers are expected to be conventionally powered.[3]

Chinese designers are working on a fourth class of carrier, Type 004. The new class will displace between 90,000 and 100,000 tons and have electromagnetically assisted launch system (EMALS) catapults. These carriers are expected to carry a large air wing of J-15 fighters, J-31 stealth fighters, KJ-600 airborne early warning and control aircraft, anti-submarine warfare helicopters, and stealth attack drones. They can launch aircraft at a faster rate, enabling them to project more power more quickly and with better protection.

In November 2017, the *South China Morning Post* reported that Beijing had achieved a technological breakthrough allowing its next carrier to use EMALS without nuclear power. Most of America's current carriers use a steam catapult system in which steam explodes into a piston attached to the plane's landing gear, powering it off the deck. Only the newer Ford-class carriers of the U.S. Navy use electromagnetic catapults to power the launch. Aircraft launched by electromagnetic catapults can get airborne quicker and with greater quantities of fuel and ammunition, giving them an advantage over planes launched by standard steam catapult. The problem is that electromagnetic catapults require more power than steam power systems. And steam catapults themselves require enormous power, which is why most CATOBAR carriers are powered by nuclear reactors. Chinese engineers are said to believe they solved this problem by developing an integrated propulsion system (IPS), which generates enough power to use EMALS. The obstacle was whether a conventionally powered carrier would be able to support EMALS. The breakthrough came when Chinese engineers used a medium-voltage, direct-current transmission network instead of a system using alternating current. This required a complete overhaul of the energy supply and distribution system — from steam boilers to the energy storage device.[4]

In building aircraft carriers, China appears to be following a policy of gradual improvements. The first domestically built carrier was very similar to the *Liaoning*. The next one, it appears, with have the electromagnetic catapult launch system. It has been speculated that the Type 003 will be nuclear-powered. While the Type 003 remains on the drawing board, it is expected to displace 110,000 tons. The Type 003 carriers will be the first ships since the 1950s built anywhere in the world to rival the largest, most powerful U.S. super carriers. Also, China will have a new generation of fighters and drones available by the time the first Type 003 is ready.

Another argument for nuclear power is that, despite Belt and Road efforts at Sri Lanka and other South Asian and East African ports, China lacks naval bases for refueling. Robert Farley, senior lecturer at the Patterson School of Diplomacy and International Commerce at the University of Kentucky, emphasizes this point: "Unlike the U.S. Navy, the PLAN does not yet have access to an array of bases and maintenance facilities that can keep a carrier battle group in fighting trim. Similarly, the PLAN lacks the experience of the USN in long-range underway replenishment. A nuclear carrier does not solve these problems — escorts will still need fuel, and the air group will still burn through equipment and fuel at a high rate. But a carrier that can travel long distances without refueling can help."[5]

Farley notes that the other reason that nuclear power could be useful is the potential for huge power generation. "Projections suggest that this will increasingly become a requirement for advanced warships, as they will depend upon lasers and other power-hungry systems for defensive and offensive weapons. It is not inconceivable, if testing and development go well, that China's first nuclear carrier could carry lasers, railguns and other such advanced equipment."[6]

China's maritime lines of communication lie in the Pacific and in the Indian Oceans. In the Indian Ocean especially, China faces potentially hostile foreign powers (India, France, the United Kingdom) on turf that geographically favors those countries. "As the core of a task force made of cruisers, destroyers and nuclear attack submarines, a Type 003 carrier could offer a formidable presence — likely more formidable than that of any navy besides the USN," Farley warns. "What the U.S. experience has demonstrated is that large aircraft carriers are extremely flexible platforms, which can support all manner of operations beyond their intended functions. Big decks with big reactors offer a nation reliable tools for resolving its security concerns," Farley added.[7]

Will this super-carrier strategy work for the Chinese? Farley notes that it may not be a slam-dunk. The Russians were trying it when the Soviet Union collapsed. "Unexpected events might change China's evolution, as well," he writes in *The National Interest*. "The People's Republic of China might suffer an economic downturn that would render its carrier fleet too expensive to push forward. China might decide that aircraft carriers aren't worth the risk, given improvements in the technologies designed to destroy them. But at the moment, the PRC has decided to allow the PLAN to push forward with an extremely ambitious carrier program, one that could eventually produce a fleet second only to the USN, and that perhaps only for a time."[8]

Escorts like the Type 055 DDG will surround China's carrier strike groups. Accompanying them will be replenishment and support replenishment ships with the speed and range needed to keep up and stay with the warships. So, the Type 901 fleet oiler is a noteworthy addition to the growing blue-water navy. Sea trials for the first Type 901 began in December of 2016. Seven hundred feet long and displacing 48,000 tons, the Type 901 has five liquid bulk cargo tanks for fuel and potable water and two dry cargo holds and a maximum cruising speed of 25 knots. She is equipped with hangar space for three heavy helicopters, as well as a sizeable flight deck. An automated logistics management system tracks and optimizes fuel consumption and the logistics replenishment needs of fleet ships. A second Type 901 is currently under construction at the Guangzhou naval shipyard.[9]

The Chinese navy commissioned three new Type 903A fleet oilers in 2016 alone (numbers 887, 963, 964) and is showing a dedicated interest to expand its fleet refueling capabilities. Replacing older ships with new, more capable fleet oilers, and expanding the total number of oilers and replenishment vessels will expand China's power projection capabilities. At 530 feet in length and displacing 23,400 tons, the first Type 904B dry cargo/general stores vessel was commissioned in 2015, and two more are currently being fitted out. These ships are ideally suited for supporting offshore island garrisons, such as those on Chinese-held islands in the South China Sea.

All the PLANs Type 904, Type 904A, and Type 904B dry cargo replenishment ships are attached to the South Sea Fleet based at Hainan Island. The Type 904 was increased in size with the Type 904A and the addition of a heavy helicopter hangar was added in the design of the Type 904B. Along with four twin 37 millimeter guns and four twin 25 millimeter guns, these ships will be able to defend themselves.

SUMMARY

It was more than 600 years ago that China possessed the world's most formidable blue-water navy, cruising the Indian and Pacific Oceans. That fleet rotted at the docks when the government's interests turned almost entirely to internal affairs. The resurgence of a Chinese blue water navy is best evidenced by the carrier battle groups that will soon cruise these oceans and beyond. Like their U.S. Navy counterparts, these battle groups will perform a prestigious function for a nation intent on demonstrating its power and capabilities.

"In an era of renewed great power competition, China's military modernization effort, including its naval modernization effort, has become the top focus of U.S. defense planning and budgeting. China's navy, which China has been steadily modernizing for more than 25 years, since the early to mid-1990s, has become a formidable military force within China's near-seas region, and it is conducting a growing number of operations in more-distant waters, including the broader waters of the Western Pacific, the Indian Ocean, and waters around Europe. China's navy is viewed as posing a major challenge to the U.S. Navy's ability to achieve and maintain wartime control of blue-water ocean areas in the Western Pacific — the first such challenge the U.S. Navy has faced since the end of the Cold War — and forms a key element of a Chinese challenge to the long-standing status of the United States as the leading military power in the Western Pacific.

China's naval modernization effort encompasses a wide array of platform and weapon acquisition programs, including anti-ship ballistic missiles (ASBMs), anti-ship cruise missiles (ASCMs), submarines, surface ships, aircraft, unmanned vehicles (UVs), and supporting C4ISR (command and control, communications, computers, intelligence, surveillance, and reconnaissance) systems. China's naval modernization effort also includes improvements in maintenance and logistics, doctrine, personnel quality, education and training, and exercises.

China's military modernization effort, including its naval modernization effort, is assessed as being aimed at developing capabilities for addressing the situation with Taiwan militarily, if need be; for achieving a greater degree of control or domination over China's near-seas region, particularly the South China Sea; for enforcing China's view that it has the right to regulate foreign military activities in its 200-mile maritime exclusive economic zone (EEZ); for defending China's commercial sea lines of communication (SLOCs), particularly those linking China to the Persian Gulf; for displacing U.S. influence in the Western Pacific; and for asserting China's status as the leading regional power and a major world power."[10]

NOTES

1. "Next Aircraft Carrier: Everything We Know (So Far)," *The National Interest*, March 31, 2017.

2. Interview with Bryan Clark, Center for Budgetary and Strategic Assessment, Interview December 21, 2018.

3. 3. Interview with Thomas Callender, Senior Fellow for Defense Programs, Heritage Foundation, Washington, D.C., January 5, 2019.

4. Interview with Bryan Clark, Center for Budgetary and Strategic Assessment, December 21, 2018.

5. Robert Farley, "The Ultimate Weapon: Could China Build a 'Nuclear' Aircraft Carrier?" *The National Interest*, September 23, 2019.

6. Robert Farley, "The Ultimate Weapon: Could China Build a 'Nuclear' Aircraft Carrier?" *The National Interest*, September 23, 2019.

7. Robert Farley, "The Ultimate Weapon: Could China Build a 'Nuclear' Aircraft Carrier?" *The National Interest*, September 23, 2019.

8. Robert Farley, "The Ultimate Weapon: Could China Build a 'Nuclear' Aircraft Carrier?" *The National Interest*, September 23, 2019.

9. "China Building a 3rd Type 901 Large Replenishment Oiler for PLAN," *Naval Defense Industry News*, January 29, 2018.

10. *China Naval Modernization: Implications for U.S. Navy Capabilities — Background and Issues for Congress*, May 21, 2020.

ON SEPTEMBER 30, 2018, the USS *Decatur*, an Arleigh Burke-class guided-missile destroyer, was conducting a routine freedom of navigation patrol in the vicinity of the Spratly Islands in the South China Sea. As the *Decatur* approached Graven Reef, a Chinese Navy Luyang III class guided missile destroyer shadowed it. The Chinese vessel closed in and passed within 150 feet of the Decatur's port bow, forcing it to maneuver sharply away to avoid collision.

A U.S. Pacific Fleet spokesman protested the Chinese vessel's aggressive maneuvers. The Chinese made no comment, and the vessels did separate and steam off. But the question lingers: What if this encounter had led to combat — even accidentally? Short of the far more urgent question of what the potentially catastrophic international consequences could have been, how would these destroyers have measured up against each other? This second question is urgent because the relative strengths of

USS Rafel and USS John Fin in the eastern Pacific Ocean. Credit: United States Navy

USS Arleigh Burke. Credit: United States Navy

the U.S. and Chinese fleets now and in the years ahead will have global implications.

The U.S. fleet now has 68 active Arleigh Burkes. The Decatur was commissioned in 1998, seven years after the commissioning of the first ship in the class. By 2005, the last of the Spruance-class destroyers, built to replace the World War II destroyers, had been decommissioned, making the Arleigh Burkes the only active destroyers. Spruance-class destroyers were just over 560 feet in length and 8,000 tons. The Arleigh Burkes overall length is somewhat less at 505 to 509 feet but have heavier displacements of 8,315 to 9,200 tons. With weaponry including over 90 missiles, they have more firepower per ton than any other ship in the fleet. Arleigh Burkes are also the first class of destroyers built around the Aegis Combat System and the SPY-1D multifunction passive electronically scanned array radar. They are designed as multi-mission ships capable of fulfilling strategic land strike roles with Tomahawk missiles. Other capabilities include anti-aircraft warfare (AAW) with Aegis radar and surface-to-air missiles and anti-submarine warfare (ASW) with towed sonar array, anti-submarine rockets and ASW helicopter and anti-surface warfare (ASUW) with Harpoon missile launchers. With upgrades to their AN/SPY-1 phased radar systems and their associated missile payloads as part of the Aegis Ballistic Missile Defense System, these ships have also begun to demonstrate some promise as mobile anti-ballistic missile and anti-satellite weaponry platforms. Some no longer have the towed sonar or Harpoon missile launcher, and their hulls and superstructures have been designed to reduce the radar cross section.[1]

Only the *Spruance,* the *Kidd* (563 ft.), and the *Zumwalt* (600 ft.) are longer. The larger Ticonderoga-class ships were constructed on *Spruance*-class hull forms but are designated as cruisers because their weapons systems and missions are radically different than the *Spruance* and *Kidd*-class destroyers. The designers of *Arleigh Burke* incorporated lessons learned from the *Ticonderoga*-class cruisers, which were deemed too expensive to continue building and too difficult to upgrade. The *Arleigh Burke* design incorporates such stealth techniques as the angled, rather than the traditional vertical hull surfaces and the tripod mainmast, making the ship more difficult to detect, particularly by anti-ship missiles. "Collective Protection" makes the Arleigh Burkes the first U.S. warships designed with an air-filtration system against nuclear, biological, and chemical (NBC) warfare. Other NBC defenses include a countermeasure wash down system. Their Aegis Combat System uses a passive electronically scanned array allowing continual tracking of targets simultaneously with area scans. The system's computer control also allows centralization of the previously separate tracking and targeting functions, and the system is also resistant to electronic counter measures. The five-inch deck gun is an anti-ship weapon which can also be used against air attack and to support forces ashore, firing 20 rounds a minute with a range of up to 20 miles. A Light Airborne Multi-Purpose (LAMPS) helicopter system improves the ship's capabilities against submarines and surface ships. The helicopters are able to support ground assaults with machine guns and Hellfire anti-armor guided missiles.[2] When retirement of the Iowa-class battleships prompted Congressional concern over the loss of the Navy's shore bombardment capabilities, a modernization program extended the range of the 5-inch deck guns. Work began on developing extended range guided munitions (EGMs) to double the current 20-mile range, but in 2008 the program was cancelled.[3]

"The Chinese began their transition from a nearly exclusive brown water navy to at least a partially blue water navy in 1999, when the first of two 8,100-ton Sovremenny-class destroyers, purchased from Russia, entered service. In 2002 two additional Sovremenny-class destroyers were acquired and entered service in 2005 and 2006. These destroyers were equipped with the highly capable Russian-made SS-N-22 Sunburn anti-ship missiles (ASCMs).

Since then, China has put into service six new classes of indigenously built destroyers, including three variations of one class. The classes are called the Luhu (Type 052A), Luhai (Type 051B), Louzhou (Type 051C), Luyang I (Type 052B), Luyang II (Type 052C), and Luyang III (Type 052D). Compared to China's remaining older Luda (Type 051) class destroyers, which entered service between 1971 and 1991, these six new indigenously built destroyer classes feature substantially more modern hull designs, propulsion systems, sensors, weapons, and electronics."[4]

Deck of Chinese Destroyer. Credit: Michael Fahey

The Luyang II-class and the Luyang III-class ships, displacing about 7,100 tons and 7,500 tons respectively, appear to feature phased-array radars somewhat similar to the SPY-1 radar used in the U.S.-made Aegis combat system. Like the older Luda-class destroyers, the six new destroyer classes are armed with ASCMs.

In August 2012, two new hulls were detected under construction at China's Changxingdao-Jiangnan Shipyard. Reconnaissance determined that they were armed with a new 130 millimeter deck gun and new AESA radar system. They were the first two ships in the Luyang III or Kumming class (Type 052A). Just five years later, this class would comprise one third of the PLAN's active destroyer fleet — one of which encountered the *Decatur* at Graven Reef.

While similar to the earlier Type 052C, the 052Ds feature reduced radar cross-section due to the superstructure sloping inward at a greater angle. The helicopter hangar, rather than being on the port side like that of the 052C, is at the center. A pair of enclosed boat/raft launching systems are on each side of the helicopter hangar, and the radar mast has been moved to the stern. There are several mounting sites for a new single barrel 30 millimeter stealthy gun mount that is fully automated. This small caliber weapon would be useful on countering non-conventional threats, such as potential terrorist attacks and anti-piracy operations.[5]

"New radar features four larger arrays, probably housing more transceivers. The curving arrays, which resulted from the need for air circulation on Type 052Cs, have been replaced by flat arrays, suggesting the adoption of a liquid cooling system instead of the mixed air and liquid cooling system. A new vertical launching system (VLS) for surface-to-air, cruise, anti-submarine, and anti-ship missiles appears similar to the U.S. Mk 41 VLS. Chinese sources have confirmed that different types of missiles can be launched by a single launching system. Like the Mk 42, launching modules includes eight launching tubes, any of which can house one to four missiles. And each launching model has a launching control unit that can simultaneously launch up to four missiles. The Type 052C's 100 millimeter gun has been replaced by a new single barrel 130 millimeter gun. Rapid firing anti-missile guns can intercept incoming anti-ship missiles up to a speed of Mach 4 with a claimed 96 percent success rate. An anti-submarine system includes two Type triple torpedo tubes and four 18-tube launchers for firing decoy rockets. The Type 052D has been described as the Chinese Aegis with radar and defensive missiles comparable to those of the Arleigh Burkes. Radar systems are capable of detecting stealth fighter aircraft, including the American F-35 Lightning II, China claims.[6]

Guided missile cruisers, like the *Ticonderoga*, are the primary air defense vessel for the U.S. fleet, particularly for carrier battle groups. China

Deck gun of Chinese Destroyer. Credit: Michael Fahey

is expected to form as many as three carrier battle groups in the next few years. A new escort vessel is under development, called the Type 055 destroyer and the Renhai class guided missile cruiser. Displacing 13,000 tons and 590 feet in length, these massive ships will feature multi-mission designs with air defense as their main role. They will have anti-submarine warfare capabilities surpassing previous Chinese surface combatants.

In April 2014, images emerged of a full-scale mock-up of the Type 055 superstructure — with an enclosed integrated mast for radar and other electronics — at the Chinese naval electronic testing range in Wuhan. Construction began on the first ship in 2014. When it was launched in June 2017, it was among the largest post–World War II warships produced in East Asia and the largest surface combatant launched by China. Within three years, six Type 055s were under construction simultaneously. A conventional flared hull on the 055 is combined with an enclosed bulbous bow, hiding mooring points, anchor chains and other equipment. The bow and main deckhouse are configured similarly to 052D destroyers with a continuous structure amidships increasing internal volume and reducing the radar cross-section. Both the radar and the infrared signature are reduced by the smokestack design. Stealthiness is also improved with reduced electromagnetic radiation signatures. The battle management system is designed to allow integration with all ships in carrier strike groups.

The OSS's additional advances over older ships include various electronic warfare support measures (ESM), electronic countermeasures (ECM) and electro-optic (EO) sensors. There is a deployment port for variable depth and towed array sonar, and the bulbous bow is thought to contain a bow sonar, larger than those of earlier Chinese surface combatants. Primary armament consists of missiles carried in 112 universal vertical launch cells (VLS), 64 forward and 48 aft with diameters of 0.85 meters. These cells support cold launches, and hot launches with concentric canisters.[7]

Available in three lengths, the cells on the Type 055 are likely nine meters, the longest variant. These are larger than strike-length Mark 41 VLS and Mark 57 Peripheral VLS cells used by the U.S. Navy. Upon entering service, the O55 is likely to carry HHAQ-9 surface-to-air, YJ-18 anti-ship, and CJ-10 land-attack cruise missiles, and missile-launched anti-submarine torpedoes.

Reconnaissance photos of the lead ship show what may be a Chinese version of the electromagnetic railgun on the forward deck. U.S. Navy artillery experts believe that if, in fact, the Chinese have developed an operational railgun, it may have the 100-mile range of the problem-plagued U.S. version but virtually no accuracy. Also, the 550 would require the installation of integrated electric propulsion to meet railgun power requirements.

SUMMARY

The new type 055 destroyer is in a killer class of warships. The question is how would the U.S. Navy do in a fight with this large ship, displacing 13,000 tons and carrying 112 vertical launch system (VLS) cells, in addition to a 130-millimeter gun and a wide array of sensors and defensive weapons. "They are the world's largest surface combatants apart from the Zumwalt class destroyers, which really are specialized land attack vessels. But apart from the Arleigh Burke Flight III ships, the U.S. Navy has no specific large combatants in its long-term plans."[8] At the moment, both the Chinese and American destroyers are equipped with the world's most sophisticated electronically scanned array systems. The American ship is armed with 96 vertical launch systems — 60 of which are dedicated to air defenses — in contrast to the Chinese ship's 64. The 052C and 052D Type destroyers are expected to become the mainstay of China's destroyer fleet. There is a gap between their capabilities and those of the Arleigh Burke-class destroyers. The Arleigh Burke can cover 4,400 nautical miles at a speed of 20 knots, while the Type 052D has a range of 4,000 nautical miles at 15 knots. The radar on Chinese destroyers has a greater capability to command different electronic systems. The Type 051D destroyer is seen as a significant upgrade to its predecessor, the Type 052C. These ships have been hailed as the most advanced ships of their type in Asia. China now has 20 Type 052D destroyers in active service. The United States currently has 66 Arleigh Burke destroyers in service.[9]

NOTES

1. *China Naval Modernization: Implications for U.S. Navy's Capabilities — Background and Issues for Congress*, May 21, 2020.

2. Thomas Callender, *The Nation Needs a 400-Ship Navy*, Washington, D.C.: Heritage Foundation, 2019.

3. "DDG-51, Arleigh Burke-Class," *GlobalSecurity.org*.

4. Interview with Bryan Clark, Center for Budgetary and Strategic Assessment, June 16, 2019.

5. *China Naval Modernization: Implications for U.S. Navy's Capabilities — Background and Issues for Congress*, May 21, 2020.

6. *Report to Congress on Navy Force Structure*, May 28, 2020.

7. Interview with James Hogge, Adm. USN (Ret.), March 16, 2010.

8. Interview with Thomas Callender, April 16, 2019.

9. Kyle Mizokami, "Can the U.S. Navy Beat China's New Type 055 Destroyer in a Fight?" *The National Interest*, Sep. 29. 2019.

17 | U.S. Attack Submarines

In late April 2014, the U.S. Naval Sea Systems Command awarded the largest contract in U.S. Navy history. For $17.8 billion, $3 billion more than the entire shipbuilding budget for that fiscal year, General Dynamics (GD) Electric Boat would build 10 Block IV Virginia-class attack submarines. The award for a 5-year period was recognition of both GD's proficiency as the prime submarine builder and of the crucial role of the Virginia class in national defense.

Since 1976, with the commissioning of the first ship of the Los Angeles class, the predecessor of the Virginia class, nuclear-powered attack submarines have excelled in their unique mission in U.S. naval strategy. With nuclear power providing limitless range, attack submarines can prowl the

Virginia class submarine. Credit: General Dynamics Electric Boat

Los Angeles submarine. Credit: General Dynamics Electric Boat

globe, invisible to adversaries' reconnaissance. They can shadow Russian and Chinese ICBM submarines, escort U.S. carrier strike groups or suddenly arrive at vital strategic locations prepared to deliver devastating missile barrages. Meanwhile, they are also covertly collecting intelligence that cannot be obtained any other way and delivering special operators ashore for secret missions.[1]

The Los Angeles class replaced the Sturgeons, a 37-ship class, built between 1963 and 1975 and in commission between 1967 and 2004. The Sturgeons were known as the workhorses of the attack submarine fleet for much of the Cold War. At 300 feet in length and displacing 4700 tons, they were considerably smaller than the attack submarines that replaced them.

Of the 61 Los Angeles class submarines deployed, 35 remain active, making up nearly 70 percent of the attack submarine fleet, comprising more active nuclear submarines than any other navy in the world. All are armed with Tomahawk missiles, but the second flight of these submarines was designed with 12 vertical launch tubes. In earlier submarines, Tomahawks had to be launched horizontally, like torpedoes. Officially they carried 25 torpedoes, as well as Mark 67, Mark 60 CAPTOR mines, and Tomahawk and Harpoon missiles.

"The last 23 built in the 688i improvement program were designed with more advanced electronics, sensors and noise reduction technology. Top speed is classified but has been estimated to be as high as 38 knots. Maximum operating depth is officially listed as 650 feet but has been estimated at 950 feet. The 688i subclass is equipped with an advanced combat system employing updated computers and interface equipment. After a series of cost and scheduling setbacks, the system was replaced with conformal passive hydrophones hard mounted to each side of the hull. The system uses frequency line integration tracking (FLIT) which hones in on precise narrowband frequencies of sound and can accurately provide firing solutions against very quiet submarines. This hull array doubled the performance of Los Angeles class predecessors.

This system has now been replaced by the Acoustic Rapid Commercial Off-The-Shelf Insertion (A-RCI), a four-phase program for transforming existing submarine sonar systems from legacy systems to a more capable and flexible COTS/Open System Architecture (OSA) that also provided a common sonar system. A single A-RCI Multi-Purpose Processor (MPP) has as much computing power as the entire Los Angeles submarine fleet combined and will allow the development and use of complex algorithms previously beyond the reach of legacy processors. The use of these technologies and systems will enable rapid periodic updates to both software and hardware."[2]

Los Angeles class submarines are equipped with light water reactors generating 35,000 shaft horsepower. Auxiliary propeller motors supply 242 KW. The life of the fuel cells is approximately 10 years. The reactor plant was originally designed to use the D1G-2 core, similar to the D2G reactor used on the Bainbridge-class guided missile cruiser. All Los Angeles class submarines were built with a D2G core. The D1G-2 cores are being replaced with D2W cores as the boats are refueled.[2]

In 1983 design work began on the Sea Wolf class of nuclear-powered fast attack submarines intended to succeed the Los Angeles class. Initially 29 submarines of this class were planned, but this number was reduced to 12 with the end of the Cold War and the resulting budget cuts. The class was dropped to three boats, a reduction which lead to the design and construction of the Virginia class.

Designed to combat the threat of such Russian submarines as the Typhoon and the Akula classes in deep ocean environment, the Sea Wolf hulls are constructed of heavier steel than previous classes and are larger, faster and quieter than Los Angeles and other previous classes of U.S. nuclear submarines. They also have twice as many torpedo tubes and up to 50 USM-109 Tomahawk cruise missiles for attacking both land and sea targets. They are powered by a single S6W nuclear reactor delivering 45,000 hp to a low-noise pump jet. Much more expensive than previous nuclear submarines, they have a projected cost $32.6 billion for 12 boats.

The USS *Jimmy Carter* is the largest of the Sea Wolf class at 453 feet in length and 12,000 tons, due to the insertion of the Multi-Mission Platform (MMP) which allows launch and recovery of remotely operated underwater vehicles (ROVs) and Navy SEALs. An underwater splicing chamber in the MMP allows for undersea fiber-optic cable tapping.[3]

Construction of the Virginia class began in 2000 with the first one commissioned in 2004. Seventeen are now active, with construction slated to go on until 2043, for a total of 66 ships. Large ships, 377 feet in length and displacing 8,700 tons, they are the same size as Arleigh Burke destroyers. Plans call for Block V Virginia-class submarines built from 2019 onward to be significantly larger than the first submarines in the class. Block V submarines have a Virginia Payload Module (VPM) and mid-body sections, increasing their overall length. The VPM will add four multipurpose Virginia Payload Tubes (VPT) replacing dozens of single purpose cruise missile launch tubes. The VPM could carry non-nuclear medium-range ballistic missiles. Adding the VPM increases the cost of each submarine by $500 million. The additional cost would be offset by reducing the total submarine force by four boats. According to most recent reports, the VPM would carry only Tomahawk SLCM and possibly unmanned undersea vehicles (UUV) with the new price tag now estimated at $360–380 million per boat. The VPM launch tubes/silos are similar in design to the ones planned for the new Columbia class ICBM submarine.

Impressively the Virginia class project has been an exercise in cost control and reduction through creative design and construction cost controls that could eventually allow badly needed expansion of the entire fleet. The Los Angeles class submarines were built by assembling pressure hulls and then installing equipment through cavities in those hulls. This approach required extensive time-consuming and dangerous construction within the narrow confines of the hull. In the Virginia class approach, modular techniques made it possible to construct large segments of equipment outside the hull. Dubbed "rafts" these segments are then inserted into hull sections. The integrated raft and hull section form a module which, when joined with other modules, forms a Virginia class sub. Block I boats are built in 10 modules, with each submarine requiring 84 months to build.[4]

Block II planning reduced the 10 sections to four, saving $300 million per boat. Block II boats are also built under a multi-year procurement agreement as opposed to the block-buy contract in Block I, resulting in savings of $80 million per boat. The SS *New Hampshire*, as a result, was finished three months ahead of schedule and $500,000 under budget.

The costliest shipbuilding contract in history involves Block IV boats. Savings for this block involved reducing major maintenance periods from four to three years, increasing each ship's total lifetime deployment by one year. Block V submarines may incorporate the VPM, which would give guided-missile capability when the Ohio class submarines are retired from service. The Block V submarines are expected to triple the capability of striking shore targets for each boat.

"In contrast to a traditional bladed propeller, the Virginia class uses pump-jet propulsors, originally developed for the Royal Navy's Swiftsure class submarines. By reducing risks of cavitation, propulsors significantly reduce the noise of operations. As the stealthiest combat systems ever built, Virginia-class submarines can travel places covertly and non-provocatively where no other U.S. submarines can go. If war threatens, a U.S. attack submarine is nearby, monitoring adversaries' communications and ready to strike land or sea targets with enemies powerless to repel them. The knowledge of that threat is a powerful deterrent, one that grows with each advance in the ever-improving attack submarine technology."[4]

Limitless range and extraordinary speed in covering vast distances put Virginia-class submarines in combat position in areas half-way around the world from home bases — such as the distance from San Diego to the Persian Gulf. This capability increased when reactors went from requiring replacement at 17-year life-of-the-ship cores of the Los Angeles submarines to 35-year life-of-the ship cores with the Virginias. With the Virginia class, food for the crew is the only consideration. Unlike the rest of the fleet, these ships require no large logistical tail.

Increased endurance comes along with improved war-fighting performance in the Virginia submarines. It is performance that is being further improved with each new production contract. Now the Virginia class has more sophisticated sonar and eavesdropping sensors, a control system that facilitates shallow-water operations, a lockout chamber for inserting special operators ashore, and an improved capacity to launch land-attack weapons.

It is generally agreed that the Virginia class's technology and war-fighting capabilities can deny our two major adversaries access to the sea, destroy targets deep in the Eurasian or African interiors without warning, and intercept the most sensitive communications, both theirs and those of lesser state adversaries and terrorists. Potentially, they could even block nuclear attacks on the United States by destroying the seagoing strategic forces, a capability no other nation can claim now or in the foreseeable future.

Current shipbuilding plans assume that Virginia-class submarines will remain in production through 2043. Since some Virginia-class submarines might be in service until 2070, the Navy has committed to a process of continuous adaptation and improvement that will import new technologies into the ship's design with each successive production contract.

This process began in 2008 when the "Block III" contract led to the re-design of bow sensors, land-attack missile launchers, and other features.[6]

Begun in 2019, the Block V contract is tripling the capacity of each submarine to attack targets ashore, further contributing to Virginia's technological evolution. Constantly reducing costs by redesigning parts, refining construction processes, and awarding multi-year contracts that facilitate long-term planning is an important part of the Virginia-class program. This emphasis on efficiency reduced costs for each successive production contract.

These construction performance triumphs, however, have tended to mask one major problem with the attack submarine fleet: Los Angeles–class boats are being retired so quickly because of age that the size of the submarine fleet is declining rapidly and, at 48 submarines, is already below the size the Navy requires. The need is for 60 attack submarines, and the Navy could actually use 70. Although 70 or even 60 may be out of reach, experts agree that the best solution would be to increase Virginia class construction from two boats per year to three, until serial production of the Columbia ICBM class begins. Although this would require increasing the shipbuilding budgets above historic levels, the fact is that naval ship construction accounts for only two percent of defense spending today. Failure to build more Virginia class submarines virtually guarantees that vital war-fighting capabilities at sea will not be available when and where they are urgently needed.[7]

USS Dakota. Credit: General Dynamics Electric Boat

SUMMARY

The Navy's attack submarine force capabilities were enhanced when a 1994 Nuclear Posture Review determined that four of the Navy's 16 ballistic missile submarines were not needed to meet the country's strategic force requirements. At that time, the Navy elected to transform the four oldest SSBNs into SSGNs, carrying both conventional land attack and special operations forces (SOF) platforms. These conversions, along with refueling, were accomplished in just five years. The four SSGNs now provide more than half of the submarine force's vertical launch payload capacity with each SSGN capable of carrying up to 154 Tomahawk land-attack cruise missiles. The missiles are loaded in seven-shot Multiple-All-Up-Round Canisters (MARCs) in 22 missile tubes. These tubes can also accommodate additional stowage canisters for SOF equipment, food, and other consumables, extending the submarine's ability to remain forward deployed. The missile tubes are also able to accommodate future payloads such as new types of missiles, unmanned aerial vehicles, and unmanned undersea vehicles.[7]

Each SSGN can accommodate up to 66 SOF personnel, more when additional berthing is installed in the missile compartment. The two forward missile tubes were permanently converted to lockout chambers that allowed clandestine insertion and retrieval of SOF personnel. Each lockout chamber can also accommodate a Dry Deck Shelter (DDS), enhancing the SSGNs' SOF capabilities.

During conversion, each SSGN received the Common Submarine Radio Room and two High-Data-Rate antennas for significantly enhanced communication capabilities. These additions allow each SSGN to serve as a forward-deployed, clandestine Small Combatant Joint Command Center.

NOTES

1. Report to Congress on Navy Force Structure, May 26, 2020.
2. Thomas Callender, "The Nation Needs a 400-Ship Navy," Washington, D.C.: Heritage Foundation.
3. Interview with Bryan Clark, Center for Budgetary and Strategic Assessment, April 13, 2019.
4. Interview with Thomas Callender, Senior Fellow for Defense Programs, Heritage Foundation, May 11, 2019.
5. Interview with Mark Lyles, June 16, 2019.
6. Interview with Andrew Evers, USN, April 24, 2019, and May 23, 2019.
7. Interview with Jerry Hendrix, Telemus Group, June 25, 2019.

18 | ICBM Submarines: The Ultimate in Lethality and Stealth

LETHALITY AND STEALTH will be the absolute essentials of naval weapons platforms in conflicts to come, and no platforms are more lethal and stealthier than Intercontinental Ballistic Missile Submarines. The 14 submarines of the Ohio class, 540-foot long, 18,750-ton monsters now deployed deep in the oceans of the world are each prepared to shower nearly 300 nuclear warheads from 24 Trident II D5 missiles on targets up to 6,000 miles away. They are the sturdiest and most potent leg of the U.S.

Ohio class submarine. Credit: General Dynamics electric Boat

nuclear triad, carrying 70 percent of U.S. nuclear weapons. In addition, design work is underway on the Ohio's successor, the Columbia class, slated to join the fleet beginning in 2031 at the rate of one a year until the projected number of 12 replaces the entire Ohio class.

The 172nd successful test firing of a D5 missile came from the Ohio-class USS *Rhode Island* submerged off the coast of Florida on May 9, 2019. The D5 is a three-stage, solid propellant ballistic missile, fitted with multiple independently targetable reentry vehicles carrying three types of warheads: the 100-kiloton W76/Mk-4, the 100 kiloton W761/Mi-4A and the 455-kiloton W88/Mk-5, the highest-yield ballistic missile warhead in the U.S. arsenal.

In 1971, the Navy began a long-term modernization plan to develop what became the D5, a missile with twice the range of the existing Poseidon (ULMS I). With the addition to a longer-range missile, the larger Ohio-class ICBM submarine replaced the James Madison– and Ben Franklin–class SSBNs in 1978. The USS *Ohio,* first in the class, was commissioned in 1981. The USS *Louisiana,* the last in the class, was commissioned in 1997 and may remain in service until 2040.

Now the Navy is extending the lives of both D5 missiles and of the Ohio-class submarines to 2040 under the D5 Life Extension Program (D5LEP). The main aim is to control costs by replacing obsolete components with commercial off-the-shelf (COTS) hardware, while maintaining the demonstrated performance of the existing D5 missiles.

Contracts totaling $848 million have been awarded to Lockheed Martin to perform this and related work, which also includes upgrading the missiles' reentry system. Another $318 million has been awarded to Draper Labs to upgrade the guidance system. In 2009 D5 missiles were upgraded with an arming, fuzzing and firing (AF&F) system that allows targeting of hardened silos and bunkers more accurately.[1]

The first flight test of D5's new guidance system, in a launch by the USS *Tennessee* in February 2012, was almost exactly 22 years after the first D5 missile was launched from the *Tennessee* in February 1990. As of 2019, the cost of the Trident program had reached $39.5 billion, which is about $70 million per missile.

In submerged submarine launches ignition of explosive charges in separate containers, which are separated by 17 titanium alloy pinnacles activated by a double alloy steam system, eject the missiles from their tubes. The energy from the blast is directed to a water tank, where the water is flash vaporized to steam. The subsequent pressure spike ejects the missile from the tube and provides enough momentum to reach and clear the water surface. Nitrogen is pressurized in the missile to prevent the intrusion of water into any internal spaces. Any water could damage the missile or add weight, destabilizing the missile.[2]

There are several safety mechanisms that can either deactivate the missile before launch or guide it through a launch phase should it fail to breach the surface. Activated upon launch, inertial motion sensors detect downward acceleration after being blown out of the water, and the first-stage motor ignites. Then the aerospike is deployed. This is a telescoping outward extension that reduces aerodynamic drag, and the boost phase begins. Within two minutes of the launch, the third-stage motor fires, and the missile is traveling 13,600 mph (Mach 18) on a sub-orbital trajectory.

Along with the D5's inertial guidance system there is a star-sighting system (a combination known as astro-inertial guidance). Together they can correct any small position and velocity errors that may have resulted from problems in the launching system or imperfect instrument calibration during the flight. Although GPS has been used on some test flights, it is assumed that the GPS system would not be available for combat missions.

Once the star sighting has been completed, the missile maneuvers to achieve the various velocity vectors that will send the deployed multiple independent reentry vehicles to their individual targets. The down-range and cross-range dispersion of the targets remain classified. In foul weather it's difficult to locate the stars. This is the vulnerability.

The D5 has a completely new design from its D4 predecessor, although some technologies have been maintained, and both missiles are within the "family" that started in 1960 with Polaris (A1, A2, and A3) and continued with the 1971 Poseidon (C3).

The first eight Ohio-class submarines were built with the D4 missile launching design. D4s were also retrofitted onto 12 SSBNs of the James Madison and Ben Franklin classes, replacing Poseidon missiles. More sophisticated and carrying a heavier payload, the D5 is accurate enough to be a first strike, or second-strike weapon. All three stages of the D5 are made of graphite epoxy, reducing the missile's weight.[3]

The D5 missile is currently carried by 14 Ohio-class and four Royal Navy *Vanguard*-class SSBNs. Along with 172 successful test firings, there have been 10 failures, the most recent being from the HMS *Vengeance*, one of Britain's nuclear-armed submarines, off the coast of Florida in June 2016. The Royal Navy operates their missiles from a shared pool together with the Atlantic squadron of the U.S. Navy. The pool of missiles at King's Bay, Georgia, where they are loaded on both the Ohio subs and the Royal Navy SSBNs is co-mingled, so the missiles are selected at random for loading on to either nation's submarines.[4]

The first Ohio-class submarine to be armed with the D5 missile was the USS *Alaska* in 2000, and by 2008 all SSBNs were D5 armed. The first eight Ohio submarines were home ported in Bangor, Maine, and Seattle,

Washington, replacing submarines carrying Polaris A3 missiles that were then being decommissioned. The remaining 10 Ohios originally had their home ports at Kings Bay, Georgia, replacing Poseidon and D4 back-fitted submarines of the Atlantic Fleet.

In 1994, the *Nuclear Posture Review* study determined that 14 Ohio-class subs would be sufficient for the country's strategic needs, and the decision was made to convert the four oldest ships in the class to SSGNs capable of conducting conventional land attack and special operations. Conversion of these subs began in 2002 and was completed in 2008 at a cost of $1 billion per submarine. They now carry 154 Tomahawk cruise missiles and 66 special operations personnel.[5]

Twenty-two of the 24 88-inch diameter Trident missile tubes were converted to contain large vertical launch systems; one configuration is a cluster of seven Tomahawks. The 154 cruise missiles carried is the equivalent of what is typically deployed in a surface battle group. Other payload possibilities include new generations of supersonic and hypersonic cruise missiles, Submarine Launched Intermediate Range Ballistic Missiles, unmanned aerial vehicles, the ADM-160 MALD sensors for anti-submarine warfare or intelligence, surveillance, and reconnaissance missions, countermine warfare payloads such as the AN/BLQ-11 Long Term Mine Reconnaissance System, and the universal buoyant launcher and stealthy affordable capsule system's specialized payload canisters.

The missile tubes also have room for stowed canisters that can extend the forward deployment time for special forces. The other two Trident tubes are converted to swimmer lockout chambers. For special operations, the Advanced SEAL Delivery System and the dry dock shelter can be mounted on the lockout chamber and the boat can host up to 66 special operations sailors or Marines, such as Navy SEALS or Marine Corps teams.

In 2006 the Conventional Trident Modification program was established as part of a broader long-term strategy to develop worldwide rapid strike capabilities and to diversify strategic options. Dubbed Prompt Global Strike, the $503 million program converted existing D5 missiles (presumably two missiles per submarine) into conventional weapons by fitting them with modified Mk4 reentry vehicles equipped with GPS for navigation update and a reentry guidance and control (trajectory correction) segment to perform impact accuracy. No explosive was to be used since the reentry vehicle's mass and hypersonic impact velocity was expected to provide sufficient mechanical energy and impact.[6]

The second conventional warhead was a fragmentation version to disperse thousands of tungsten rods, obliterating everything within 3,000 square feet. Together these were expected to make accurate conventional strikes with little warning and flight time.

There were serious drawbacks, however. It would be virtually impossible for radar to distinguish between conventionally tipped ballistic missiles and nuclear-tipped missiles, creating the possibility that other nuclear-armed countries might mistake it for a nuclear launch and provoke a counterattack.

For that reason, this project raised a substantial debate both before Congress for the FY07 Defense budget and internationally. Russian President Vladimir Putin, among others, warned that the project would increase the danger of accidental nuclear war. "The launch of such a missile could provoke a full-scale counterattack using strategic nuclear forces," Putin said in May 2006.[7]

The decision to replace the Ohios with the Columbia class was not automatic. The analyses included a variety of replacement platforms, including designs based on the highly successful Virginia-class attack submarine program and the current Ohio-class. Neither passed muster. "It's been speculated that the required survivable deterrence of intercontinental ballistic submarines could be achieved more cost effectively with the Virginia-based option or by restarting the Ohio-class SSBN production line," noted Rear Adm. Richard Breckenridge, Director of Undersea Warfare. "Both of these ideas make sense at face value — which is why they were included among the alternatives assessed — but the devil is in the details. When we examined the particulars, each of these options came up short in both military effectiveness and cost efficiency. Adm. Breckenridge cited these shortcomings with the Virginia-based SSBN design, modified with a large-diameter missile compartment for the D5 missile. The design would not meet survivability (stealth) requirements due to poor hull streamlining and lack of a drive train able to quietly propel a much larger ship."[8]

Other problems with the Virginia-based SSBN design:

- It will not meet at-sea availability requirements due to longer refit times (since equipment is packed more tightly within the hull, it requires more time to replace, repair and retest)

- It will not meet availability requirements due to a longer mid-life overhaul (refueling needed).

- It will require a larger number of submarines to meet the same operational requirement.

- It will reduce the deterrent value needed to protect the country (fewer missiles, warheads at-sea).

- It will be more expensive than other alternatives due to extensive redesign of Virginia systems to work with the large missile compartment.

"We'd be spending more money (on more ships) to deliver less deterrence (reduced at-sea warhead presence) with less survivability (platforms that are less stealthy)," Adm. Breckenridge summed up.

What about a Virginia-based SSBN design with a smaller missile? "Some have encouraged the development of a new, smaller missile to go with a Virginia-based SSBN," he acknowledged. "But this would carry forward many of the shortfalls of a Virginia-based SSBN and add to it a long list of new issues." The life of the D5 was deliberately extended to de-couple and de-risk the complex and costly missile development program from the new replacement submarine program. Additionally, a smaller missile means a shorter employment range requiring longer SSBN patrol transits.

"This would compromise survivability, require more submarines at sea and ultimately weaken our deterrence effectiveness," the admiral explained. "With significant cost, technical and schedule risks, there is little about this option that is attractive." As to the proposal that the Ohio-class production be reopened, he noted that this simply could not be done because there was no Ohio-class production line. "It's long since been re-tooled and modernized to build state-of-the-art Virginia-class, using computerized designs and modular, automated construction techniques," he pointed out.

Is it desirable to redesign the Ohio so that a ship with its legacy performance could be built using the new production facilities? The admiral answered this question with a resounding no, since an Ohio-based SSBN would

- Not provide the required quieting due to Ohio design constraints and use of a propeller instead of propulsion (which is the standard for virtually all new submarines);

- Require 14 instead of 12 SSBNs by reverting to Ohio class operational availability standards (incidentally creating other issues with the New START treaty limits); and

- Suffer from reduced reliability and costs associated with the obsolescence of legacy Ohio system components.

"Once again, the end result would necessitate procuring more submarines (14) to provide the required at-sea presence and each of them would be less stealthy and less survivable against foreseeable 21st century threats," Admiral Breckenridge warns. All those involved in the decision-making process agreed the right answer was to come up with a new SSBN design improving on the Ohio: the Columbia.

What has emerged from the Navy's exhaustive analysis is an Ohio replacement submarine that starts with the foundation of the proven per-

Columbia class submarine. Credit: General Dynamics Electric Boat

formance of the Ohio SSBN, its Trident II D5 strategic weapons system and its operating cycle.

To this it adds:

- Enhanced stealth as necessary to keep pace with emerging threats expected over its service life.

- Systems commonality with Virginia (pumps, valves, sonars, etc.) wherever possible, enabling cost savings in design, procurement, maintenance, and logistics.

- Modular construction and use of COTS equipment consistent with those used in today's submarines to reduce the cost of fabrication, maintenance, and modernization.

- Total ownership cost reduction (for example, investing in a life-of-the-ship reactor core enables providing the same at-sea presence with fewer platforms).

"The Ohio replacement takes the best lessons from 50 years of undersea deterrence from the Ohio, from the Virginia, from advances in shipbuilding efficiency and maintenance, and from the stern realities of needing to provide survivable nuclear deterrence," the admiral concluded. "The result is a low-risk, cost-effective platform capable of smoothly transitioning from the Ohio and delivering effective 21st century undersea strategic deterrence."[8]

Echoing the admiral, the U.S. Naval Institute has stated ensuring Columbia class subs remain survivable throughout their 40-year life spans they will have to be fitted with the most up-to-data capabilities including such additional design features as:

- X-shaped stern control surfaces (hydroplanes)

- Off-the-shelf equipment developed for previous submarine designs (Virginia-class SSNs), including pump-jet propulsion, anechoic coating and a Large Aperture Bow (LAB) sonar system.

- A Submarine Warfare Federated Tactical System (SWFTS), a cluster of systems that integrate sonar, optical imaging and weapons control.

- Electric drive. Conceptually, electric drive is only a segment of the propulsion system (it does not replace the nuclear reactor or the steam turbines). Instead, it replaces reduction gearing (mechanical drive) used on earlier nuclear-powered submarines. The Defense Science Board has long envisaged a nuclear-powered submarine that would use an advanced electric drive, eliminating the need for reduction gearing.

Northrop Grumman will be the prime designer and manufacturer of the Columbia-class turbine generator units. Turbine generators convert mechanical energy from the steam turbines into electrical energy, which is then used for powering onboard systems as well as for propulsion via electric motor. Various electric motor designs have been considered, but the permanent magnet motors being developed by General Dynamics and Newport News Shipbuilding are expected to be used for the Columbia. These motors developed by Siemens AG are now in service in the German and Italian navies.

The Royal Navy's Dreadnought-class submarine slated to replace the Vanguard-class may have submarine shaftless drive (SSD) with an electric motor mounted outside the pressure hull. The U.S. Navy has evaluated SSD, but it is unknown whether it will be included in the Columbia design. That design change improves stealth by eliminating the need for relatively noisy reduction gears in the linkage between the steam turbines and the shaft rotating the propeller/pump-jet propulsion.

With SSD, steam from turbines drives electric turbo generators connected to a non-penetrating electric junction at the aft end of the pressure hull. A watertight electric motor mounted externally, possibly an Integrated Motor Propulsion arrangement, powers the pump-jet propulsion, although SSD concepts without pump-jet propulsions also exist.

Recent data, including a Columbia scale model, indicates that these submarines will feature pump-jet propulsions visually similar to those used on Virginia-class. The class will share components from the Virginia-class in order to reduce risk and cost of construction. The design and technology development of the Columbia-class is projected to cost $4.2 billion (fiscal 2010 dollars), although technology and components from the Ohio and Virginia classes are to be included where possible to save money. The cost to build Columbia, the lead boat of the class, will be an estimated $6.2 billion (fiscal 2010 dollars).

The Navy has a goal of reducing the average cost of the remaining 11 planned hulls in the class to $4.9 billion. The total lifecycle cost of the entire class is estimated at $347 billion, cutting deeply into the shipbuilding budget.

In March 2016, the Navy announced that General Dynamics Electric Boat had been chosen as the prime contractor and lead design yard. Electric Boat will carry out the majority of the work on all 12 submarines, including final assembly, just as it did on all 18 Ohio-class submarines. Huntington Ingalls Industries' Newport News Shipbuilding will serve as the main subcontractor, participating in the design and construction and performing 22 to 23 percent of the required work.

By late 2016, some 3,000 employees were involved in the detailed design phase of the program, with the delivery of the first submarine scheduled for 2021. Completion of the first submarine iss scheduled for 2030, followed by its entry into service in 2031. All 12 submarines are expected to be completed by 2042 and remain in service until 2085.[9]

SUMMARY

The nuclear ballistic missile submarine's sole mission is strategic nuclear deterrence, for which it carries long-range submarine-launched ballistic missiles. They provide the most survivable leg of America's strategic nuclear deterrence with 70 percent of the nation's accountable nuclear warheads and its only assured second-strike or retaliatory nuclear strike capability. The Navy's force structure assessment establishes a requirement for a minimum of 12 Columbia-class nuclear ballistic missile submarines to replace the Ohio-class submarines.[10]

The Columbia-class design incorporates several new technologies to increase its stealth and operational availability. The submarine and its life-of-ship reactor core have been designed for a 42-year service life as opposed to the Ohio-class which was extended from 30 years to 42 years. Additionally, the submarine's electric drive propulsion motor and other stealth technologies will ensure the nation's SSBN force will remain undetectable survivable against evolving threats into the 2080s.[11]

Should Russia, China, or any other adversary develop capabilities for locating and destroying U.S. ICBM submarines, the consequences could be devastating. With 70 percent of the country's nuclear retaliatory power jeopardized, the probabilities of nuclear attack do not just increase but rise significantly. The greatest barrier to this surge is the extraordinary stealth designed into the Columbia. So, the greatest danger lies between now and 2031, when the Columbia will be deployed. That is a long period of terrifying vulnerability. Nothing should be done to slow the development and deployment of the Columbia class, and we should support any opportunities to speed it up.[12]

NOTES

1. U.S. Navy, Office of the Chief of Naval Operations, Deputy Chief of Naval Operations (Warfare Systems) (N9), Report to Congress on the Annual Long Range Plan for Construction of Naval Vessels for Fiscal Year 2019, February 2018.

2. Interview with Bryan Clark, Center for Budgetary and Strategic Assessment, February 12, 2010.

3. Megan Eckstein, "Ohio-Class Subs Approaching Several Firsts," *USNI News*, February 3, 2015.

4. "Vanguard Class Ballistic Missile Submarine," *Seaforces.org*.

5. 1994 Nuclear Posture Review, Nautilus Institute, June 6, 2019.

6. James Acton, "Conventional Prompt Global Strike," Independent Military Review, October 4, 2013.

7. Stuart Galbraith, "Cold War — the Reimaging Series," *Tank Net*, July 3, 2019.

8. Navy Columbia (SSBN-826) Class Ballistic Missile Submarine Program: Background and Issues for Congressional Research Service, June 5, 2020.

9. "DOD Asks Congress for Two Sub Columbia Class Buy," *DefenseNews.com*, May 13, 2020.

10. U.S. Navy, Executive Summary: 2016 Navy Force Structure Assessment.

11. "Navy Columbia Class Ballistic Missile Submarine Program: Background and Issues for Congress," Congressional Research Service Report for Members and Committees of Congress, May 17, 2019.

12. "Navy Columbia Class Ballistic Missile Submarine Program: Background and Issues for Congress," Ronald O'Rourke, Congressional Research Report for Member and Committees of Congress, May 7, 2019.

19 | Anti-Submarine Warfare

STEALTH ACHIEVED by virtually silencing the power and propulsion noise from the Virginia- and Columba-class nuclear submarines will not make them undetectable or invulnerable to our adversaries' anti-submarine warfare forces. New and rapidly developing sonar technologies can locate and track the quietest submarines. A growing array of highly accurate and destructive torpedoes and missiles, along with sonar-equipped mines, are now available to attack our submarines throughout the oceans of the world.[1]

Chinese government hackers stole massive amounts of highly sensitive data related to undersea warfare, including secret plans to develop a supersonic anti-ship missile for use on U.S. submarines by 2020. The hacks took place in January and February 2018 and targeted an unidentified contractor working for the Naval Undersea Center in Newport, Rhode Island. Taken were 614 gigabytes of material relating to a closely held project known as "Sea Dragon," as well as signals and submarine radio information relating to cryptographic systems and the Navy's electronic warfare library. (See Chapter 10, Cyber Warfare Threat.)

It was not long ago that Anti-Submarine Warfare (ASW) technology had advanced only to hull-mounted sonars (HMS) and tube-launched lightweight torpedoes, systems capable only of short-range, last-ditch detection and engagement. ASW surface ships were equipped with towed array sonar system (TASS) providing significantly longer-range detection and engagement potential than HMS.

The Russian and Chinese navies have advanced this technology to variable depth sonar (VDS) and longer ranged missile/rocket torpedo systems. Even now most U.S. ASW surface ships are equipped only with long linear-type passive towed sonar arrays. New VDSs, along with bow HMS arrays, can "ping" from within or below the thermal layers concealing submarines, leaving them nowhere to hide from low-frequency sonar to flashing LEDs — plus big data computing power that enhances the faint signals they pick up.

These new technologies for detecting submarines are analogous to what is being pursued in the electromagnetic spectrum against stealth aircraft. In both air and water, the advantage provided by stealth will continue to diminish. Russia's Project 1124M anti-submarine warfare (ASW) ships (aka: the Grisha V-class corvettes) are designed to enhance ASW operational capability of navies across the world. Currently in service with both the Lithuanian and the Russian navies, ASW can search, track, and destroy enemy submarines in deep waters.

Displacing 1,000 tons and just over 200 feet long, the ships require crews of only 80 but feature an aft-flight deck large enough for a medium-sized helicopter. Up-to-date electronics include MGK-335EM-03 Vesta-K sonar, Pozitiv-ME1.2 radar, and a Gorizont-25E INS Sigma-E combat management system. Two DTA-53 twin torpedo launchers enable Grishas to destroy deep-water submarines. The Osa-MA2 surface-to-air missile (SAM) system on the vessel can engage aerial targets, such as aircraft and helicopters.

The active and passive countermeasures systems include a TK-25E ship-borne electronic suppression system and four PK-10 decoy systems. The ship is also equipped with a towed ship-based acoustic torpedo counter-measures system. Also available for export to the navies of the world is Russia's new APR-3M air-launched ASW missile. "All the trials of the APR-3M missile have been completed, the process of its serial production has been organized, and its deliveries to the Russian Defense Ministry are under way," a missile manufacturer's CEO recently told Russian state media in announcing the export program. "The APR-3M is integrated into the armament of a Ka-27M modernized ASW helicopter."[3]

The Russian Navy is reportedly testing a compact hydro-acoustic station that can be fitted on almost any type of warship or civilian vessel. This module is unique in that it has been designed to fit into a conventional shipping container. The system apparently works with use of a trawl-antenna with hydrophones. A computer control post collects all the data and creates an operational picture of the underwater situation. The capabilities of this module allow Russia to rapidly expand its anti-submarine forces.

Concealment in containers is a feature of this system and there is concern that Russia's containerized ASW system could be sold to other potential U.S. adversaries. Development like this could threaten U.S. submarine superiority, so the sub force should be large enough to carry out its missions despite battle loses.

Bryan Clark, of the Center for Strategic and Budgetary Assessments, himself a career submariner and former top aide to the CNO, takes U.S. submarine vulnerability a step further. He concludes that instead of enemy submarines operating alone, they could operate together in underwater networks. Manned submarines would lurk out of missile range, 200 nautical miles from hostile shores, and serve as mother ships for unmanned mini-submarines and even aerial drones that push ahead into enemy anti-access/area denial defenses. This networked force (aka: a new wolf pack) would take advantage of America's lead in computing, communications, and autonomous systems — just as Russia and China are starting to catch up on numbers and sophistication of submarines.

Clark notes that with improved sensors and processing the advantages of submersion may disappear because sound bends with the curvature of the earth giving these sensors and processing greater range than radar.[5]

Big data is a big part of the new detection methods. Navies normally use active sonars with frequencies higher than 1,000 Hz, because lower frequencies require longer wavelengths that are less precise, even though lower frequencies carry farther. With the right algorithms and plenty of computing power, however, you can refine a fuzzy picture to the point that low-frequency sonar becomes tactically useful. It is similar to how improvements in processing power might make low-frequency radar able to target stealth aircraft.

Big data also enables more exotic techniques. Instead of standard sonar, sub-hunters could use lasers or even light from LEDs, carefully tuned to frequencies that carry best underwater. Active sensing altogether and passively monitors changes in the ocean environment, such as changes in background noise from sea life or tiny ripples on the surface from a submarine passing underneath. These indirect detection methods also have their anti-aircraft counterparts, where "passive radar" looks for stealth aircraft by analyzing disturbances in the background chatter of radio transmissions that are part of modern life.

Overall, the new methods for detecting submarines are similar to those being developed in the electromagnetic spectrum for detecting stealth and other aircraft, notes Clark. "Advantages provided by stealth will diminish."[6]

That does not mean submarines or F-35 fighters become irrelevant, however, because platforms without stealth features will fare far worse. Stealth will become the price of entry into the warzone rather than a ticket to penetrate undetected into enemy defenses.

As a result, in Clark's view, we need to start combining stand-off and stealth: Keep the manned stealth platform at a distance — where it's harder to detect and has more time to evade attack — and send in unmanned, relatively expendable, but also stealth platforms to do the close-in tactical work. Larger drones and unmanned underwater vehicles (UUVs) would deploy on their own from surface ships, while smaller systems could be launched from the submarines themselves.[7]

In the early 2010s, China started producing a number of ships that challenged ASW surface combatant platforms. The most important of these include the 052D DDG, the 054A FFG, and the 056/A corvette. Their transformation of PLAN ASW capability was a result of their mass fielding of new ASW sensors and weaponry. A new type of VDS was observed aboard the 17th 054A FFG (sometimes unofficially called the 054A+), and the same type of VDS has been fitted aboard the 052D as standard equipment beginning with the lead ship. The VDS has also been sighted aboard a variant of the 056 corvette, dubbed 056A.

By early September 2018, the PLAN's VDS equipped warships were composed of the following:

- 8–10 052Ds in service, out of a total of 14 launched and fitting out, with production continuing at shipyards in both Dalian and Shanghai.

- Approximately 20 056A corvettes in service, with another 10 in various stages of launch and fitting out. A total of 60 056 ships is expected to be produced by 2020, of which approximately the first 20 were built as standard 056 "no-VDS" corvettes, while the latter 40 are expected to be 056As.

Also, the new 055 large DDGs in production have been identified with a similar-sized opening in its aft indicative of a VDS and will almost certainly be equipped with a similar or superior ASW suite on existing ships.

Significantly, all the VDS equipped surface combatants are "two-tailed," fielding both a towed VDS and a linear TASS. These ASW sensor arrangements are not standard ASW fit for most surface combatants around the world and are reserved instead for more dedicated ASW warships. Therefore, the speed and breadth with which this type of sensor outfit has proliferated among recent PLAN warships has been impressive. Each of these warships also features an HMS as well, but as mentioned above, the utility of such a sensor for modern ASW is limited. The qualitative capability of the two-tail VDS and TASS outfit is not known. However, generally the modern PLAN has procured systems in large numbers only if they reach a level of adequate technology and competitive capability.

The benefits of VDS include greater detection ranges, the ability to alter submerged depth for optimal detection and tracking, and operation across a wide range of ocean environments. Therefore, the two tail VDS and TASS systems offer a vast advancement in ASW sensing capability compared with older ships equipped with only HMS and TASS. So, the two tail VDS and TASS aboard the 1,500-ton 056A corvette are almost certainly technically superior to the 052C DDG, which is equipped only with TASS and lacks a VDS.

Prior to March 2014, the PLAN surface combatant fleet fielded no two-tail surface combatants. But just over four years later, there are 42 two tail warships in service, of which about 20 are 056A corvettes intended for near-seas missions, and 22 were blue water capable 052D DDGs and 054A+ FFGs. It is likely that at least a total of 40 056As will enter service by 2020, with the last two 054A+ hulls entering service by 2020 as well. An indeterminate number of 052Ds and 055s are being produced and the expected 054B frigate will field an ASW suite at least as capable as what is currently in service.

Backing up the fleet of two-tail ships is a large number of single-tail DDGs and FFGs equipped only with a TASS. These ships include the standard first 16 054A FFGs, as well as six 052C and two 052B DDGs, and various older refitted DDGs and FFGs. A single-tail TASS is the standard ASW fit for many general-purpose warships around the world, and some leading surface combatants lack even a TASS.

The cover of a 2014 issue of *Modern Ships* showed a Type 056 from the stern quarter deploying a prominent variable depth sonar (VDS) as it hunted for a nearby adversary submarine. A variety of sources took note of this major design adjustment for the Type 056 with the first of these ASW-optimized light frigates, featuring the much larger aperture in its stern for the VDS. It is true that Beijing has been experimenting with towed arrays since the 1980s. But most new surface vessels have deployed with long linear-type passive towed arrays. The new VDS will give the 056 additional active sonar capabilities (along with the bow array) that can "ping" more effectively from within or below thermal layers.

According to the *Modern Ships* rendering, surface ships that employ active sonar methods of operation will render submarines unable to hide. Coupled with the possibility of new weapons, such as homing depth bombs or even a new type of ASW missiles, these forces promise a much more formidable challenge. Undoubtedly, a Chinese move toward more regularized "far seas operations" — quite visible in a variety of realms — will require a renewed emphasis on airborne ASW. Quite simply, fixed-wing and rotary-wing aircraft make for highly potent ASW platforms because of their speed, range, search rate and near invulnerability to submarine-launched weapons. Despite these advantages, aerial ASW has long been the Achilles heel of the Chinese Navy — a fact widely acknowledged in Chinese naval circles.

The PLAN's advances in shipboard ASW weapons have been equally impressive, particularly with two new ship launched ASW rocket and missile systems. The first of these is the Yu-8, a weapon similar to the U.S. Navy's VL-ASROC that can be vertically launched from the 054A's vertical launch system. This system has a range of about 30 miles and carries either a Yu-7 or Yu-11 lightweight torpedo. A 30-mile-ranged weapon greatly extends the capability of a surface ship to organically engage a submarine at safer distances, especially when paired with more capable sensor suites such as the two-tail VDS and TASS outfit.

Furthermore, the Yu-8 is almost certainly capable of being equipped aboard all 054A ships, not merely the two-tail "054A+" ships, which greatly expands the ASW lethality of single-tail 054A FFGs as well. There is currently no evidence that Yu-8 has been integrated into the universal VLS that equips the 052D and 055.

Less is known about the second weapon, a cruise missile that has been test fired from the ST-16M slant launcher. The launcher typically carries YJ-83 family anti-ship missiles and is widely fielded aboard PLAN warships, including all 054As, 056/As, and older DDGs and FFGs. This weapon is equipped with foldout wings, a ventral air intake, and a light-weight torpedo. It is not known if this system is currently in service, though its development implies the PLAN is looking to greatly expand the ASW engagement envelope that some warships can enjoy. If a vertically launched variant of this weapon is developed, it will likely be too large for the 054A's VLS but the more spacious universal VLS aboard the 052D and 055 may be able to accommodate it.

While adding these large destroyers and aircraft carriers, in its transition from a brown water to a blue water navy, the PLAN has created targets for enemy submarines — resulting in even greater urgency to strengthen its ASW capabilities. On July 10, 2019, the *South China Morning Post* reported that "China is developing large, smart and relatively low-cost unmanned AI-enabled submarines that can roam the world's oceans to perform a wide range of missions." ASW is almost certainly one of those missions.

The article said that the robot submarines are not intended to fully replace manned submarines. And, at least for now, they will not make entirely autonomous attack decisions. A military officer will have to approve whether to attack another ship. Still, the article notes, "the robotic submarines are aimed particularly at the U.S. forces in strategic waters like the South China Sea and western Pacific Ocean."

China already has small-unmanned underwater vehicles. Besides having limited range and payload capabilities, they are launched from another ship or submarine. The researchers who talked to SCMP noted the new robotic submarines — which China hopes to deploy by 2021, the 100-year anniversary of the Chinese Communist Party — are much larger and more autonomous. "They station in dock as conventional submarines," the report said. "Their cargo bay is reconfigurable and large enough to accommodate a wide range of freight, from powerful surveillance equipment to missiles or torpedoes. The larger boats are also powered by diesel-electric engines and other sources that give them greater endurance."[8]

One of the most attractive features of AI-enabled submarines is their low cost. As the SCMP article notes, manned submarines must have a high level of stealth to ensure survival, while also taking care of various safety and comfort level issues for its submariners. These AI boats will not have to worry about many of these issues. Thus, China can build and deploy a lot of them to perform reconnaissance missions, target other submarines or surface ships, and ram into other ships. This will be especially useful in waters near China where the boats can be programmed to operate in familiar terrain.

One curious part of the SCMP report is the sudden transparency. The People's Liberation Army (PLA) has a well-deserved reputation for opacity in military developments. The article quoted Lin Yang, a chief scientist at 912 Project, a "classified" program to develop the AI-enabled submarines. Elsa B. Kania, an expert on Chinese AI and defense innovation at the Center for a New American Security, noted that a "senior scientist being willing to discuss a 'classified' military program for an English-language publication surprises me. Assuming that Lin Yang is not about to be charged under China's National Security or Counterespionage Laws, he must have received official permission."[9]

Kania believes this permission was likely granted for signaling purposes. She suggests that since it is nearly impossible to confirm the level of maturity or actual capabilities of these submarines, it may be that China is revealing details about this program to make it seem more advanced than it really is. She has pointed out elsewhere, however, that the PLA recognizes a potential opportunity to undermine current U.S. dominance in undersea warfare. In that regard, it is interesting to note that the Department of Defense's latest annual report on China's military did not mention Beijing's relative weakness in ASW, and it noted that China has been taking steps to strengthen its ASW capabilities.

SUMMARY

Anti-submarine warfare and mine warfare are core naval competencies that need new directions if they are to keep pace with developments in other warfare areas and allow the Navy to have relatively unencumbered maneuver and action with acceptable risk. The engineering and technical challenge will be to develop affordable and cost-effective approaches that can readily make the transition into the fleet.

"These are four principal elements of an effective ASW program:

1. Distributed ASW sensor networks to provide adequate surveillance cueing against submarines

2. New technologies to counter mines

3. Advanced undersea vehicles (both unmanned and minimally manned) for a variety of mission applications

4. New system and technology developments that reflect increased emphasis on warship self-protection against undersea threats, including defense against torpedoes and mines

ASW advances mandate the kind of advances U.S. submarine capabilities demonstrated in design and development of the Virginia-class attack submarines and the Columbia ICBM submarines. The fact is that we may never know — until hostilities begin — how effective our ASW arrays will be in combatting their subs and/or how effective our newest submarines will be in eluding theirs. What we must never do is drop our guard in research, development and necessary spending."[10]

NOTES

1. Interviews with Bryan Clark, Center for Strategic and Budgetary Assessments, May 15 and 22, 2019.
2. Project 1124M Anti-Submarine Warfare Ships, *www.naval technology.com*.
3. "Russia Launches Serial Production of New APR Anti-Submarine Missile," *Russian Aviation*, May 13, 2019.
4. Interviews with Kyle Goldstein, Naval War College, April 12, 2019, and May 15, 2019.
5. Interview with Bryan Clark, Center for Strategic and Budgetary Assessments, June 12, 2019.
6. Interview with Bryan Clark, Center for Strategic and Budgetary Assessments, interview on June 12, 2019.
7. Interview with Bryan Clark, Center for Strategic and Budgetary Assessments, on July 11, 2019.
8. Bill Gertz, *South China Morning Post*, July 14, 2019.
9. Mike Giglio, "Inside the U.S. China Espionage War," *The Atlantic*, Aug. 22, 2019.
10. *Assessing Threats to U.S. Vital Interests: China*, Washington, D.C.: Heritage Foundation, Oct. 30, 2019.

20 | Sea-Mine Warfare: Inexpensive, Easy to Use, and Deadly

DAMAGE TO FOUR OIL TANKERS in the Persian Gulf, caused by limpet mines that Iranian Special Forces are suspected of having planted, was a mild preview of what destruction and chaos Iranian mining could cause. Iran is easily capable of laying a field of far larger mines to block the Strait of Hormuz, shutting off 20 percent of the world's oil supply, and causing global economic turmoil. Advances in mine technology have made preventing this kind of a blockade extremely difficult.

The Iranians have an estimated arsenal of 20,000 mines, many supplied by Russia and China. These countries have also helped North Korea build up an arsenal of 50,000. Iranians are no novices to mine warfare. On February 18, 1991, three days before the ground war began in Iraq, a large formation of U.S. Navy ships escorting the carriers USS *Midway* and USS *Ranger* was cruising north in the Persian Gulf along the Kuwaiti coast. On the left, between the formation and the shore, was the USS *Princeton*, a Ticonderoga-class Aegis cruiser bristling with missiles for protection against anticipated air and missile attacks.

At 9 a.m., the *Princeton* was ordered to reverse course and midway through the turn, she struck two mines. Casualties were light with only three crew members helicopered off for medical attention. The ship had to be towed to port, and it was more than three years later that repairs were completed. At the time of the explosion, the *Princeton*'s mission included protecting a nine-ship mine sweeping operation. Earlier that morning, the USS *Tripoli*, an Iwo Jima-class helicopter carrier and flagship of the minesweeping group, struck a mine, ripping a 16-foot-by-25-foot hole 10 feet below the water line and flooding several compartments. As with the *Princeton*, there were no serious casualties, but the *Tripoli* had to be towed back to port, and she was out of commission for years.

While mine blockades — except for one blocking the Strait of Hormuz — can usually be skirted, unsuspected mine fields like those that damaged the *Princeton* and *Tripoli* are much more of a threat to naval forces. The *Tripoli* had literally "bumped into" a M-08 contact mine, a type developed by Czarist Russia in 1908. While the M-08 is an advance in mine technology that dates back hundreds of years, these mines are only detonated by actual contact with a ship. They are anchored in relatively shallow water and easily detected by properly equipped mine sweeping vessels and helicopters. But they still make up most of the mines in naval arsenals. Why the *Tripoli* failed to detect the mine that nearly sank her is unclear.

What damaged the *Princeton* was an Italian made "manta" mine lying on the bottom in 60 feet of water. A type of "influence" mine, the manta is set off, not by contact, but by pressure typical of a caveating propeller or a ship's bow wave. The pressure wave caused by the *Princeton*'s propellers is believed to have detonated the second mine and the explosion lifted her stern out of the water. That mine set off a second mine off her starboard bow and caused the ship to rock vigorously back in the other direction. The explosions left the ship dead in the water with damage to the propeller shaft, piping and the air conditioning system, which temporarily shut down the air defense radar and missiles system, and leaving her a big metal target extremely vulnerable to attack.[1]

The likelihood of many Navy ships becoming big metal sitting targets or worse increases with mine technology. The original broadband acoustic mines of World War II have been replaced by more sensitive and selective narrow band sensors programmed to listen for specific acoustic signatures. With sophisticated digital signal processing capabilities, the latest electronic mine fuses prevent detonation by electronic countermeasures. Modern "influence" mines can quickly load new acoustic signatures into fuses or programs that enable them to detect a single, highly distinctive target signature and ignore friendly vessels and small enemy vessels. Or the mine can be programmed to ignore all surface vessels and just target submarines. To conserve power in their long-life lithium batteries, "influence" mines can remain semi-dormant until an unpowered or low-powered sensor detects the presence of a vessel, triggering the fuse to power up and the acoustic sensors to begin operating. "Bottom" mines are effective against surface vessels in waters 200 feet deep and against submarines at more than 650 feet. Usually using several different kinds of detections systems (e.g., combinations of acoustic, magnetic, and pressure sensors), they are effective against most kinds of ships. They are much harder to detect and sweep and can carry a much larger explosives than a moored mine. But most modern mine systems are moored. "Homing" mines, containing either a rocket or a torpedo as a warhead, are among the most vexing new developments in mine warfare. One Russian model fires a homing high-speed rocket at a passing vessel. There are also "torpedo" mines which pursue their intended targets and "mobile" mines which, once launched, proceed to a predetermined location in a harbor or channel at distances of up to 10 miles. Most concerning of all are mines equipped with tactical nuclear warheads. These were tested during the Cold War but never put into production. There are reports, however, they are being developed by North Korea.[2]

Pitting mines worth a few thousand dollars against ships worth billions and anti-mine measures worth hundreds of millions have brought asymmetrical warfare to sea in the starkest way. The manta mines that disabled the *Princeton* for three years cost only $25,000 each. Since the end of World War II, mines have damaged or sunk more U.S. Navy ships than any other weapons. One of the oldest naval weapons, they are usually the cheapest and most available to maritime nations around the world.

China

Much discussion among East Asian security analysts now centers on Beijing's potential development and deployment of aircraft carriers. While photos of a first home-build Chinese carrier will no doubt cause a stir, the Chinese Navy has in recent times focused much attention upon a decidedly more mundane and non-photogenic arena of naval warfare: sea mines.

This focus has, in combination with other asymmetric forms of naval warfare, had a significant impact on the balance of power in East Asia. People's Liberation Army Navy (PLAN) strategists contend that sea mines are easy to lay and difficult to sweep; their concealment potential is strong; their destructive power is high; and the threat value is long-lasting. The key objectives for a Chinese offensive mine strategy would be blockading enemy bases, harbors and sea lanes; destroying enemy sea transport capabilities; attacking or restricting warship mobility; and crippling and exhausting enemy combat strength. For future littoral warfare, it is said that sea mines constitute the main threat to every navy, and especially for carrier battle groups and submarines.[3]

This emphasis corresponds to the PLAN evaluation that, relative to other combat mission areas, the U.S. Navy's mine warfare capabilities are extremely weak. When military experts cast their gaze on the vast sea battle area, submarines attacking in concealment with torpedoes and the ingenious deployment of mines are still the main battle equipment of a modern navy. These PLAN experts call for making full use of units that can "force their way into enemy ports and shipping lines to carry out minelaying on a grand scale. China is engaged in a significant effort to upgrade its mine warfare prowess. Submarines are large and difficult to hide, and various intelligence agencies of other powers are no doubt attuned to the scope and dimensions of these important developments.

By contrast, mine warfare capabilities are easily hidden and thus constitute a true 'assassin's mace.' Relying heavily on sea mines, the PLAN is already fully capable of blockading Taiwan and other crucial sea lines of communication in the western Pacific area. Taiwan's relative trade dependence, the inherent difficulty in clearing mines, and the extreme weakness of American mine-clearing capacity, particularly in the Pacific theater, all make blockading Taiwan a tempting strategy for China. Sea mines, used to complement a variety of other capabilities, constitute a deadly serious challenge to U.S. naval power in East Asia.[4]

Russia

Developed in the late 1950s, Russia's modern "bottom" mines are considered state of the art. Equipped with multichannel exploders fitted with sensors responding to acoustic, magnetic, hydrodynamic, and electric fields, they operate on the principle of a highly sensitive influence exploder activated by passing ships. In combination with delayed arming, ship counting, channel selection, and telecontrol devices, this makes these mines extremely hard to sweep. Hidden in the sea mud, they can detect and destroy underwater mine-hunting vehicles normally operated ahead of mine sweepers.

Russia's submarine-laid bottom mines, which appeared in the 1970s, are self-propelled and menace adversaries' forces even in areas where submarine defenses are strong. The first Russian self-propelled a propulsion plant drives mine, designated MDS-1, originally designed for a torpedo. Comprised of a mine module and carrier, the module consists of a warhead charge and an equipment section with sensors responding to the target's physical fields, influence equipment, power supplies, and safety and functional devices. This mine is detonated as soon as the target-ship or submarine comes within a range where the intensity of the physical fields produced by it is sufficient to activate the mine's influence exploder.

Russia's self-propelled seabed mine (SMDM) functions like a standard bottom mine after it has been fired from a submarine's torpedo tube, runs the prescribed distance, and lands on the seabed at the required depth. The primary advantage of propelled mines is that, after being laid on the seabed, they are difficult to detect by mine-hunting sonars of submarines and surface ships, as well as by underwater mine-hunting vehicles.

Russia's moored mines are designed to destroy surface ships. The PM-2 moored mine is specifically designed to counter submarines under ice, with an antenna system consisting of three antennas: upper, middle and lower, each with two electrodes. The mine's influencer is activated when a target submarine enters the danger zone. The development and deployment of U.S. ICBM submarines spurred the development of Russia's anti-submarine mines. In addition to mines, special-purpose mine-hunting sonars and deep-water sweeps, as well as various mine hunting and killing assets, came into service.

"Russia's shipborne rocket-assisted ascending mine features a passive-active acoustic system capable of detecting and classifying a surface or submerged target, transmitting commands for warhead separation and igniting the rocket motor to transport the warhead to the sea surface and on to the target's location. The PRM-type moored rocket-assisted mine can be used against submarines of various classes, including low-acoustic-signature boats cruising at depths of 200 to 2,000 feet at any speed. This mine is armed with three rockets controlled through a flexible wire while it is running towards the target. The RM-1 and RM-2 rocket-assisted ascending mines run towards the target along a straight path. Their hydroacoustic influence system determines the target's relative depth. They are highly reliable and attempts by other countries to imitate them have failed. The PMR-2 anti-submarine rocket-assisted mine and the PMK-1 mine system (the export version) are basically combinations of moored mines and fast underwater automatically targeted rockets. The distinguishing feature of these systems is that, although they are basically active mines, they attack targets themselves. Their systems detect and classify underwater targets, determine their courses and running depths, optimize the target intercept trajectories and generate commands to launch either a rocket or torpedo. The warheads are sealed in launchers planted at great depths, and there are no effective countermeasures. Their great operational depth, wide target engagement zone and short time of attack, deprive targets of countermeasures or evasive maneuvers. These mine systems have given the Russians capabilities no other weapons system of prolonged action against an enemy can provide." [5]

North Korea

Russia has been North Korea's source of mines since the start of the Korean War, which saw the regime effectively blockading ports against U.N. naval activity. Today North Korea is able to secure mines relatively high up on Russia's mine technology scale. A decade ago, reports began circulating that the North Koreans had broken from major power mine conventions and begun developing nuclear mines.

Dissident North Koreans contend that a special group of researchers as the National Defense Technology Institute is developing underwater weapons using nuclear warheads. While their contentions were unconfirmed, according to a "secret" Wikileaks cable, a Chinese diplomat told a U.S. diplomat that North Korea failed to report "critical information about secret underwater nuclear facilities located on North Korea's coast."[6] Adding to the sense of stress in the United States have been "theoretical" Chinese naval analyses concerning arming sea mines with tactical nuclear weapons. One such analysis notes that nuclear sea mines could sink adversary nuclear submarines from a range of over one mile. A second points out that a nuclear payload is one logical method to increase the destructive power of sea mines. A third argues that nuclear mining is especially promising for future deep-water ASW operations, stating, that at this time, various countries are actively researching this extremely powerful nuclear-armed sea mine. There is no direct evidence of the existence of such naval tactical nuclear weapons programs in either North Korea or China, but these articles signal the need to closely monitor any efforts by these or any other countries in this direction.[7]

Iran

"Iran has a large supply of anti-ship mines, including modern mines that are far superior to the simple world-War I-style contact mines that it used in the 1980s. In addition to expanding the quantity of its mines from an estimated 1,500 during the Iran-Iraq war to at least 6,000 and possibly up to 20,000. Tehran has increased their quality. It has acquired significant stocks of 'smart mines' including versions of the Russian MDM-6, Chinese MC-52, EM-11, EM-31 and EM-55 mines. One of Iran's most lethal mines is the Chine-designed EM-52 'rocket' mine which remains stationary on the sea floor and fires a homing rocket when a ship passes overhead."[8]

The "manta" mines that Iran used to damage the *Princeton* and the contact mine that damaged the *Tripoli* were known to be imported, but Iran is thought to have annual domestic mine production capabilities of a few hundred mines, probably mostly contact. According to the CIA, Iran would now use mines against Arab gulf ports, particularly those of Kuwait, because of their high traffic and vulnerability. The CIA disputes the notion that the Iranians would mine the Gulf of Hormuz arguing that they rely too heavily on shipping through that waterway. The CIA also believes they would be unlikely to mine areas outside of the Persian Gulf. Iranian leaders have denounced mining of the Red Sea, and they probably recognize that mining beyond the Gulf would likely result in economic sanctions even more stringent than what they are enduring now. Kuwait and Saudi Arabia would turn to the U.S. and other Western countries for help because of their lack of modern maritime anti-mine warfare equipment and expertise.

Mine Warfare Defenses

An investigation of the limitations of U.S. mine clearing capacity must center on the 224-foot Avenger-class that the Navy has relied on for nearly 40 years. Because they are lightly armed and lack the flexibility to perform major roles other than mine sweeping, Avengers are out of favor in naval circles, and plans call for the decommissioning them over the next few years. The same plans called for the Avengers to be replaced in their minesweeping mission by littoral combat ships (LCSs). But these mine sweeping plans are now insufficient for the troubled LCS program, which has been cut back from 55 to 30 or fewer ships. Frustration is building in naval circles because of the growing need for mine detection and sweeping capabilities and the promise of technologies now being developed. Developers of Unmanned Underwater Vehicles (UUVs), for example, are testing an intriguing variety of candidates, discussed below.

The Barracuda

"The Barracuda is a semi-autonomous, unmanned, underwater vehicle that identifies and destroys near-surface, volume and bottom sea mines. It can operate in shallow water, using an expendable, modular neutralizer with a kill mechanism, propulsion, sensors and communications buoy, which transmits wirelessly back to the host ship. Initially it will be launched from an unmanned surface vessel operating from a Littoral Combat Ship, but in the future, it could be launched from almost any platform with an A-sized sonobuoy launcher. This UUV's mission is called Single Sortie Detect-to-Engage (SSDTE), which combines the search-detect-identify and elements of a mine countermeasure mission on a single platform executing a single outing, or sortie, so mine detection and neutralization can be conducted in a single pass of an area, a procedure that can be accomplished in days or hour instead of the weeks and month that were needed before. With this system, an unmanned surface vehicle launched from a LCS can spot mines from any angle and in high definition. The towed pod, known as AN/AQS-20, incorporates four separate sonars in a compact and lightweight body. It uses advanced imaging sonars, signal processing and computer algorithms to provide real-time, computer-aided detection and classification against the full spectrum of mines. In other words, it pinpoints mine-like objects and a visual image. If an object is determined to be a mine, a number of actions can be taken, including detonation."[9]

The Knifefish

This is an autonomous unmanned underwater vehicle designed to sweep mine-infested areas and chart minefields, employing low-frequency broadband sonar sensors to scan the bottom for mines. Launched and recovered from a Navy ship, the Knifefish operates independently in shallow water. Plans call for the Knifefish to replace the marine mammals now used to detecting mines. A vital component of the Knifefish is software based. The drone is equipped with automated target recognition software technology developed by the Naval Research Laboratory. This saves mine hunters an important step: While marine mammals could only locate mines, Knifefish will tell the Navy exactly what kind of mines they are, allowing them to begin a process of disposing them before seen by human eyes. Importantly, Knifefish is the only mine hunting system carried by the LCSs that can detect mines buried in the seabed.[10]

If the Navy discovers a possible minefield, an LCS will deploy its Knifefish drones from a safe distance and let the drone do all the detection work. This eliminates the physical danger to human crews. Dive crews or shipboard weapons can then destroy the mines in place. For now, only eight LCSs will carry mine counter measures (MCM) mission modules that include UUVs, Unmanned Surface Vessels (USVs), and a MQ-8 Fire Scout drone as well as a manned MH-60 Seahawk helicopter. This is even less mine sweeping capacity than the sweeping "Sea Dragon" helicopters. There would be just four LCSs on each coast. So, with typical Navy cycles of maintenance, training at home, and deployment abroad that would mean that only 2.3 of these ships would be ready for deployment at any time.

A major transition to what may well be the minesweeping vessels of the future appears to have begun. These vessels will likely be far larger than Avengers or LCSs. In the early spring of 2019 off the coast of Virginia, a U.S. MCM team embarked on the *Mounts Bay*, a 579-feet-long Royal Fleet Auxiliary amphibious transport ship.[11] The U.S. team included LCS Squadron 2 operating unmanned boats and submarines, Helicopter Sea Combat Squadrons 2 and 28 with MH-60S helicopters equipped with laser mine-detection systems plus a naval explosive-ordnance-disposal unit with its own small boats and robots. The team did not test the effectiveness of the systems to find mines, but concentrated on these areas:

- Whether a single-task group could command and control all the people and platforms at once;

- Whether the vehicles could be launched, recovered, and operated together without getting in each other's way; and

- Whether their data could be combined into a single operating picture to allow the task group commander to make decisions about how to clear a minefield.

Concerns were overcome about the potential difficulties and hazards of helicopters trying to operate from the flight deck and two units trying to move their unmanned systems and boats around the deck without slowing each other down or hurting any of the equipment.

Rather than Bay-class ships, most future MCM teams will be going to U.S. ships like the Expeditionary Sea Base (ESB), a 764-foot support ship which will be capable of carrying four huge MH-53 counter-mine helicopters, drones, small craft, other equipment and all their support staff. The USS *Puller* is the Navy's first purpose-built expeditionary sea base (ESB) in decades and already the byproduct of innovation. At a cost of $650 million, the ship provides a four-spot flight deck for helicopters and tiltrotor aircraft, a massive mission bay with cranes and equipment for small boat and unmanned vehicle operations, and still has a great deal of unused space.

On the MCM mission, the crew of the *Puller* had had little experience in mine warfare, just having worked with the airborne mine countermeasures such as MH-53E helicopters to determine how the ship could best support them and how it could be best reconfigured to optimize those operations. The *Puller* also worked with Avenger-class MCM ships in 5th Fleet to see if she can help refuel them or support them in any other way. Officers wanted experience with a carrier and other ships to become proficient in working with them. There were empty spaces in and on the big ship available to be filled. The costs would only be the engineering needed to design and build it. With each of the existing ESBs being permanently attached to a numbered fleet, each could make different alterations based on what operations and capabilities are most in-demand in that region of the world.

A second candidate to succeed the Avengers and the LCSs is the Expeditionary Fast Transport (EPF), a high-speed catamaran. Although these are much smaller than the ESBs (340 feet), they are much faster (43 knots) and their 12-foot drafts allow them to get much closer to shore. Their roomy multi-purpose bays are capable of carrying a wide variety of equipment, as well as a helicopter pad. But they are unstable in rough seas and at high speeds and are not considered suitable for blue water operations.[12]

Perhaps far more likely than the EPF to take over MCM missions, are virtually all the Navy's outright warships: amphibious ships, destroyers, and even aircraft carriers. All these types of ships can operate the Navy's workhorse helicopter, the MH-60S Seahawk, which can be fitted with lasers to detect mines and mini-torpedoes to destroy them. The *Seahawk* could be easily modified to carry UUVs and drop them from the air to hunt mines, dramatically expanding their reach. Unmanned minehunters deployed directly from destroyers and other ships could also carry an Expeditionary Mine Counter Measure Team (ExMCM), using inflatable boats, UUVs, and divers.

"All U.S. Navy ships should be prepared to operate in mined waters," insists Brian Clark, noting that this is essential with the ongoing ship from dedicated MCM forces to organic capability residing in each warship. And it is especially important for fast attach subs that will be the first in the fight." Because over 90 percent of the world's oceans depths are a mile or more, mining effectiveness is confined to the relatively narrow, shallow areas around continents and islands. For this reason, the enormous fire power of ocean-launched missiles by subs and surface ships and of carrier air wings is not affected by sea mining. In the relatively shallow areas where mines are effective, however, the advances in mine fuzzing and the virtual invisibility of bottom mines make them a threat to naval forces that even the most advanced mine detection and mine sweeping technologies cannot totally overcome. Continuously improving these technologies and spreading them across the fleet are the best counter measures.[13]

SUMMARY

In conversations about modern warfare tactics and weaponry, sea mines get lost in all the talk about satellite surveillance, stealth aircraft, and high-tech artillery. But those in the business of sea mine countermeasures warn that sea mines are more dangerous than ever and could be a key warfare component for countries and terrorist groups in future conflicts. Of the 19 U.S. Navy ships sunk or seriously damaged since World War II, 15 were the victims of sea mines.

China has reportedly prepared to deploy 80,000 sea mines to help it claim control of the seas during any potential conflict. North Korea is reportedly developing nuclear sea mines with an eye toward neutralizing the naval supremacy of the United States and its allies in the event of a conflict.

Russia has thousands of "smart" mines ready to be planted at a moment's notice. The importance of having a credible counter-mine capability is critical for the U.S. Navy and our allies. To address the very real threat, the United States will replace its fleet of 14 minesweepers over the next 15 years with multifunction vessels, including 24 that can be outfitted to find and eliminate surface and underwater explosives.

NOTES

1. Dave Majumdar, "Sea-Mines: The Most Lethal Naval Weapon on the Planet," *The National Interest*, Sep. 1, 2016.

2. *Assessing threats to U.S. Vital Interests: Iran, China, Russia*, Washington, D.C.: Heritage Foundation, Oct. 30. 2019.

3. *Chinese Mine Warfare: A PLA Navy 'Assassin's Mace' Capability*. U.S. Naval War College Digital Commons, June 2009.

4. Andrew S. Erickson, Lyle J. Goldstein, and William S. Murray, *Chinese Mine Warfare: A PLA Navy 'Assassin's Mace' Capability*. U.S. Naval War College Digital Commons, June 2009.

5. *Assessing Threats to U.S. Vital Interests: Russia*, Washington, D.C.: Heritage Foundation, Oct. 30. 2019.

6. Rebecca Perring, "North Korea's Secret Weapon — Kim's Stockpile of Explosive Sea Mines," *Express*, Nov. 23, 2017.

7. Greg Mapson, "The Looming Threat of Sea Mines," *The Strategist*, April 15, 2020.

8. *Assessing Threats to U.S. Vital Interests: Iran*, Washington, D.C.: Heritage Foundation, Oct. 30, 2019.

9. *Clean sweep: New Tech Can Transform Naval Mine Countermeasures, Raytheon Missiles & Defense*, Sep. 16, 2019.

10. Matthew Cox, "Navy's Knifefish Mine-Hunting Drone Sub Approved for Production," *Military.com*, Aug. 29, 2019.

11. David Axe, "America Is Getting Rid of their Minesweepers," *The National Interest*, Aug. 3, 2019.

12. Expeditionary Fast Transport (EPF) Department of the Navy, Nov. 11, 2019.

13. Interview with Brian Clark, Center for Budgetary and Strategic Assessment, Sept. 29, 2019.

21 | The Future Navy: Unmanned Warships

IN EARLY 2019, USS *Sea Hunter* became the first ship to autonomously navigate from San Diego to Pearl Harbor and back without a single crew member onboard, except for very short duration boarding by personnel from an escort vessel to check electrical and propulsion systems. This long-range mission demonstrated to the U.S. Navy that autonomous technology is ready to move from the developmental and experimental stages to advanced mission testing. Leidos Defense Group, builder of the *Sea Hunter*, has been awarded a $43.5 million contract to develop *Sea Hunter II*, which is currently under construction in Mississippi.[1]

Today two-thirds of the U.S. fleet is made up of Large Surface Combatants, monolithic and multi-mission platforms (e.g., destroyers and carriers) designed to perform many missions at once in self-contained kill chains existing within single hulls, which are expensive to man and

Sea Hunter. Credit: United States Navy

maintain. The likely future alternative is a transition to unmanned systems capable of taking the place of manned platforms in some situations. Two unmanned systems could take the place of one destroyer and one frigate at a substantially lower cost.

The problem is that maintaining the existing fleet is becoming too expensive, so the Navy is looking for ways of reducing the size of the fleet as measured in traditional ways like the number of manned hulls. They are looking for new ways of providing naval capability delivered by a combination of manned and unmanned platforms.[2]

The Navy is transitioning from a war-of-attrition approach to a strategy of out missiling adversaries. The goal is to create and mosaic of capabilities that will confuse enemies enough to forestall conflict or to win should conflict be unavoidable.

The service is so sure that it needs USVs for its future operations that it is pouring $2.7 billion into researching and buying 10 large USVs over the next five years. The overall plan is to buy 232 unmanned surface, underwater, and aerial vehicles of all sizes in the next five years. With much still unknown about the capabilities of USVs, why is the Navy risking such major investment? According to Vice Adm. Bill Merz, the Deputy Chief of Naval Operations for Warfare Systems (OPNAVN9), this lack of knowledge is precisely the reason.

> "We have a lot to learn on the unmanned surface vehicles," he explains. "We've all said that in testimony, but we're at the point where we really have to get them out there to start understanding how tough are these things, how robust, and how are they going to integrate them with the fleet, what kind of policies are going to surround these systems when you start talking about potentially separating weapons from humans. We're cautious on that side, but we're very aggressive in getting it out there, and run these parallel paths and illuminate these challenges and start resolving them.
>
> This commitment will send a tremendous message to the shipbuilding industry, crucial to companies making the investments needed to meet the Navy's coming requirements, he continues. "Every study we have done, several of them directed by Congress, have told us we have to develop these capabilities. We have to be more distributed, more lethal, more cost-imposing, all to complement the 355-ship Navy," Merz said.

Among the specific missions the Navy is contemplating for unmanned surface vessels:

- Mine counter measures to be carried out by small USVs;

- Sensors for the fleet carried out by medium USVs, akin in size to the *Sea Hunter*; and

- Weapons platforms by large USVs, similar size to smaller manned ships like the Offshore Support Vessel.

The Pentagon's Strategic Capabilities Office (SCO) has already purchased two large USVs with its own funding. Beginning in 2021, the Navy will work closely with industry to understand what possible and what kind of design and capabilities is to pursue. After two years of experience at sea, the Navy could go to industry and say, "Now you know what we want it to do. We've run these things around, you've all seen them, you know what we're after; give us some options. And we'll start working with industry on what the rest of them will look like. And then from there we will quickly transition them out of the research and development accounts and send it into a procurement account," Merz said.

For now, unmanned vessels are not considered battle force ships and would not replace any that are. But Merz stressed that this could quickly change in the future if efforts to build USVs and integrate them into the fleet are successful. "They may be battle force ships someday, but we have to get through all those technical and policy questions before we get to the point of calling them ships," he said. "What happens if you come through a storm and you had four and now you only have three? And the missing one was full of very valuable payloads. Where did it go? Who has it? Is it on the ocean floor? How are we going to let the fleet use these? These are very active discussions. But we don't have the direction yet. So,

Unmanned Underwater Vehicle. Credit: United States Navy

until we come through all of that, we can't start the discussion on which ships might be replaced. So, I'd say, we are 10 years away from replacing battle force ships with unmanned ships," he continued. "We don't really see the hurry. These are just enabling capabilities, so to us it's an accounting question, but it really doesn't change the pace of how we're getting after the capability."[2]

Where do our potential adversaries stand with development of unmanned surface ships? At just over a third the length of the *Sea Hunter*, China's JARI USV unmanned "warship" is boasted by the PLAN to have the firepower of an Arleigh Burke destroyer. Electronics and armaments are said to include an electro-optical sensor atop a superstructure, a phased array radar, a dipping sonar, eight vertical launch system cells, a torpedo launcher and a forward mounted machine gun and rocket launcher for counter-surface engagement.[3]

Western Naval experts are skeptical. Similar to commercially available unmanned harbor patrol boats, they can mount a machine gun on their forward decks and can also carry vertically launched rockets or small missiles on their rear decks. According to the product video, the drone appears to be modular and reconfigurable for the different mission areas, but it is unclear what missions are permanently integrated into the system. In the video, JARI is shown alternately shooting down an aerial drone, sinking a submarine, machine-gunning a RHIB full of adversaries trying to steal it (after firing warning shots) and sinking a surface ship that looked a little like a littoral combat ship.

Although the JARI may be nothing close to the clearly exaggerated descriptions of the PLAN, China's plans for unmanned warships are clearly extensive. It is part of the government's ambitious plan to boost the country's naval power with AI technology. In Zhuhai, Guangdong province, China has built the world's largest testing facility for surface drone boats.[4]

Russian development of unmanned surface vessel appears limited, at this time, to cargo ships which would be safer and more economical to operate in Arctic waters than manned ships. Their studies have shown that significant improvements can be made in the hulls of the ships if they can be constructed without providing space for crew members. Cargo can be placed in the bow, the dimensions of the vessels will be optimized in a more favorable way, making the voyage more effective in Arctic waters. One of Russia's powerful nuclear-powered icebreakers would sail first opening the ice for a convoy of unmanned vessels en route either to or from a domestic Arctic port or in transit between Asia and Europe.[5]

Unmanned Submarines

It now appears that unmanned submarines may become battle force factors more quickly than their surface counterparts. Under a contract announced in early 2019 Boeing got $43 million for fabrication, test, and delivery of four Orca Extra Large Unmanned Undersea Vehicles (XLUUVs) and associated support elements. The Orca is based on the Echo Voyager technology demonstration submarine. That boat is an unmanned diesel electric submarine launched and recovered from a pier. It has a range of 6,500 nautical miles and can run completely alone for months at a time. It measures 51 feet in length and weighs 50 tons. The submarine features an inertial navigation system, depth sensors, and can surface to get a fix on its position via GPS. It uses satellite communications to phone home and report information or receive new orders. Echo Voyager can dive to a maximum depth of 11,000 feet and has a top speed of eight knots.

One crucial feature of Echo Voyager is the modular payload system that allows it to take on different payloads to support different missions. The unmanned submarine has an internal cargo volume of 2,000 cubic feet with a maximum length of 34 feet and a capacity of eight tons. It can also support external payloads hanging off the hull.[6]

How much Orca will improve upon the technology already inside Echo Voyager is unknown. U.S. Naval Institute News reports that Orca will be capable of mine countermeasures, anti-submarine warfare, anti-surface warfare, electronic warfare, and strike missions. Orca could carry sonar payloads, detect enemy submarines, and send location data to friendly helicopters and surface ships.

Orca could even pack a MK-46 lightweight torpedo for use against an enemy submarine. It could also carry MK-48 torpedoes to attack surface ships. It would even carry anti-ship missiles. It could drop off cargos on the seabed and detect, or even lay, mines. The modular hardware payload system and open architecture software ensures Orca could be rapidly configured based on need.

This sort of versatility in a single, low-cost package is at this point unheard of in military spending. The nearest rough equivalent is the $584 million Littoral Combat Ship, which requires a crew of 40. While the LCS is faster and carries a larger payload, the autonomous Orca is cheaper by orders of magnitude.

For missions such as anti-submarine warfare, dozens of cheaper Orcas could saturate an area, potentially a far more effective strategy than that provided by a single surface ship or a manned submarine. Several Orcas could be controlled by a single shore-based crew, allowing the autono-

217

mous submarines to operate independently for days or even weeks at a time.[7]

Another benefit of unmanned submersibles is that they are more or less disposable and able to operate in dangerous waters without risking human lives. Orca could pretend to be a full-size submarine: waiting for an enemy submarine to take a shot while a real Virginia-class nuclear-powered attack submarine sits back, waiting to ambush it. Orca could take on the most dangerous missions, such as laying mines in heavily defended waters. They would be leaving behind a deadly surprise for enemies convinced that mine laying in their waters is simply too dangerous for manned submarines.

It is still not known whether an Orca system can become a full-fledged part of the fleet, although the Navy's purchase of four indicates that there are plans for using them for real-world missions. The Navy may be purchasing enough to continue testing while having a few on hand for actual use. Inexpensive systems like Orca could go a long way towards one of the most understated promises of unmanned air, land, and sea drones: reversing the out-of-control costs of today's weapons systems.

While China's development of unmanned surface vessel may just be getting started developing unmanned surface ship, researchers in AI projects report that the country is developing large, smart, and relatively low-cost unmanned submarines that appear to be capable of performing a wide range of missions, from reconnaissance to mine placement to even suicide attacks against enemy vessels. Expected to be deployed in the early 2020s and not intended to entirely replace human-operated submarines, these submarines are intended to contest U.S. Naval forces in strategic waters like the South China Sea and Western Pacific Ocean.

At the testing facility at Zhuhai, Guangdong province, military researchers are also reportedly developing an AI-assisted support system for submarine commanders. The new class of unmanned submarines is expected to join the other autonomous or manned military systems on water, on land, and in orbit to carry out missions in coordinated efforts, according to the researchers.[8]

With no human operators on board, these subs will handle their assignments and return to base on their own. While they may establish contact with the ground command periodically for updates, they will be designed to completing missions without human intervention. According to researchers, the AI-powered subs are "giants" compared to the normal UUVs. Their cargo bays are reconfigurable and large enough to accommodate a wide range of freight, from powerful surveillance equipment to missiles or torpedoes. Their energy supply comes from diesel-electric engines or other power sources that ensure continuous operation for months.

The Chinese unmanned submarine would not be nuclear-armed, and their main advantage is that they can be produced and operated on a large scale at a relatively low cost. While not presently developing unmanned submarines, Russia has something of an equivalent with the Poseidon, deemed a "doomsday weapon" by the Pentagon back when the drone-bearing torpedo was still known as the Status-6 Oceanic Multipurpose System.

The operational status of Poseidon was confirmed by President Putin during his March 2018 State of the Nation address, in which he touted work on "unmanned submersible vehicles that can move at great depths — I would say extreme depths — intercontinentally, at a speed multiple times higher than the speed of submarines, cutting-edge torpedoes and all kinds of surface vessels, including some of the fastest. They are quiet, highly maneuverable and have hardly any vulnerability for the enemy to exploit. There is simply nothing in the world capable of withstanding them."[9]

SUMMARY

We must leverage technology to expand our reach, lethality, and warfighter awareness. This means an increase in funding for experimentation and development of technologies to advance autonomous systems employment in undersea, surface, and air warfare. We must develop and incorporate unmanned systems to make the fleet more survivable and resilient and increase the lethal challenges and operational dilemmas we pose to an adversary, especially in terms of transforming, moldering, and revolutionizing warfare.

Maximum impact, minimum vulnerability. That could be the motto of the Navy in the decades ahead. Electronics and weapons platforms that can carry out the missions at minimal cost and with minimal exposure of equipment and personnel will be the keys to assuring both coastal protection and ocean supremacy when adversaries have reconnaissance capabilities and fire power to locate and destroy virtually any target.

NOTES

1. U.S. Senate Committee on Appropriations, "Department of Defense Appropriations Bill, 2018: Omnibus Agreement Summary," August 12, 2018.
2. *2020 Index of Military Strength*, Washington, D.C.: Heritage Foundation.
3. Interview with Thomas Callender, Senior Fellow for Defense Programs, Heritage Foundation, Washington, D.C., June 15, 2019.

4. Interview with Bryan Clark, Center for Budgetary and Strategic Assessment, June 4, 2019.

5. U.S. Department of Defense, Joint Chiefs of Staff, "Current list of CJCSG/I/M/Ns," May 4, 2018.

6. Ronald O'Rourke, *Navy Force Structure and Shipbuilding Plans: Background and Issues for Congress*, Congressional Research Service Report for Members and Committees of Congress, July 31, 2018

7. "An Assessment of U.S. Military Power: U.S. Navy," in *2018 Index of U.S. Military Strength*, Washington, D.C.: Heritage Foundation, 2017.

8. Interview with Thomas Callender, Senior Fellow for Defense Programs, Heritage Foundation, Washington, D.C., July 12, 2019

9. "Russia to Tests Doomsday Drone in High Arctic," *Asian Times*, May 26, 2020.

THE USS *ZUMWALT* was going to be the United States' 21st-century, cruiser-sized, super destroyer that would allow us to dominate the world's oceans and littorals for the next 50 years. The Navy said it would be able to supply the Naval Surface Fire Support (NSFS) capability that it has been promising the Marines since it retired the last of the modernized Iowa-class battleships in 1992.

The biggest of the fleet's Large Combat Ships (LCSs) was going to anchor the Navy's ability to project power into the littorals. Its 16,000-ton displacement would be crammed full of new and revolutionary technologies such as the integrated power system, the Linux-powered Total Ship Computing Environment Infrastructure (TSCEI) as well as the rail gun or even just the Advanced Gun System (AGS). The massive electrical

USS *Zumwalt*. Credit: United States Navy

generating capacity would allow it to power the energy-hungry lasers and other weapons of the future. The ship's defining glory, its stealth, would allow the *Zumwalt* to undertake missions that other ships could not.

The first ship in the class was commissioned while still incomplete and years from being ready for combat. In April 2016, the total program cost was $22.5 billion, with an average cost of $7.5 billion per ship. The dramatic per-unit cost increases eventually triggered cancellation of further production. Proof of the critics' concerns about the *Zumwalt* was demonstrated in her initial voyage from East Coast ports to San Diego. She broke down in the Panama Canal when both propellers seized up, and she had to be towed the rest of the way.

"Speed Kills" was the motto of the BAE Systems' project that designed a compact electromagnetic railgun for the Zumwalt class. Firing a 7-pound projectile at Mach 6 (about 4,000 miles an hour) would have been the first time in history that such a level of performance was achieved. Unfortunately, failure to reach an acceptable rate of fire with railguns mounted on the *Zumwalt* prevented the ship from achieving its goal. The expectation of projectile speed and the failure to achieve it may have killed the Zumwalt, at least for its primary intended purpose of shore bombardment.[1]

Rail-gun technology employs a pair of parallel conductors, or rails, along which the electromagnetic effects of a current accelerate a sliding armature that flows down one rail, into the armature and then back along the other rail. The velocity of the projectile fired is so high that it destroys the target on impact, and no explosive charge is needed. The advantages over conventional guns are several. The range is far greater, and the absence of both explosive propellants and warheads allows lower storage and handling costs. It also eliminates the bane of warships since the beginning of the gunpowder age: secondary explosions after the ship is hit by enemy fire.

The initial cost estimates were $1.34 billion per ship with total costs of $46 billion for 32 ships. Subsequent higher cost estimates prompted the Navy to lower the projected class size to 16 ships. Four years later that dropped to seven and a few years after that to three. Although the ship's electrical generating capacity was ready for the rail gun, the gun itself was years away from practical naval capabilities. In anticipation of this predicament, work began on the AGS by BAE Systems' Armaments Systems and was delivered to the Navy in May 2010. AGS turrets have now been installed on all three of the Zumwalt-class ships. The AGS uses the same 155 millimeter caliber as most American field artillery forces. But AGS cannot use ammunition designed for existing artillery, so ammunition must be specially designed and manufactured. The only type available is the Long-Range Land Attack Projectiles (LRLAP) for which procurement was cancelled when the cost reached a staggering $800,000 per

USS *Somerset*. Credit: United States Navy

round. Modifying all six guns on the three ships for different ammunitions would cost $250,000 in engineering work alone, and there is no plan in place for replacing the ammunition-less AGSs.[2]

Capable of the same 10-rounds-per-minute rate of fire expected for the rail gun, ASGs have been mounted in turrets specifically designed for the Zumwalt class, with fully automated ammunition supply and operation. The turret itself is designed to be stealthy, allowing the entire length of the barrel to be enclosed within the turret housing when not firing. The AGS is more capable of supporting ground forces and striking land targets than conventional naval guns. The 10-round per minute capacity will deliver the firepower of a battery of six 155-mm howitzers.

At the current, albeit rejected, cost of $800,000 per round, the LRLAP would deliver the same 24 pounds of high explosive as the conventional 155-mm round. That's a difference of 1100 times the cost for admittedly better range and accuracy. A $1-million Tomahawk cruise missile delivers a 1,000-pound warhead with 15 times the range of the LRLAP. So now officials at Naval Sea Systems Command and Naval Operations will monitor new technologies that could be incorporated into the BAE Systems-built 155-mm AGS.

There is as yet no plan for a material-specific solution, and the Navy continues to monitor industry developments, like the hyper-velocity projectile. At one point the Navy considered modifying the Raytheon Excalibur guided 155-millimeter artillery round but found that the unique low-twist nature of the AGS barrel would make the modification of the system to accommodate a new round extremely difficult. With no new round on the horizon and the fielding of a hyper-velocity projectile a decade away, the focus of the ship will now be on long-range surface and land-strike missions.

In addition to the AGS, each ship in the class fields 80 Mk 54 vertical launch system cells that are capable of fielding the Tomahawk Land Attack Missile, the Standard Missile-2, and the anti-air Evolved Sea Sparrow Missile (ESSM). Kirk and Smith would not confirm if the ship would eventually field the SM-6 but said there would soon be additional clarity on the changes under consideration. Vice Adm. Tom Rowden, Commander of U.S. Surface Forces, said that combat systems activation was not going as rapidly as planned.

Another weapon Navy official envision putting on the Zumwalts is a 150-kilowatt laser made possible by the ships' Integrated Power Systems generating up to 78 megawatts. While these lasers would not be powerful enough to seriously damage larger ships, they could be effective against Iran's Revolutionary Guards' small boats, drones, and incoming missiles. Lasers can also burn holes in ship hulls, torch flying drones, slice off control surfaces, and explode the propellants or warheads of incoming missiles.[3]

Crew member performance should be fairly easy to assess because the crew is small. The Zumwalt class was expected and intended to demonstrate the Navy's minimal- or optimal manning initiative, intended to reduce the Navy's shipboard-manpower requirements and cut long-term costs. Instead of requiring a crew of 400 to 600, as is traditional for ships of this size, the *Zumwalt* requires only 95. With less money spent on crews, more could be devoted to building ships.

No actual analysis was ever presented showing that a crew of 95 would be sufficient. But the number was routinely cited as being attainable until the design team was forced to accept a crew size of 147, not including air detachment of about 30 sailors. Critics warn that there is no way a large surface combatant can operate with a crew as small as 95. Should the ship sustain major damage, like a hull breach, it would be impossible for a crew that size to conduct the necessary ship-saving and recovery operations. The peak of the optimal manning argument may have come when it was argued the post of ship's cook be eliminated and the ship go to sea stocked with pre-prepared meals.

With the major increase in the ship's crew came the need to make it as stealthy as possible. This led to their odd-to-modern-eyes tumblehome hull design, which gives it a radar cross-section roughly the same as that of a 50-foot fishing vessel.

Stealth, however, has come with some major disadvantages. Tumblehome hulls the size of the *Zumwalt* are very expensive to maintain and less stable at sea than conventional ships with convex hulls. They could capsize in rough and windswept seas. The mounting of guns, sensors, communications arrays, and other equipment became so expensive that the decision was made to have the *Zumwalt* go with less stealthy externally mounted sensors and antennas, similar to those of the Arleigh Burke-class, rather than having them built into the superstructure.

Zumwalt skeptics also point out another question about stealth concerns: The primary mission of these ships is to dominate close-to-shore areas. But these waters are crowded with fishing boats, freighters, tankers, pleasure craft, foreign naval ships, submarines, and aircraft, both civilian and military. While the *Zumwalt* might be harder to see on radar, it would be very visible from shore and nearby watercraft. Even if it escaped prying eyes, once it began bombardments there would be no mistaking where and what it was.

Curiously, realization of the Zumwalt's deficiencies came well after it probably should have. In 2012, Obama Defense Secretary Ashton Carter enthused that the soon-to-be-launched first ship in the class that the Navy was preparing promised "game-changing capabilities to confound potential enemies." But those potential enemies remain unimpressed, at least by this particular weapon and weapon platform.[4]

The Chinese, one of those potential enemies, may have mounted their own, perhaps more advanced version of the railgun on the 550, their own massive new destroyer. Some optimists remain positive about the railgun and the potential for the *Zumwalt* to achieve effectiveness in its intended purpose of shore bombardment. Adm. James Hogge, USN (Ret) a former commander of the New Jersey, one of the four Iowa-class battleships built during World War II, believes the railgun could be perfected to achieve its intended range and rate of fire within the next 10 years. However, the media has piled on with negative coverage, as so often happens when a highly touted and unexpectedly expensive initiative appears to have failed.

"After more than a decade of research and development and more than $500 million, the Office of Naval Research's (ONR) much-hyped electromagnetic rail-gun prototype is finally capable of flexing its futuristic muscles — but despite the swirl of science-fiction excitement surrounding the muscular new cannon, it will likely never see combat," reported *Task & Purpose*. According to interviews with several congressional and military sources, the supergun has come under scrutiny from lawmakers and military planners thanks to the Strategic Capabilities Office.[5]

With SCO's interest drawn to other weapons systems, ONR may end up without the necessary funding to push the exceedingly complex rail-gun toward a critical testing milestone. This delay, along with increasing budget pressures and the DOD's shifting strategic priorities, could condemn the decade-long project to an inescapable limbo of research and tinkering far from any ship. "People at SCO don't want to fund the railgun because they're simply not buying it," one senior legislative official with direct knowledge of the project told Task & Purpose. "They are imparting that priority on to Big Navy, which is pulling the money away from ONR."[6]

SUMMARY

Is the *Zumwalt* a disaster? It's hardly a triumph as a frontline warship. With its guns neutered, it now seems to be a ship without a mission. If that is the case, how will the Navy use this ship? Eric Wertheim, author and editor of the U.S. Naval Institute's *Guide to Combat Fleets of the World*, noted, "With only three ships, this class of destroyers could become something of a very expensive technology demonstration project." He is not alone in this judgment. Adm. Elmo "Bud" Zumwalt Jr., former Chief of Naval Operations, deserved better.

NOTES

1. Interview with Thomas Callender, Senior Fellow for Defense Programs, Heritage Foundation, Washington, D.C, Interviews December 4, 2018, March 5, 2019.

2. Interview with Bryan Clark, Center for Budgetary and Strategic Assessment .

3. Interview with Thomas Callender, Senior Fellow for Defense Programs, Heritage Foundation, Washington, D.C. April 5, 2019.

4. "Carter's Strategic Capabilities Office: Hiding in Plain Sight," *Ius Curators*, February 6, 2016, *Inside Unmanned Systems*.

5. Jared Keller, "The Navy's Much-Hyped Electromagnetic Railgun May End Up Dead in the Water," *Task & Purpose*, December 4, 2017.

6. Jared Keller, "The Navy's Much-Hyped Electromagnetic Railgun May End Up Dead in the Water," *Task & Purpose*, December 4, 2017.

23 | Super Carriers: Fearsome Warships or Expensive Targets?

ON JULY 22, 2017, the U.S. Navy accepted into service the USS *Gerald Ford*, the first of up to four new fleet carriers. The 1,100-foot-long vessel will carry 60 aircraft, including 24 F-35 Lightning stealth fighters and 24 FA-18 Super Hornets. It features faster elevators for positioning planes and moving munitions, new electromagnetic launch catapults and arresting hooks to increase the speed of flight operations while reducing maintenance costs.

U.S. Super Carriers are by far the biggest and most expensive warships ever built. Towering 15 stories above the waterline and displacing more than 100,000 tons, they are nearly one-third larger than the enormous battleships built by Japan and the United States in World War II. At a

USS *Gerald Ford*. Credit: United States Navy

cost of over $14 billion, not including the air wing, the USS *Gerald Ford* is nearly twice as expensive as the Nimitz-class carriers in dollar figures adjusted for inflation. Some cost reduction is expected through simultaneous construction procedures now being employed for the USS *John F. Kennedy* and the USS *Enterprise*, the next two carriers of the Ford-class.

228

These nuclear-powered fleet carriers serve as potent symbols of American military power, capable of unleashing tremendous sustained firepower. The challenge facing carrier strike groups today is that new anti-ship missiles are becoming faster, longer-range, and more widespread, and they can be deployed from platforms including long-distance planes and bombers, small and stealthy fast-attack submarines and boats, and even shipping containers concealed on freighters or in harbors. Advances in missile and submarine technology raise questions as to whether such large and expensive ships are survivable when operating within striking distance of an enemy coastline. That striking distance is dictated by the 700-mile combat radius of the carrier's F-35C stealth fighters, with a shorter range for the Super Hornets. Sailing a carrier strike group close enough for its fighters to attack coastal targets places the it within range of deadly new missiles.

China's DF-21D IRBM has a range of 900 miles and possesses a high degree of accuracy with the capability of hitting a moving target, like an aircraft carrier. Their greater range means new missiles can safely be lobbed at carriers without entering within range for easy retaliation. The greater speed means they are harder to shoot down. The ability to deploy them from a variety of platforms makes the missile-launching units difficult to detect. Even more troubling for a carrier's air defenses is a new generation of hypersonic missiles with reported speeds of 4,600 miles per hour.[1]

China and Russia both have submarines that can hunt for carriers across regional waters. The Russian Oscar-class submarines do not have to get close to a carrier group's surface escorts with its P-700 Granit missiles that have a range of 400 miles and travel at supersonic speeds.

With both Russia and China rapidly acquiring new naval, missile, and air capabilities, it is also unlikely is that the strategies and tactics we used in 1995 and 1996 would deter them. At that time, the Aegis-class cruiser *Bunker Hill* had been off the south coast of Taiwan monitoring a series of missile tests China had been conducting from mid–July 1995 through early 1996. Another set of missile firings, accompanied by live ammunition exercises, occurred in August 1995. Chinese naval exercises were followed by highly publicized amphibious assault exercises in November 1995.

In March 1996, President Clinton ordered additional ships into the region in the biggest display of American military might in Asia since the Vietnam War. Two aircraft carrier battle groups centered on the USS

Nimitz and the USS *Independence* arrived along with the amphibious assault ship USS *Belleau Wood*. The *Nimitz* with her battle group of destroyers and cruisers and the *Belleau Wood* sailed through the Taiwan Strait, forcing the Chinese leadership to acknowledge its inability to stop U.S. forces from coming to Taiwan's assistance. These U.S. naval movements had come in the face of a warning from China for foreign ships and aircraft to stay out of the area during an upcoming round of live-ammunition military exercises.

"Should the foreign forces support and connive with the attempt by the Taiwan authorities to create independence or to split the motherland, then it could lead to a chaotic situation in Taiwan," China announced. "Should the foreign forces refrain, then there is no need to worry about tensions." China was seeking to intimidate Taiwan on the eve of the island's first direct presidential election, hoping to discourage the pro-democracy movement by raising voters' fears that any drive for formal independent status could lead to war with China. Naval deployments were the Clinton administration's favorite response to China's saber rattling.[2]

As the *Nimitz* sailed through the strait, U.S. officials declined to connect the action to American displeasure with China's Taiwan policy. But Washington had now dropped any pretense about the purpose of U.S. naval activity in the region. In their interviews, U.S. officials declined to say whether the U.S. would come to Taiwan's aid militarily if it were attacked. Rather, they stressed repeatedly that any attack would bring "grave consequences" for China.

A third set of PLA tests just before the election sent missiles within 25 to 35 nautical miles of Taiwan's ports of Keelung and Kaohsiung. Over 70 percent of commercial shipping passed through the targeted ports, which were disrupted by the proximity of the tests. Flights to Japan and trans-Pacific flights were prolonged by 10 minutes because airplanes needed to detour away from the flight path. Ships traveling between Kaohsiung and Hong Kong had to take a two-hour detour.

One Chinese response to the U.S. actions was to purchase Sovremenny-class destroyers from Russia, a Cold War–era class designed to counter U.S. Navy carrier battle groups. China also arranged to buy Kilo-class attack subs and some warplanes to counter the U.S. Navy's carrier groups. The missile tests and military exercises also strengthened the argument for further U.S. arms sales to Taiwan and led to the strengthening of military ties between the United States and Japan, increasing the role Japan would play in defending Taiwan.

Much has changed in the years since these events. The PLAN has developed from a brown-water navy of numerous small and mostly older ships to a potent blue-water force of increasing numbers of large modern surface combatants, both nuclear and highly sophisticated diesel-electric subs and now even a developing aircraft carrier force. The reach of PLAN weaponry now extends to over 1,000 miles off the coast and includes the Dong Feng-21 "carrier killer" ballistic missile. The *Nimitz* and the *Independence* would be in serious jeopardy in the waters around Taiwan today.

"The previous approach of using large, high-end platforms such as aircraft carriers to support the whole range of naval operations will not be effective at providing the prompt, survivable, high-capacity firepower that might be required to deter aggression in the South or East China Seas," notes the *Restoring American Sea Power* (*RASP*) published by the Center for Strategic and Budgetary Assessments. "It may be better to rely upon submarines and surface combatants as the primary instruments of deterrence and reassurance and to deploy aircraft carriers from the open ocean where they can maneuver to engage the enemy once aggression occurs."[3]

The *RASP* goes on to stress that U.S. allies in Asia, including Japan, Australia, South Korea, and the Philippines, are growing worried about China's maritime build-up and increasingly aggressive behavior at sea. These allies will need to be reassured with evidence of conventional deterrence by the U.S. Navy.

For China the threat could be Taiwan or the Senkakus. For Russia, the Baltic nations. For Iran, the Strait of Hormuz. These potential U.S. adversaries could attack these targets quickly and with little warning. All may lack the core personnel and equipment they would need to quickly replace losses and repair damaged equipment. They would probably be unable to confront secondary threats—unexpected military reactions from U.S. allies that could develop during the conflicts. But those problems might be overcome simply by the proximities of the targets.

RASP notes that China has a larger military than our other potential adversaries and would be better able to meet these force-structure demands. But it also notes that only a small fraction of the enormous forces of the PLA and the PLAN would be needed, even for complex military operations like invasions of Taiwan or the Senkakus. Given these capabilities and their geographic advantages, China might believe that it could achieve its military objectives before U.S. and Allied forces are able to mobilize their massive, albeit delayed, response.

RASP also predicts that China and other potential aggressors might further calculate that they would have another crucial advantage: the reluctance of the international community to support a conventional offensive to dislodge them, given the number of additional casualties, damage, and disruption the operation would entail. Then there is the likelihood, under these circumstances, of nuclear escalation. As a result, these aggressors might hope to achieve what Russia did with its annexation of Crimea in 2014.

How would the Navy react should China make an all-out attack on Taiwan? Attack submarines and surface combatants of the containment force positioned within a few hundred miles of the Chinese coast could launch Tomahawk missiles. But the missile arsenals on these ships would be quickly exhausted, and the ships would have to return to Japan or Guam to be rearmed. Next in the line of "defense," the maneuver force would be a Super Carrier or carriers at least 1,000 miles offshore. That distance would put it some 400 miles beyond the strike range of the carriers' air wings—the distance dictated by range of Chinese anti-ship missile salvos that may or may not be stopped by the anti-missile defenses of the carrier strike group's escorts and air wing.

Super carriers' significance extends well beyond their size, their cost, and even their military potency. Speaking at the Heritage Foundations 2019 seminar "The Future of the U.S Aircraft Carrier — Fearsome Warship or Expensive Target," Jerry Hendrix, vice president of Telemus Group, noted that carriers have gone beyond being naval platforms to becoming "near mystical symbols of American national power" and perceived as aspects of national prestige.[4]

"If we purchased a *Ford* carrier in one year it would represent 80 percent of our entire ship-building budget," Dr. Kendrix noted. "Presidents may be hesitant to introduce carriers inside the enemy's threat environment for fear of loss of both national prestige and political power. Because of this, over the past 50 years, the Navy has become increasingly focused on defending the carrier."

Defending the carrier means keeping these ships out of range of enemy missiles, which, in a conflict with China, could mean keeping them well out in the Western Pacific. Bryan McGrath, a retired Navy Arleigh Burke commander and another speaker at the Heritage Foundation Conference, sees that positioning as advantageous. "Super-carriers well out in the Western Pacific would have the advantage of continuously practicing tactics with their combined air wings, making up a force of 200 or more attack aircraft. Such a force, armed with our most up-to-date missiles and flown by pilots carefully trained to use these weapons to maximum advantage, would be extraordinarily formidable," McGrath said.[5]

The problem of limited range remains, however. Coming in from the Pacific, the carriers would still have to remain beyond the range of Chinese missiles. So this enormous combined air wing has to be refueled during its approach to targets. Unmanned aircraft tankers flown off the same carrier decks would provide the refueling. But the tankers to accomplish this are four or five years away. Even once they are available, there is the question of how the refueling process of all these attack planes would be protected from Chinese aircraft and missiles.

Supporters of the super carriers believe that in time these questions will be answered. They suggest that filling the gap between our Toma-

F-18E Super Hornet. Credit: United States Navy

hawk launching submarines and surface combatants would be a force of smaller carriers carrying contingents of vertical takeoff F-35 B fighters. As described by *RASP* co-author Bryan McGrath, Senior Fellow, Center for Strategic and Budgetary Assessments, they would "initially" be built on the backbone of amphibious assault ships — which now carry helicopters — with the helicopters being redistributed to a more numerous amphibious force.

The USS *Wasp* and the USS *Essex*, both amphibious assault ships with six F-35Bs aboard, have been assigned to the Pacific fleet. There are no plans for building 50,000-ton light carriers, and there is some skepticism about the combat capabilities of the F-35Bs. Another problem is that a fixed-wing airplane in vertical takeoff mode can carry only a limited amount of fuel and weapons.

McGrath counters that the limits on the airplane's fuel load could be made up by an increased range on the missiles it fires. What seems certain, however, is that there may be no near-term solution to the gap between today's limited deterrence force of submarines and surface combats and the two-distant super-carriers.

What might happen if the Chinese should decide to move against Taiwan before the hoped-for deterrence fleet is ready? Bryan Clark sees a "grey zone" action on islands in the Taiwan Strait as the most likely site for conflict. Right now, Taiwan has a defense force of small patrol boats, fighter aircraft, and attack helicopters to oppose an invasion. But Clark believes that the Chinese might not conduct an invasion, at least not right away.

Clark notes that Taiwan may not want to use its military to counter that because it would be seen as disproportionate. Taiwan lacks the tools at the lower levels of escalation that would be suited for that. China's Central Military Commission has command and control over all these quasi-military assets.

"By virtue of their ability to use these civilian and paramilitary forces and their long-range air defense and surface-to-surface missiles on the mainland, they can go up and down the escalation ladder, whereas the U.S. and our allies do not have many tools, except at the high end of escalation. And, of course, they would be reluctant to use them in situations where the actions are carried out on groups of civilians," Clark added.

"Occupying an island? You're not going to want to defend that with air strikes. Our war games show that China has a superior position, mainly because the U.S. and its allies like Taiwan have not invested in the kinds of tools that could be used for a lower level response. These are non-kinetic weapons, like high-power microwave and electronic warfare or smaller ships to be used to block theirs. Having no investment in these, we have few options when the Chinese take these gray zone actions," Clark said.

Fortification of the Taiwan Strait islands would proceed slowly at first as China did on the Spratlys. It took a long time before China began installing infrastructure and military capability there. They wanted to see how far they could go before the United States or the Philippines pushed back. Because they did not get much resistance, they just kept going. In the Taiwan Strait, they can put a lot of the maritime militia out to encircle the island, preventing easy access by the Taiwanese. They can establish

F-35 Lightning. Credit: United States Navy

conditions on the water that make it seem like China is in control. Then they might establish a non-manned outpost or one that would not be continually manned. Eventually they would put people on it, build up the island slowly by adding features to make it more militarily relevant as they perceive they are not being resisted by the Taiwanese or the United States.[6]

"I don't think of Taiwan as China's Crimea, demonstrating President Xi's aggressiveness," Clark continued. "Putin's gradualist approach was in the Ukraine. Crimea emerged as an opportunity, but it was not what Russia had in mind at the start. The probability of failure was very low because of the instrumentalist approach Putin took. He could always have dialed that back if there was the possibility of it not going well," Clark said.

"Taiwan would be an all-or-nothing proposition. It's a big country. Its military is capable but not very good at power projection. The Strait is 90 miles wide with difficult oceanography. There are not many good beaches to land on. It would be pretty easy for the Taiwanese to determine which areas to defend. An invasion would be a very fraught proposition. It's not likely Xi would want to go through that to deal with a domestic problem because they could end up failing and make it worse," Clark added.[6]

The Chinese might impose blockade or partial blockade because their military could do it, and the Taiwanese would not necessarily be able to defeat it. Clark believes that the U.S. Navy would be unlikely to come in on Taiwan's side unless it was seen as an existential threat. If Xi put some pressure on Taiwan to make some further capitulations to Chinese rule and the Taiwanese resisted, China might invent a situation where the blockade was seen as retaliation. That could build up nationalist support for Xi's administration. This is the more likely scenario. It is low risk. It would pay off in nationalist sentiment, and Xi could always dial it back, whereas a failed invasion attempt would be a bad situation. Once you are in, either you bring it to completion, or you lose face because you backed off. Meanwhile Taiwan would not have the capability to reach out and lift a blockade.

SUMMARY

The answer to the question "Fearsome Warships or Expensive Targets?" unfortunately seems to be "targets." Until carrier airwings are made up of attack aircraft with far greater ranges than those currently available, carriers like the Navy's other large combat ships are targets in long-range missile dominated conflicts. The real question is why so much of the Navy's budget is devoted to building and operating carriers when the best and the only truly effective warships will have to operate beneath the ocean surface. The money spent building one Ford-class carrier would fund four Virginia-class submarines, and the costs of operations would be significantly lower.

NOTES

1. Heritage Foundation Conference, "The Future of the U.S. Aircraft Carrier: Fearsome Warship or Expensive Target?" June 9, 2019,

2. James Risen, "U.S. Warns China on Taiwan, Sends Warships to Area," *Los Angeles Times*, March 11, 1996.

3. Bryan Clark, Peter Haynes, Jesse Sloman, Timothy Walton, Feb. 9, 2017, *Restoring American Sea Power* (*RASP*), Center for Strategic and Budgetary Assessments.

4. "The Future of the U.S Aircraft Carrier–Fearsome Warship or Expensive Target?" Heritage Foundations 2019 seminar.

5. "The Future of the U.S Aircraft Carrier–Fearsome Warship or Expensive Target?" Heritage Foundations 2019 seminar.

6. Terrence Kelly, David Gompert, Duncan Long, "Exploiting U.S. Advantages to Prevent Aggression," Feb. 8, 2017, Rand Corporation.

24 | Naval Training: Are the Right People Being Held Accountable for Ship Collisions?

Commanders Bryce Benson and Alfredo Sanchez, former commanders of the USS *Fitzgerald* and the USS *John S. McCain* respectively, faced charges of negligent homicide after the deaths of 17 sailors in the collisions of their ships with merchant vessels in June and August of 2017. The *Fitzgerald* was about 80 nautical miles southwest of Tokyo when the collision occurred. The *McCain* was in the Straits of Malacca. Their defense attorneys were expected to ask just whose negligence was responsible. At that time of the collisions, the vice chief of naval operations called these accidents especially alarming because, as part of the Seventh Fleet, the crews of these ships were among the best trained and most experienced in the Navy.[1] The Navy dropped charges on Aug. 11, 2019, against Cmdr. Benson and Lt. Natalie Combs for what it determined was an avoidable accident caused by numerous leadership failures.[2] Negligent homicide charges filed against Cmdr. Alfredo, CO of the *McCain* at the time of the collision, were dropped on May 23, 2018.[3]

Admiral John R. Richardson, Chief of Naval Operations, contended that the collisions were avoidable in a summary of the reports issued in November 2017. "Both of these accidents were preventable and the respective investigations found multiple failures by watch stands that contributed to the accidents. We are a Navy that learns from mistakes and the Navy is firmly committed to doing everything possible to prevent an accident like this from happening again. We must never allow an accident like this to take the lives of such magnificent young sailors and inflict such painful grief on their families and the nation."[4]

Reports of the two collisions ware filled with missed warnings, chains of errors, and frantic American sailors fighting to save their fellow shipmates. What had gone wrong? In the case of the *Fitzgerald*, the Navy determined that the crew and leadership on board failed to plan for safety, to adhere to sound navigation practices, to carry out basic watch prac-

USS *Fitzgerald*. Credit: United States Navy

tices and to respond effectively in a crisis and placed responsibility on Commander Benson's faulty judgement and decision making.

In the case of the *John S. McCain*, things began to go wrong at 5:20 a.m. on August 21, 2017, as the ship approached the Straits of Malacca, one of the busiest shipping lanes in the world. The moon had set beneath an overcast sky and a three-foot swell rolled under the 505-foot-long, *Arleigh Burke*, a guided missile destroyer. The ship's commanding officer, Cmdr. Alfredo J. Sanchez, had been on the bridge since 1:15 that morning. He noticed that the sailor steering the ship was having difficulty managing the helm and the complex arrangement of throttles that controlled the power to the *McCain*'s twin propellers. He ordered that the tasks be divided, one sailor steering at one station, another manning the throttles at another. The move, intended to make operating the ship more manageable, ended up taking away the helmsman's ability to steer. A secondary effect of the decision was the inadvertent transfer of steering to the console, now designated to control the throttles.

The helmsman, confused and apparently with no control of the ship, said he lost steering. As the ship began turning to the left, Commander Sanchez ordered a reduction in speed. The sailor operating the throttles tried to slow the ship but managed only to reduce power to one of the propellers, meaning only one reduced speed while the other continued at regular propulsion. The mismatch lasted for more than a minute, causing the *McCain* to veer left and into the path of the *Alnic*, a 600-foot merchant ship. "Although the *McCain* was now on a course to collide with *Alnic*, the Commanding Officer and others on the ship's bridge lost situational awareness. No one on the bridge clearly understood the forces acting on the ship, nor did they alter the *Alnic*'s course and speed relative to *John S McCain* during the confusion"[5]

The crew eventually managed to synchronize the ship's steering and throttles, but it was too late, The *Alnic*'s bow slammed into the *McCain*'s left side, punching a 28-foot-wide hole in the warship that spanned deep under the waterline. The vessels remained welded together for several minutes before breaking free. The 10 sailors who perished were in a berthing area situated below the *McCain*'s waterline, near the point of impact. The 15-foot wide space filled with water immediately and was completely submerged in under a minute. The *McCain* report concluded that the collision resulted from a loss of situational awareness while responding to mistakes in the operation of the ship's steering and propulsion system while in highly trafficked waters.

The *Fitzgerald* was within sight of land around 1:00 a.m. on June 17, 2017, when officers on the bridge failed to realize how close their ship had come to the *Crystal*, a merchant freighter. In the minutes before the collision, two additional ships came close to the *Fitzgerald*. But the officers did not change course, mistaking the *Crystal* for one of the ships they believed was farther away. By the time they realized the mistake, it was

USS McCain. Credit: United States Navy

too late. The *Crystal* struck the *Fitzgerald* at 1:30 a.m., and within seconds sailors were waist deep, then neck deep in water. Of the 35 trapped sailors, seven would not survive. The report attributed the collision to failure to maneuver the ship away from the approaching freighter, failure to sound the danger signal and failure to contact the Crystal. Navy investigators described a bridge team that was overworked and exhausted. The crew's workday began at 6:00 a.m. on June 16, 2017, and it involved a full schedule of demanding tasks. By the time the crew arrived at their bridge for their four-hour shift, they were fatigued and without adequate rest, the report said.[6]

Within days of the *McCain* collision, Vice Adm. Joseph Aucoin, commander of the 7th Fleet, was removed from his command, along with Rear Adm. Charles Williams, the commander of Task Force 70 and Capt. Jeffrey Bennet, Destroyer 15 commander. Under the Navy's "charge of command," the commanding officer bears absolute responsibility for the "safety, well being and efficiency" of their command. The CO of a naval vessel must answer for everything that happens on board. The question remains however: Are the right people being held accountable? Admiral Aucoin claimed that the 7th Fleet was frequently tasked with missions on short notice. Even when he had said he would not recommend the mission, he was ordered to execute it anyway, he said.[7]

Some Navy officials believe the problems began in 2011 when Congress required nearly $1 trillion in cuts to projected defense spending over a decade. Spending cuts have left the U.S. Navy and Marines ill-prepared to deal with a sudden conflict, and continuing reductions may mean ships and troops arrive late to the fight and without the training and arms they need, Admiral Jonathan Greenert, then Chief of Naval Operations, warned a Senate hearing on March 10, 2015. Admiral Greenert said budget cuts had forced the Navy to reduce operations and create maintenance backlogs. At the same time, General Joseph Dunford, the Marine commandant, said tight budgets had required his force to prioritize training and equipment for units that were deploying abroad.[8]

The late senator John McCain, then chairman of the Senate Armed Services Committee, pointed to the automatic budget cuts, a process known as sequestration, as one of the primary culprits behind the combined 17 deaths abroad the Fitzgerald and the McCain. "We've deprived them of the funds to do it and we're putting those men and women in harm's way to be wounded or killed because we refuse to give them the sufficient training and equipment and readiness. It's a failure of Congress. It's on us."[9]

A study provides a number of answers: the fleet is too small and has too few sailors to meet the nation's ever-increasing operational demands; the professional development regimen for surface warfare personnel no longer provides the intensive navigation and mariner skills training formerly offered officers and sailors; the extremely high operational demands on forward-deployed ships has left no dedicated time to formally train and evaluate the proficiency of crew members and officers; ships were often tasked to perform missions based on availability, not fitness — much less certification — for missions; and years of budget cuts has forced Navy leadership to reduce or delay spending on near-term operations and maintenance.[10]

A House Armed Services Committee hearing convened to explore what is behind the rash of naval collisions (there had been two others in the year prior to those of the *Fitzgerald* and the *McCain*). The hearing brought additional troubling issues to light. Government Accountability Office testimony revealed that the number of expired warfare certifications among the Japan-based destroyers and cruisers has increased five-fold in the two years prior to the hearings. Moreover, eight of those 11 ships have expired seamanship certifications. It was also revealed that the Surface Fleet Leadership, from ships' commanding officers all the way up to the Naval Surface Warfare Commander, had approved waivers and risk mitigation plans for these expired certifications to meet operational requirements.[11]

At these hearing, it was pointed out that in the Navy — as in all military culture — it is extremely hard to say "no" to tasking. So, leaders have had to take a hard look at the quantity and priority of operational tasking versus the availability and proficiency of Navy ships and say "no" when there is an obvious deficit. Moreover, commanding officers need clear "red lines" of required proficiency certifications and acceptable risk, so they know when to tell their superiors "no" to assigned tasking.

A recent internal review conducted by senior U.S. surface fleet leaders found some significant concerns with the ship-handling skills of nearly 85 percent of its junior officers. Many struggled to react decisively to extricate ships from danger when there was an immediate risk of collision, according to the report.[12]

"Of the 164 officers who were evaluated, only 27 passed with "no concerns." Another 108 completed with "some concerns," and 29 had "significant concerns." The evaluations raise distressing questions about the level of ship-handling training junior officers get both prior to their arrival at their first command. Among the shortfalls identified in the checks:

- Officers struggled with operating radars and the associated tools at hand, an issue that emerged in the wake of the Fitzgerald accident.

- Officers had a firm grasp of the international rules of the road for navigating ships at sea, but struggled to apply them practically during watch standing, especially in low-visibility situations.

- Most officers were able to keep clear of close encounters with other ships in the simulator but those who found themselves in extremes were often not equipped to take immediate action to avoid collisions, a factor that was a direct contributor to the loss of life in both the *McCain* and *Fitzgerald* collisions.

Vice Admiral Richard Brown, the Navy's top Surface Warfare Officer, said the report should be a call to action for the surface community to get after its shortcomings. In the case of *McCain*, confusion and indecision took hold on the bridge at the precise moment when the ship had to take immediate actions to avoid a collision. In the case of *Fitzgerald*, both the bridge and the combat information center showed a lack of basic understanding of the radar they were using and failed to use the tools at hand effectively."[13]

Expensive as it is to build, train, and maintain a credible blue-water force, that force provides the capability of global power projection and enduring presence in forward areas throughout the world. The question now, in view of the Seventh Fleet collisions and other preventable mishaps in the fleet, is whether that capability may be seriously eroding, not because of shortcoming of vessel design and capabilities, but because of inadequate training and management of the crews.

SUMMARY

While these questions are being sorted out, China is rapidly building up its naval capabilities and is bent on achieving parity, if not superiority, to ours in the Pacific theater. China's leadership under Xi is placing emphasis on maritime interests and operations to sustain them. Beijing has declared that the traditional mentality that land outweighs sea must be abandoned and more emphasis must be placed on managing the seas and oceans. This building emphasis on sea power will mean vastly improved training and proficiency of PLAN crews. Allowing the proficiency of U.S. Navy crews to stagnate and diminish at a time when the naval personnel of our major foreign adversary are rapidly improving could be disastrous. The collisions of the *Fitzgerald* and the *McCain* should be all the warning we need to provide the funding needed for the U.S. Navy to maintain the best trained and most proficient sailors in the world.

NOTES

1. Megan Rose, Kengo Tsutsumi, and T. Christopher, "The *Fitzgerald* and *McCain* Collisions Left Sailors Traumatized," *Propublica, Task Purpose*, Feb. 13, 2020.

2. Vanessa Romo, "Navy Drops Criminal Charges Against Officers in USS *Fitzgerald* Collision Case," *NPR*, April 11, 2019.

3. Geoff Ziezulewicz, "The Navy Dropped A Homicide Charge Against the Former *McCain* CO and No One's Sure Why," *Navy Times*, May 23, 2018.

4. "Navy Releases Collision Report for USS *Fitzgerald* and USS *John S McCain* Collisions," Navy Office of Information, Nov. 1, 2017.

5. "Navy Releases Collision Report for USS *Fitzgerald* and USS *John S McCain* Collisions," Navy Office of Information, Nov. 1, 2017.

6. Section 1, Administration of Discipline, Department of the Navy, 1990.

7. Interviews with Thomas Callender, Senior Fellow for Defense Programs, Washington, D.C.: Heritage Foundation, June 5, 2019 and July 11, 2019.

8. Eric Schmitt, Thomas Gibbons-Neff, and Helene Cooper, "Navy Collisions That Killed 17 Sailors Were 'Avoidable,' Official Inquiry Says," *The New York Times*, Nov. 1, 2017.

9. *2019 Index of U.S. Military Strength*, Washington, D.C.: Heritage Foundation.

10. Interview with Bryan Clark, Center for Budgetary and Strategic Assessment, May 16, 2019.

11. Interview with Thomas Callender, Senior Fellow for Defense Programs, Heritage Foundation, Washington, D.C., August 12, 2019.

12. 2019 Index of U.S. Military Strength, Washington, D.C.: Heritage Foundation.

13. "Navy Releases Collision Report for USS *Fitzgerald* and USS *John S McCain* Collisions," Navy Office of Information, Nov. 1, 2017.

243

25 | Shortcomings in Naval Maintenance and Repair

Docked at Norfolk Naval Shipyard for over three years, the USS *Boise* has become the poster ship for excessive U.S Navy maintenance backlogs. Nor is it simply the length of time the *Boise* has spent idle at dockside that has earned her poster ship status. A fast attack submarine, one of 49 in a fleet that badly needs 68 of them, is out of service awaiting routine certification for submerged operations. Expiration of that certification was entirely predictable when it arrived in 2016. Continued delays resulting from the also entirely predictable overhauls of two other attack submarines, the USS *Helena* and the USS *Columbus,* mean that the *Boise* remains without even an official start date for her maintenance.

During a May 9, 2019, readiness hearing, Adm. Francis Moran informed Congress that the Navy had deferred Boise's depot maintenance until FY 2020 due to problems with funding and shipyard capacity.

Maintenance, repair funding, and shipyard capacity are the unclothed emperors in the room as arguments rage on about the need for a 350-ship Navy. Former Mississippi governor and Navy Secretary Ray Mabus liked to say that "quantity has a quality all of its own," even as Navy Undersecretary Janine Davidson repeatedly told him that the Navy was plowing money into buying new ships while its current fleet was falling dangerously into disrepair. While it will take years and even decades to expand the fleet, with five years normally elapsing between approved funding and completed sea trials, the risks are immediate.

Secretary Malbus left his post just months before the Navy's repair load shot up with the collisions of the *Fitzgerald* and the *McCain*. Undersecretary Davidson also moved on, at considerable cost to naval readiness. Having grown up in a Navy family and been commissioned as an Air Force second lieutenant in 1988, she had become a legitimate warrior. She had flown combat support, airdrop, and humanitarian air mobility missions in the Pacific, Europe, and the Middle East. After serving as an instructor pilot at the Air Force Academy, she was designated a Distinguished Graduate of Air Force Squadron Officers' School and was the first woman to fly the Air Force's tactical C-130.

While Davidson was serving as Undersecretary, Adm. Thomas Rowden, then overseeing surface ship readiness, confided in her that maintenance problems were getting worse. The Navy, she concluded at the time, was "sleepwalking into a level of risk" they did not even realize they had. Beyond shortcomings with ships, she found that pilot training was below necessary levels and that there was a growing backlog in fighter jet repairs. One reflection of an $800 million shortage in the maintenance budget was a 50 percent increase in aviation mishaps between 2013 and 2015.

"'What? How does that happen?'" Davidson remembers saying to herself. It had begun to happen some years before in the halls of Congress. Beginning in 2009 and for the next eight years, the Department of Defense operated under Continuing Resolutions (CRs) that forced the Navy to operate at reduced spending levels and severely limited abilities to complete required ship and aircraft maintenance and training. It was not until fiscal year 2019 that the Navy was not hampered by CR limitations for at least part of the year. The consequences of not having a full year to plan and execute maintenance and operations have been profound.[1]

In April 2018 Adm. John Richardson, CNO, testified before the Senate Armed Services Committee that restoring fleet readiness to an "acceptable" level would take until 2021 or 2022 and that the continued lack of "stable and adequate funding" would delay these efforts. It is extremely difficult to assess the readiness of individual naval ships and crews. First, the official readiness data on each Navy ship, which will also vary significantly over a 36-month cycle as the ship conducts various maintenance, training, and certifications in preparation for its operational deployment, is maintained and promulgated via the classified Defense Readiness Reporting Network Navy. Because of the sometimes-opposing demands of material readiness and operational readiness these two critical readiness components may not always be synchronized. For example, while the operational readiness of a ship's crew just completing an overseas deployment may be very high, material readiness could be significantly lower due to periodic maintenance and repairs that could not be completed while deployed.[2]

Inadequate funding or insufficient shipyard capacity may lead to maintenance deferral, which can have a ripple effect on the whole fleet. The material condition of ships may be worse when delayed maintenance begins. So, the work takes longer than the time scheduled, leading to delays in maintenance for the next ships in line. "Correcting these maintenance backlogs will require sufficient and stable funding to defray the

costs of ship maintenance and modernize the public shipyards,"
reads the Heritage Foundation's Design for Maintaining Maritime Superiority, Version 2.0. "These maintenance and readiness
issues also affect capacity by significantly reducing the numbers of
operational ships and aircraft available to support the combatant
commanders."

The Design notes that between 2012 and 2018 ship maintenance
delays resulted in the loss of 1,207 aircraft carriers, 18,581surface
ships, and 7,321 submarine operational days. Those losses, the report
continues, were the equivalent of losing 0.5 aircraft carriers, 7.3
surface ships, and 2.9 submarines from fleet operations each year.
"Even with additional readiness funding in FY 2018, maintenance
delay days increased for aircraft carriers, surface ships and submarines in FY 2018."

The nearly six-month long FY 2018 CR had a significant effect on
delaying the start of new depot maintenance that year. The domino
effect of cascading deferred maintenance has resulted in a surface
ship and submarine depot maintenance funding shortfall of $763
million in FY 2020. "Funding ship maintenance at the maximum
executable capacity of both public and private shipyards in FY 2020
can address only 95 percent of the required maintenance, a decrease
from a 96 percent execution in FY 2019," the Design continues.
"Funding FY 2020 aviation maintenance at the maximum executable
level of the depots can meet only 95 percent of the requirement."[3]

When will the Navy overcome this maintenance backlog? No
time soon. The backlog will continue to grow until maintenance
enterprise capacities exceed the annual maintenance requirements.
As the fleet grows to 355 ships over the next 15 years, the mounting maintenance will not only stress shipyard repair capacity, but
also exceed likely future Navy budgets. Public shipyard workforce
increases of 1,414 workers are funded in the FY 2019 budget while
the Navy budget requested 1,223 workers beyond that. But even with
the hiring of additional shipyard workers over the past three years,
the public (government-owned) shipyards failed to keep up with the
ship and submarine maintenance demands.[4]

Then too, shipyard productivity is beyond the Navy's control.
Training newly hired workers to the necessary skill levels requires
an average of five years. To accelerate this process, it was recommended that the Navy:

- Complete its Shipyard Optimization and Recapitalization
  Plan recognizing the importance of the Navy's four public
  shipyards to fleet readiness and national defense. This plan,

which had a target date of 2018, laid out the framework and investment needed to modernize the public shipyards through three primary focus areas: dry dock recapitalization ($4 billion); facility layout and optimization ($14 billion); and capital equipment modernization ($3 billion).

- Commence a $21 billion, 20-year public shipyard optimization plan in FY 2019. Entitled the Long-Range Plan for the Maintenance and Modernization of Naval Vessels for Fiscal Year (FY) 2020 this is intended to "Sustain the Navy the Nation Needs." It complements the Navy's annual 30-year shipbuilding plan and describes the Navy's continued challenges with "high-tempo operations that have resulted in a maintenance backlog and reduced readiness rates for Navy ships."

- Develop a long-range maintenance and modernization requirement based on technical analysis and condition assessment of the fleet driven by the number of ships in the FY 2020 Shipbuilding Plan. A long-term maintenance and modernization plan is intended to efficiently leverage both public and private shipyard capacity to reduce maintenance backlogs while supporting a growing fleet size.

Having several years to plan depot-level maintenance, private shipyards will be able to do more thorough maintenance planning and dry-dock utilization, ultimately resulting in shorter and more cost-effective maintenance availabilities. Similar improvements are planned for the maintenance of carrier air wings. As of April 2018, planned maintenance intervals for Super Hornets had been reduced from 120 to 60 days.

Shipyard repair efficiency has received increased scrutiny after the fires on the SSN *Miami* and the destroyer *Oscar Austin*, the collisions at sea of the *McCain*, the *Fitzgerald*, and the USS *Lake Champlain* and the grounding of the *Antietam*.

The *Miami* was undergoing an overhaul at the Portsmouth Naval Shipyard in 2012 when fire deliberately set by an emotionally unstable employee caused such extensive damage that repair costs were estimated at $700 million, and the submarine was scrapped. The electrical fire that erupted on the *Oscar Austin* while she was undergoing a $41.6 million modernization at BAE Systems Norfolk Ship Repair facility was accidental but will keep the guided missile destroyer out of commission until at least 2022. "There was significant fire and smoke damage as well as water damage from the fire-fighting efforts," explained a NAVSEA spokeswoman. Once the original work is complete, the ship will transit to Naval Station Norfolk to complete remaining restoration of affected equipment and spaces. Due to the complexity, availability and fabrication or refurbishment of the waveguides and cabinets, the restoration and testing schedule remains under review.[5]

The *Austin Martin* was set to receive an Aegis Baseline 9 upgrade, allowing the ship to conduct ballistic missile defense missions as well as perform traditional air warfare missions simultaneously. Fortunately, the computer infrastructure for the Baseline 9 upgrade had not been installed when the fire occurred, but existing computer equipment required for the upgrade was severely damaged by either the fire or fire control efforts.

Following the fire, NAVSEA announced it has worked with the shipyard to improve its fire safety. "Since the incident, the Navy worked with BAE to establish additional prevention and safety measures. Enhanced training was implemented for all BAE employees associated with hot work and fire watch. Permit Authorizing Individual training was also increased as were the number of hot work permits audits. Administratively, BAE implemented measures to ensure site turnover is conducted between shifts, work boundaries are clearly delineated, and the BAE supervisors have properly communicated work scope."[6]

Similar fire safety improvement may be overdue at the Ingalls Shipbuilding Yard in Pascagoula, Mississippi, where the *Fitzgerald* is undergoing a projected $534-million repair effort following its collision with a container ship. Cmdr. Garrett Miller, the *Fitzgerald* commanding officer, has noted a series of more than 15 fire safety incidents aboard the ship since it arrived. "The lack of fire safety is a major concern on this project, and I am extremely concerned we are on a path to have a catastrophic fire event on board. NSA (Naval Supervisory Authority) and KTR (a contractor) leadership have taken measures to curtail, but they have been marginally effective. I have seen improvements in government [oversight] in the past few months, but little change in craft deck plate compliance. The most recent incident is uncomfortably like the recent USS *Oscar Austin* fire."

Huntington Ingalls Industries has stressed the Yard is taking measures to keep work on the ship safe. "Safety is and always will be the number one priority at Ingalls Shipbuilding. We have strict procedures and guidance relative to fire prevention and protection on every single ship built or repaired at our facility. These types of incidents happen in an industrial environment where, on this ship alone, approximately 23,000 hot work items have been conducted over an 18-month period," reads the statement.

"Regardless, our goal remains zero incidents on all our ships. We knew and were prepared for the challenging work associated with an extensive repair project on USS *Fitzgerald*, and to that end, assigned double the number of trained and qualified fire and safety personnel to the ship.

Additionally, twice a day an Ingalls safety representative conducts a fire prevention and housekeeping walk through on the ship with our Navy customer."

Miller stated that the numerous fire incidents aboard *Fitzgerald* while in the yard involved poorly staffed fire watches, a smoldering deck, combustible material catching on fire, the discovery of previously unreported burnt-cable spot fires and fires that melted equipment. The Naval Supervisory Authority included comments from Miller's report and concurred with his assessment. Ingalls Shipbuilding hired more fire marshals to review hot work areas, and the new process has resulted in a slight improvement in compliance.

In October 2017, at the direction of the vice chief of Naval Operations, Adm. Phil Davidson, then Commander, Fleet Forces Command, completed a Comprehensive Review of Recent Surface Force Incidents to determine the improvements or changes needed to make the surface force safer and more effective. The Review addressed training and professional development; "operational and mission certification of deployed ships with particular emphasis on ships based in Japan"; "deployed operational employment and risk management"; "material readiness of electronic systems to include navigation equipment, surface search radars, propulsion and steering systems"; and "the practical utility and certification of current navigation and combat systems equipment including sensors, tracking systems, displays and internal communication systems." There are 58 recommended actions to correct deficiencies across the "Doctrine, Organization, Training, Material, Leadership and Education, Personnel, and Facilities (DOTMLPF)" spectrum.[7]

Former Secretary of the Navy Richard V. Spencer directed a team of senior civilian executives and former senior military officers to conduct a Strategic Readiness Review. They examined issues of governance, accountability, operations, organizational structure, manning, and training over the past three-plus decades to identify trends and contributing factors that have compromised performance and readiness of the fleet.

Broad strategic recommendations that the Navy must address to arrest the erosion of readiness and reverse the "normalization-of-deviation" that led to a gradual degradation of standards of the following:

- Creation of combat ready forces must take equal footing with meeting the immediate demands of Combatant Commanders.

- Establishment of realistic limits regarding the number of ready ships and sailors and, short of combat, not acquiescing to emergent requirements with assets that are not fully ready.

- Realignment and streamlining command and control structures to tightly align responsibility, authority, and accountability.

"Learn and create the structures and processes that fully embrace this commitment," the Review advises. "Despite the fact that the Navy implemented several maintenance and training reforms to improve fleet and aviation readiness, it will take several years of Navy leadership oversight and stable funding to ensure the Navy's sailors and platforms are ready to compete and win against Great Power competitors if called upon."

251

SUMMARY

To responsibly grow and dynamically operate the fleet, we must effectively maintain it, in peacetime and in conflict. As we have learned over the past decade, it is cheaper to maintain readiness than to buy it back. Our toughest challenge is reversing the trend of delivering only 40 percent of our ships from maintenance on time. We must further develop and implement better productivity metrics, identifying key levers to deliver all depot availabilities on time. The goal is to improve productivity, to reduce lost days though depot availability extensions by 80 percent in FY20 compared with FY19, and to eliminate lost days through depots extensions by the end of FY21.

NOTES

1. Interviews with Thomas Callender, Senior Fellow for Defense Programs, Heritage Foundation, Washington, D.C., January 2, 2019, andApril 18, 2019.

2. Interview with Bryan Clark, Center for Budgetary and Strategic Assessment, April 25, 2019.

3. A Design for Maintaining Maritime Superiority, Version 2.0, The Heritage Foundation, Conference August, 5, 2019.

4. U.S.N. Long-Range Plan for the Maintenance and Modernization of Naval Vessels for FY 2020.

5. Maintenance Policy for Navy Ships, OPNAV Instruction, 4700.7M, May 8, 2019.

6. Ben Werner, "USS Oscar Austin Fire Damage Repairs Will Stretch into 2022," *USNI News*, June 4, 2019.

7. Comprehensive Review of Recent Surface Force Incidents, Heritage Foundation, April 4, 2019.

THE NINE AIR WINGS (CVWs) rotating among the fleet's 11 nuclear super carriers constitute the tip of the spear of the U.S. Navy's aircraft striking power. Each wing is made up of some 70 aircraft, including more than 40 F/A-18 fighters, E-2D early-warning planes, EA-18G radar-jamming planes, C-2 cargo planes, and helicopters. Over the next few years, MQ-25 tanker drones and V-22 cargo tiltrotors will be added. As potent as the tip may be, the shaft of this spear is too short for the Navy's current challenges and responsibilities. During the Cold War, the A-6 bombers and F-14 fighters of the air wings had ranges of 1,800 miles with seven-ton payloads. These ranges were no longer needed for raids on terrorist training camps in the asymmetric conflicts of the 1990s and the early 2000s. Today the payloads have increased to nine tons, but the ranges have shrunk to 1,300 miles, just 650 miles to and from targets. Meanwhile both China and Russia have developed anti-ship missiles accurate at over 1,000 miles.

Clearly CVWs must be able to operate at longer ranges than they have for the past two decades. The MQ-25 tanker drone, designed and built by Boeing, marks an effort to extend that range. Expected to join the fleet in 2023–24, the drones could virtually double the ranges of the strike aircraft. But there are some serious drawbacks. Refueling would almost certainly have to take place in contested areas, so both drone and refueling strike aircraft would be highly vulnerable to air and/or missile attacks when neither would be maneuverable enough to avoid them. Also, a drone could only refuel two aircraft, so six drones would be needed to refuel just 12 of a carrier's 40 strike aircraft. The number of drones needed to support a CVW's air wing would take up a significant portion of a carrier's limited aircraft storage space.[1]

The fundamental shortcoming of the MQ-23 is to be found, however, it its initial conception, which was not as a refueling vehicle but as an unmanned strike fighter. What the Navy's senior leadership has done in

FA-Growler takes off from the Harry S. Truman. Credit: United States Navy

agreeing to commit $805 million to four aerial tankers is also to create a test-bed platform for learning how to integrate unmanned platforms into the air wing. But, as Bryan Clark of the Center for Strategic and Budgetary Assessments (CSBA) points out, rather than thinking of it as a prototype-plus, the Navy needs to move forward on implementing up to eight Stingrays per air wing into the fleet as soon as possible, so it can push out existing fourth-generation fighters to farther ranges.

Robert Work, former Deputy Secretary of Defense under the Obama administration, agrees that the MQ-25 should be able to push a few Hornets out to the ranges suggested in Clark's study, but argues that approach is not a long-term solution.[2] "They are going to be able to drag some forces out pretty far, but the air wing is not going to be able to sustain a large number of aircraft at 1,000 nautical miles," Work notes.[3]

Clark believes that the Navy could sustain larger numbers of aircraft off the carrier if it began integrating 12 to 15 MQ-25s in each air wing. He acknowledges, however, that in doing so the Navy would pack its hanger bay so full of tankers that the whole effort would eat into how much strike capacity the service could retain on any given carrier. Still, he insists, that would offer the Navy at least a near-term fix.

The longer-term fix for the Navy is whatever comes next. For Work, the Navy must focus on range if it is to recapture relevance in a potential fight with China. And range means unmanned fighters. "So now the focus should be on the F/A-XX. If you really want range that has to be the platform you are shooting for, because with the Navy buying the F-35Cs and the Block III Super Hornets, and the Marine Corps buying the F-35Bs, you are not going to be able to afford two or three programs. The F/A-XX is the one you need to focus on. And if the analysis shows you need range, that points to unmanned planes."[4]

The F/A-XX is described as an air superiority fighter with multi-role capabilities. Sometime in the 2030s, they would replace the F/A-18E/F Super Hornet and EA-18G Growler aircraft, while complementing the F-35C Lighting 11 and UCLASS unmanned aircraft, that can operate in anti-access/anti-denial environments. Primary missions include air combat, ground attack, surface warfare, close air support and additional missions could include air-to-air refueling, reconnaissance, surveillance, target acquisition (RSTA), and electronic attack.

Manned, unmanned, and optionally manned platforms are under consideration. Just as the F-35C will replace aging F/A Hornets and complement Super Hornets, the F/A-XX will replace aging Super Hornets in the 2030s and complement the F-35C.

Clark notes that an unmanned combat air vehicle, or UCAV, could have a range of up to 3,000 nautical miles without refueling and has the ability to perform missions from anti-submarine and electronic warfare to anti-surface and land target strikes. Manned fighters would still be needed for command-and-control capabilities in environments where communications were jammed or nonexistent.

"There is still going to be a need for manned fighters to do close-air support, but mostly to do command and control of other platforms that are perhaps unmanned inside a communication-denied environment," says Clark. "So, you send some loitering missiles or you send UCAVs up forward; you would expect them to be managed by someone who is able to maintain communications with them. That would be a human in a fighter that is able to remain close enough."[3]

For that, Clark suggests a retooled F-35 fighter jet, one that switches out internal payload space for fuel. "The F-35 folks, when you talk to them about what it would take to make it a longer-range command-and-control aircraft, they're pretty optimistic because most of the challenge in doing these kinds of changes is in the software," he says. "And the software isn't dramatically different because it's really just changing how it manages the fuel, not any of the other functions."

The Navy has experimented with its Northrop Grumman–developed X-47B unmanned demonstrator aircraft, which made history in 2013 as the first unmanned aircraft to make a carrier landing. In 2015, the X-47B demonstrated the first unmanned aerial refueling. But the program, which was fiercely debated internally, moved away from delivering a penetrating strike aircraft or a long-range reconnaissance aircraft, instead evolving into the less ambitious MQ-25 tanker, with the goal being to get something on deck as quickly as possible with a minimum of requirements.

Work, who was involved in the decision to proceed with a tanker, notes that cost was the main consideration at the time. "Consider the F-35 program," he says. "The Navy plans to buy new carrier onboard delivery aircraft while the Marine Corps is acquiring heavy-lift CH-53K helicopters." With all of that happening simultaneously, the dollars didn't add up, especially in a time of spending cuts. "There was no way — with all the other things going on — unless we wanted to totally cancel the F-35C. We could have said: 'We're out of the F-35C business, we're going to stop building it and we're going to go whole hog into another aircraft.' The costs would have been extraordinary, and the Navy needed stealth on the deck of the carriers. The F-35C was going to give them stealth."[5]

This is why the effort to get a long-range unmanned aircraft with deadly capabilities was delayed. Clark insists, however, that the Navy must start pumping money into its unmanned systems for aircraft carriers to remain relevant. "The near-term fix is to get more tankers," he says. "The mid-term fix is to start investing in a longer-range unmanned aircraft. Because the idea of having to have 12 or so tankers just so your fighters can get to 1,000 miles means you have to have a lot of your deck and hanger space being taken up by tankers and not strike aircraft. This way you can use the tankers you've developed for other missions — either strike or intelligence, surveillance and reconnaissance on their own — or free up that deck space for other aircraft."

It's either that, or, as his study put it: "If the Navy is unable to transform its carrier air wings, Navy leaders should reconsider whether to continue investing in carrier aviation or shift the fleet's resources to more relevant capabilities." So, while the MQ-25 might be the answer to solving the near-term issues of CVW's limited range, better, long-term solutions are under active consideration. The CSBA has proposed adding the FA-XX to the CVWs before 2040. Addressing the space-available issue, the new drones could be smaller than an F/A-18, allowing carriers to embark more aircraft during crises than they can today.

"Although the proposed 2040 CVW includes a few more aircraft than today's CVW, it would only take up 60 F/A-18C-sized spots compared to the 70 spots in today's CVW," points out Clark. "The maximum number of spots available in a Nimitz-class is about 98 to 104, enabling the future CVW to incorporate additional aircraft to address emergent mission requirements.

"The proposed 2040 CVW will cost more than Navy's planned CVW, but the Navy may have no choice but to incur these additional costs or decide to relegate carrier aviation to a niche capability dedicated to permissive operations against less stressing threats," Clark said. Pointing out that the Pentagon could free up some money for new aircraft by reducing the number of CVWs to eight, he warns that, "If the Navy doesn't enhance its carrier wings, it risks the wings — and, by extension, the carriers — losing relevance. If the Navy is unable to transform its CVWs, Navy leaders should reconsider whether to continue investing in carrier aviation or shift the fleet's resources to more relevant capabilities."[6]

The carrier air wing of the future will also need to be able to hunt submarines, serving as a replacement for the S-3 Viking aircraft, provide surveillance and targeting, and destroy ships and land targets with standoff weapons, all while fighting at nearly double the range of today's air wing. If the Navy wants to counter China's anti-ship cruise missiles and increasing naval capabilities, it must resurrect the Cold War–era "outer-air battle" concept, which focused on longer-range aircraft to counter Russia's bombers. However, "instead of fighting at 200-plus nautical miles, the air wing will have to fight at 1,000 nautical miles," according to Clark.

In some contrast to concerns about radically extending the range of CVW aircraft, *A Design for Maintaining Maritime Superiority, Version 2.0* focuses on achieving and maintaining superiority with existing aircraft in the immediate future. Design points out that the Navy's long-range strike capability derives from its ability to launch various missiles and combat aircraft and warns that naval aircraft are much more expensive and difficult to modernize as a class than missiles. After the carrier air fleet was winnowed down to the F/A-18, the last Navy legacy Hornet squadron completed its final operational deployment in April 2018, and the last operational legacy Hornet squadron transitioned to more capable and modern F/A-18E/F Super Hornets in February 2019.

"The F/A-18E/F Super Hornet has longer range, greater weapons payload, and increased survivability than the F/A-18A-D Legacy Hornet and will be the numerically predominant aircraft in CVWs into the mid-late 2030's," Design states flatly. "The Navy's FY 2020 budget request includes 24 F/A-18E/F Super Hornets, and an additional 84 Block III Super Hornets over the next five years, in an attempt to mitigate shortfalls in its strike aircraft inventory."[6]

Design also points out that the Navy has been addressing numerous incidents, or physiological episodes (PEs), of dizziness and blackouts by F/A-18 and T-45 aircrews over the past several years. Navy investigators have identified "multiple interrelated causal factors" and have instituted mitigation efforts that include "software modifications, personnel education, and equipment changes."

The T-45 training aircraft have undergone a significant reduction in

USS America, an amphibious ship. Credit: United States Navy

PE rate with only 14 events in over 100,000 hours flown since the aircraft returned to operation. Two events are still under investigation, while seven have been attributed to human factors. In addition to correcting an identified engine flow problem, the Navy is integrating an Automatic Backup Oxygen System (ABOS) to improve oxygen generating system performance overall.

The Navy's largest aviation modernization program is the F-35, a fifth-generation fighter (all F/A-18 variants are considered fourth generation). Greater stealth capabilities and state-of-the-art electronic systems allow this plane to sense its tactical environment and communicate with multiple other platforms more effectively.

Design notes that the Navy plans to purchase 273 F-35Cs and 67 Marine Corps F-35Bs. "The F-35 can accomplish a wide spectrum of missions including strike, close air support, counter air, escort, and suppression of enemy air defenses. The Navy's objective is to attain a 2 + 2 mix of two F-35C squadrons and two F/A-18E/F Block III squadrons per CVW by the mid–2030s."

Operational capability (IOC) of the F-35C was declared in February 2019. In a released statement, Navy officials stated that in order to declare IOC, the first operational squadron "must be properly manned, trained and equipped to conduct assigned missions in support of fleet operations." This includes having 10 Block 3F, F-35C aircraft, requisite spare parts, support equipment, tools, technical publications, training programs, and a functional Autonomic Logistic Information System

(ALIS). Additionally, the ship that supports the first squadron must possess the proper infrastructure, qualifications, and certifications. IOCs for the Marines Corps' and Air Force F-35 were declared three and four year earlier, respectively. Program development delays and the Navy's unique requirement for block 3F-equipped F-35C aircraft postponed the F-35C IOC. The first operational F-35C deployment is scheduled for FY 2021, as part of Carrier Air Wing 2 onboard USS *Carl Vinson*.

The Navy's carrier-based Airborne Early Warning and Battle Management Command and Control aircraft is the E-2D Advanced Hawkeye, which forms the hub of the Naval Integrated Control-Counter Air system and provides critical Theater Air Missile and Missile Defense capabilities. Procurement of four aircraft with an additional 14 aircraft over the next three years is called for in the Navy's FY 2020 budget.

A land-based, high-altitude, long-endurance UAV, the MQ-4C Triton, fills a vital role for the Joint Forces Maritime Component Commander by delivering persistent and netted maritime ISR and furthers our plan to retire legacy EP-3E aircraft. Two Tritons are called for in the Navy's FY 2020 budget and five in FY 2021, and the eventual requirement is for 68 Tritons. The planned initial deployment of two Triton UAVs to Guam in FY 2019 was delayed following the September 2018 MQ-4C crash landing due to technical issues with the aircraft.

What about the MQ-25? *Design* states that the focus on the return to Great Power Competition and building a more lethal force is manifested in the Navy's FY 2020 budget prioritization on developing and fielding new capabilities in the areas of unmanned vehicles, directed energy [weapons], artificial intelligence, hyper sonics, and other advanced weapons technology.

It appears that the evolution of the MQ-25 into the F/A-XX and a CVW with 3,000-mile range strike aircraft remains decades down the road.

SUMMARY

With the costs of building a Ford class aircraft carrier and furnishing it with a CVW and a highly trained crew of 5,200 approaching if not exceeding $29 billion, there are serious questions about whether the country can afford 11 of these enormous fighting machines. Those questions assume even greater urgency when no answers to are whether carrier planes now available or expected to be available within the next decade will be capable of reaching likely targets. So while carriers will continue to be objects of national pride and prestige, there should be serious and continuing reviews as to whether this major portion of the Navy budget might be more advantageously spent on different, smaller and probably submersible or unmanned weapons platforms.

NOTES

1. "What's Killing the US Navy's Air Wing?" *Navy League*, May 5, 2019.
2. David B. Larter, "With the Future of the US Carrier Wings Murky, Congress Demands a Plan, *Defense News*, June 12, 2019.
3. "US Navy and Boeing Use Manned Jet to Control Growlers," *C4ISR*.
4. David B. Larter, "What's Killing the US Navy's Air Wing?" *Navy League*, May 5, 2019.
5. David B. Larter, "US Navy and Boeing Use Manned Jet to Control Growlers," Feb. 4, 2019, *C4ISR*.
6. *A Design for Maintaining Maritime Superiority, Version 2.0*, U.S. Navy.

Chapter 27 | Maintaining Maritime Superiority

ON OCTOBER 21, 1805, the destruction of the combined French and Spanish fleets at the battle of Trafalgar left the Royal Navy in virtually undisputed command of the oceans for over a century. On June 7, 1942, destruction of four aircraft carriers at the Battle of Midway ended Japanese efforts to control the Western Pacific, total defeat three years later and the U.S. Navy's global supremacy ever since. On December 11, 2018, Chief of Naval Operations Admiral John M. Richardson described how the U.S. Navy would maintain this supremacy:

"Our Navy will protect America from attack and preserve America's strategic influence in key regions of the world. U.S. naval forces and operations—from the sea floor to space, from deep water to the littorals, and in the information domain — will deter aggression and enable peaceful resolution of crises on terms acceptable to the U.S. and our allies and partners. If deterrence fails, the Navy will conduct decisive combat operations to defeat any enemy."[1]

Such a mission would still be inconceivable for any other country. It has been U.S. determination and commitment to deter aggression and enable peaceful resolution of crises throughout the Cold War and beyond that has resulted in the formation and maintenance of just such a Navy. The question today is whether this can continue with the proliferation of weapons and weapon platform technologies and the naval build-ups of potential adversaries, particularly the PLAN.

As the abilities of potential adversaries to contest U.S. actions have improved, the sea services (i.e., the Navy, the Marines and the Coast Guard) have had to revisit their assumptions about gaining access to key regions. Together the functional areas of power projection, sea control, maritime security, deterrence, and domain access constitute the basis for the Navy's strategy. Achieving and sustaining the ability to excel in these functions drives Navy thinking and programmatic efforts. As the U.S. military's

The Freedom-variant literal combat ships the USS *Detroit* and the USS *Gridley*. Credit: United States Navy

primary maritime arm, the Navy provides the enduring forward global presence that enables us to respond quickly to crises around the world.

The Navy's unique flexibility qualifies it to handle this role. Unlike ground or air forces that require fixed, large support bases necessitating host nation consent, the Navy can operate freely at sea across the globe and shift its presence wherever needed without any other nation's permission. Naval forces are often the first to respond to a crisis and, through their persistent forward deployments, continue to preserve U.S. security interests long after conflict formally ends.

The Navy's ability to project combat power rapidly anywhere in the world during peacetime supports missions that include securing sea lines of communication for the free flow of goods and services, assuring U.S. allies and friends, deterring adversaries, and providing a timely response to crises short of war. The Heritage Foundation's 2020 *Design for Maintaining Maritime Superiority* notes that the Navy and Marine Corps primary combat force contributors are two Carrier Strike Groups (CSGs) and two Amphibious Ready Groups (ARGs) are positioned in key areas at all times. Backing them up are three additional CSGs and ARGs in ready use or able to deploy within 30 days.[2]

The report also notes that naval ships, submarines, and aircraft must possess the most modern war fighting capabilities including weapons, radar, and command and control systems to maintain a competitive advantage over potential adversaries. These naval platforms must be properly maintained and their sailors must be adequately trained to ensure that they are ready to fight tonight.

"Failure in any one of these critical performance measures drastically increases the risk that the U.S. Navy will not be able to succeed in its mission and ensure the security of the nation and its global interests," the report states. "For example, if the fleet is sufficiently large but has out-of-date equipment and weapons, and if its sailors are not proficient at war fighting, the Navy will fail to deter adversaries and succeed in battle." Naval capacity is measured by the number of ships rather than the number of sailors, and not all ships are counted equally. For example, the capabilities and contribution to combat operations of aircraft carriers and their associated air wings are significantly greater than those of a littoral combat ships (LCSs). The Navy focuses mainly on the size of its "battle force," which is composed of ships it considers to be directly related to its combat missions.

A "benchmark" of 400 ships is considered the minimum battle force fleet required to handle two simultaneous or nearly simultaneous major regional conflicts (MRCs) with a 20 percent margin held in reserve. This benchmark provides a peacetime global forward presence to deter potential aggressors and assure our allies and maritime partners that the nation remains committed to defending its national security interests and alliances.[3]

This minimum battle force fleet determination includes an independent review of previous force structure assessments, historical naval combat operations, Navy and Marine Corps guidance on naval force composition, current and near-future maritime threats, U.S. naval strategy, and enduring naval missions. A 400-ship battle force provides:

- 13 carrier strike groups and 15 expeditionary strike groups (ESGs) required to meet the simultaneous two-MRC construct.

- An historical steady-state demand of approximately 100 ships constantly forward deployed in key regions around the world.

- Sufficient capacity to properly maintain the Navy's ships and ensure its sailors are adequately trained to fight immediately.

While this represents a significant increase both from the language of the fiscal year 2018 National Defense Authorization Act (NDAA), which specified an official U.S. policy of not fewer than 355 battle force ships and the Navy's own 2016 Force Structure Assessment, the Navy's recent fleet readiness issues and the 2018 NDS's focus on the reemergence of long-term strategic competition point to the need for a much larger and more capable fleet.[4]

The Navy's nuclear ballistic missile submarine's (SSBN) sole mission is strategic nuclear deterrence, for which it carries long-range submarine-launched ballistic missiles. They provide the most survivable leg of America's strategic nuclear deterrent force with 70 percent of the nation's accountable nuclear warheads and its only assured second-strike or retaliatory nuclear strike capability.

The Navy's force structure assessment and the 2018 *Nuclear Posture Review* established a requirement for a minimum of 12 Columbia-class nuclear ballistic missile submarines (SSBNs) to replace the legacy Ohio-class SSBN. With an average acquisition cost of $7.1 billion, production of the Columbia-class submarines will require a significant portion of the Navy's shipbuilding funding if the overall budget is not increased.

The Navy's FY 2013 budget deferred procurement of the lead boat from FY 2019 to FY 2021, with the result that the Navy's SSBN force will drop to 11 or 10 boats for the period FY 2030–FY2040.The Navy may have increased difficulty maintaining U.S. Strategic Command's requirement for a minimum of 10 operational SSBNs as it strives to maintain the legacy Ohio-class SSBN fleet to the end of their 42-year service life.

The Columbia-class design incorporates several new technologies to increase its stealth and operational availability. The submarine and its ship reactor core have been designed for a 42-year service life as opposed to the Ohio-class, which was extended from 30 years to 42 years. Twelve Columbia-class SSBNs are needed to meet the requirement for 10 operational boats, because the midlife overhauls of Columbia-class boats, which will not include a nuclear refueling, will require less time (about two years) than the midlife refueling overhauls of Ohio-class boats. Additionally, the submarine's electric drive propulsion motor and other stealth technologies will ensure the nation's SSBN force will remain undetectable and survivable against evolving threats into the 2080s.[5]

The report notes that the vast distances of the world's oceans and the relatively slow average transit speeds of naval warships (15 knots) require that the U.S. Navy maintain sufficient numbers of ships constantly forward deployed in key regions around the world to respond quickly to crises and deter potential aggression. This larger fleet not only includes additional small surface combatants (SSCs) to support the strike groups, but also a significant increase in combat logistics force (CLF) ships to ensure that distributed forces deployed in peacetime and in combat operations can receive timely fuel, food, and ammunition resupply.

Most important, the fleet must be large enough to provide the requisite number of CSGs and ESGs when called upon as the primary elements of naval combat power during an MRC operation. Although a 400-ship fleet may be difficult to achieve based on current department of defense fiscal constraints and the present shipbuilding industrial base capacity, this benchmark is "budget agnostic" and based strictly on assessed force-sizing requirements.

There are now 289 ships in the battle force fleet, up from 284 in 2018. This, of course, is still well below both the goal of 355 ships and the 400-ship fleet required to fight and win two MRCs. The FY 2019 NDAA provided $24.2 billion for the construction of 13 new ships, including one additional Littoral Combat Ship (LCS); one additional Flight III *Arleigh Burke* guided missile destroyer (DDG); one additional Fast Replenishment Oiler (T-AO); one Expeditionary Fast Transport (T-EPF); and one towing, salvage and rescue ship (T-ATS). The Navy has requested the procurement of 12 ships in FY 2020, marking the largest shipbuilding budget request in over 20 years. But it will be some time before these ships join the fleet. On average, depending on the ship class, a ship is commissioned and joins the fleet three to five years after it is purchased by the Navy.

The commissioning of 17 ships is expected in fiscal years 2019 and 2020, including 4 Arleigh Burke-class DDGs, 3 Virginia-class nuclear attack submarines (SSN), 2 LCS, and 1 TEPF. Five battle force ships will be retired including two Los Angeles-class SSNs and three mine countermeasure ships (MCM). Decommissioning will increase significantly as additional Los Angeles-class SSNs and MCMs reach the end of their service lives and expected service-life extensions of eight Ticonderoga-class guided missile cruisers are cancelled.

The largest proportional shortfall in the fleet in 2020 is among small surface combatants. The Navy's current inventory of 28 SCSs (17 LCSs and 11 MCMs) is 24 below the objective requirement of 52. The attack submarine inventory stands at 51 (31 Los Angeles-class, 3 Seawolf-class, and 17 Virginia-class), 15 below the requirements of 66. Several factors make this the most challenging and most important force level issue for the Navy, the report states:

1. The growing anti-access/area denial capabilities of great power competitors like China and the ability of submarines to penetrate these long-range defenses have made attack submarines a critical component to joint force missions such as power projection and sea control.

2. Geographic combatant commanders have repeatedly expressed concerns that the Navy cannot meet their operational demands for attack submarines. Admiral Davidson, U.S. Indo-Pacific Command Commander, stated that his Pacific forces receive slightly over 50 percent of their submarine mission requests.

What is especially concerning about the submarine force shortfall is that, while submarines provide the greatest advantage over great power competitors Russia and China, the submarine industrial base has very limited excess capacity over the next 30 years to accelerate attack submarine production. The Navy's FY 2020 30-year shipbuilding plans only provide for three additional Virginia-class submarines over the next six years and an additional nine next-generation SSNs between FY 2037 and FY 2049.[6]

The current aircraft carrier force of 11 is two below the two-MRC requirement of 13. According to the Congressional Research Service (CRS) "increasing aircraft carrier procurement from the currently planned rate of one ship every five years to a rate of one ship every three years would achieve a 12-carrier force on a sustained basis by about 2030." The Navy has stated that, with its current fleet of 11 carriers, it cannot meet the requirement to maintain two carriers deployed at all times and three ready to deploy within 30 days.[7]

The carrier force only reached 11 with the commissioning of the USS *Gerald R. Ford* (CVN-78) on July 22, 2017. But while the *Ford* is considered part of the fleet battle force, it will not be operationally deployed until 2022. In addition, through 2037, one Nimitz-class carrier at a time will be in a four-year refueling and complex overhaul (RCOH) to modernize the ship and refuel the reactor to support its full 50-year service life. Carriers on RCOH are counted as battle force ships but are not operationally deployable.

The combination of these two factors means that only nine aircraft carriers will be operationally available until 2022. The Navy's FY 2020 budget request was notable for its apparent contradiction regarding the required size of its aircraft carrier fleet. On the one hand, the budget included a two-ship aircraft carrier procurement of CVN 80 and CVN 81 in FY2020, realizing an estimated $3.9 billion in savings over buying the ships separately.[8]

The Navy's final force objective of 355 ships as recommended by the FSA is based on a minimum force structure that complies with current defense planning guidance, meets approved war fighting response timelines and delivers future war fighting requirements.

The final recommendation for a 355-ship force is an increase of 47 in the minimum number of ships from the previous requirement of 308. The most significant increases are

- Aircraft carriers, from 11 to 12;

- Large surface combatants (guided missile destroyers [DDG] and cruisers [CG]), from 88 to 104 to deliver increased air defense and expeditionary BMD (ballistic missile defense) capacity and provide escorts for the additional carrier;

- Attack submarines (SSNs), from 48 to 66 to provide the global presence required to support national tasking and prompt war fighting response;

- Amphibious ships from 34 to 38; and

- 12 Columbia-class nuclear ballistic missile submarines (SSBNs) to replace the legacy Ohio-class SSBN.

Significantly, remarks by Navy leadership during Congressional testimony have indicated that the mix of ship types is expected to change to provide an increased number of small surface combatants (frigates), unmanned ships and undersea vehicles, and logistics ships to support more dispersed maritime operations. Enthusiasts for this change have cautioned, however, the while the FSA may discuss unmanned ships and undersea vehicles, it will almost certainly not establish an unmanned force size or replace manned ships with unmanned vessels.

The Navy released its Report to Congress on the Annual Long-Range Plan for the Construction of Naval Vessels for Fiscal Year 2020 (or the 30-year shipbuilding plan) in March 2019. This updated plan provided the foundation for building the Navy the nation needs and ultimately achieving the congressionally mandated requirement for 355 battle force ships. It includes 55 ships within the Future Years Defense Program (FYDP) FY 2020–2024 and 304 ships over the period FY 2020–2049. The FY 2019 plan also buys 55 ships over FY 2020–2024 period but only builds 301 ships over the next 30 years.[9]

So although the FY 2020 plan achieves 355 ships by FY 2034, approximately 20 years earlier than the FY 2019 plan, it is achieved primarily through the service life extension of all Arleigh Burke–class DDGs to 45 years and not increased numbers of new ships. This 335-ship fleet will not achieve the desired force mix as defined in the 2016 FSA. It will consist of significantly more large surface combatants than needed (i.e., destroyers and cruisers), but have fewer aircraft carriers, attack submarines and amphibious ships than required.

The FY 2020 shipbuilding plan also includes several significant changes to the Navy's shipbuilding profile over the next five years. It accelerates the acquisition of two additional Ford-class carriers while adding an additional Virginia-class submarine and FFG(X) frigate. The plan also decreases the number of amphibious warships purchased over the next five years from four to two. The 30-year shipbuilding plan also includes service life extensions (SLEs) for qualified candidate vessels as a key tool to increase fleet size more rapidly. The Navy's FY 2019 budget submission included SLEs for six Ticonderoga-class cruisers, four mine countermeasure (MCM) ships, and the first of potentially seven improved Los Angeles–class attack submarines.

Extension of the entire Arleigh Burke destroyer class to a service life of 45 years was announced on April 12, 2018, by Vice Adm. William Merz, Deputy Chief of Naval Operations for Warfare Systems, at a meeting of the House Armed Services. While the FY 2020 shipbuilding plan includes the DDG-51-class life extension and plans to refuel two Los Angeles–class attack submarines over the next five years, it also removes funding for the SLEs for the six oldest Ticonderoga–class cruisers in favor of readiness and other lethality investments.[10]

The FY 2020 plan also removes the planned life extensions for four mine counter measure (MCM) ships and accelerates the retirement of all the Avenger-class MCMs by FY 2023. The Navy states its transition to a broad-spectrum, cross-domain, expeditionary approach that includes dedicated LCS-based MCM ships, MCM modules for use aboard Vessels of Opportunity (VOO), small expeditionary MCM teams, and undersea vehicles. supports this accelerated transition from legacy MCM ships.

While the mine mission package aviation assets have been certified for operation on Independence variant LCS ships, the certification of Freedom-variant ships occurred at the end of FY 2019. Certification of additional undersea MCM assets on Independence-variants is expected by the end of FY 2019 and on Freedom-variants by FY 2020.[11]

Taken alone, total fleet size can be a misleading statistic. Related factors must also be taken into account when considering numbers of ships. One such important factor is the number of ships that are forward deployed to meet operational demands. On average, the Navy maintains approximately one-third of the total fleet deployed at any given time (90–100 ships).

The type or class of ship is also important. Operational commanders must have the proper mix of capabilities deployed to enable a timely and effective response to emergent crises. Not all ships in the battle force are at sea at the same time. The majority of the fleet is based in the continental U.S. (CONUS) to undergo routine maintenance and training, as well as to limit deployment time for sailors. However, given the CCDRs' requirements for naval power presence in each of their regions, there is an impetus to have as many ships forward deployed as possible.

As of May 20, 2019, the Navy had 92 Deployed Battle Force Across the Fleet Including Forward Deployed Submarines. While the Navy remains committed to deploying roughly a third of its fleet at all times, capacity shortages have caused the current fleet to fall below the levels needed to fulfill both the Navy's stated forward presence requirements and below the levels needed for a fleet that is capable of projecting power at the two-MRC level.

The Navy has attempted to increase forward presence by emphasizing non-rotational deployments having a ship Home Ported (the ships, crew, and their families are based abroad) or Forward Stationed (rotating blue and gold crews, effectively doubling the normal forward deployment time).

Formal agreements with allies are required for these deployment options, but both enable one ship to provide a greater level of presence than four ships based in CONUS. The Navy's planning assumptions assume a forward deployed presence rate of 19 percent for a CONUS-based ship compared to a 67 percent presence rate for an overseas Home Ported ship.

Capability Scoring the U.S. Navy's overall ability to protect U.S. interests globally is not simply a matter of counting the fleet. Admiral Francis Moran, Vice Chief of Naval Operations, provided an annual update on the progress of the RROC in February 2019, highlighted accomplishments included the following:

- Our Force Generation strategy, the process by which we certify ships for sea, was completely restructured. Today, any operations outside the guidance established by the Surface Force Commander require notification of a Four-Star Fleet Commander to ensure visibility and accountability.

- Fleet Commanders conducted Ready-for-Sea Assessments to ensure they possess appropriate manning levels, training certification, and equipment status for every operational ship at sea. Fifteen of eighteen Forward Deployed Naval Force-Japan (FDNF-J) ships were assessed as ready for sea. The three remaining ships were immediately sidelined for additional training and maintenance prior to getting underway.

- Prioritized Navy manning in support of Operational Requirements. Currently across FDNF, at-sea billets are filled at 100 percent in the aggregate, compared to the Navy-wide average of 95 percent.

- Surface Warfare Officer Training (SWO): The revised SWO career path will increase time at sea during an officer's first sea tour (48 total months).

Although the Navy has made strides in arresting its readiness decline since Admiral Moran expressed his concerns about the Navy's ability to handle two major crises, the gains have not been sufficient to assume that his concerns do not still hold true today. The escalating depot maintenance demands of a growing fleet, coupled with several attack submarine refueling overhauls in the near future, have the potential to amplify ship maintenance backlogs before the effects of shipyard modernization and a larger maintenance workforce are felt.

The Navy's FY 2020 shipbuilding plan and modernization efforts forecast a larger and more lethal fleet. However, funding limitations will make it extremely difficult for the Navy to both increases capacity and field new lethal capabilities in the near-term. Unless DOD leadership and Congress can provide the Navy a sustained increase in procurement and research and development funding, the plans to build a bigger and better Navy will be curtailed. This could result in future degradation in the Navy's capacity and capability scores.

A major amount of new weapons platform spending will be devoted to designing and building the Columbia-class ICBM submarines to replace the aging Ohio class. While these will not hit the water until 2027, the up-front costs will absolutely limit spending on promising new projects like the F/A-XX. This may stretch out the evolution of the MQ-25 into the F/A-XX — and the eventual development of CVWs with 3,000-mile-range strike aircraft — for over a decade.[12]

From the perspective of our major adversaries, the existence of un-detectable weapons platforms lurking somewhere in the depths of the oceans and capable of wiping them entirely off the face of the earth will be far more concerning than flights of F-35 and F-18 strike fighters lifting off carriers decks and attempting to evade ever more sophisticated air defenses to attack heavily defended military targets.

SUMMARY

We need a Navy that is ready to win across the full range of military operations in competition, crisis, and contingency by persistently operating with agility and flexibility in an all-domain battlespace. Our Navy must be the best when the national needs it the most. On a daily basis, our objective is to have our fleet manned, trained, equipped and integrated into the Joint Force. We must be ready to meet requirements directed by the Secretary of Defense. Our fleet must be a potent, formidable force that competes around the world every day, deterring those who would challenge us while reassuring our allies and partners.

The future of the United States depends on the Navy's ability to rise to this challenge. China and Russia are deploying all elements of their national power to achieve their global ambitions. In addition, our competitors have been studying our methods over the past 20 years. In many cases, they are gaining a competitive advantage and exploiting our vulnerabilities. Their activity suggests that Eurasia could once again be dominated by rivals of the United States, our allies, and partners. China and Russia seek to accumulate power at America's expense and may imperil the diplomatic, economic, and military bonds that link the United States to its allies. While rarely rising to the level of conflict, Chinese and Russian actions are frequently confrontational. And these actions are not only directed at the United States: China and Russia seek to redefine the norms of the entire international system on terms more favorable to themselves.

This global competition extends to the maritime domain, including the seabed, and importantly, to newer domains: space and cyber. The new security environment is shaped by the following five facts:

1. Our competitive advantage has shrunk and, in some areas, is gone altogether. We do not have the margins we once enjoyed.

2. Twenty-first century competition takes place over a wide range of conceptual approaches — from peaceful competition to violent conflict. This competition involves all elements of national power.

3. The competitive space has expanded to new domains, fueled by technological advances as well as the amount and availability of information.

4. The pace of competition has accelerated in many areas, achieving exponential and disruptive rates of change. As this pace drives yet more unpredictability, the future is becoming increasingly uncertain. Identifying mid- and near-term outcomes will become more challenging.

5. We cannot become overwhelmed by the blistering pace. This is a long-term competition. We must think in terms of infinite, instead of finite, time frames. Only sustainable approaches will prevail."[13]

NOTES

1. John Richardson, Chief of Naval Operations, Statement before the House Armed Services Committee on Fiscal Year 2020 Navy Budget, April 10, 2019,

2. *Design for Maintaining Maritime Superiority,* USN, Dec. 2018.

3. *Comparison of Navy's 355-Ship Goal, 346-Ship Navy Goal from 1993 BUR, and 346-Ship Navy Goal from 2010 QDR Review Panel,* Navy Force Structure and Shipbuilding Plans.

4. "Sense of Congress on Accelerated Production of Aircraft Carriers," in H.R. 5515, John S. McCain National Defense Authorization Act for FY-2019.

5. *Attack Submarine Procurement: Background and Issues for Congress*, Congressional Research Service Report for Members and Committees of Congress, May 17, 2019.

6. U.S. Department of Defense, Department of the Navy, Office of the Chief of Naval Operations, "Optimized Fleet Response Plan," OPNAV Instruction 3000.15A, May 20, 2019.

7. *Navy Force Structure and Shipbuilding Plans: Background and Issues for Congress*, Congressional Research Service, June 3, 2020

8. Thomas Callender, *The Nation Needs a 400-Ship Navy,* The Heritage Foundation, Special Report No. 205, October 26, 2018.

9. *Executive Summary: 2016 Navy Force Structure Assessment*, U.S. Navy.

10. "Life of All Arleigh Burke DDGs to Be Extended 45 Years," *Seapower Magazine,* April 14, 2018.

11. *Report to Congress on the Annual Long- Range Plan for Construction of Naval Vessels for Fiscal Year 2020,* U.S. Department of the Navy, Naval Sea Systems Command.

12. *Report to Congress on the Annual Long- Range Plan for Construction of Naval Vessels for Fiscal Year 2020,* U.S. Department of the Navy, Naval Sea Systems Command.

13. *Design for Maintaining Maritime Superiority,* USN, Dec. 2018.

THE PRIOR ADMINISTRATION did not raise the alarm to a situation that has been building up over many years. Russia and China saw a power vacuum in the Arctic and moved in, according to John Buche, retired State Department official.[1] Russia, with its vast northern reaches, dominates the Arctic, and U.S. officials complain of Moscow's aggressive behavior there: refitting submarines, boarding ships, reopening bases and claiming exclusive rights to certain waterways. Russia's current development of three new nuclear-powered icebreakers to add to its already large fleet is further deepening concerns that the United States lacks the conviction to push back. These concerns are heightened by the fact that while Russia has some 40 icebreakers and China recently commissioned the lead vessel of a new class of icebreakers, Type 272 Hai-Bin, into its Northern Fleet the U.S. icebreaker fleet consists of the *Polar Star*, a 43-year-old "rust bucket" that often breaks down on or between its annual voyages to Antarctica. Another ice breaker, the Healy is newer than the Polar Star but is a medium ice breaker and struggles with breaking thick ice. After years of warnings, Congress approved $750 million to build one new heavy icebreaker in February 2018. Unfortunately, however, it could be years before the new ship is deployed, and nobody thinks just one new icebreaker will be enough. It is certainly a problem if you see Russia and China building tens of icebreakers and the United States doesn't do anything about it.

President Trump released a new directive on June 16, 2020, prioritizing a growing fleet of icebreakers to defend the Polar Regions for years to come. Pointing out that the current fleet is not large enough to meet the growing needs in the Arctic, the directive calls for six icebreakers with at least three in the heavy class. The directive sets the goal of a ready, capable, and available fleet of polar security icebreakers that is operationally tested and fully deployable by Fiscal Year 2029. "When deployed, this fleet will provide persistent presence in both the Arctic and Antarctic to

USCG *Polar Star*. Credit: United States Coast Guard

secure U.S. interests and support allies. Given the activity in the Polar Regions of Russia and China, the U.S. cannot afford to wait forever for a new fleet." The directive also looks at domestic and international basing locations for the fleet to operate from.[2]

The Trump Administration has used every available opportunity on the international stage to raise awareness of Chinese ambition in the Arctic. During a trip to Iceland, Vice President Mike Pence made Chinese economic activity in the Arctic one of the focal points of his visit. During the 2019 Arctic Council meeting, Secretary of State Pompeo highlighted the threat China poses to U.S. interests in the region. Meanwhile, Russia is investing heavily in militarizing its Arctic region.

Rapidly melting sea ice, which is opening up important new sea lanes, oil and gas reserves, and possible sites for military action, is, of course, what is spurring international ambitions in the Arctic. But no navy will be able to operate effectively in the area without extensive ice-breaking capabilities. After decades of showing little interest in the Arctic, the Navy sent the aircraft carrier USS *Harry Truman* to the Norwegian Sea in 2018 and made a point of steaming across the Giuk Gap, a waterway around Greenland, Iceland, and the United Kingdom considered to be a crucial naval chokepoint. The U.S. Navy also resurrected the Second Fleet to counter increased Russian activity in the Atlantic Ocean and the Arctic.

Current anxieties center on China, which describes itself as a "near

Arctic" country, although Beijing is nearly 2,000 miles from the Arctic Circle. In recent years China has made major investments in Iceland, built scientific research centers in Norway, and sought to build airports and buy mines and naval facilities in Greenland. This is all clearly part of a strategy to develop what has been entitled the "Polar Silk Road." It plans to open shipping routes made accessible by climate change, prepare to exploit oil and gas fields and possibly base submarines there. While not an official member of the Arctic Council, which consists of Canada, Denmark, Greenland, Finland, Iceland, Norway, Russia, Sweden, and the United States, China was granted observer status in 2013.[3]

More than 3,000 miles from home, Chinese crews drill for gas under the Kara Sea off Russia's northern coast. Every summer for the last five years, Chinese cargo ships have steamed through the ice packs off the Russia coast. Aleksi Harkonen, Finland's Ambassador for Arctic Affairs, believes that China's ambitions in the Far North mirror its ambitions in Africa, Asia, and the Middle East. China's rapidly developing partnership with Russia comes at a time of rising hostilities between China and the United States over issues like trade, territorial claims, and allegations of espionage. In its 2018 report to Congress on China's military power, the Pentagon for the first time included a section on the Arctic and assessed the risks of a growing Chinese presence in the region. Prominent among the risks is the expected deployment of nuclear submarines.[4]

The Pentagon's assessment cited Denmark's expressions of concern about China's interest in Greenland and its proposals to establish a research station and a satellite ground station, and to renovate airports and expand mining. Civilian research could support a strengthened Chinese military presence in the Arctic Ocean, which could include deploying submarines to the region as a deterrent against nuclear attacks.

The Pentagon report noted the PLAN's high priority in modernizing its submarine fleet, which currently consists of 4 nuclear-powered ballistic missile submarines, 6 nuclear-powered attack submarines, and 50 conventionally powered attack submarines. "The submarine force will likely grow to between 65 and 70 submarines by 2020," the report predicted, adding that China has built 6 Jin-class submarines, with 4 operational, and 2 under construction at Huludao shipyard.[5]

In a January 2019 report, the Pentagon's Defense Intelligence Agency said the Chinese Navy would need a minimum of five Jin-class submarines to maintain a continuous nuclear deterrence at sea. At a meeting of foreign ministers in Rovaniemi, Finland, Secretary of State Mike Pompeo assailed China for aggressive behavior in the region and stated that Beijing has much to gain, strategically, in a warming Arctic. China, he insisted, focuses on the long game, pouring money into nearly every Arctic country and investing billions into extracting energy from beneath the Yamal peninsula in northern Russia. China is also drilling for gas in Russian waters and is prospecting for minerals in Greenland.

In 2013 China struck a free-trade deal giving Iceland an enormous market for fish, its major export. Also, a Chinese company proposed to partner with Greenland in rebuilding airports, a proposal that prompted Denmark to step in and underwrite the project instead. In addition, Chinese ships are sailing the Northern Sea Route. The China Ocean Shipping Company, which is state-owned, has sent its cargo vessels across the Arctic multiple times since 2013, and a company official told a recent Arctic affairs meeting in Shanghai that the northern route takes 10 days less than Asia to Europe routes through the Indian Ocean and the Suez Canal. He also noted with climate change warming the Arctic twice as fast at the global average, the northern route is open longer each year. Finally, and perhaps most importantly, China is partnering with the leading expansionist power in the region, Russia, which sees the Arctic as key to its future wealth and power.

Russia's wariness of competition in the Arctic has given way to a new openness with China. "Though Russia and China would be natural competitors for Arctic resources and influence, they have started cooperation knowing that together they can outcompete the West," notes energy expert Agnia Griga. "China's need for energy sources and Russia's economic dependence on fossil fuel exports depends on this."[6]

President Vladimir Putin has met with his Chinese counterpart, Xi Jinping, more than any other foreign leader, and Putin is said to be personally cultivating investments from Chinese companies in energy and transport infrastructure across Russia. In a joint appearance with the Chinese president, Putin proposed linking the thawing Northern Sea Route in Russian waters with China's Belt and Road infrastructure plan.

By providing crucial financial backing to the huge natural gas project on the Yamal peninsula, China has secured access for its domestic market. The first shipment of liquid natural gas sent by the Northern Sea Route from Russia arrived in China in the summer of 2018. The establishment of a joint Russia–China research center to study changes in ice conditions along the Northern Sea route is being planned, and China's plan to build a deep-water port in Arkhangelsk on Russia's Arctic coast is under consideration.

But relations between the Russia and China are not entirely harmonious. Russia rents out its large icebreaker fleet to assist foreign vessels navigating the Northern Sea Route and is cool to the Chinese icebreaker construction program. Russia is leery of China's plans to build a deep-water Navy to protect its expanding interests around the world. Where Chinese strategic investments are made, the rapidly expanding PLAN is likely to follow. Most experts believe that China has time on its side. As sea ice retreats, much larger portions of the Arctic become navigable. The days of Russia ruling the waters of the Far North may be numbered.

Some argue that Washington should expand its presence in the region and work with international forums to bring together governments in the region. Greenland is emerging as the centerpiece of the State Department's effort to block China's Arctic ambitions. The U.S. Air Force base in Thule, 750 miles north of the Arctic Circle, hosts radar systems that scan for nuclear missile launches against the U.S. homeland.

The Trump Administration wants to foster warmer diplomatic and commercial relations with the Danish territory, which is eager to diversify its economy beyond fishing. Alarmed by China's growing Arctic ambitions, Denmark rejected their offer to buy an abandoned naval base in Gronnedal on Greenland's southwestern tip. In 2018 the Uniteed States convinced Denmark to counter Chinese offers to help build three international airports in Greenland, intended to allow direct flights to the United States and Europe. The Danish government welcomed the Pentagon's promise to invest in airports in Greenland that could be used for both civilian and military purposes.

U.S. Ambassador to Denmark, Carla Sands, said that Denmark, a NATO ally, is claims that ally is willing to do what many allies will not, and Pompeo warns frequently about China's playbook in the Arctic. Despite this high-level encouragement, however, there is widespread skepticism that the United States is prepared to finance the initiatives needed. U.S. efforts have been no match for Russia's, which over the past decade include more than a dozen new airfields and deep-water ports. Russian jets have buzzed NATO fighters. In 2015, the Russian military established an Arctic command to coordinate its growing activities.

The previous administration tried to have a more cooperative approach with Russia in the Arctic, according to John Buche. The Russians were not all that receptive, and invasion of the Ukraine derailed the limited prospects for cooperation. "The Russians punch you in the face right away. The Chinese are more subtle," Buche said.[7]

One Russian punch in the face could be their newest military outpost, the Northern Clover military base on Kotelny Island in the Arctic. Built to house up to 250 servicemen with enough supplies to last over a year, the Kotelny outpost is one of three new Russian bases above the 75th parallel and part of Russian President Putin's effort to flex his country's military muscle across its Arctic coastline. Russia has built 475 military sites in the past six years, spanning from the country's western frontier with NATO borders to the Bering Strait in the east. The base is already equipped with coastal defense missile systems and Arctic-adapted

Pantsir medium-range surface-to-air missile systems able to operate in temperatures as low as −50 C. The Russian military plans to further bolster its positions in the Arctic by testing a "polar" version of the S-400 anti-aircraft systems.

Owning 50 percent of the total Arctic coastline and bidding with the United Nations to claim some 1.2 million square kilometers more of the Arctic shelf, Russia's ambitions are obvious. Putin has created a new Ministry for Far East and Arctic and described the Arctic as the most important region for Russia's future. In a presidential decree issued shortly after his 2018 inauguration, he ordered a tenfold increase of shipping traffic via Northern Sea Route by 2024.

In 2018, NATO staged drills with 40,000 troops, its biggest military exercise in Norway in more than a decade. In January 2019 former U.S. Navy Secretary Richard Spencer said the Navy was working out a plan to reopen Adak base in Alaska and to send surface ships into the Arctic waters for the first time in the summer. The Russians plan large-scale exercises in the Arctic archipelagos of Novaya Zemlya and New Siberian Islands in 2020. The exercises will be a serious test of the battle capacities of its Arctic forces, according to Russian military authorities.[8]

SUMMARY

Now early in the 21st century, we are seeing specific areas where our Navy cannot assure the presence of ships and other assets likely to be necessary in the next few decades. Russia, with its long-established Arctic dominance, and China, with its rapidly escalating Arctic capabilities, present truly daunting competition. The funding Congress has approved to date to close this gap is insufficient. Correcting this lapse will be increasingly difficult as the ice caps melt and Arctic maritime activities increase rapidly in the years ahead.

"As other nations devote resources and assets in the Arctic region to secure their national interests, America cannot afford to fall behind. America's very real interests in the Arctic region will only increase in the years to come. The melting of some of the Arctic ice during the summer months each year is creating security challenges, but also new opportunities for economic development. Reduced ice will mean new shipping lanes, increased tourism, and further natural resource exploration. This increase in economic activity will also mean a larger military presence by more actors than ever before. As the U.S. prepares for future security challenges in the Arctic region it must continue to invest in necessary military and security capabilities, deepen its bilateral relations with friendly Arctic countries, focus NATO's attention on the Arctic, and continue to highlight Russia and China's malign role in the region. America's very real interests in the Arctic region will only increase in the years to come. As other nations devote resources and assets in the region to secure their national interests, America cannot afford to fall behind. The U.S. must champion an agenda that advances the U.S. national interest and devotes the required national resources to the Arctic region."[9]

NOTES

1. Interviews with John Buche, U.S. State Department, Foreign Service Officer (ret),July 2, 2018 and February 22, 2019.

2. James Di Pane, "Trump's Mew Directive Will Keep the Arctic Safe for America," *The Daily Signal*, June 16, 2020.

3. U.S. Department of the Navy, Office of Budget, Highlights of the Department of the Navy, FY 2019 Budget.

4. U.S. Department of Defense, Joint Chiefs of Staff, *Current List of CJCSG/I/M/Ns*, May 4, 2018.

5. "China's Submarine Capabilities," *NTI Building a Safer World*, October 9, 2019.

6. "Latest Arena for China's Growing Global Ambitions: The Arctic," *New York Times*, May 24, 2019.

7. U.S. Department of the Navy, Office of Budget, Highlights of the Department of the Navy FY 2019 Budget, 2018.

8. Interview with John Buche, U.S. State Department, Foreign Service Officer (ret), August 30, 2019.

9. Luke Coffey, Daniel Kochis, and James Di Pane, *Arctic Security Is Not About Preparing for War, But About Preparing for the Future*, The Heritage Foundation, Jan. 22, 2020.

29 | Meeting Our Greatest Threats

"CHINA WILL CONTINUE ITS EXPANSION as a maritime and naval power which will complicate maritime activity in the Western Pacific and eventually in the Indian Ocean. The probability of Taiwan becoming a military flashpoint through misstep or Chinese aggression will increase." These were among the warnings and recommendation made by Admiral Gary Roughead, former Chief of Naval Operations, in an appearance before the House Armed Services Committee on June 4, 2020. He said that submarines are our winning hand but cautioned that China and Russia will emphasize programs and investments to counter our undersea advantage and will become more proficient in anti-submarine warfare. "Our submarines are extraordinary assets whether used for intelligence, surveillance and reconnaissance, strike missions, special operations support or sea control against adversary surface ships or submarines. Using a chess analogy, our nuclear submarines are like an invisible queen on a chessboard. They enjoy great flexibility, versatility, and endurance, yet their location is unknown, complicating an adversary's calculus."[1]

Roughead expressed concern with the dip in the number of submarines in the coming years. "Submarine requirements in the Pacific and Atlantic will burden the force, and it is likely our submarines will be further taxed in the Arctic in the coming years." He recommended that we field new technologies such as artificial intelligence, hypersonic systems, and defense systems against adversaries' developments. "The need for high-end surface combatants will be greatest in the Western Pacific with a low to high mix appropriate for the Middle East. The Atlantic will require high-end undersea warfare capability and capacity to monitor and counter Russian submarine operations. Unmanned systems are ideally suited to fulfilling these needs and can be deployed from distant, safe bases. We have been slow in prototyping, experimenting and accelerating unmanned concepts and systems into the Fleet largely for reasons of cost, culture and process. Every effort must be made to increase their numbers and accelerate deployment and greater flexibility and tolerance for unmanned programs."

Roughead warned that our maritime industrial base, from craftsman to seafarer, is extremely fragile. "As a nation, we underappreciate the skill, competence and dedication of those who envision, design, and build the ships and aircraft our sons and daughters take in harm's way. Enhancing the base, making it more attractive for young people to pursue, and returning manufacturing of key maritime components to the U.S. will only be possible if it is economically worthwhile and if those who chose to support our maritime needs and interests see a predictable and fulfilling future."

When Kenneth Braithwaite was sworn in as Navy Secretary on May 20, 2020, he said the worst seven words in the English language: "That's the way we've always done it. We're stopping things," Braithwaite continued. "We're reviewing everything from the bottom up and from the top down. We're going to assess it: Is it adding value?"[2]

In December of 2018, Chief of Naval Operations John M. Richardson stated, "The United States Navy will be ready to conduct prompt and sustained combat incident to operations at sea. Our Navy will protect America from attack and preserve our strategic influence in key regions of the world. U.S. naval forces and operations — from the sea floor to space, from deep water to the littorals, and in the information domain — will deter aggression and enable peaceful resolution of crises on terms acceptable to the United States and our allies and partners. If deterrence fails, the Navy will conduct decisive combat operations to defeat any enemy."[3]

There is something discordant in these statements by the Navy's two top officials. Secretary Braithwaite's comments sound somewhat aspirational, conceding that the way things have been done will not be the way of keeping the Navy the worlds' best and preventing war by discouraging potential adversaries from initiating conflicts. CNO Richardson bristles with confidence, as the service's top officer should: We have been ready, we are ready, and we will be ready.

But are we ready and will we be ready?

James Carafano of the Heritage Foundations points out that, right now, the Navy is deeply engaged in comprehensive assessments of the changing security environment, as well as the implications of the National Defense Strategy (NDS) and its direction to re-orient itself, from sustained irregular warfare to competition among great powers. "This means re-assessing operating forces in terms of the equipment, they use and the design of units and formations, how their forces might be employed, and what they will need in the future," he notes. "There is also the need to free up resources within existing budget limits in order to start research and development for new capabilities, or to have the legal authority to re-allocate funding from one previously approved project to a newly identified need."[4]

Will Congress in its defense funding decisions properly calculate how difficult it will be to analyze these changing threats and operational challenges?

The challenge for Congress is to appreciate the uncertainty that accompanies these efforts at analyzing the changing operational and threat environments. How will politicians "determine which portions of existing force capabilities meet requirements and which need to be eliminated, and what type of new capabilities are suggested by experimentation and operational concept development," asks Peter Brooks. Senior Research Fellow, Heritage Foundation. "The Navy is asking the right questions and has committed itself to figuring out what it will need. At the same time, the Navy has a good sense of what it will *not* need, and which programs need to accelerate, sustain, truncate, or end. They will be reluctant to request funding for items that would ultimately be a waste of taxpayer monies."[5]

Over the past three fiscal years the Navy supported more proficient surface-ship operations, better ship and aviation depot maintenance and more flying hours, as well as additional ships and aircraft purchases with the increased funding Congress provided, notes Heritage Foundation's Thomas Spoehr. "The Navy has also done a good job of increasing its end strength, which has helped it correct manning shortfalls on its ships. Although these larger defense appropriations have helped the Navy to address readiness and modernization challenges, it will take years to restore complete readiness, increase fleet capacity, and field new capabilities. The most optimistic projections do not envision a fleet of 355 ships until 2034, and even then, only by extending the life of all DDG 51 Arleigh Burke-class destroyers."[6]

Increase funding for faster procurement of Virginia-class nuclear-powered attack submarines (SSNs) is urgently needed. The Navy now has 51 attack submarines carrying out missions requiring 66. Recommendations are for Congress to add one Virginia-class submarine from the Navy's unfunded priority list to the FY 2021 request and for the Navy to procure two Virginia-class SSNs in FY 2021 and two each year until the fleet reached needed attack submarine strength. It is also urgent that Congress provides full funding for the Columbia-class ballistic missile submarine program, the nation's top defense priority. The 12 Columbia submarines will carry a staggering 70 percent of the country's nuclear arsenal when they are completed. And Congress should fully fund the Navy's Shipyard Infrastructure Optimization Plan, a 20-year project of shipyard modernization that will replace and improve obsolete dry docks and production-facilities. This modernization will be essential both for reducing current ship maintenance backlogs and for meeting a larger fleet's maintenance requirements. Full funding should be approved for research and development in FY 2021, especially the research that will be needed to define the Navy's unmanned platform requirements. The Integrated Naval Force Structure Assessment (INFSA) will define the extent to which unmanned systems, both surface and undersea, could contribute to the Navy's vision of distributed operations. The INFSA will also explore how unmanned platforms could improve the ability of a distributed naval force to compete against an adversary's fleet.

Assessments of the Marine Corps' capabilities and missions in the *2020 Index* was made before the February 29 announcement by Commandant Gen. David Berger that the Corps' 2021 budget request includes a plan to drop the service's end strength from 186,200 to 184,100. The plan to shed thousands from the Marine Corps' ranks next year won't be the only cut. Nor will it be the biggest reduction the force will face either, the general told lawmakers.

"I think every service chief would love to have a bigger force, but you need us to be lethal," Berger said. "You need us to be mobile. It needs to be integrated with the Navy. So, we're going to reduce the size of the Marine Corps some this year, more next year." Berger said the work to reshape the service to deal with a near-peer threat will be ongoing. "We know the size of the Marine Corps we think we'll need 10 years from now." he said. "You'll see the impacts to programs I think later this summer and into the spring of next year."

The future Marine Corps will look radically different than the one in place right now. To get better, the general said, the Corps needs to get smaller. "We need the resources," he said. "When we shrink a little bit in structure, we're going to take that money and pour it into the Marine Corps that the country needs."[7]

The *2020 Index* rates the Navy Weak in Capacity, Marginal in Capability and Marginal in Readiness. The current Marine Corps got the same three ratings. Both had overall scores of Marginal. The Army scores were also Weak in Capacity and Marginal in Capability. But the Army rated an impressive Very Strong in Readiness.

United States Army

The U.S. Army is rated the strongest and most capable ground force in world. It must be. Its assigned task is to be capable of deterring and defeating both China and Russia, and, presumably, with both hands tied behind its back, of fighting off both Iran and North Korea and any extremist groups and any other challenges that might crop up. A major problem is that, for most of the last two decades, the Army's organization, equipment, training, and doctrine have been shaped by the conflicts in Iraq and Afghanistan. And. while a major focus is now on restoring capabilities for large scale conflicts, these Middle East and Asian conflicts and responsibilities continue.

"Army budgets and end strength were sharply reduced during the period 2011 to 2016 as a consequence of the Budget Control Act and the prior Administration's priorities," the *2020 Index* points out. "Readiness was poor, equipment aging, and manpower dwindling. Significant funding increases in 2017 through 2019 have helped the Army change its trajectory, and end strength is slowly growing, albeit constrained by a tough recruiting environment.

"Army leaders have gone on the record to say that the Army is too small. Chief of Staff General Mark Milley has said the Regular Army should be about 540,000 (from 478,000 today) with similar increases in the National Guard and Army Reserve. Additionally, the allocation of forces between its components — Regular, Guard, and Reserve — over time has become distorted. In the past, the Army has had the luxury to develop concepts and doctrine based on a single monolithic adversary (e.g., the Soviet Union) operating in a defined geographic area (e.g., Central Europe). The situation today could not be more different, which requires the Army to consider many more potential scenarios and environments."[8]

There have, of course, been some conspicuous accomplishments in equipment development and improvements during the Iraq and Afghanistan conflicts. Battle deaths and the severity of injuries have been significantly reduced by the development of counter improvised explosive device (IED) systems, vehicle and body armor and unmanned aerial vehicles. But the value of these in open battle against a conventional enemy would be limited.

"Just as the Army's manpower and budget have changed, so, too, has its posture," points out Frederico Bartels, a policy analyst for the Center for National Defense, Heritage Foundation. "In 1985, the Army had over one-third of its forces permanently stationed overseas. Today that number is around 10 percent. Efforts to plan and execute successful modernization should be informed by prior Army initiatives. Some efforts launched to great fanfare ultimately fell short. Others that were fortunate enough to take place outside major conflict and budget drawdowns, and that were patiently led and shepherded through many obstacles, succeeded. The development of Air-Land Battle doctrine, Force XXI capabilities, Stryker Brigade Combat Teams, and Task Force Modularity features prominently among the successful efforts to modernize and adapt the Army."[9]

While the Army scaled back its growth goals in 2020 due to missed recruiting goals in 2018, it did manage to achieve an actual strength of 483,941, but if growth continues at a rate of only 2,000 soldiers a year, a strength of 500,000 will not be reached until 2030. "That is too long a time to accept risk," the *2020 Index* states. "The Army appears to have now found the key to better recruiting methods, and Congress should take advantage of this success to increase the size of the Army by 3,000 in 2021, putting the Army on a path to reach 500,000 by the mid-2020s."

"Congress should direct the Army to establish an additional armored brigade combat team (ABCT) by 2023. This additional ABCT would be the 12th Regular Army ABCT, bringing the total of Regular Army BCTs from 31 to 32. Since ABCTs are being employed in a 'heel-to-toe' rotation plan in both Korea and Europe, they are one of the Army units most in demand. In 2019, the Army will only field 31 active BCTs, 19 below the 50 that Heritage Foundation defense analysts assessed as necessary for meeting a two-major-regional-contingency (MRC) requirement."[10]

THE UNITED STATES AIR FORCE

The Air Force is rated as marginal right across the board: Capacity, Capability, and Readiness. Despite billions of dollars spent on research and development, the service "lacks the capacity to meet the challenges laid out in the 2018 National Defense Strategy," the *Index* states flatly.

"Making do with a minimal, aging force structure while searching for the next revolutionary change puts the United States at risk, not just for the present, but also during an almost 20-year acquisition cycle. The Air Force of 2040 will be comprised of current weapons systems and those that can be acquired from active production lines or those that are nearing production. The Air Force needs to acquire as many leading-edge weapons systems as it can now, while the current surge in funding is available."[11]

The primary role of the Air Force is to respond quickly with sustained offensive and defensive air operations demanded anywhere in the world. While the other services can be optimized for specific regions or theaters, the Air Force must be able to conduct combat operations in Europe, the Pacific, the Middle East, or any other region. "The Air Force must have the ability to see not only over the next hill, but also over a horizon of much greater depth than that viewed by the other Services," notes Peter Brooks, Senior Research Fellow, Weapons of Mass Destruction, Heritage Foundation. "That vantage, coupled with extraordinary technology, gives the Air Force the ability to find, fix, and target an enemy anywhere on or near the face of the Earth. The speed, radius of action, and advantages inherent to the air domain allow the Air Force to be the first to a region of conflict or instability, and those same traits often compel it to be the last of the services to depart."

How much airpower does the nation need? "The 2018 National Defense Strategy (NDS) directed the services to prepare for a large-scale, high-intensity conventional war with China or Russia," Brooks continues. "That mission requires a force that, with little advanced warning, can rapidly deploy, fight, and defeat a regional threat or peer competitor anywhere in the world. In 2018, the Air Force released a strategic vision for the capacity and capabilities it needs to execute the NDS called *The Air Force We Need* (*TAFWN*). Based on thousands of war-game simulations, the plan assessed that the service needed, among other things, one additional strategic airlift squadron, seven additional fighter squadrons, five additional bomber squadrons, and 14 additional tanker squadrons to execute that strategy and win such a war," Brooks said.

"With today's explosion in technology, some fear that a commitment to fielding relevant, leading-edge technologies like those mapped out by *TAFWN* will prevent the service from funding a game-changing technology when it emerges. Almost every technological innovation has been born with that same fear; but if the history of land and naval warfare is any guide, the nature of air combat will be changed around the edges over the coming years, not fundamentally transformed by a new breakthrough," Brooks said.

Brooks notes that the Air Force now has the fewest combat squadrons in its history. There are less than half the numbers in service when the Cold War ended, the last time the country had a peer competitor. "Due to readiness and mobilization challenges, today's Air Force would likely be able to deploy just 30 of its 50 available total force fighter squadron equivalents to fight a peer competitor, although even those numbers would allow the Air Force to thwart an attack by either China or Russia if they were appropriately positioned forward in each region and rapidly reinforced."

The combination of the lack of forward presence and low stateside readiness levels, however, would prevent a rapid response. "And, later in the campaign, 30 squadrons would be too few to force an aggressor nation to retreat back within its borders. Not only that, deployment of all 30 would leave no air cover to defend against a cruise missile attacks. We're now at a point where an obsolete U.S. Air Force fleet would have to battle a peer competitor," Brooks warned.[12]

The *2020 Index* notes that, from its inception during World War I through today, the Air Force has been guided by more than 40 plans and strategic concepts. Each was designed to put the service on a better footing for the next conflict, but just three went on to infuse the service with the most advanced equipment available in numbers sufficient to execute the missions the nation expected of its Air Force. Their success was based on three principal elements: a plan to acquire the most advanced field-able technology, commensurate funding to acquire weapons systems in numbers sufficient for the mission set, and exceptionally well-trained airmen to employ those systems.

Remarkably, the service has managed to get by without seemingly suffering the effects of a debilitated weapons system, a series of major mishaps, or significant combat loss, the *2020 Index* notes. "Two decades of such accomplishments have given rise to external expectations that the service can maintain that record without significant reinvestment. After years of senior Air Force leaders fighting those expectations, it appears that this mindset has been embraced by an Air Force that is preparing to fight a different kind of enemy."

"It is one thing for the Air Force to engage an adversary that has little ability to shoot back, as it has for the past 28 years; it is quite another to fight a nation-state that possesses capabilities that can challenge every perceived U.S. advantage in the air and space domains. Building and sustaining the capacity and capability required to fight and defeat a peer competitor requires a plan to increase readiness levels and to refresh and grow the service's fleet of aircraft with relevant capacity — systems with the most advanced, fieldable technology available in numbers sufficient to fulfill standing Operational Plans (OPLANs) in support of the 2018 NDS. That force is defined by *The Air Force We Need*, and the service needs to move immediately to acquire those systems and posture itself for the conflict on the horizon while the current surge in funding is available."[13]

During the Air Force Association's 2018 annual conference, Secretary of the Air Force Heather Wilson announced the results of a study to determine how large the Air Force needs to be in order to meet the 2018 NDS that directs the services to prepare for strategic competition with China and Russia. Based on thousands of war-game simulations, the study determined that the Air Force needs one additional strategic airlift squadron, seven additional fighter squadrons, five additional bomber squadrons, and 14 additional tanker squadrons to execute that strategy and win such a war. This list equates to at least 15 more tanker aircrafts, 50 more bombers, 182 more fighters, and 210 more refueling aircraft than the Air Force currently has in its inventory.[14]

So, building and sustaining the capacity, capability, and readiness levels required to fight and defeat a peer competitor are the main challenges facing the Air Force in implementing the NDS. This will require plans to increase readiness levels, as well as to refresh and expand the air fleet and dedicated leadership.

The Air Force should execute the plan detailed in *The Air Force We Need* immediately. The emphasis should be on acquiring one additional strategic airlift, seven additional fighter squadrons, five additional bomber squadrons, and 14 additional tanker squadrons. Congress should accelerate the acquisition of the most modern and deployable weapons systems currently available, including 100 F-35s in FY 2021, 110 in FY 2022, and 120 in FY 2023; and 18 KC-46 tankers in FY 2021, 20 in FY 2022, and 25 in FY 2023.

The Air Force should sustain the current fleets of B-1, B-2, and KC-10 aircraft until it accepts the delivery of sufficient B-21 and KC-46 aircraft to fulfill the airframe requirements of *TAFWN*. Bringing the B-21 Raider up to initial operating capability standards and fielding that jet in the numbers required to support an operational plan will not likely occur until well into the 2030s, which means that the Air Force will rely on the B-1s, B-2s, and B-52s that it currently has in its inventory to support any war plan through the mid-2030s. The current buy plan for the KC-46 is capped at 179 aircraft. Assuming the Air Force acquires all 179 KC-46 aircraft and sustains its entire fleet of KC-10 and KC-46 refuelers, it will still fall 31 refueling platforms short of *TAFWN*.

Congress should increase Air Force end strength to 337,100 airmen in 2021, and to 350,000 by 2025. New airmen billets will be filled as recruiting capacity and training pipelines expand, but graduation rates across the spectrum of Air Force career fields need to accelerate to meet the need. Gaining the end strength required to manifest the Air Force Secretary's vision is critically important and it must be done methodically. Yet, if the Air Force is to be ready for a full-out war with a near-peer competitor in the 2020s, accepting further delay in accelerating the pipeline for most career fields can no longer be tolerated.[15]

SUMMARY

In these doomsday categories, the country's efforts are rated mostly Marginals with a few Strongs. In the nuclear weapons category Nuclear Test Readiness is rated Weak and Reliability of Delivery Platforms, Nuclear Warhead Modernization, Nuclear Weapons Complex, and Personnel Challenges Within the National Nuclear Laboratories are all Marginal. But Readiness of Forces, Current Nuclear Stockpile, and Nuclear Delivery System are Strong. The Missile Defense category gives no ratings, but the conclusion is stark and worrisome:

By successive choices of post–Cold War Administrations and Congresses, the United States does not have in place a comprehensive set of missile defense systems that would be capable of defending the homeland and allies from robust ballistic missile threats. U.S. efforts have focused on a limited architecture protecting the homeland and on deploying and advancing regional missile defense systems. The pace of the development of missile threats, both qualitative and quantitative, outpaces the speed of missile defense research, development, and deployment. To make matters worse, the United States has not invested sufficiently in future ballistic missile defense technologies, has canceled future missile defense programs like the Airborne Laser and the Multiple Kill Vehicle, and has never invested in space-based interceptors that would make U.S. defenses more robust and comprehensive.[16]

NOTES

1. Statement of Admiral Gary Roughhead, U.S. Navy (Retired) before the House Armed Services Committee Subcommittee on Seapower and Projections Forces, June 4, 2020.

2. Megan Eckstein, "New SECNAV Braithwaite Focused on the Next Fleet, Changing Navy Culture," *USNI News* June 11, 2020.

3. John M. Richardson, *A Design for Maintaining Maritime Superiority, Version 2.0*, U.S. Navy, Office of the Chief of Naval Operations, December 2018.

4. James Carafano, *Preparing National Security Strategy for 2020 and Beyond*, Heritage Foundation Special Report No. 214, May 23, 2019.

5. Peter Brooks, Senior Research Fellow, Heritage Foundation.

6. Thomas Spoehr, Director, Center for National Defense, Heritage Foundation.

7. Gina Harkins, "More Marine Corps Personnel Cuts Are Coming, Commandant Says," *Military News*, February 27, 2020.

8. *2020 Index of U.S. Military Strength*, Washington, D.C.: Heritage Foundation.

9. Frederico Bartels, Policy Analyst, Defense Budgeting, Heritage Foundation.

10. *2020 Index of U.S. Military Strength*, Washington, D.C.: Heritage Foundation.

11. *2020 Index of U.S. Military Strength*, Washington, D.C.: Heritage Foundation.

12. Peter Brooks. Senior Research Fellow, Heritage Foundation.

13. *2020 Index of U.S. Military Strength*, Washington, D.C.: Heritage Foundation.

14. *2020 Index of U.S. Military Strength*, Washington, D.C.: Heritage Foundation.

15. General Arnold W. Bunch, Jr., Air Force Materiel Command, "The Air Force We Need," July 20, 2019.

16. *Deterrence and Missile Defense in the Center for National Defense*, Heritage Foundation.

"THERE IS ONLY ONE THING WORSE THAN FIGHTING WITH ALLIES and that is fighting without them," Winston Churchill once said in referring to the squabbles between General Bernard Montgomery and his American allies during world War II.[1]

NATO's response to the coronavirus pandemic shows that the Alliance can play a positive supporting role in helping member states respond to health emergencies. Now the Alliance should gather the lessons it is now learning regarding its response to the pandemic, especially as it relates to maintaining a high level of readiness to respond to any threats to allies.[2]

As a military alliance, NATO's responsibility during the coronavirus pandemic, as well as any future pandemics, is to ensure the readiness of Alliance forces to carry out combat operations at a moment's notice. Military readiness relies on training. If they cannot train, they will be less prepared to fight. COVID-19 has already affected readiness on both a strategic and a tactical level. On the strategic level, a major exercise in Norway called "Exercise Cold Response 20" was cancelled because of the coronavirus outbreak. On the tactical level, if soldiers cannot do basic training, such as going to the rifle range because they are restricted to military bases or to the barracks, their readiness levels go down.[3]

President Donald Trump maintained his pressure on the NATO Allies to increase their defense spending to 2 percent of their respective GDPs. "What good is NATO if Germany is paying Russia billions of dollars for gas and energy? Why are there only 5 out of 29 countries that have met their commitment?" President Trump tweeted.[4]

NATO has faced criticism from President Trump for failing to live up to pledges for military expenditures. He pointed out that all members of NATO have pledged to devote 2 percent of its GDP to defense. Germany invests only 1.2 percent of its GDP while the U.S. spends 4.3 percent of its GDP on defense. President Trump also criticized a trade agreement that calls for Germany to buy billions of dollars in natural gas from Russia. The deal, made by then Chancellor Gerhard Schroeder, authorized a natural gas pipeline to Germany controlled by Russia's Gazprom Corporation. Today Schroeder is Chairman of Rosneft, a Russian oil company that controls 50 percent to 75 percent of Germany's consumption of natural gas. "It certainly doesn't seem to make sense that Germany pays billions of dollars to Russia and we have to defend them against Russia," President Trump said.[5]

Although the collective NATO countries and the United States have roughly the same GDP, the United States paid 71.7 percent of NATO's total cost in 2017. The United States contributed more funds to NATO than Germany, France, Italy, Spain, the United Kingdom, and Canada combined. Only the United States, Greece, the United Kingdom, Estonia, Poland, and Romania met NATO requirements.

President Trump also must be given credit for NATO's willingness at last to address China's growing influence in Europe. The Europeans have ignored China's inroads into their territory, but countries like Greece have welcomed Beijing's help in solving their economic woes.[6]

"NATO is suffering brain death," French President Emmanuel Macron stated on November 7, 2019. "There has been no NATO planning, nor any coordination concerning Turkey's military operations against Kurdish forces in northern Syria," Macron warned NATO members. Macron also suggested that European nations seek a rapprochement with Moscow, which regards NATO with suspicion since the alliance was set up to counter the former USSR. He said that NATO did not reexamine its future in the early 1990s, after the collapse of the Soviet Union. "If we want to build peace in Europe, to rebuild European strategic autonomy, we need to reconsider our position with Russia," he said.[7]

"NATO has survived seven decades of external threats and internal strife and will continue to be the cornerstone of European security, despite Macron's comments. Through NATO, the U.S. is obliged by treaty to come to the aid of the alliance's European members. Russia represents a threat to NATO member countries in Eastern and Central Europe. It continues to sow discord among NATO member states. It uses cyberattacks, espionage and propaganda to undermine the alliance."[8]

Russia has also demonstrated a willingness to use military force to change the borders of modern Europe. When Kremlin-backed Ukrainian President Viktor Yanukovych failed to sign an Association Agreement with the European Union (EU) in 2013, months of demonstrations led to his ouster early in 2014. Russia responded by violating Ukraine's territorial integrity, sending troops to occupy the Crimean Peninsula under the pretext of protecting the Russian people. This led to Russia's annexation of Crimea, the first such forcible annexation of territory in Europe since World War II.[9]

Russia continues to exploit ethnic divisions and tensions to advance pro-Russian policies at odds with NATO's goals in the region. Russia has deployed 28,000 troops to Crimea and is restoring airfields and new radars there. Control of Crimea has allowed Russia to use the Black Sea as a platform to launch naval operations in the Gulf of Aden and the Eastern Mediterranean. It has stationed warships there, including two frigates equipped with Kaliber-NK long-range cruise missiles with a range of 2,500 kilometeres.[10]

In the Donbas region of eastern Ukraine, Russia has supported a separatist movement with advanced weapons, technical training, and financial support. Russian-backed separatists continually violate the Minsk cease-fire agreements signed in February 2015. The war in Ukraine has cost thousands of lives and displaced 1.7 million people.[11]

Russia has doubled its troops on western borders and recently deployed four S-400 air defense systems. The overall effect is to produce a line of substantial Russian combat forces along the western border. Considering Russia's aggression in Georgia and Ukraine, a conventional attack against a NATO member cannot be ruled out.[12]

Recently Russia launched its biggest war games since the fall of the Soviet Union with more than 300,000 troops taking part. Thousands of Chinese and Mongolian service personnel were also involved in the drills, which included mock airstrips and the testing of cruise missile defense systems. Shortly before the drills began, Russian President Vladimir Putin met his Chinese counterpart, Xi in the eastern city of Vladivostok and told him the two countries were based "in trust in the spheres of politics, security and defense."[13]

China sent 3,200 troops, 900 tanks, and 30 jets and helicopters to take part in the exercise, signifying a geopolitical shift in the region. Up until this time, Moscow had previously viewed China, its richer and more populous neighbor, with suspicion. While Moscow said the exercises were purely "defensive in character," it heightened tensions between NATO and Russia.[14]

Allies in the Pacific

The assumption that allies in the Pacific would join the United States in a conflict with China is dependent on whether the U.S. or China is the dominant power at the time. If China reaches military parity with the U.S., Australia, Korea, Japan, the Philippines and Thailand will always act in their own self-interests. Only a fool would ignore Lord Palmerston's famous warning in the British Parliament in 1848: "There are no permanent allies and there are no permanent enemies, only permanent interests."[15]

Burgeoning trade in the area has benefited all of them and satisfactory relations with China are necessary for it to continue. During the Cold War, the United States' treaties in the Pacific were a true expression of power balancing against the threat of communism. The Pacific Allies are no longer a united block, and there are many opportunities for China to promote fence sitting or influence defections.[16]

Below is a breakdown of the current relationships of the United States with countries in the Pacific.

Australia

Australia–China relations are characterized by strong trade bonds. China is Australia's largest trading partner and Australia is a leading source of resources for China. More recent trends show that Australian exports are now expanding well beyond the resource sector. Politically the relationship has had its ups and downs. In recent years there have been concerns over Chinese investment in Australia, Beijing's establishment of an Air Defense Identification Zone in the East China Sea, and the arrest of ethnically Chinese Australian citizens in China, among others. But there have also been high points to the political relationship. In 2013, China and Australia agreed to establish a prime-ministerial level dialogue between the two countries, which makes Australia one of only a handful of countries to have such a dialogue.[17]

The United States and Australia have fought together since World War I. The alliance has always been strong, but the assumption that Australia would back the United States in a war with China is no longer certain. Australia is already playing both sides. Three years ago, it joined the Asian Infrastructure Investment Bank, despite strong opposition from the Obama Administration. It also leased the Darwin Port to China for 99 years. The Australian government has also refused to take a hard stance to China's expansion in the South China Sea. Since trade with China is vital to the Australian economy, war with China's would be particularly painful for Australians. Although the Australia–U.S. Alliance is strong now; there is no guarantee that it will continue as China is now the United States' greatest threat.[18]

China-Australia relations hit a new low recently over China's handling of coronavirus. Australian Prime Minister has called on the World Health Organization to conduct an investigation, a move that brought threats of retaliation from China. No other country is as dependent on China as Australia. In 2019, China accounted for more than one-third of Australian merchandise exports and one-fifth of service trade.[19]

However, Australians may be rapidly losing trust in China and are concerned about relying on Chinese trade, a survey by a think tank in Sydney has found. The poll surveyed 2,130 Australian adults nationwide over a two-week period in March 2019. Only 32 percent of Australians trust China to act responsibly, according to the annual opinion poll by the Lowy Institute — a 20-point plunge compared to last year and the lowest percentage recorded since the survey began in 2005.

In all, 74 percent of respondents said Australia was too economically dependent on China, which receives nearly one-third of Australian exports, while 79 percent saw China's infrastructure investments in Asia as part of plans to dominate the region. In a sign of rising hawkish sentiment in Australia, 77 percent of those surveyed said the government should do more to challenge Chinese military activities in the region, even if it affected economic ties; this number is up 11 points since 2015.[20]

Japan

In 2013, China declared a formal Air Defense Identification zone covering airspace over islands in the East China Sea, called the Senkaku by Japan and the Diaoyu by China. Japan scrambled two F-15 fighter jets along with two early warning aircraft warplanes on May 19, 2017, after four Chinese coastguard ships and a drone aircraft entered territory around the disputed islands. It marked the first time Beijing used an unmanned aircraft in the dispute over the islands. The Senkaku chain lies almost 1,900 kilometers (1,180 miles) southwest of Japan. Although the islands are uninhabited, Japan has exclusive mineral and fishing rights in the waters.[21]

Japan's Prime Minister Shinzo Abe, came to power in 2007, vowing to prepare his country to cope with an increasingly powerful China. Abe hopes to achieve a free and open Indo-Pacific, with India and Australia as key partners. Abe knows that the military and economic gap between Japan and China is wide and getting wider. Until recently, Abe had been handicapped by years of pacifism following Japan's defeat in 1945. Threatened by an aggressive China and a growing North Korean nuclear threat, Abe's administration passed a law allowing Japan to defend allies and approving a new mutual defense plan to formalize the nation's armed forces' existence.[22]

Japan now has 240,000 personnel called the Self-Defense Force (SDF) with an annual budget of $50 billion, divided among land, sea, and air forces. Japan's navy is considered the most formidable of these three branches and is among the most sophisticated in the world. The air force is currently working with the United States to develop a Theatre Missile Defense System (TMDS) and is also expanding its long-range precision missile technologies.

The SDF's naval and air forces face significant constraints under current Japanese law. The Navy is not allowed to have nuclear submarines, which are considered offensive weapons. The United States has long pressured Japan to take a more robust military posture, and the country is responding. On April 30, 2010, Japan launched the JS *Izumo*, the largest vessel in Japan's fleet. The *Izumo* represents the bold new military future Japan is embarking on. The Japanese government has announced plans to convert the *Gizmo* into a full-fledged aircraft carrier.[23]

The new legislation is seen as an effort for Japan to become a closer ally to the United States in containing Chinese aggression. This was not Japan's first effort to contain the Chinese. In 2007, Prime Minister Abe and the George W. Bush Administration pitched the idea of a naval alliance among Japan, India, the Philippines, and the United States. The idea fell apart after intense Chinese protests. Recently the United States, Japan, India, and the Philippines challenged Beijing in the South China Sea with a joint show of force. The U.S. guided missile destroyer *William P. Lawrence* conducted drills with the Japanese aircraft carrier Izumo, two Indian naval ships and a Philippine patrol vessel in the waterway claimed by China. During the week of joint drills, two other U.S. warships sailed near islands in the region claimed by China, prompting a protest from Beijing, which said the action infringed its sovereignty.[24]

China has continued to proceed south through the South China Sea toward the Strait of Malacca, a critical chokepoint for global maritime trade and the place where all four countries' interests overlap the most. Japan's dependence on energy imports through the Strait is a major driver of its push to shed its constitutional constraints on offensive military capabilities. India relies on the free flow of commerce through the waters and is looking for ways to counter China's growing presence in the Indian Ocean. Japan has a lot to lose in a war with China, and its power balancing indicates an awareness of the threat. Arguably Japan would be the United States' most dependable ally in a war with China.[25]

Vietnam

Vietnam shares a 1,200-kilometer land border with China. Even a negotiated land border puts a very different complexion on the bilateral relationship. Although Vietnam emerged stronger than China in the border war, Hanoi must live, uniquely among Southeast Asia's South China Sea territorial claimants, with strategic vulnerability. Beijing could position forces on the border to pressure Hanoi in a crisis.

Hainan Province, where many of China's most-advanced naval and air assets are already concentrated, flanks the North Vietnamese coast in semi-encirclement. Hanoi is 173 kilometers from the Chinese border and would be immediately vulnerable if general hostilities broke out. Vietnam should be more subservient to China than it is. Instead, the country has demonstrated a very high tolerance of strategic risk, including during the confrontation over China's positioning of an energy rig in 2014, within disputed waters. Vietnam chose to challenge China by mobilizing its modest maritime forces. In the end, China backed down.[26]

In an all-out conflict, Vietnam's armed forces have little hope of prevailing against China's PLA. Nonetheless, Hanoi has directed scarce resources to maritime and air acquisitions in recent years, giving Vietnam's Navy and Air Force sharpened teeth with the aim of fielding a credible conventional deterrent. Vietnam is now the eighth-largest arms importer in the world. This ambitious build-up in Vietnam is being carried out despite defense spending that is roughly equal to Malaysia's in dollar terms and slightly higher than the Philippines's.

Beyond the deterrent value of raising costs for China in a military sense, Vietnam understands the complex interplay between diplomacy and military power. This includes psychological aspects, above all the capacity for independent action that is embodied in a national defense capability maintained at high readiness. Vietnam's defense inventory includes Israeli-made radars, Russian S-300 surface-to-air missiles, and Su-27 and Su-30MK2 strike aircraft and Kilo submarines equipped with land-attack cruise missiles. This resembles a thrifty but still potent version of China's own "anti-access" and sea denial dispositions vis-à-vis the United States.

"Hanoi further avoids the flip-flop mentality by maintaining depth in its international relations, avoiding dependence on a single ally, and ensuring that alternatives are available when a comprehensive strategic partner like Russia might prove unreliable. Vietnam consciously pursues diversified economic partners, courting investment from a wide base and strategic agreements like the Trans-Pacific Partnership to balance its trade dependence on China. Hanoi closely tracked the Philippine legal case against China in the South China Sea, hinting it will launch proceedings of its own if pushed too far. History naturally pervades Vietnam's strategic behavior. The struggles of its people have conditioned the Vietnamese to calculate strategic risk and to embrace it. Relative to past sacrifices, the risk of standing up to China in the South China Sea appears acceptable. Intuitively, Hanoi grasps that an approach based simply on conflict avoidance and de-escalation with China is doomed to failure. Vietnam's real skill lies in showing that it is possible to have a coherent approach towards China that combines competition with bouts of confrontation and sustained political engagement."[27]

Philippines

The official U.S. stance is that the U.S.–Philippine alliance remains strong, but Philippine President Rodrigo Duterte has pursued relationships with China and Russia. Tensions between the Philippines and the U.S. reached an all-time low during the previous administration when Duterte met with Chinese President Xi to pursue an alliance with China.[28]

The Philippines view China not as a major security threat, but as a relatively benign power. The assumption that the Philippines would join the United States in a war with China is no longer valid. Instead, the country may take a fence-sitting position. President Duterte is negotiating an agreement with China to share oil and natural-gas resources in the disputed waters of the South China Sea, a deal that would be a major policy victory for Beijing. It would open the door for China to push for similar arrangements with other Southeast Asian nations that have challenged its expansive claims and would potentially lock Western oil companies out of the resource-rich region. It would also fortify Beijing's control over the strategic waters, where tensions between the United States and China have surged.[29]

Under the Trump administration, relations between the United States and the Philippines have improved. Duterte is well aware of the benefits his country receives through its relationship with the United States. But the question remains: In the event of war with China, would the Philippines sacrifice blood and treasure, or would it be a fair-weather ally?[30]

Thailand

While the U.S. State Department considers Thailand to be a key U.S. security ally in Asia, there is growing evidence that Thailand does not feel the same way. In fact, Thailand's security focus is in areas such as counter-terrorism, counterinsurgency, and peacekeeping. China's influence with Thailand is increasing, while U.S. influence is declining. China is Thailand's biggest trading partner. Two-way trade between the partners is expected to jump to $120 billion in 2020. Thailand has agreed to build a maintenance and production center for Chinese weapons in Thailand. Thailand has purchased three Chinese-made Yuan class S26T submarines and a number of battle tanks from China. In 2015 Thailand denied the United States the use of a base at the urging of the Chinese. Of all our allies in the Pacific, Thailand is seen as the most likely to defect in a war with China.[31]

Republic of Korea

The Republic of Korea is resolute in its commitment to the United States in the event of war with China. The problem is the mutual-defense treaty between North Korea and China. If China calls on North Korea's support in a conflict with the United States, it is almost certain that North Korea would honor its commitment. North Korea's entry would force the Republic of Korea to defend the Korean peninsula, effectively side-lining them in a war with China.[31]

SUMMARY

Too many nations of the world have substituted the United States for their own police forces. Europe has ample funds to provide for the common defense. The EU GDP is $19.9 trillion, compared to the United States with $19.4 trillion. A bigger question is does Europe have the motivation to defend itself from an attack by Russia? Leaders of EU member nations believe that no major conflict will ever embroil the European continent in a war again.

"For seven decades, NATO has preserved peace and stability in Europe, promoted democratic values, and been a consistent and significant force multiplier for the United States, both politically and militarily. We must remain steadfast in our alliances and partnerships, which remain indispensable in any future fight. Operating and exercising together, we must build on existing intelligence and partnerships with allied nations to broaden and strengthen global maritime awareness and access. Although we are not exchanging fire with our competitors, we are fighting for influence and positional advantage. But the degree to which the "allies" of the U.S. have come to rely on U.S. protection is now excessive, and the Trump administration is fulfilling a long overdue rebalancing of alliances. Today the enemy to peace and prosperity is isolation, and we cannot afford to let the strength of our bond abate for the lack of dialogue and communication. We must work together to neutralize shared threats, overcome our policy differences, and increase our gains from trade and innovation as we build a secure and free society."[32]

The Trump Administration has improved security in Europe. "The U.S. has helped push back a revanchist Russia and strengthened transatlantic defense. U.S. bases in Europe provide American leaders with flexibility, resilience and options in a dangerous multipolar world. The huge garrisons of American service personnel in Europe are no longer the fortresses of the Cold War, but rather the forward operating bases of the 21st century. The U.S. needs to have the tools to react to events in America's interests, whether in Europe, the Middle East or Asia."[33]

NOTES

1. Winston S. Churchill, *Triumph and Tragedy*, Rosetta Books, New York, 2002.
2. Jim Garamond, "NATO Takes Steps to Combat Coronavirus," DOD, April 6, 2020.
3. Robein Emott, "NATO Scales Down Exercises Due to Coronavirus, *Reuters*, March 19, 2020.
4. "Trump Pushes Allies for Immediate Military Spending Increase," *UPI*, July 11, 2018.
5. Jonathan Lemire and Jill Corvin, "'They're paying billions': Donald Trump says Germany is being 'controlled' by Russia," *AP*, July 11, 2018.
6. Frank Holmes, "China's Belt and Road Initiative Opens Up Unprecedented Opportunities," *Forbes*, Sep. 4, 2018.
7. Ludovic Marin, "France's Macron Says NATO Suffering 'Brain Death' Questions U.S. Commitment," *Reuters*, Nov. 7, 2019.
8. Daniel Kochis and Luke Coffey, *Global Politics*, The Heritage Foundation, May 5, 2020.
9. "Annexation of Crimea by the Russian Federation," *Study.com*, March 16, 2014.
10. Alex Schneider, "Russia's Black Sea Buildup," *The Maritime Executive*, March 29, 2017.
11. Cristina Maza, "Russia vs. Ukraine War: Cease-fire Violations and Evidence of Russian Interference as Conflict Enters Fifth Year," *Newsweek*, Jan. 10, 2019.
12. Tom Balmforth, "Putin Says Russia's defense with China Based on Trust, *Reuters*, Sep. 11, 2018.
13. Sebastian Kettley, "A Danger for Europe; Tensions High after Putin Sends 100,000 Soldiers to Russia's borders," *Express*, Feb. 13, 2017.
14. Vickie Oliphant, "A Clear Provocation' Ukraine's War Games Near Crimea Border Sparks Fears of New Conflict," *Express*, Feb. 11, 2017.
15. *Threats to U.S. Vital Interests, 2020*, Washington, D.C.: Heritage Foundation.
16. Daniel Coates, *Worldwide Threat Assessment of the U.S. Intelligence Community, 2020*, Washington, D.C.: Heritage Foundation.
17. "China and Australia — Who Really Holds the Power?" *ABC News*, May 25, 2020.
18. David Rowe, "China-Australia Relations Hits New Low in Spat Over Handling of Coronavirus," *The Conversation*, April 28, 2020.
19. Kelsey Munro, "Poll: Australians Sour on China," *The Diplomat*, June 26, 2019.
20. Michael MacArthur Bosack, "China's Senkaku Islands Ambition," *The Japan Times*, June 12, 2019.
21. Daisuke Akimoto, "Japan's Emerging Multi-Domain Defense Force," Daisuke Akimoto, *The Diplomat*, March 18, 2020.
22. Prashanth Parameswaran, "Japan Launches New Helicopter Destroyer," *The Diplomat*, Aug. 29, 2015.

23. Jon Sharman, "US, Japan, India and Philippines Challenge Beijing in South China Sea with Joint Show of Force," *Independent*, May 9, 2019.

24. Interview with Thomas J. Christensen, Professor of Public and International Affairs and Director of the China and the World Program at Columbia University, Oct. 10, 2019.

25. Rajeswari Pillai Rajagopalan, "Vietnam Confronts China, Alone," *The Diplomat*, Sep. 26, 2019.

26. *Threats to U.S. Vital Interests, 2020*, Washington, D.C.: Heritage Foundation, Washington, D.C.

27. Ben Blanchard, "Duterte Aligns Philippines with China, Says U.S. Has Lost," *Reuters*, Oct. 20, 2016.

28. Arianne Merez, "Duterte OK with 60–40 Sharing in Joint Oil Exploration with China, *ABS-N News*, Aug. 8, 2019.

29. Mary Louise Kelly, "The U.S.–Philippine Relationship Under Trump," *NPR*, Sep. 29, 2017.

30. Ron Corben, "Thailand Expanding Relations with China Amid Pivot to Other Nations," *VOA*, Dec. 27, 2016.

31. *The 2020 Worldwide Threat Assessment of the U.S. Intelligence Community*, The Heritage Foundation., Washington, D.C.

32. Kim R. Holmes, "The Value of NATO in the 21st Century," *Heritage Foundation*, Sep. 14, 2018.

33. Daniel Kochis, "Basing Troops in Europe is About U.S. Security. A Pullout Would be Unwise," *Heritage Foundation*, June 9, 2020.

Why and How the United States Should Stop Financing China's Bad Actors

Roger W. Robinson, Jr.
Chairman, Prague Security Studies Institute

IN THE EARLY 1980S, I served on President Reagan's National Security Council. Prior to my time at the White House, I was a vice president at Chase Manhattan Bank, in charge of its USSR and Eastern Europe division. It was my job to assess the creditworthiness of the countries in that part of the world, and I had come to realize that the Soviet Union had relatively modest hard currency income — and that what little it had come largely from the West.

In 1982, the Soviets had an empire stretching from Havana to Hanoi, but their hard currency revenue totaled only about $32 billion a year — roughly one-third the annual revenue of General Motors at the time. They were spending about $16 billion more annually than they were making, with the funding gap — the USSR's life support — being financed by Western governments and banks.

President Reagan had long believed that the Soviet Union was economically vulnerable, because he knew it lacked the entrepreneurship, technological dynamism, and freedoms that are the prerequisites of a strong modern economy. And when he learned that we in the West were financing its brutal regime, he committed to slowing, and ultimately terminating, that flow of discretionary cash.

Our European allies had a completely different approach. Their belief in *Ostpolitik*, as the Germans called it, presupposed that commercial bridge building would lead to geopolitical cooperation. If the West would offer financing and trade with the Soviets, peace and prosperity would result. Meanwhile, the Soviets were using the proceeds of Western loans, hard currency revenue streams, and technological support to build up their military, expand their empire, and engage in anti-Western activities.

The Reagan administration drew the line on a project called the Siberian Gas Pipeline, a 3,600-mile twin-strand pipeline that stretched from Siberia into the Western European gas grid. If completed, not only would it become the centerpiece of the Soviets' hard currency earnings structure, but Western Europe would become dependent on the USSR for over 70 percent of its natural gas, weakening Western Europe's ties to the United States and leaving the continent open to Kremlin extortion. Moreover, the pipeline was being financed on taxpayer-subsidized terms, since France and Germany viewed the USSR as a less developed country worthy of below-market interest rates.

The United States at the time had a monopoly on oil and gas technology that could drill through permafrost — which we had developed for Alaska's North Slope — and we imposed oil and gas equipment sanctions on the USSR and European companies that were helping to build the Siberian pipeline. At one point, despite the strain it placed on relations with our NATO allies, we closed the U.S. market entirely to companies that continued to supply the pipeline project over our objections. Four of the six affected companies went under within six months, and Europeans woke up to the fact that they could do business with us or the Soviets, but not both.

As a result of these efforts we capped Soviet gas deliveries to Western Europe at 30 percent of total supplies, delayed the first strand of the pipeline by years, killed the second strand, and eventually helped dry up the bulk of Western credits to the USSR. In a secret deal, we also persuaded the Saudis to pump an additional two million barrels of oil per day and decontrolled prices at the wellhead in this country, knocking oil prices down to about $10 a barrel — significant because for every dollar decrease in the price of a barrel, the Soviets lost some 500 million to one billion dollars. In short, the Soviet Union never recovered from these economic and financial blows. It defaulted on some $96 billion in Western hard currency debt shortly before the total collapse of the Soviet empire.

The story with China today has certain similarities, but with one big difference: the United States has been playing the role of the naive Europeans. Since adopting the Kissinger policy of engaging with China in the 1970s, our government has operated on the assumption that economic and financial relations with China would lead Beijing to liberalize politically. And since 2001, when we backed China's entry into the World Trade Organization, the pace at which we have given China access to our best technology and capital and trade markets has accelerated. Yet China has shown no signs of embracing individual freedoms or the rule of law.

Instead, with our support, the Chinese have launched a massive campaign to become the world's leading superpower. We know about the "Belt and Road Initiative," a strategic undertaking to place huge segments of the world under China's influence or outright control. We know about "Made in China 2025," a strategy designed to dominate key technology sectors — from artificial intelligence and quantum computing to hypersonic missiles and 5G. We know about China's practice of forced technology transfers: requiring American companies to share their trade secrets and R&D in order to do business in China. We know about China's predatory trade practices. We know many of these things only because President Trump has brought them to the forefront of national attention, for which he deserves credit. And the ongoing tariff war is a good thing in the sense that we've finally begun to take a stand.

But there is an issue more critical than trade that Americans, by and large, do *not* know about: China has over 700 companies in our stock and bond markets or capital markets. It has about 86 companies listed on the New York Stock Exchange, about 62 in the NASDAQ, and over 500 in the murky, poorly regulated over-the-counter market. Among these companies are some egregious bad actors. Hikvision, for example, is responsible for facial recognition technology that identifies and monitors the movement of ethnic Uyghurs, persecuted Muslims living in China's northwest. It also produces the surveillance cameras placed atop the walls of Chinese concentration camps holding as many as two million Uyghurs in Xinjiang. Both its parent company and Hikvision itself are on the U.S. Commerce Department Entity List (what many describe as the "Blacklist").

Do any of us have the financing of concentration camps in mind when we transfer money into our retirement and investment accounts? This sounds difficult to believe, but it is an empirical fact: the majority of American investors are unwittingly funding Chinese concentration camps, weapons systems for the People's Liberation Army (PLA), and more. This is because the U.S. has no security-minded screening mechanism for our capital markets, which have roughly $35 trillion under management.

When it comes to screening Chinese investments in U.S. companies, we have the Committee on Foreign Investment in the United States, which was recently strengthened with the Foreign Investment Risk Review Modernization Act of 2018. Congress expanded its reach because it was properly worried about China undermining our security and stealing our technology.

Our capital markets, on the other hand, are completely unprotected. There are serial violators of U.S. sanctions in our markets today. There are proliferators to our adversaries of advanced ballistic missiles. There are manufacturers of sophisticated weapons systems for the PLA. There are companies that are militarizing the illegal islands in the South China Sea. There are companies helping maintain the North Korean nuclear threat. There are companies that have been indicted or whose employees have been arrested for espionage as well as known cyber criminals. Do we find any of these material risk factors in the risk section of our prospectuses? No. Are we hearing about these concerns from our financial planners or fund managers? No. Nor has there ever once been a hearing on this topic in Congress.

The trade war is hurting China — this is positive and long overdue. But the Chinese can manage it. What would hurt them immeasurably more would be any contraction in their access to our investment dollars. The Chinese are estimated to have attracted nearly two trillion dollars of American investment in equities alone. We do not even know the extent of our real exposure to China, because it has dollar-denominated bonds issued elsewhere in the world that are ending up in Americans' bond portfolios — our investment banks buy them overseas to utilize a loophole in our regulatory structure. But I can tell you that in the next 36 months, if nothing is done, our exposure will be two to three trillion dollars more than it is today. The Chinese are moving as fast as they can into the investment portfolios of the American people because they are in desperate need of our dollars. That's what China is knowingly working towards — and that's called "checkmate."

The so-called China lobby is large and formidable today — consider how the NBA was cowed into silence regarding Chinese repression of the freedom movement in Hong Kong. But it is nothing compared to where things are headed if Americans become more heavily invested in China. And we remain largely blind to this development, just as we were blind — prior to Reagan's election in 1980 — to the extensive financing of the Soviet Union by the West. So here we go again — another authoritarian villain waging economic and financial warfare against us and our allies — but this time even more aggressively and capably.

Astoundingly, Americans are even investing in China's sovereign bonds — bonds issued directly by the Chinese. A company's stock will likely decline when it becomes known that the company is providing surveillance cameras for concentration camps or producing ICBMs targeting American cities. You would think that demanding this kind of disclosure would be unobjectionable — but then why is it so hard? Is it because China would be offended?

Beyond the need for dollars, consider the fact that roughly 150 to 180 million Americans have investments in our capital markets. What if these scores of millions of Americans wake up one morning and discover that 15, 18, or 22 percent of their retirement accounts are in Chinese securities? That's not far-fetched — indeed, it is almost certain to happen if nothing is done. And if that happens, those scores of millions of Americans will have a vested financial interest in opposing any future sanctions or other penalties against China, irrespective of the severity of China's offenses or the overall threat it poses to America's national war effort.

Today Americans are buying Chinese sovereign bonds to finance our own potential destruction — *anti-Liberty Bonds*. The California State Teachers' Retirement System, to cite just one example, owns Chinese sovereign bonds valued at over $4 million. The Prague Security Studies Institute is finding examples like this throughout our state public employee retirement systems. Or look at university endowments. The University of Michigan has 44 percent of its $12.2 billion in assets in private equity and venture capital; of the venture capital portion, one-third of the investments are Chinese. This is not to single out or excoriate the University of Michigan. Its investment portfolio is quite typical of what we're finding elsewhere.

Where is the disclosure related to these Chinese investments? Where is the due diligence on the part of fund managers and index providers? There are all kinds of investment policies and standards that prohibit the financing of concentration camps, human rights abuses, the PLA, organizations engaged in espionage, and violators of U.S. sanctions — but it's happening anyway. State legislatures need to take this up as a matter of urgent concern.

So far, we've talked mostly about private capital. What about our tax dollars? The Federal Thrift Savings Plan (TSP) — the retirement system for all federal employees — totals roughly $578 billion. It is the largest retirement fund in the country, with 5.7 million enrollees — including U.S. military personnel. For a long time, TSP managers were using a specific index for TSP's $50 billion international portfolio. Morgan Stanley Capital Investment (MSCI) has a whole range of indexes, and TSP was using an index containing only companies in developed countries — largely industrialized democracies. But in November 2017, the TSP Board had the idea of changing its index to capture yields from emerging markets. A Wall Street consulting firm introduced them to the MSCI All Country World Index, which includes China. Indeed, it includes companies such as AVIC, which makes fighter aircraft for the PLA and is China's largest producer of ballistic missiles, and China Mobile, which has been barred from U.S. government procurement for national security reasons. The decision was made to begin moving the TSP international fund to this MSCI All Country World Index beginning next year.

So what's to be done? The first urgent matter is to reverse the TSP Board decision before it is implemented. This should not be a partisan issue. Even leaving aside China's brutal repression of its own people, does anyone in America, Democrat or Republican, want to fund the production of weapons designed to kill American soldiers, sailors, and marines? Does any American want to underwrite the Chinese militarization of the South China Sea? Or finance U.S. sanctions violators, benefiting Iran and North Korea? Do Americans want to finance the destruction of their own liberty and the ruin of everything they hold dear? I think most Americans would react with outrage, if they knew the facts.

Next, it is urgent that Chinese bad actors be excluded from accessing U.S. capital markets — or at least be forced to disclose their malevolent past activities because of the material risks involved. To be candid, when it comes to China, there is a question whether one can even speak of *good* actors. Article 7 of the National Intelligence Law of China allows every commercial entity to be instantly weaponized — to commit espionage, technology theft, or whatever else is deemed to be in China's national interest — by simple order of the government. That's a matter of public record. In other words, for some fund managers who wish to eliminate bad actors from their portfolios, one solution is simply to eliminate Chinese enterprises. For others, careful, security-minded diligence is required.

Some detractors of this initiative will object that it is detrimental to the free flow of global capital — that it contracts the investable universe of fund managers, narrowing what they can buy in seeking a better yield. "Don't politicize the markets," will be a popular refrain. It's an unfortunate fact that you can't appeal to Wall Street on the basis of patriotism, doing the right thing, and safeguarding America's security interests. You'll generally get a big yawn.

So instead we need to speak to them in market terms: "Where's the prudent risk management? Where's the required disclosure of material risks? Where's the good corporate governance? Where's the concern over share value, corporate reputation, and brand?"

That's Wall Street's lingo. It's much more difficult for them to ignore. Failure to disclose material risks is illegal. And although the SEC apparently doesn't consider egregious corporate human rights and national security abuses as material risks, the kind of material risk I am talking about is based on the idea that a company's stock will likely decline when it becomes known that the company is providing, for example, surveillance cameras for concentration camps or producing ICBMs targeting American cities. You would think that this kind of disclosure would be unobjectionable — but then why is it so hard? Is it because China would be offended?

The good news is that we can win this economic and financial war. America dominates the global economic and financial domain — period. Our capital markets are roughly the size of the rest of the worlds combined, and we hold about 60 percent of the world's liquidity. Wall Street might argue that if we safeguard value our capital markets, China will just go to another international exchange, in which case our country will be the one hurt. The problem with that argument is that no other country has anywhere near the depth and volume of our markets. China's need for dollars is so voracious that it would likely use up the volume of a Frankfurt or London in months, not years. There is nowhere else for a player the size of China to go. Just as in the early 1980s, when we had a monopoly on oil and gas equipment and technology for Arctic-like conditions, we have most of the world's money today — and the leverage that goes with it.

The bottom line is clear. The Chinese are waging economic and financial warfare against us every day. We are in a position to prevail. The problem is that we've not seriously taken the field. In terms of our capital markets, we're not even at the stadium. It's time to mobilize our national assets and declare, "Not on my watch." After all, it's our money.

This essay was adapted from a speech delivered at Hillsdale College on September 9, 2019, during a conference on the topic, "Understanding China." Reprinted with permission of Imprimis, *a publication of Hillsdale College, Hillsdale, MI.*

Roger W. Robinson, Jr. is president and CEO of RWR Advisory Group and co-founder and chairman of the Prague Security Studies Institute. He earned a B.A. from Duke University and an M.A. from George Washington University. He served as senior director of international economic affairs on President Reagan's National Security Council, where he was the principal architect of the secret economic and financial strategy that proved decisive to the defeat of the Soviet Union. He later served as chairman of the Congressional U.S.–China Economic and Security Review Commission. Prior to his government service, he was a vice president in the international department of the Chase Manhattan Bank.

Acronyms Index
Heritage Foundation, Washington, D.C.

AFSB Afloat Forward Staging Base

AIMD Aircraft Intermediate Maintenance Department (or Detachment)

AK Auxiliary, Cargo, class/type of ship. An attack transport.

AS Auxiliary, Submarine Tender, class/type of ship

AS Aviation Support Equipment Technician

ASAU Air Search and Attack Unit

ASR Auxiliary, Submarine Rescue, class/type of ship

ASUW Anti-Surface Warfare

ASW Auxiliary Seawater system

ASW Anti-Submarine Warfare

ASWO Anti-Submarine Warfare Officer

ATS Auxiliary, Towing and Salvage, class/type of ship

AUTEC Atlantic Undersea Test and Evaluation Center

AUXO Auxiliaries Officer

AVCM Master Chief Avionics Technician

AVGAS Aviation Gasoline

BCM Beyond Capable Maintenance. Equipment status that indicates the item cannot be repaired and must be sent out for rework or disposed.

BUSANDA Bureau of Supplies and Accounts

BUWEPS Bureau of Naval Weapons

CA Cruiser, Attack, class/type of ship. Heavy Cruiser (outdated)

CAG Cruiser, Attack, Guided Missile, class/type of ship. Guided Missile Heavy Cruiser (outdated)

CAG Commander, Air Group

CBMU Construction Battalion Maintenance Unit

CC Cruiser, class/type of ship.

CDO Command Duty Officer

CENTCOM U.S. Central Command (USCENTCOM)

CG Cruiser, Guided Missile, class/type of ship

CGN Cruiser, Guided Missile, Nuclear, class/type of ship (outdated)

CIC Combat Information Center

CICO Combat Information Center Officer

CIWS Close-In Weapon System

CMC Commandant of the Marine Corps or Chaplain of the Marine Corps or Command Master Chief

CNATRA Chief of Naval Air Training

CNET Command Naval Education and Training

CNO Chief of Naval Operations

312

CO Commanding Officer

COD Carrier Onboard Delivery

COMCVW Commander, Carrier Air Wing

COMDESGRU Commander, Destroyer Group

COMDESRON Commander, Destroyer Squadron

COMLANTFLT Commander, U.S. Atlantic Fleet

COMMO Communications Officer

COMNAVAIRES Commander, Naval Air Force, Reserve

COMNAVAIRFOR (also CNAF) Commander, Naval Air Forces

COMNAVAIRLANT (also CNAL) Commander, Naval Air Force Atlantic

COMNAVAIRPAC Commander, Naval Air Force Pacific

COMNAVRESFOR Commander, Navy Reserve Forces

COMNAVSEASYSCOM Commander, Naval Sea Systems Command

COMNAVSECGRU Commander, Naval Security Group

COMPACFLT Commander, Pacific Fleet (formerly CINCPACFLT)

COMPATRECONGRU Commander, Patrol and Reconnaissance Group

COMSEC Communications Security

COMSUBFOR Commander, Submarine Forces

COMSUBLANT Commander, Submarine Force Atlantic

COMSUBPAC Commander, Submarine Force, U.S. Pacific Fleet

COMTACGRU Commander, Tactical Air Control Group

COMTRAWING Commander, Training Air Wing

COS (also CoS) Flag Officer's Chief of Staff

CRG Coastal Riverine Group

CS Culinary Specialist

CSEC Computerized Self Evaluation Checklist

CSMC Combat Systems Maintenance Center

CSOSS Combat Systems Operational Sequencing Systems

CV Aircraft Carrier, class/type of ship.

CVA Aircraft Carrier, Attack, class/type of ship.

CVAN Aircraft Carrier, Attack, Nuclear, class/type of ship

CVN Nuclear-powered Aircraft Carrier (Cruiser, heavier-than-air aircraft, nuclear)

CVW Carrier Air Wing

DCAG Deputy Air Wing Commander (see CAG)

DCC Damage Control Central

DD Destroyer

DDG Guided Missile Destroyer

DDR Radar Picket Destroyer

DE Destroyer Escort

DESDIV Destroyer Division

DESRON Destroyer Squadron

DOD (also DoD) Department of Defense

DoN Department of the Navy

EM Emergency Management

EMCON Emissions Control

EMO Electronics Material Officer

EOOW Engineering Officer of the Watch

EOS Enclosed Operating Space

EOSS Engineering Operational Sequencing Systems

ET Electronics Technician

EW Electronic Warfare

EXW Expeditionary Warfare

FAC Forward Air Controller

FAC/A Forward Air Controller/Airborne

FBM Fleet Ballistic Missile

FDO Flight Deck Officer

FF Frigate, class/type of ship

FFG Frigate, Guided Missile, class/type of ship

FICEURLANT Fleet Intelligence Center Europe & Atlantic

FLEACT Fleet Activity

FLTMPS Fleet Training Management and Planning System

FMF Fleet Marine Force

FOD Foreign Object Damage (Debris and Detection also used
in some cases)

FRC Fleet Readiness Center

FRS Fleet Replacement Squadron (Formerly RAG)

FSA Food Service Attendant

FT Fire control technician

FTB Fire Control Technician Ballistic Missile

GCCS-M Global Command and Control System-Maritime

GSE Gas Turbine Systems Technician Electrical

GSM Gas Turbine Systems Technician Mechanic

HAC Helicopter Aircraft Commander

HEDSUPPACTLANT Headquarters, Support Activity Atlantic

HELO Helicopter

HS Helicopter Squadron, Anti-Submarine Warfare
(HS-4 Black Knights)

HT Hull Maintenance Technician

IC Interior Communications Electrician

ITS Information Technology Submarines

JBD Jet Blast Deflector (carriers)

JP-5 Jet Propellant no. 5, standard Navy jet fuel (F-44, AVCAT)

JTF Joint Task Force

JTFEX Joint Task Force Exercise

LANTCOM Atlantic Command

314

LAWS Laser Weapon System

LCAC Landing Craft, Air Cushion.

LCC Amphibious Command Ship.

LCM Landing Craft, Mechanized, class/type of boat. Usage: LCM-4, LCM-6, LCM-8

LCPL Landing Craft, Personnel Launch, class/type of boat.

LCS Littoral Combat Ship, class/type of ship.

LHA Landing, Helicopter, Assault, class/type of ship.

LHD Landing, Helicopter, Dock, class/type of ship.

LKA Landing, Cargo, Attack, class/type of ship.

LPD Landing, Personnel, Dock, class/type of ship.

LPA Landing, Personnel, Attack, class/type of ship.

LPOD Last Plane On Deck

LRAD Long Range Acoustic Device

LS Logistics Specialist

LSD Landing Ship, Dock, class/type of ship.

MALS Marine Aviation Logistics Squadron

MC Mass Communication Specialist

MMCO Maintenance/Material Control Officer

MO Maintenance Officer (pronounced "Moe")

MPA Military Patrol Craft (P-3 Orion, etc.)

MRDB Material Readiness Database

MSG Message

MSW Main Seawater System

MT Missile Technician

NAB Naval Amphibious Base

NAF Naval Air Facility

NALCOMIS Naval Aviation Logistics Command Management Information System

NAS Naval Air Station

NAVAIR Naval Air Systems Command

NAVCOMP Comptroller of the Navy

NAVFAC Naval Facilities Engineering Command

NAVMAT Naval Material Command

NAVSEA Naval Sea Systems Command

NAVSECGRUACT Naval Security Group Activity

NAVSTA Naval Station

NAVSUBASE Naval Submarine Base

NAVSUP Naval Supply Systems Command

NAWCAD Naval Air Warfare Center, Aircraft Division

NAWCWD Naval Air Warfare Center, Weapons Division (formerly Pacific Missile Test Center)

NCDU Navy Combat Demolition Unit

316

SSES Ships Signals Exploitation Space. A compartment on a ship where embarked NAVSECGRU personnel, known a Cryptologic Technicians, do their work.

SSGN Submersible Ship Guided Missile Nuclear. Hull classification symbol for cruise missile submarine.

SSN Submersible Ship Nuclear. Hull classification symbol for general-purpose fast attack submarines.

SUBRON Submarine Squadron

SWCC (swick) Special Warfare Combatant-craft Crewmen, the Special Operations Forces who operate and maintain an inventory of boats used to conduct special operations missions or to support special operations missions conducted in maritime environments, particularly those of the U.S. Navy SEALs.

SWO Surface Warfare Officer

TF Task Force

TG Task Group

TSP Troubled Systems Process

TU Task Unit

UAV Unmanned Aerial Vehicle

UCT Underwater Construction Team

UDT Underwater Demolition Team

UNREP Underway Replenishment

VAQ Fixed Wing Electronic-Attack Squadron

VAW Fixed Wing Airborne Early Warning Squadron

VDS Variable Depth Sonar

VFA Fixed Wing Strike Fighter Squadron

VLS Vertical Launching System

VX Air Test & Evaluation Squadron (VX-4 Evaluators)

WTC Watertight Compartment

INDEX

Page numbers in *italics* indicate figures.